The Riddles
of Philosophy

The Riddles
of Philosophy

Rudolf Steiner

SteinerBooks

Originally published in German under the title
Die Rätsel der Philosophie, 1961, volume 18
in the Collected Works of Rudolf Steiner.

This authorized translation published by kind
permission of the Rudolf Steiner Nachlassverwaltung,
Dornach, Switzerland.

Published in the United States of America
by SteinerBooks / Anthroposophic Press, Inc.

Originally published in 1973.
This reprint copyright © 2009, SteinerBooks.

www.steinerbooks.org

ISBN 978-0-88010-711-2

All rights reserved.
No part of this book may be reproduced in any form
without the written permission of the publisher, except
for brief quotations embodied in critical
reviews and articles.

TABLE OF CONTENTS

	Page
Introduction by Fritz C. A. Koelln	vii
Preface to the 1923 Edition	xiii
Preface to the 1918 Edition	xix
Preface to the 1914 Edition	xxiii

Part I

I	Guiding Thoughts on the Method of Presentation	3
II	The World Conception of the Greek Thinkers	12
III	Thought Life from the Beginning of the Christian Era to John Scotus Erigena	50
IV	The World Conceptions of the Middle Ages	55
V	The World Conceptions of the Modern Age of Thought Evolution	63
VI	The Age of Kant and Goethe	91
VII	The Classics of World and Life Conceptions	151

v

VIII	Reactionary World Conceptions	185
IX	The Radical World Conceptions	209

Part II

	Introductory Remarks to the 1914 Edition . .	237
I	The Struggle Over the Spirit	242
II	Darwinism and World Conception . . .	284
III	The World as Illusion	314
IV	Echoes of the Kantian Mode of Conception . .	352
V	World Conceptions of Scientific Factuality . .	360
VI	Modern Idealistic World Conceptions . . .	375
VII	Modern Man and His World Conception . .	401
VIII	A Brief Outline of an Approach to Anthroposophy	445
	Index	471

Introduction

Rudolf Steiner's *Riddles of Philosophy, Presented in an Outline of Its History* is not a history of philosophy in the usual sense of the word. It does not give a history of the philosophical systems, nor does it present a number of philosophical problems historically. Its real concern touches on something deeper than this, on riddles rather than problems. Philosophical concepts, systems and problems are, to be sure, to be dealt with in this book. But it is not *their* history that is to be described here. Where they are discussed they become symptoms rather than the objects of the search. The search itself wants to reveal a process that is overlooked in the usual history of philosophy. It is the mysterious process in which philosophical thinking appears in human history. Philosophical thinking as it is here meant is known only in Western Civilisation. Oriental philosophy has its origin in a different kind of consciousness, and it is not to be considered in this book.

What is new here is the treatment of the history of philosophic thinking as a manifestation of the evolution of human consciousness. Such a treatment requires a fine sense of observation. Not merely the thoughts must be observed, but behind them the thinking in which they appear.

To follow Steiner in his subtle description of the process of the metamorphosis of this thinking in the history of philosophy we should remember he sees the human consciousness in an evolution. It has not always been what it is now, and what it is now it will not be in the future. This is a fundamental conception of anthroposophy. The metamorphosis of the consciousness is not only described in Steiner's anthroposophical books but in a number of them directions are given from which we can learn to participate in this transformation actively. This is explicitly done not only in his *Knowledge of the Higher Worlds and its Attainment* but also in certain chapters of his *Theosophy*, *An Outline of Occult Science* and several other of his anthroposophical books.

The objection may be raised at this point that the application of concepts derived from spiritual exercises is not admissable in a field of pure philosophical studies, where every concept used should be clearly comprehensible without any pre-conceived ideas. Steiner's earlier philosophical books did not seem to imply any such presuppositions and his anthroposophical works therefore appear to mark a definite departure from his earlier philosophical ones.

It is indeed significant that the anthroposophical works appear only after a long period of philosophic studies. A glance at Rudolf Steiner's bibliography shows that it is only after twenty years of philosophical studies that his anthroposophy as a science of the spirit appears on the scene. The purely philosophical publications begin with his *Introductions to Goethe's Natural Scientific Writings* (1883–97) and with the *Fundamental Outline of a Theory of Knowledge Implicit in Goethe's World Conception* (1886). They are followed by his own theory of knowledge presented in *Truth and Science* in 1892 and his *Philosophy of Freedom* (also translated as *Philosophy of Spiritual Activity*) of 1894. This work presents clearly the climax of Steiner's philosophy and it should be studied carefully by anyone who intends to arrive at a valid judgment of his later anthroposophy. It is, however, still several years before the books appear that contain the result of his spiritual science. Not only his book on *Nietzsche, a Fighter against his Time* of 1895 and his *Goethe's World Conception* of 1897 but also his *World- and Life-Conceptions in the Nineteenth Century* of 1900 and even his *Mysticism at the Dawn of the Modern Age and Its Relation to Modern World Conception* of 1901 could have been understood as merely historical descriptions.

With Steiner's next work we seem to enter an entirely different world. *Christianity as Mystical Fact and the Mysteries of Antiquity* clearly begin the series of his distinctly anthroposophic works. Like his *Theosophy* (1904), his *Knowledge of the Higher Worlds* (1905/08) and his *Occult Science* (1910) it could only have been written by an occultist who spoke from a level of consciousness that one did not have to assume as the source of his earlier books.

To the casual reader it could appear that there was a distinct break in Steiner's world conception at the beginning of the century, and this is also the conclusion drawn by some of his critics.

Rudolf Steiner's own words, however, as well as a study of both phases of his work leave no doubt that there was no such break in his world conception. He clearly states that knowledge derived from a higher level of consciousness was always at his disposal, also at the time of his early philosophical publications. His deep concern was the question: How could one speak about worlds not immediately accessible to scarcely anybody else in an age in which materialism and agnosticism ruled without any serious opposition. He found both so deeply rooted in Western Civilisation that he had to ask himself at times: Will it always be necessary to keep entirely silent about this higher knowledge.

In this time he turned to the study of representative thinkers of his time and of the more recent past in whose conceptions of world and life he now penetrated to experience their depth and their limitations. In Goethe's world he found the leverage to overcome the basic agnosticism and materialism to which the age had surrendered. In Nietzsche he saw the tragic figure who had been overpowered by it and whose life was broken by the fact that his spiritual sensitivity made it impossible for him to live in this world and his intellectual integrity forbade him to submit to what he had to consider as the dishonest double standard of his time.

Neither Rudolf Steiner's Nietzsche book nor his writings on Goethe's conception of the world are meant to be merely descriptive accounts of philosophical systems or problems. They reveal an inner struggle of the spirit that is caused by the spiritual situation of their time and in which the reader must share to follow these books with a full understanding. When these studies are then extended to comprise longer periods of time as in the *World and Life Conceptions of the Nineteenth Century* and in *Mysticism at the Dawn of the Modern Age* soul conditions under which the individual thinkers have to work become more and more visible.

When Rudolf Steiner published the present work in 1914 as *The Riddles of Philosophy* he used the book on the *World and Life Conception of the Nineteenth Century* as the second part, which is now preceded by an outline of the entire history of philosophy in the Western world.

At this time Steiner's anthroposophical books had appeared in which the evolution of human consciousness plays an important role. It could now be partly demonstrated in an outline of the philosophic thinking of the Western world.

Rudolf Steiner's approach to history is symptomatological, and it is this method that he also applies to the history of philosophy. The thoughts developed in the course of this history are treated as symptomatic facts for the mode of thinking prevalent in a given time. He sees four distinct phases in the course of Western thought evolution. They are periods of seven to eight centuries each, beginning with the pre-Socratic thinkers in Greece.

Here pure thought as such free of images develops out of an older form of consciousness that is expressed in myths and symbolic pictures. It reaches its climax in the classical philosophies of Socrates, Plato and Aristotle and ends with the Hellenistic period.

A second phase begins with Christianity and reaches as far as the ninth century A.D. This time Rudolf Steiner characterizes as the age of the awakening self-consciousness and he is convinced that an intense historical study of this period will more and more prove the adequacy of that term. The emergence of a greater self-awareness at this time diminishes the importance of the conceptional thinking as the religious concern of the soul with its own destiny grows. The emerging self-consciousness of this phase is intensely felt, but does not lead to an intellectual occupation with the concept of this *"self."* In a third period a new concern becomes prevalent when the scholastic philosophers become more and more confronted with the tormenting question of the reality of thought itself. What is often regarded as an aberration into mere verbal quarrels, the medieval discussions of the significance of the universal concepts, is now seen as a soul struggle of a profound human concern. Thus the long war between Realism and Nominalism appears in a new light. As the nominalists seem to emerge more and more as the victors the thought climate for the fourth phase is gradually prepared.

Since the Renaissance natural science proceeds to develop a world conception in which the self-conscious ego must experience itself as a foreign element. The emergence of this experience leads to a new inner struggle in which the fourth phase of the history of philosophy is from now on deeply engaged in its predominant thought currents: It is the phase of consciousness in which we still live. The various forms of idealistic materialistic and agnostic philosophies are subject to the tension caused by the indicated situation. As Steiner characterizes them he points out that the different thinker personalities can be quite unconscious of the currents that manifest themselves in their thinking although their ideas and thought combinations receive direction and form from them.

In the last chapter of the second part of the book Steiner describes his own philosophy as he had developed it in his earlier books *Truth and Science* and *Philosophy of Freedom.* In this description the relation between his philosophical works and his anthroposophical ones also becomes clear. As a philosophy of spiritual activity, the *Philosophy of Freedom* had not merely given an analysis of the factors involved in the process of knowledge, nor had the possibility of human freedom within a world apparently determined on all sides, merely been logically shown. What the study of this book meant to supply was at the same time a course of concentrated exercise of thinking that was to develop a new power through which man really *becomes* free. As Aristotle's statement (Metaph. XII, 7) that *the actuality of thinking is life* in this way becomes a real experience of the thinker, human freedom is born. Man becomes free in his actions in the external world, developing the moral imagination necessary for the situation in which he finds himself. At the same time his spirit frees itself from the bodily encasement in which thoughts had appeared as unreal shadows. The process of his real spiritual development has begun.

In this way the *Riddles of Philosophy* may be considered as a bridge that can lead from Steiner's early philosophical works into the study of anthroposophy. The undercurrents characterized in the four main phases of the evolution of thought lead from potentiality to ever increasing actuality of the awakening spirit. And for the exercises described in the specific anthroposophic books there can be no better preparation than the concentrated study of Rudolf Steiner's *Philosophy of Spiritual Activity.*

FRITZ C. A. KOELLN

Bowdoin College
Brunswick, Maine
April, 1973

Preface to the
1923 Edition

When, on the occasion of its second edition in 1914, I enlarged my book, *World and Life Conceptions of the Nineteenth Century*, the result was the present volume, *The Riddles of Philosophy*. In this book I intend to show those elements of world conceptions that appear historically and that move the contemporary observer of these riddles to experiences of greater depth of consciousness as he encounters the feelings with which they were experienced by the thinkers of the past. Such a deepening of the feelings is of profound satisfaction to one who is engaged in a philosophical struggle. What he in his own mind is striving for is strengthened through the fact that he sees how this endeavor took shape in earlier thinkers on whom life bestowed viewpoints that may be close to, or far from, his own. In this way I intend in this book to serve those who need a presentation of the development of philosophy as a supplement to their own paths of thought. Such a supplement will be valuable to anyone who, in his own mode of thinking, wishes to feel himself at one with the intellectual work of mankind, and who would like to see that the work of his own thoughts has its roots in a universal need of the human soul. He can grasp this when he allows the essential elements of the historical world conceptions to unfold before his eye.

For many observers, however, such a display has a depressive effect. It causes doubt to invade their minds. They see thinkers of the past contradicting their predecessors and contradicted by their successors in turn. It is the intention in my account of this process to show how this depressing aspect is extinguished by another element. Let us consider two thinkers. At first glance the contradiction of their thoughts strikes us as painful. We now take these thoughts under a closer inspection. We find that both thinkers direct their attention to entirely different realms of the world. Suppose one thinker had developed in himself the frame of mind that concentrates on the mode in which thoughts unfold in the inner weaving of the soul. For him it becomes a riddle how these inward soul processes can become decisive in a cognition concerning the nature of the external world. This point of departure will lend a special color to all his thinking. He will speak in a vigorous manner of the creative activity of the life of thought. Thus, everything he says will be colored by idealism. A second thinker turns his attention toward the processes accessible to external sense perception. The thought processes through which he holds these external events in cognitive perception do not themselves in their specific energy enter the field of his awareness. He will give a turn to the riddles of the universe that will place them in a thought environment in which the ground of the world itself will appear in a form that bears semblance to the world of the senses.

If one approaches the historical genesis of the conflicting world views with presuppositions that result from such a thought orientation, one can overcome the deadening effect these world perspectives have on each other and raise the point of view to a level from which they appear in mutual support.

Hegel and Haeckel, considered side by side, will at first sight present the most perfect contradiction. Penetrating into Hegel's philosophy, one can go along with him on the path to which a man who lives entirely in thoughts is bound. He feels the thought element as something that enables him to comprehend his own being as real. Confronted with nature, the question arises in him of the relation in which it stands toward the world of thought. It will be possible to follow his turn of mind if one can feel what is relatively justified and fruitful in such a mental disposition. If one can enter into Haeckel's thoughts, one can again follow him part of the way. Haeckel can only see what the senses grasp and how it changes. What is and changes in this way he can acknowledge as his reality, and he is only satisfied when he is able to comprise the entire human being, including his thought activity, under this concept of being and transformation. Now let Haeckel look on Hegel as a person who spins airy meaningless concepts without regard to reality. Grant that Hegel, could he have lived to know Haeckel, would have seen in him a person who was completely blind to true reality. Thus, whoever is able to enter into both modes of thinking will find in Hegel's philosophy the possibility to strengthen his power of spontaneous, active thinking. In Haeckel's mode of thought he will find the possibility to become aware of relations between distant formations of nature that tend to raise significant questions in the mind of man. Placed side by side and measured against one another in this fashion, Hegel and Haeckel will no longer lead us into oppressive skepticism but will enable us to recognize how the striving shoots and sprouts of life are sent out from very different corners of the universe.

Such are the grounds in which the method of my presentation has its roots. I do not mean to conceal the contradictions in the history of philosophy, but I intend to show what remains valid in spite of the contradictions.

That Hegel and Haeckel are treated in this book to reveal what is positive and not negative in both of them can, in my opinion, be criticized as erroneous only by somebody who is incapable of seeing how fruitful such a treatment of the positive is.

Let me add just a few more words about something that does not refer to the content of the book but is nevertheless connected with it. This book belongs to those of my works referred to by persons who claim to find contradictions in the course of my philosophical development. In spite of the fact that I know such reproaches are mostly not motivated by a will to search for truth, I will nevertheless answer them briefly.

Such critics maintain that the chapter on Haeckel gives the impression of having been written by an orthodox follower of Haeckel. Whoever reads in the same book what is said about Hegel will find it difficult to uphold this statement. Superficially considered, it might, however, seem as if a person who wrote about Haeckel as I did in this book had gone through a complete transformation of spirit when he later published books like *Knowledge of the Higher World and Its Attainment, An Outline of Occult Science*, etc.

But the question is only seen in the right light if one remembers that my later works, which seem to contradict my earlier ones, are based on a spiritual intuitive insight into the spiritual world. Whoever intends to acquire or preserve for himself an intuition of this kind must develop the ability to suppress his own sympathies and antipathies and to surrender with perfect objectivity to the subject of his contemplation. He must really, in presenting Haeckel's mode of thinking, be capable of being completely absorbed by it. It is precisely from this power to surrender to the object that he derives spiritual intuition. My method of presentation of the various world conceptions has its origin in my orientation toward a spiritual intuition. It would not be necessary to have actually entered into the materialistic mode of thinking merely to theorize about the spirit. For that purpose it is sufficient simply to show all justifiable reasons against materialism and to present this mode of thought by revealing its unjustified aspects. But to effect spiritual intuition one cannot proceed in this manner. One must be capable of thinking idealistically with the idealist and materialistically with the materialist. For only thus will the faculty of the soul be awakened that can become active in spiritual intuition.

Against this, the objections might be raised that in such a treatment the content of the book would lose its unity. I am not of that opinion. An historical account will become the more faithful the more the phenomena are allowed to speak for themselves. It cannot be the task of an historical presentation to fight materialism or to distort it into a caricature, for within its limits it is justified. It is right to represent materialistically those processes of the world that have a material cause. We only go astray when we do not arrive at the insight that comes when, in pursuing the material processes, we are finally led to the conception of the spirit. To maintain that the brain is not a necessary condition of our thinking insofar as it is related to sense perception is an error. It is also an error to assume that the spirit is not the creator of the brain through which it reveals itself in the physical world through the production and formation of thought.

*Preface to the
1918 Edition*

The thoughts from which the presentation of the content of this book have grown and that form its basic support have been indicated in the Preface of the 1914 edition following this. To what was said then, I should like to add something connected with a question that lives more or less consciously in the soul of one who turns to a book on the riddles of philosophy. It is the question of the relation of philosophical contemplation to immediate *life*. Every philosophical thought that is not demanded by this life is condemned to remain barren even if it should attract for awhile a few readers of contemplative inclination. A fruitful thought must have its roots in the processes of development that mankind as a whole has to undergo in the course of its historical evolution. Whoever intends to depict the history of the evolution of philosophical thought from any kind of viewpoint can, for this purpose only, rely on such thoughts as are demanded by life itself. They must be thoughts that, when carried into the conduct of life, will penetrate man in such a way that he gains from them energies capable of directing his knowledge. They must become his advisors and helpers in the task of his existence. Because mankind needs such thoughts, philosophical world views have come into existence. If it were possible to master life without them, man would never have been inwardly justified to think of the "Riddles of Philosophy." An age that is unwilling to think such thoughts shows through this fact merely that it does not feel the need to form human life in such a way that it can really unfold itself in all directions according to its original destination. But for such a disinclination, a heavy penalty must be paid in the course of human evolution. Life remains undeveloped in such ages, and men do not notice their sickly state because they are unwilling to recognize the demands that nevertheless continue to exist deeply seated within them and that they just fail to satisfy. A following age shows the effect of such a neglect. The grandchildren find in the formation of a stunted life something that was caused by the omission of the grandparents. This omission of the preceding age has turned into the imperfect life of the later time into which the grandchildren find themselves placed. In life as a *whole,* philosophy must rule. It is possible to sin against this demand, but it is inevitable that this sin will produce its effects.

We shall only understand the course of the development of philosophical thought, the existence of the "Riddles of Philosophy," if we have a feeling for the significance that the philosophical contemplation of the world possesses for a whole, full human existence. It is out of such a feeling that I have written about the development of the riddles of philosophy. I have attempted to show through the presentation of this development that such a feeling is inwardly justified.

Against this feeling there will emerge from the outset in the minds of some readers a certain dampening objection that at first sight seems to be based on fact. Philosophical contemplation is supposed to be a necessity of life, but in spite of this, the endeavor of human thought in the course of its development does not produce clear-cut and well-defined solutions to the riddles of philosophy. Rather are they ambiguous and apparently contradictory. There are many historical analyses that attempt to explain the only too apparent contradictions through superficially formed ideas of evolution. They are not convincing.

To find one's way in this field, evolution must be taken much more seriously than is usually the case. One must arrive at the insight that there cannot be any thought that would be capable of solving the riddles of the universe once and for all times in an all-comprehensive way. Such is the nature of human thinking that a newly found idea will soon transform itself in turn into a new riddle. The more significant the idea is, the more light it will yield for a certain time; the more enigmatic, the more questionable it will become in a following age.

Whoever wants to view the history of human thought development from a fruitful point of view must be able to admire the greatness of an idea in one age, and yet be capable of producing the same enthusiasm in watching this idea as it reveals its shortcoming in a later period. He must also be able to accept the thought that the mode of thinking to which he himself adheres will be replaced in the future by an entirely different one. This thought must not divert him from recognizing fully the "truth" of the view that he has conquered for himself. The disposition of mind that is inclined to believe that thoughts of an earlier time have been disposed of as imperfect by the "perfect" ones of the present age, is of no help for understanding the philosophical evolution of mankind.

I have attempted to comprehend the course of human thought development by grasping the significance of the fact that a following age contradicts philosophically the preceding one. In the introductory exposition, *Guiding Thoughts of the Presentation*, I have stated which ideas make such a comprehension possible. The ideas are of such a nature that they will necessarily find a great deal of resistance. At first acquaintance they will have the appearance of something that just occurred to me and that I now wanted to force in a fantastic manner on the whole course of the history of philosophy. Nevertheless, I can only hope that one will find that the ideas are not thought up as preconceived and then superimposed on the view of philosophical development, but that they have been obtained in the same way in which the natural scientist finds his laws. They have their source in the *observation* of the evolution of philosophy. One has no right to reject the results of an observation because they are in disagreement with ideas that one accepts as right because of some kind of inclination of thought without observation. Opposition to my presentation will be based on the superstitious denial of the existence of forces in human history that manifest themselves in certain specific ages, and dominate effectively the development of human thought in a meaningful and necessary way. I had to accept such forces because the observation of this development had proved their existence to me, and because this observation made apparent to me the fact that the history of philosophy will only become a science if one does not shrink back from recognizing forces of this kind.

It seems to me that it is only then possible to gain a tenable attitude toward the riddles of philosophy, fruitful for life at the present time, if one knows the forces that dominated the ages of the past. In the history of thought, more than in any other branch of historical reflection, it is necessary to let the present grow out of the past. For in the comprehension of those ideas that satisfy the demand of the present, we have the foundation for the insight that spreads the right light over the past. The thinker who is incapable of obtaining a philosophical viewpoint that is adequate to the dominating impulses of his own age will also be unable to discover the significance of the intellectual life of the past. I shall here leave the question undecided whether or not in some other field of historical reflection a presentation can be fruitful that does not at least have a picture of the present situation in this field as a foundation. In the field of the history of thought, such a procedure would be meaningless. Here the object of the reflection must necessarily be connected with the immediate life, and this life, in which thought becomes actual as practice of life, can only be that of the present.

With these words I have meant to characterize the feeling out of which this presentation of the riddles of philosophy grew. Because of the short time since the last edition, there is no occasion for change or additions to the content of the book.

RUDOLF STEINER

May 1918

*Preface to the
1914 Edition*

I did not have the feeling that I was writing a "centennial book" to mark the beginning of the century when I set about to outline the *World and Life Conceptions of the Nineteenth Century*, which appeared in 1901. The invitation to present this book as a contribution to a collection of philosophical works only provided me with the challenge to sum up results of the philosophical developments since the age of Kant, at which I had arrived long ago, and which I had meant to publish. When a new edition of the book became necessary and when I re-examined its content, I became aware of the fact that only through a considerable enlargement of the account as it was originally given could I make completely clear what I had intended to show. I had at that time limited myself to the characterization of the last one hundred and thirty years of philosophical development. Such a limitation is justifiable because this period indeed constitutes a well-rounded totality that is closed in itself and could be portrayed as such even if one did not mean to write a "centennial book." But the philosophical views of the last century lived within me in such a way that, in presenting its philosophical problems, I felt resounding as undertones in my soul the solutions that had been attempted since the beginning of the course of the history of philosophy. This sensation appeared with greater intensity as I took up the revision of the book for a new edition. This indicates the reason why the result was not so much a new edition but a new book.

To be sure, the content of the old book has essentially been preserved word for word, but it has been introduced by a short account of the philosophical development since the sixth century B.C. In the second volume the characterization of the successive philosophies will be continued to the present time. Moreover, the short remarks at the end of the second volume entitled, *Outlook*, have been extended into a detailed presentation of the philosophical possibilities of the present. Objections may be raised against the composition of the book because the parts of the earlier version have not been shortened, whereas the characterization of the philosophies from the sixth century B.C. to the nineteenth century A.D. has only been given in the shortest outline. But since my aim is to give *not only* a short outline of the history of philosophical problems but to discuss these problems and the attempt at their solution themselves through their historical treatment, I considered it correct to retain the more detailed account for the last period. The way of approach in which these questions were seen and presented by the philosophers of the nineteenth century is still close to the trends of thought and philosophical needs of our time. What precedes this period is of the same significance to modern soul life only insofar as it spreads light over the last time interval. The *Outlook* at the end of the second volume had its origin in the same intention, namely, that of developing through the account of the history of philosophy, philosophy itself.

The reader will miss some things in this book that he might look for in a history of philosophy—the views of Hobbes and others, for instance. My aim, however, was not to enumerate all philosophical opinions, but to present the course of development of the philosophical problems. In such a presentation it is inappropriate to record a philosophical opinion of the past if its essential points have been characterized in another connection.

Whoever wants to find also in this book a new proof that I

have "changed" my views in the course of years will probably not even then be dissuaded from such an "opinion" if I point out to him that the presentation of the philosophical views that I gave in the *World and Life Conceptions* has, to be sure, been enlarged and supplemented, but that the content of the former book has been taken over into the new one in all essential points, literally unchanged. The slight changes that occur in a few passages seemed to be necessary to me, not because I felt the need after fifteen years of presenting some points differently, but because I found that a changed mode of expression was required by the more comprehensive connection in which here and there a thought appears in the new book, whereas in the old one such a connection was not given. There will, however, always be people who like to construe contradictions among the successive writings of a person, because they either cannot or else do not wish to consider the certainly admissable extension of such a person's thought development. The fact that in such an extension much is expressed differently in later years certainly cannot constitute a contradiction if one does not mean by consistency that the latter expression should be a mere copy of the earlier one, but is ready to observe a consistent development of a person. In order to avoid the verdict of "change of view" of critics who do not consider this fact, one would have to reiterate, when it is a question of thoughts, the same words over and over again.

RUDOLF STEINER

April 1914

THE RIDDLES OF PHILOSOPHY

Part I

Chapter I

*Guiding Thoughts on
the Method of Presentation*

If we follow the work of the mind invested by man in his attempts to solve the riddle of world and life, the words, "Know Thyself," which were inscribed as a motto in the temple of Apollo, will suggest themselves to the soul in its contemplation. The understanding for a world conception rests on the fact that the human soul can be stirred by the contemplation of these words. The nature of a living organism involves the necessity of feeling hunger. The nature of the human soul at a certain stage of its development causes a similar necessity. It is manifest in the need to gain from life a certain spiritual return that, just as food satisfies hunger, satisfies the soul's challenge, "Know Thyself." This feeling can lay hold on the human soul so powerfully that it can be forced to think, "Only then am I *fully human* in the true sense of the word when I develop within myself a relation to the world that expresses its fundamental character in the challenge, 'Know Thyself.'" The soul can reach the point where it considers this feeling as an *awakening* out of the dream of life that it dreamt before this particular experience.

During the first period of his life, man develops the power of memory through which he will, in later life, recollect his experiences back to a certain moment of his childhood. What lies *before* this moment he feels as a dream of life from which he awoke. The human soul would not be what it should be if the power of memory did not grow out of the dim soul life of the child. In a similar way the human soul can, at a more developed stage, think of its experience of the challenge expressed in the words, "Know Thyself." It can have the feeling that a soul life that does not awake out of its dream of life through this experience does not live up to its inner potentialities.

Philosophers have often pointed out that they are at a loss when asked about the nature of philosophy in the true sense of the word. One thing, however, is certain, namely, that one must see in philosophy a special form of satisfying the need of the human soul expressed in the challenge, "Know Thyself." Of this challenge one can know just as distinctly as one can know what hunger is, although one may be at a loss to give an explanation of the phenomenon of hunger that would be satisfactory to everybody.

It was probably a thought of this kind that motivated Johann Gottlieb Fichte when he stated that the philosophy a man chooses depends on the kind of man he is. Animated by this thought, one can examine the attempts that have been made in the course of history to find solutions for the riddles of philosophy. In these attempts one will find the nature of the human being himself revealed. For although man will try to silence his personal interests entirely when he intends to speak as a philosopher, there will, nevertheless, immediately appear in a philosophy what the *human personality* can make out of itself by unfolding those forces that are most centrally and most originally its own.

Seen from this viewpoint, the examination of the philosophical achievements with regard to the world riddles can excite certain expectations.

We can hope that such an examination can yield results concerning the nature of human soul development, and the writer of this book believes that in exploring the philosophical views of the occident he has found such results. Four distinctly discernible epochs in the evolution of the philosophical struggle of mankind presented themselves to his view. He had to recognize the difference of these epochs as distinct as the difference of the species of a realm of nature. This observation led him to acknowledge in the realm of the history of man's philosophical development the existence of objective spiritual impulses following a definite law of evolution of their own, independent of the individual men in whom they are observed. The achievements of these men as philosophers thus appear as the manifestation of these impulses that direct the courses of events under the surface of external history. The conviction is then suggested that such results arise from the *unprejudiced* observation of the historical facts, much as a natural law rests on the observation of facts of nature. The author of this book believes that he has not been misled by preconceptions to present an arbitrary construction of the historical process, but that the facts force the acknowledgment of results of the kind indicated.

It can be shown that in the evolutionary course of the philosophical struggle of mankind, periods are distinguishable, each of which lasts between seven and eight centuries. In each of these epochs there is a distinctly different impulse at work, as if it were under the surface of external history, sending its rays into the human personalities and thus causing the evolution of man's mode of philosophizing while taking its own definite course of development.

The way in which the facts support the distinction of these epochs is to be shown in the present book. Its author would like, as far as possible, to let the facts speak for themselves. At this point, he wants to offer a few guiding lines from which, however, the thoughts expressed in this book *did not take their departure*; they are the *results* of this book.

One can be of the opinion that these guiding lines correctly should have been placed at the end of the book because their truth follows only from the content of the complete presentation. They are, however, to precede the subject matter as a preliminary statement because they justify the inner structure of the book. For although they were the result of the author's research, they were naturally in his mind before he wrote the book and had their effect on its form. For the reader, however, it can be important to learn not only at the end of the book *why* the author presents his subject in a certain way, but to form his judgment concerning this method of presentation already during the reading. But only so much is to be stated here as is necessary for the understanding of the book's arrangement.

The first epoch of the development of philosophical views begins in Greek antiquity. It can be distinctly traced back as far as Pherekydes of Syros and Thales of Miletos and it comes to a close in the age of beginning Christianity. The spiritual aspiration of mankind in this age shows an essentially different character from that of earlier times. It is the age of awakening thought life. Prior to this age, the human soul lived in imaginative (symbolic) thought pictures that expressed its relation to the world and existence.

All attempts to find the philosophical thought life developed in pre-Greek times fail upon closer inspection. Genuine philosophy cannot be dated earlier than the Greek civilization. What may at first glance seem to resemble the element of thought in Oriental or Egyptian world contemplations proves, on closer inspection, to be not real thought but parabolic, symbolic conception. It is in Greece that the aspiration is born to gain knowledge of the world and its laws by means of an element that can be acknowledged as *thought* also in the present age. As long as the human soul conceives world phenomena through pictures, it feels itself intimately bound up with them. The soul feels itself in this phase to be a member of the world organism; it does not think of itself as an independent entity separated from this organism. As the pure pictureless thought awakens in the human soul, the soul begins to feel its separation from the world. Thought becomes the soul's educator for independence.

But the ancient Greek did not experience thought as modern man does. This is a fact that can be easily overlooked. A genuine insight into the ancient Greek's thought life will reveal the essential difference. The ancient Greek's experience of thought is comparable to our experience of a perception, to our experience of "red" or "yellow." Just as we today attribute a color or tone percept to a "thing," so the ancient Greek perceives thought *in* the world of things and as adhering to them. It is for this reason that thought at that time still is the connecting link between soul and world. The process of separation between soul and world is just beginning; it has not yet been completed. To be sure, the soul feels the thought within itself, but it must be of the opinion to have received it from the world and it can therefore expect the solution of the world riddles from its thought experience. It is in this type of thought experience that the philosophical development proceeds that begins with Pherekydes and Thales, culminates in Plato and Aristotle and then recedes until it ends at the time of the beginning of Christianity. From the undercurrents of the spiritual evolution, thought life streams into the souls of man and produces in these souls philosophies that educate them to feel themselves in their self-dependence independent of the outer world.

A new period begins with the dawn of the Christian era. The human soul can now no longer experience thought as a perception from the outer world. It now feels thought as the product of its own (inner) being. An impulse much more powerful than the stream of thought life now radiates into the soul from the deeper currents of the spiritual creative process. It is only now that self-consciousness awakes in mankind in a form adequate to the true nature of this self-consciousness. What men had experienced in this respect before that time had really only been harbingers and anticipatory phenomena of what one should in its deepest meaning call inwardly experienced self-consciousness.

It is to be hoped that a future history of spiritual evolution will call this time the "Age of Awakening Self-Consciousness." Only now does man become in the true sense of the word aware of the whole scope of his soul life as "Ego." The full weight of this fact is more instinctively felt than distinctly known by the philosophical spirits of that time. All philosophical aspirations of that epoch retain this general character up to the time of Scotus

Erigena. The philosophers of this period are completely submerged in religious conceptions with their philosophical thinking. Through this type of thought formation, the human soul, finding itself in an awakened self-consciousness entirely left to its own resources, strives to gain the consciousness of its submergence in the life of the world organism. Thought becomes a mere means to express the conviction regarding the relation of man's soul to the world that one has gained from religious sources. Steeped in this view, nourished by religious conceptions, thought life grows like the seed of a plant in the soul of the earth, until it breaks forth into the light.

In Greek philosophy the life of thought unfolds its own inner forces. It leads the human soul to the point where it feels its self-dependence. Then from greater depths of spiritual life an element breaks forth into mankind that is fundamentally different from thought life—an element that filled the soul with a new inner experience, with an awareness of being a world in itself, resting on its inner point of gravitation. Thus, self-consciousness is at first *experienced, but it is not as yet conceived in the form of thought.* The life of thought continues to be developed, concealed and sheltered in the warmth of religious consciousness. In this way pass the first seven or eight hundred years after the foundation of Christianity.

The next period shows an entirely different character. The leading philosophers feel the re-awakening of the energy of thought life. For centuries the human soul had been inwardly consolidated through the experience of its self-dependence. It now begins to search for what it might claim as its innermost self possession. It finds that this is its thought life. Everything else is given from without; thought is felt as something the soul has to produce out of its own depth, that is, the soul is present in full consciousness at this process of production. The urge arises in the soul to gain in thought a knowledge through which it can enlighten itself about its own relation to the world. How can something be expressed in thought life that is not itself merely the soul's own product? This becomes the question of the philosophers of that age. The spiritual trends of Nominalism,

Realism, Scholasticism and medieval Mysticism reveal this fundamental character of the philosophy of that age. The human soul attempts to examine its thought life with regard to its content of reality.

With the close of this third period the character of philosophical endeavor changes. The self-consciousness of the soul has been strengthened through century-long work performed in the examination of the reality of thought life. One has learned to feel the life of thought as something that is deeply related to the soul's own nature and to experience in this union an inner security of existence. As a mark of this stage of development, there shines like a brilliant star in the firmament of the spirit, the words, "I think, therefore I am," which were spoken by Descartes (1596–1650). One feels the soul flowing in thought life, and in the awareness of this stream one believes one experiences the true nature of the soul itself. The representative of that time feels himself so secure within this existence recognized in thought life that he arrives at the conviction that true knowledge could only be a knowledge that is experienced in the same way as the soul experiences thought life resting on its own foundation. This becomes the viewpoint of Spinoza (1632–1677).

Now philosophies emerge that shape the world picture as it must be imagined when the *self-conscious* human soul, conceived by the life of thought, can have its adequate position within that world. How must the world be depicted so that within it the human soul can be thought to correspond adequately to the necessary concept of the self-consciousness? This becomes the question that, in an unbiased observation, we find at the bottom of the philosophy of Giordano Bruno (1548–1600). It is also distinctly the question for which Leibnitz (1646–1716) seeks the answer.

With conceptions of a world picture arising from such a question the fourth epoch in the evolution of the philosophical world view begins. Our present age is approximately in the middle of this epoch. This book is to show how far philosophical knowledge has advanced in the conception of a world picture in which the self-conscious soul can find such a secure place, so that it can understand its own meaning and significance within the existing world. When, in the first epoch of philosophical search, philosophy derived its powers from the awakening thought life, the human soul was spurred by the hope of gaining a knowledge of a world to which it belongs with its true nature, which is not limited to the life manifested through the body of the senses.

In the fourth epoch the emerging natural sciences add a view of nature to the philosophical world picture that gradually senses its own independent ground. As this nature-picture develops, it retains nothing of a world in which the self-conscious ego (the human soul experiencing itself as a self-conscious entity) must recognize itself. In the first epoch the human soul begins to detach itself from the experienced external world and to develop a knowledge concerned with the inner life of the soul. This independent soul life finds its power in the awakening thought element. In the fourth period a picture of nature emerges that has detached itself in turn from the inner soul life. The tendency arises to think of nature in such a way that nothing is allowed to be mixed into its conception that has been derived from the soul and not exclusively from nature itself. Thus, the soul is, in this period, expelled from nature, and with its inner experiences confined to its subjective world. The soul is not about to be forced to admit that everything it can gain as knowledge by itself can have a significance only for itself. It cannot find in itself anything to point to a world in which this soul could have its roots with its true being. For in the picture of nature it cannot find any trace of itself.

The evolution of thought life has proceeded through four epochs. In the first, thought is experienced as a perception coming from without. In this phase the human soul finds its self-dependence through the thought process. In the second period, thought had exhausted its power in this direction. The soul now becomes stronger in the experience of its own entity. Thought itself now lives more in the background and blends into self knowledge. It can no longer be considered as if it were an external perception. The soul becomes used to experiencing it as its own product. It must arrive at the question of what this product of inner soul activity has to do with an external world. The third period passes in the light of this question. The philosophers develop a cognitive life that tests thought itself with regard to its inner power. The philosophical strength of the period manifests itself as a life in the element of thought as such, as a power to work through thought in its own essence. In the course of this epoch the philosophical life increases in its ability to master the element of thought. At the beginning of the fourth period the cognitive self-consciousness, on the basis of its thought possession, proceeds to form a philosophical world picture. This picture is now challenged by a picture of nature that refuses to accept any element of this self-consciousness. The self-conscious soul, confronted with this nature picture, feels as its fundamental question, "How do I gain a world picture in which both the inner world with its true essence and the external nature are securely rooted at the same time?" The impulse caused by this question dominates the philosophical evolution from the beginning of the fourth period; the philosophers themselves may be more or less aware of that fact. This is also the most important impulse of the philosophical life of the present age.

In this book the facts are to be characterized that show the effect of that impulse. The first volume of the book is to present the philosophical development up to the middle of the nineteenth century; the second will follow that development into the present time. It is to show at the end how the philosophical evolution leads the soul to aspects toward a future human life in cognition. Through this, the soul should be able to develop a world picture out of its own self-consciousness in which its true being can be conceived simultaneously with the picture of nature that is the result of the modern scientific development.

A philosophical future perspective adequate to the present was to be unfolded in this book from the historical evolution of the philosophical world view.

CHAPTER II

*The World Conception
of the Greek Thinkers*

With Pherekydes of Syros, who lived in the sixth century B.C., a personality appears in the Greek intellectual-spiritual life in whom one can observe the birth of what will be called in the following presentation, "a world and life conception." What he has to say about the problems of the world is, on the one hand, still like the mythical symbolic accounts of a time that lies before the striving for a scientific world conception; on the other hand, his imagination penetrates through the picture, through the myth, to a form of reflection that wants to pierce the problems of man's existence and of his position in the world by means of *thoughts*. He still imagines the earth in the picture of a winged oak around which Zeus wraps the surface land, oceans, rivers, etc., like a woven texture. He thinks of the world as permeated by spiritual beings of which Greek mythology speaks.

But Pherekydes also speaks of three principles of the world: Of Chronos, of Zeus and of Chthon.

Throughout the history of philosophy there has been much discussion as to what is to be understood by these three principles. As the historical sources on the question of what Pherekydes meant to say in his work, *Heptamychos*, are contradictory, it is quite understandable that present-day opinions also do not agree. If we reflect on the traditional accounts of Pherekydes, we get the impression that we can really observe in him the beginning of philosophical thought but that this observation is difficult because his words have to be taken in a sense that is remote from the thought habits of the present time; its real meaning is yet to be determined.*

Pherekydes arrives at his world picture in a different way from that of his predecessors. The significant fact is that he feels man to be a *living soul* in a way different from earlier times. For the earlier world view, the word, "soul," did not yet have the meaning that it acquired in later conceptions of life, nor did Pherekydes have the idea of the soul in the sense of later thinkers. He simply *feels* the soul-element of man, whereas the later thinkers want to speak clearly about it (in the form of thought) and they attempt to characterize it in intellectual terms. Men of earlier times do not as yet separate their own soul experience from the life of nature. They do not feel that they stand as a special entity beside nature. They experience *themselves* in nature as they experience lightning and thunder in it, the drifting of the clouds, the course of the stars or the growth of plants. What moves man's hand on his own body, what places his foot on the ground and makes him walk, for the prehistoric man, belongs to the same sphere of world forces that also causes lightning, cloud formations and all other external events. What he at this stage feels, can be expressed by saying, "Something causes lightning, thunder, rain, moves my hand, makes my foot

---

* This book, which is to give a picture of the world and life conceptions of the nineteenth century is, in its second edition, supplemented by a brief account of the preceding philosophies insofar as they are based on an *intellectual* conception of the world. I have done this because I feel that the ideas of the last century are better shown in their inner significance if they are not taken by themselves, but if the highlights of thought of the preceding ages fall on them. In such an "introduction" not all the "documentary materials" can be given that must form the basis of this short sketch. If I should have the opportunity to develop the sketch into an independent book, it would become clear that the appropriate basis really exists. I also have no doubt that others who want to see in this sketch a suggestion for new viewpoints will find the documentary evidence in the historical sources that have been traditionally handed down to us.

step, moves the air of my breath within me, turns my head." If one expresses what is in this way experienced, one has to use words that at first hearing seem to be exaggerated. But only through these exaggerations will it be possible to understand what is intended to be conveyed.

A man who holds a world picture as it is meant here, experiences in the rain that falls to the ground the action of a force that we at the present time must call "spiritual" and that he feels to be of the same kind as the force he experiences when he is about to exert a personal activity of some kind or other. It should be of interest that this view can be found again in Goethe in his younger years, naturally in a shade of thought that it must assume in a personality of the eighteenth century. We can read in Goethe's essay, *Nature*:

> She (nature) has placed me in life; she will also lead me out of it. I trust myself into her care. She may hold sway over me. She will not hate her work. It was not I who spoke about her. Nay, what is true and what is false—everything has been spoken by her. Everything is her fault, everything her merit.

To speak as Goethe speaks here is only then possible if one feels one's own being imbedded in nature as a whole and then expresses this feeling in *thoughtful reflection*. As Goethe thought, so man of an earlier time felt without transforming his soul experience into the element of thought. He did not as yet experience thought; instead of thought there unfolded within his soul a symbolic image. The observation of the evolution of mankind leads back to a time in which thought-like experiences had not yet come into being but in which the symbolic picture rose in the soul of man when he contemplated the events of the world. Thought life is born in man at a definite time. It causes the extinction of the previous form of consciousness in which the world is experienced in pictures.

For the thought habits of our time it seems acceptable to imagine that man in archaic times had observed natural elements—wind and weather, the growth of seeds, the course of the stars—and then poetically *invented* spiritual beings as the active creators of these events. It is, however, far from the contemporary mode of thinking to recognize the possibility that man in older times experienced those pictures as he later experienced thought, that is, as an inner reality of his soul life.

One will gradually come to recognize that in the course of the evolution of mankind a transformation of the human organization has taken place. There was a time when the subtle organs of human nature, which make possible the development of anN independent thought life, had not yet been formed. In this time man had, instead, organs that represented for him what he experienced in the world of pictures.

As this gradually comes to be understood, a new light will fall on the significance of mythology on the one hand, and that of poetic production and thought life on the other. When the independent inner thought experience began, it brought the picture-consciousness to extinction. Thought emerged as the tool of truth. This is only one branch of what survived of the old picture-consciousness that had found its expression in the ancient myth. In another branch the extinguished picture-consciousness continued to live, if only as a pale shadow of its former existence, in the creations of fantasy and poetic imagination. Poetic fantasy and the intellectual view of the world are the two children of the one mother, the old picture-consciousness that must not be confused with the consciousness of poetic imagination.

The essential process that is to be understood is the transformation of the more delicate organization of man. It causes the beginning of thought life. In art and poetry thought as such naturally does not have an effect. Here the picture continues to exert its influence, but it has now a different relation to the human soul from the one it had when it also served in a cognitive function. As *thought* itself, the new form of consciousness appears only in the newly emerging philosophy. The other branches of human life are correspondingly transformed in a different way when thought begins to rule in the field of human knowledge.

The progress in human evolution that is characterized by this process is connected with the fact that man from the beginning of thought experience had to feel *himself* in a much more pronounced way than before, as a separated entity, as a "soul." In *myth* the picture was experienced in such a way that one felt it to be in the external world as a reality. One experienced this reality at the same time, and one was united with it. With *thought,* as well as with the poetic *picture,* man felt himself separated from nature. Engaged in thought experience, man felt himself as an entity that could not experience nature with the same intimacy as he felt when at one with thought. More and more, the definite feeling of the contrast of nature and soul came into being.

In the civilizations of the different peoples this transition from the old picture-consciousness to the consciousness of thought experience took place at different times. In Greece we can intimately observe this transition if we focus our attention on the personality of Pherekydes of Syros. He lived in a world in which picture-consciousness and thought experience still had an equal share. His three principal ideas—Zeus, Chronos and Chthon—can only be understood in such a way that the soul, in experiencing them, feels itself as belonging to the events of the external world. We are dealing here with three inwardly experienced pictures and we find access to them only when we do not allow ourselves to be distracted by anything that the thought habits of our time are likely to imagine as their meaning.

Chronos is not time as we think of it today. Chronos is a being that in contemporary language can be called "spiritual" if one keeps in mind that one does not thereby exhaust its meaning. Chronos is alive and its activity is the devouring, the consumption of the life of another being, Chthon. Chronos rules in nature; Chronos rules in man; in nature and man Chronos consumes Chthon. It is of no importance whether one considers the consumption of Chthon through Chronos as inwardly experienced or as external events, for in both realms the same process goes on. Zeus is connected with these two beings. In the meaning of Pherekydes one must no more think of Zeus as a deity in the sense of our present day conception of mythology, than as of mere "space" in its present sense, although he is the being through whom the events that go on between Chronos and Chthon are transformed into spatial, extended form.

The co-operation of Chronos, Chthon and Zeus is felt directly as a picture content in the sense of Pherekydes, just as much as one is aware of the idea that one is eating, but it is also experienced as something in the external world, like the conception of the colors blue or red. This experience can be imagined in the following way. We turn our attention to fire as it consumes its fuel. Chronos lives in the activity of fire, of warmth. Whoever regards fire in its *activity* and keeps himself under the effect, not of independent thought but of image content, looks at Chronos. In the activity of fire, not in the sensually perceived fire, he experiences *time* simultaneously. Another conception of time does not exist before the birth of thought. What is called "time" in our present age is an idea that has been developed only in the age of intellectual world conception.

If we turn our attention to water, not as it is as water but as it changes into air or vapor, or to clouds that are in the process of dissolving, we experience as an image content the force of Zeus, the spatially active "spreader." One could also say, the force of centrifugal extension. If we look on water as it becomes solid, or on the solid as it changes into fluid, we are watching Chthon. Chthon is something that later in the age of thought-ruled world conception becomes "matter," the stuff "things are made of"; Zeus has become "ether" or "space," Chronos changes into "time."

In the view of Pherekydes the world is constituted through the co-operation of these three principles. Through the combination of their action the material world of sense perception—fire, air, water and earth—come into being on the one hand, and on the other, a certain number of invisible supersensible spirit beings who animate the four material worlds. Zeus, Chronos and Chthon could be referred to as "spirit, soul and matter," but their significance is only approximated by these terms. It is only through the fusion of these three original beings that the more material realms of the world of fire, air, water and earth, and the more soul-like and spirit-like (supersensible) beings come into existence. Using expressions of later world conceptions, one can call Zeus, space-ether; Chronos, time-creator; Chthon, matter-producer—the three "mothers of the world's origin." We can still catch a glimpse of them in Goethe's *Faust*, in the scene of the second part where Faust sets out on his journey to the "mothers."

As these three primordial entities appear in Pherekydes, they remind us of conceptions of predecessors of this personality, the so-called *Orphics*. They represent a mode of conception that still lives completely in the old form of picture consciousness. In them we also find three original beings: Zeus, Chronos and Chaos. Compared to these "primeval mothers," those of Pherekydes are somewhat less picture-like. This is so because Pherekydes attempts to seize, through the exertion of thought, what his Orphic predecessors still held completely as image-experience. For this reason we can say that he appears as a personality in whom the "birth of thought life" takes place. This is expressed not so much in the more thought-like conception of the Orphic ideas of Pherekydes, as in a certain dominating mood of his soul, which we later find again in several of his philosophizing successors in Greece. For Pherekydes feels that he is forced to see the origin of things in the "good" (Arizon). He could not combine this concept with the "world of mythological deities" of ancient times. The beings of this world had soul qualities that were not in agreement with this concept. Into his three "original causes" Pherekydes could only think the concept of the "good," the perfect.

Connected with this circumstance is the fact that the birth of thought life brought with it a shattering of the foundations of the inner feelings of the soul. This inner experience should not be over-looked in a consideration of the time when the intellectual world conception began. One could not have felt this beginning as progress if one had not believed that with thought one took possession of something that was more perfect than the old form of image experience. Of course, at this stage of thought development, this feeling was not clearly expressed. But what one now, in retrospect, can clearly state with regard to the ancient Greek thinkers was then merely felt. They felt that the pictures that were experienced by our immediate ancestors did not lead to the highest, most perfect, original causes. In these pictures only the less perfect causes were revealed; we must raise our thoughts to still higher causes from which the content of those pictures is merely derived.

Through progress into thought life, the world was now conceived as divided into a more natural and a more spiritual sphere. In this more spiritual sphere, which was only now felt as such, one had to conceive what was formerly experienced in the form of pictures. To this was added the conception of a higher principle, something thought of as superior to the older, spiritual world and to nature. It was to this sublime element that thought wanted to penetrate, and it is in this region that Pherekydes meant to find his three "Primordial Mothers." A look at the world as it appears illustrates what kind of conceptions took hold of a personality like Pherekydes. Man finds a harmony in his surroundings that lies at the bottom of all phenomena and is manifested in the motions of the stars, in the course of the seasons with their blessings of thriving plant-life, etc. In this beneficial course of things, harmful, destructive powers intervene, as expressed in the pernicious effects of the weather, earthquakes, etc. In observing all this one can be lead to a realization of a dualism in the ruling powers, but the human soul must assume an underlying unity. It naturally feels that, in the last analysis, the ravaging hail, the destructive earthquake, must spring from the same source as the beneficial cycle of the seasons. In this fashion man looks through good and evil and sees behind it an original good. The same good force rules in the earthquake as in the blessed rain of spring. In the scorching, devastating heat of the sun the same element is at work that ripens the seed. The "good Mothers of all origin" are, then, in the pernicious events also. When man experiences this feeling, a powerful world riddle emerges before his soul. To find the solution, Pherekydes turns toward his Ophioneus. As Pherekydes leans on the old picture conception, Ophioneus appears to him as a kind of "world serpent." It is in reality a spirit being, which, like all other beings of the world, belongs to the children of Chronos, Zeus and Chthon, but that has later so changed that its effects are directed against those of the "good mother of origin." Thus, the world is divided into three parts. The first part consists of the "Mothers," which are presented as good, as perfect; the second part contains the beneficial world events; the third part, the destructive or the only imperfect world processes that, as Ophioneus, are intertwined in the beneficial effects.

For Pherekydes, Ophioneus is not merely a symbolic idea for the detrimental destructive world forces. Pherekydes stands with his conceptive imagination at the borderline between picture and thought. He does not think that there are devastating powers that he conceives in the pictures of Ophioneus, nor does such a thought process develop in him as an activity of fantasy. Rather, he looks on the detrimental forces, and immediately Ophioneus stands before his soul as the red color stands before our souls when we look at a rose.

Whoever sees the world only as it presents itself to image perception does not, at first, distinguish in his thought between the events of the "good mothers" and those of Ophioneus. At the borderline of a thought-formed world conception, the necessity of this distinction is felt, for only at this stage of progress does the soul feel itself to be a separate, independent entity. It feels the necessity to ask what its origin is. It must find its origin in the depths of the world where Chronos, Zeus and Chthon had not as yet found their antagonists. But the soul also feels that it cannot know anything of its own origin at first, because it sees itself in the midst of a world in which the "Mothers" work in conjunction with Ophioneus. It feels itself in a world in which the perfect and the imperfect are joined together. Ophioneus is twisted into the soul's own being.

We can feel what went on in the souls of individual personalities of the sixth century B.C. if we allow the feelings described here to make a sufficient impression on us. With the ancient mythical deities such souls felt themselves woven into the imperfect world. The deities belonged to the same imperfect world as they did themselves.

The spiritual brotherhood, which was founded by Pythagoras of Samos between the years 549 and 500 B.C. in Kroton in Magna Graecia, grew out of such a mood. Pythagoras intended to lead his followers back to the experience of the "Primordial Mothers" in which the origin of their souls was to be seen. It can be said in this respect that he and his disciples meant to serve "other gods" than those of the people. With this fact something was given that must appear as a break between spirits like Pythagoras and the people, who were satisfied with their gods. Pythagoras considered these gods as belonging to the realm of the imperfect. In this difference we also find the reason for the "secret" that is often referred to in connection with Pythagoras and that was not to be betrayed to the uninitiated. It consisted in the fact that Pythagoras had to attribute to the human soul an origin different from that of the gods of the popular religion. In the last analysis, the numerous attacks that Pythagoras experienced must be traced to this "secret." How was he to explain to others than those who carefully prepared themselves for such a knowledge that, in a certain sense, they, "as souls," could consider themselves as standing even higher than the gods of the popular religion? In what other form than in a brotherhood with a strictly regulated mode of life could the souls become aware of their lofty origin and still find themselves deeply bound up with imperfection? It was just through this feeling of deficiency that the effort was to be made to arrange life in such a way that through the process of self-perfection it would be led back to its origin. That legends and myths were likely to be formed about such aspirations of Pythagoras is comprehensible. It is also understandable that scarcely anything has come down to us historically about the true significance of this personality. Whoever observes the legends and mythical traditions of antiquity about Pythagoras in an all-encompassing picture will nevertheless recognize in it the characterization that was just given.

In the picture of Pythagoras, present-day thinking also feels the idea of the so-called "transmigration of souls" as a disturbing factor. It is even felt to be naive that Pythagoras is reported to have said that he knew that he had already been on earth in an earlier time as another human being. It may be recalled that that great representative of modern enlightenment, Lessing, in his *Education of the Human Race*, renewed this idea of man's repeated lives on earth out of a mode of thinking that was entirely different from that of Pythagoras. Lessing could conceive of the progress of the human race only in such a way that the human souls participated repeatedly in the life of the successive great phases of history. A soul brought into its life in a later time as a potential ability what it had gained from experience in an earlier era. Lessing found it natural that the soul had often been on earth in an earthly body, and that it would often return in the future. In this way, it struggles from life to life toward the perfection that it finds possible to obtain. He pointed out that the idea of repeated lives on earth ought not to be considered incredible because it existed in ancient times, and "because it occurred to the human mind before academic sophistry had distracted and weakened it."

The idea of reincarnation is present in Pythagoras, but it would be erroneous to believe that he—along with Pherekydes, who is mentioned as his teacher in antiquity—had yielded to this idea because he had by means of a logical conclusion arrived at the thought that the path of development indicated above could only be reached in repeated earthly lives. To attribute such an intellectual mode of thinking to Pythagoras would be to misjudge him. We are told of his extensive journeys. We hear that he met together with wise men who had preserved traditions of oldest human insight. When we observe the oldest human conceptions that have come down to us through posterity, we arrive at the view that the idea of repeated lives on earth was widespread in remote antiquity. Pythagoras took up the thread from the oldest teachings of humanity. The mythical teachings in picture form appeared to him as deteriorated conceptions that had their origin in older and superior insights. These picture doctrines were to change in his time into a thought-formed world conception, but this intellectual world conception appeared to him as only a part of the soul's life. This part had to be developed to greater depths. It could then lead the soul to its origins. By penetrating in this direction, however, the soul discovers in its inner experience the repeated lives on earth as a *soul perception*. It does not reach its origins unless it finds its way through the repeated terrestrial lives. As a wanderer walking to a distant place naturally passes through other places on his path, so the soul on its path to the "mothers" passes the preceding lives through which it has gone during its descent from its former existence in perfection, to its present life in imperfection. If one considers everything that is pertinent in this problem, the inference is inescapable that the view of repeated earth lives is to be attributed to Pythagoras in this sense as his inner perception, not as something that was arrived at through a process of conceptual conclusion.

Now the view that is spoken of as especially characteristic of the followers of Pythagoras is that all things are based on numbers. When this statement is made, one must consider that the school of Pythagoras was continued into later times after his death. Philoaos, Archytas and others are mentioned as later Pythagoreans. It was about them especially that one in antiquity knew they "considered things as numbers." We can assume that this view goes back to Pythagoras even if historical documentation does not appear possible. We shall, however, have to suppose that this view was deeply and organically rooted in his whole mode of conception, and that it took on a more superficial form with his successors.

Let us think of Pythagoras as standing before the beginning of intellectual world conception. He saw how thought took its origin in the soul that had, starting from the "mothers," descended through its successive lives to its state of imperfection. Because he felt this he could not mean to ascend to the origins through mere thought. He had to seek the highest knowledge in a sphere in which thought was not yet at home. There he found a life of the soul that was beyond thought life.

As the soul experiences proportional numbers in the sound of music, so Pythagoras developed a soul life in which he knew himself as living in a connection with the world that can be intellectually expressed in terms of numbers. But for what is thus experienced, these numbers have no other significance than the physicist's proportional tone numbers have for the experience of music.

For Pythagoras the mythical gods must be replaced by thought. At the same time, he develops an appropriate deepening of the soul life; the soul, which through thought has separated itself from the world, finds itself *at one* with the world again. It experiences itself as *not* separated from the world. This does not take place in a region in which the world-participating experience turns into a mythical picture, but in a region in which the soul reverberates with the invisible, sensually imperceptible cosmic harmonies. It brings into awareness, not its own thought intentions, but what cosmic powers exert as their will, thus allowing it to become conception in the soul of man.

In Pherekydes and Pythagoras the process of how thought-experienced world conception originates in the human soul is revealed. Working themselves free from the older forms of conception, these men arrive at an inwardly independent conception of the "soul" distinct from external "nature." What is clearly apparent in these two personalities—the process in which the soul wrests its way out of the old picture conceptions —takes place more in the *undercurrents* of the souls of the other thinkers with whom it is customary to begin the account of the development of Greek philosophy. The thinkers who are ordinarily mentioned first are *Thales* of Miletos (640–550 B.C.), *Anaximander* (born 610 B.C.), *Anaximenes* (flourished 600 B.C.) and *Heraclitus* (born 500 B.C. at Ephesus).

Whoever acknowledges the preceding arguments to be justified will also find a presentation of these men admissible that must differ from the usual historical accounts of philosophy. Such accounts are, after all, always based on the unexpressed presupposition that these men had arrived at their traditionally reported statements through an imperfect observation of nature.

Thus the statement is made that the fundamental and original being of all things was to be found in "water," according to Thales; in the "infinite," according to Anaximander; in "air," according to Anaximenes; in "fire," in the opinion of Heraclitus.

What is not considered in this treatment is the fact that these men are still really living in the process of the genesis of intellectual world conception. To be sure, they feel the independence of the human soul in a higher degree than Pherekydes, but they have not yet completed the strict separation of the life of the soul from the process of nature. One will, for instance, most certainly construct an erroneous picture of Thales's way of thinking if it is imagined that he, as a merchant, mathematician and astronomer, thought about natural events and then, in an imperfect yet similar way to that of a modern scientist, had summed up his results in the sentence, "Everything originates from water." To be a mathematician or an astronomer, etc., in those ancient times meant to deal in a practical way with the things of these professions, much in the way a craftsman makes use of technical skills rather than intellectual and scientific knowledge.

What must be presumed for a man like Thales is that he still experienced the external processes of nature as similar to inner soul processes. What presented itself to him like a natural event, as did the process and nature of "water" (the fluid, mudlike, earth-formative element), he experienced in a way that was similar to what he felt within himself in soul and body. He then experienced in himself and outside in nature the effect of water, although to a lesser degree than man of earlier times did. Both effects were for him the manifestation of *one* power. It may be pointed out that at a still later age the external effects in nature were thought of as being akin to the inner processes in a way that did not provide for a "soul" in the present sense as distinct from the body. Even in the time of intellectual world conception, the idea of the temperaments still preserves this point of view as a reminiscence of earlier times.

One called the melancholic temperament, the earthy; the phlegmatic, the watery; the sanguinic, the airy; the choleric, the fiery. These are not merely allegorical expressions. One did not feel a completely separated soul element, but experienced in oneself a soul-body entity as a unity. In this unity was felt the stream of forces that go, for instance, through a phlegmatic soul, to be like the forces in external nature that are experienced in the effects of water. One saw these external water effects to be the same as what the soul experienced in a phlegmatic mood. The thought habits of today must attempt an empathy with the old modes of conception if they want to penetrate into the soul life of earlier times.

In this way one will find in the world conception of Thales an expression of what his soul life, which was akin to the phlegmatic temperament, caused him to experience inwardly. He experienced in himself what appeared to him to be the world mystery of water. The allusion to the phlegmatic temperament of a person is likely to be associated with a derogatory meaning of the term. Justified as this may be in many cases, it is nevertheless also true that the phlegmatic temperament, when it is combined with an energetic, objective imagination, makes a sage out of a man because of its calmness, collectedness and freedom from passion. Such a disposition in Thales probably caused him to be celebrated by the Greeks as one of their wise men.

For Anaximenes, the world picture formed itself in another way. He experienced in himself the sanguine temperament. A word of his has been handed down to us that immediately shows how he felt the air element as an expression of the world mystery. "As our soul, which is a breath, holds us together, so air and breath envelop the universe."

The world conception of Heraclitus will, in an unbiased contemplation, be felt directly as a manifestation of his choleric inner life. A member of one of the most noble families of Ephesus, he became a violent antagonist of the democratic party because he had arrived at certain views, the truth of which was apparent to him in his immediate inner experience. The views of those around him, compared with his own, seemed to him to prove directly in a most natural way, the foolishness of his environment. Thus, he got into such conflicts that he left his native city and led a solitary life at the Temple of Artemis. Consider these few of his sayings that have come down to us. "It would be good if the Ephesians hanged themselves as soon as they grew up and surrendered their city to those under age." Or the one about men, "Fools in their lack of understanding, even if they hear the truth, are like the deaf: of them does the saying bear witness that they are absent when present."

The feeling that is expressed in such a choleric temperament finds itself akin to the consuming activity of fire. It does not live in the restful calm of "being." It feels itself as one with eternal "becoming." Such a soul feels stationary existence to be an absurdity. "Everything flows," is, therefore, a famous saying of Heraclitus. It is only apparently so if somewhere an unchanging being seems to be given. We are lending expression to a feeling of Heraclitus if we say, "The rock seems to represent an absolute unchanging state of being, but this is only appearance; it is inwardly in the wildest commotion; all its parts act upon one another." The mode of thinking of Heraclitus is usually characterized by his saying, "One cannot twice enter the same stream, for the second time the water is not the same." A disciple of Heraclitus, Cratylus, goes still further by saying that one could not even enter the same stream once. Thus it is with all things. While we look at what is apparently unchanging, it has already turned into something else in the general stream of existence.

We do not consider a world conception in its full significance if we accept only its thought content. Its essential element lies in the mood it communicates to the soul, that is, in the vital force that grows out of it. One must realize how Heraclitus feels himself with his own soul in the stream of becoming. The world soul pulsates in his own human soul and communicates to it of its own life as long as the human soul knows itself as living in it. Out of such a feeling of union with the world soul, the thought originates in Heraclitus, "Whatever lives has death in itself through the stream of becoming that is running through everything, but death again has life in itself. Life and death are in our living and dying. Everything has everything else in itself;

only thus can eternal becoming flow through everything." "The ocean is the purest and impurest water, drinkable and wholesome to fishes, to men undrinkable and pernicious." "Life and death are the same, waking and sleeping, young and old; the first changes into the second and again into the first." "Good and evil are one." "The straight path and the crooked . . . are one."

Anaximander is freer from the inner life, more surrendered to the element of thought itself. He sees the origin of things in a kind of world ether, an indefinite formless basic entity that has no limits. Take the Zeus of Pherekydes, deprive him of every image content that he still possesses and you have the original principle of Anaximander: Zeus turned into thought. A personality appears in Anaximander in whom thought life is borne out of the mood of soul that still has, in the preceding thinkers, the color of temperament. Such a personality feels united as a soul with the life of thought, and thereby is not so intimately interwoven with nature as the soul that does not yet experience thought as an independent element. It feels itself connected with a world order that lies *above* the events of nature. When Anaximander says that men lived first as fishes in the moist element and then developed through land animal forms, he means that the spirit germ, which man recognizes through thinking as his true being, has gone through the other forms only as through preliminary stages, with the aim of giving itself eventually the shape that has been appropriate for him from the beginning.

The thinkers mentioned so far are succeeded historically by *Xenophanes* of Kolophon (born 570 B.C.); *Parmenides* (460 B.C., living as a teacher in Athens), younger and inwardly related to Xenophanes; *Zenon* of Elea (who reached his peak around 500 B.C.); *Melissos* of Samos (about 450 B.C.).

The thought element is already alive to such a degree in these thinkers that they demand a world conception in which the life of thought is fully satisfied; they recognize truth only in this form. How must the world ground be constituted so that it can be fully absorbed within thinking? This is their question.

Xenophanes finds that the popular gods cannot stand the test of thought; therefore, he rejects them. His god must be capable of being *thought*. What the senses perceive is changeable, is burdened with qualities not appropriate to thought, whose function it is to seek what is permanent. Therefore, God is the unchangeable, eternal unity of all things to be seized in thought.

Parmenides sees the Untrue, the Deceiving, in sense-perceived, external nature. He sees what alone is true in the Unity, the Imperishable that is seized by thought. Zeno tries to come to terms with, and do justice to, the thought experience by pointing out the contradictions that result from a world view that sees truth in the change of things, in the process of becoming, in the multiplicity that is shown by the external world. One of the contradictions pointed out by Zeno is that the fastest runner (Achilles) could not catch up with a turtle, for no matter how slowly it moved, the moment Achilles arrived at the point it had just occupied, it would have moved on a little. Through such contradictions Zeno intimates how a conceptual imagination that leans on the external world is caught in self-contradiction. He points to the difficulty such thought meets when it attempts to find the truth.

One will recognize the significance of this world conception, which is called the "eleatic view" (Parmenides and Zeno are from Elea), if one considers that those who hold this view have advanced with the development of thought experience to the point of having transformed it into a special art, the so-called dialectic. In the "art of thought" the soul learns to feel itself in its self-dependence and its inward self-sufficiency. With this step, the reality of the soul is felt to be what it is through its own being. It experiences itself through the fact that it no longer, as in earlier times, follows the general world experience with its life, but unfolds independent thought experience within itself. This experience is rooted in itself and through it, it can feel itself planted into a pure spiritual ground of the world. At first, this feeling is not expressed as a distinctly formulated thought but, in the esteem it enjoyed, it can be sensed vividly as a feeling in this age. According to a Dialogue of Plato, the young Socrates is told by Parmenides that he should learn the "art of thought" from Zeno; otherwise, truth would be unattainable for him. This "art of thought" was felt to be a necessity for the human soul intending to approach the spiritual fundamental grounds of existence.

Whoever does not see how, in the progress of human development toward the stage of thought experience, real experiences—the picture experiences—came to an end with the beginning of this thought life, will not see the special quality of the Greek thinkers from the sixth to the fourth pre-Christian centuries in the light in which they must appear in this presentation. Thought formed a wall around the human soul, so to speak. The soul had formerly felt as if it were within the phenomena of nature. What it experienced in these natural phenomena, like the activities of its own body, presents itself to the soul in the form of images that appeared in vivid reality. Through the power of thought this entire panorama was now extinguished. Where previously images saturated in content prevailed, thought now expanded through the external world. The soul could experience itself in the surroundings of space and time only if it united itself with thought.

One senses such a mood of soul in *Anaxagoras* of Clazomenae in Asia Minor (born 500 B.C.). He found himself deeply bound up in his soul with thought life. His thought life encompassed what is extended in space and time. Expanded like this, it appears as the *nous,* the world reason. It penetrates the whole of nature as an entity. Nature, however, presents itself as composed only of little basic entities. The events of nature that result from the combined actions of these fundamental entities are what the senses perceive after the texture of imagery has vanished from nature. These fundamental entities are called *homoiomeries.* The soul experiences in thought the connection with the world reason (the nous) inside its wall. Through the windows of the senses it watches what the world reason causes to come into being through the action of the homoiomeries on each other.

Empedocles (born 490 B.C. in Agrigent) was a personality in whose soul the old and the new modes of conception clash as in a violent antagonism. He still feels something of the old mode of being in which the soul was more closely interwoven with external existence. Hatred and love, antipathy and sympathy live in the human soul. They also live outside the wall that encloses it. The life of the soul is thus homogeneously extended beyond its boundaries and it appears in forces that separate and connect the elements of external nature—air, fire, water and earth—thereby causing what the senses perceive in the outer world.

Empedocles is, as it were, confronted with nature, which appears to the senses to be deprived of life and soul, and he develops a soul mood that revolts against this extirpation of nature's animation. His soul cannot believe that nature really is what thought wants to make of it. Least of all can it admit that it should stand in such a relation to nature as it appears according to the intellectual world conception. We must imagine what goes on in a soul that senses such a discord in all its harshness, suffering from it. We shall then be capable of entering into the experience of how, in this soul of Empedocles, the old mode of conception is resurrected as the power of intimate feeling but is unwilling to raise this fact into full consciousness. It thus seeks a form of existence in a shade of experience hovering between thought and picture that is re-echoed in the sayings of Empedocles. These lose their strangeness if they are understood in this way. The following aphorism is attributed to him. "Farewell. A mortal no longer, but an immortal god I wander about . . ·. and as soon as I come into the flourishing cities I am worshipped by men and women. They follow me by the thousands, seeking the path of their salvation with me, some expecting prophecies, others, curative charms for many diseases."

In such a way, a soul that is haunted by an old form of consciousness through which it feels its own existence as that of a banished god who is cast out of another form of existence into the soul-deprived world of the senses, is dazed. He therefore feels the earth to be an "unaccustomed place" into which he is cast as in punishment. There are certainly other sentiments also to be found in the soul of Empedocles because significant flashes of wisdom shine in his aphorisms. His feeling with respect to the "birth of the intellectual world conception" is characterized, however, by the thought mood mentioned above.

The thinkers who are called the atomists regarded what nature had become for the soul of man through the birth of thought in a different way. The most important among them is *Democritus* (born 460 B.C. in Abdera). *Leucippus* is a kind of forerunner to him.

With Democritus, the homoiomeries of Anaxagoras have become, to a considerable degree, more material. In Anaxagoras, one can still compare the entities of the basic parts with living germs. With Democritus, they become dead indivisible particles of matter, which in their different combinations make up the things of the outer world. They mix freely as they move to and fro; thus, the events of nature come to pass. The world reason (nous) of Anaxagoras, which has the world processes grow out of the combined action of the homoiomeries like a spiritual (incorporeal) consciousness, with Democritus, turns into the unconscious law of nature (*ananke*). The soul is ready to recognize only what it can grasp as the result of simple thought combinations. Nature is now completely deprived of life and soul; thought has paled as a soul experience into the inner shadow of inanimate nature. In this way, with Democritus, the intellectual *prototype* of all more or less materialistically colored world conceptions of later times has made its appearance.

The atom world of Democritus represents an external world, a nature in which no trace of soul life can be found. The thought experiences in the soul, through which the soul has become aware of itself, are mere shadow experiences in Democritus. Thus, a part of the fate of thought experiences is characterized. They bring the human soul to the consciousness of its own being, but they fill it at the same time with uncertainty about itself. The soul experiences itself in itself through thought, but it can at the same time feel that it lost its anchorage in the independent spiritual world power that used to lend it security and inner stability. This emancipation of the soul was felt by the group of men in Greek intellectual life known as "Sophists." The most important among them is *Protagoras* of Abdera (480–410 B.C.). Also to be noted besides him are Georgias, Critias, Hippias, Trasymachus and Prodicus.

The sophists are often presented as men who superficially played with their thinking. Much has been contributed to this opinion by the manner in which Aristophanes, the playwright of comedies, treated them, but there are many things that can lead to a better appreciation of the sophists. It is noteworthy that even Socrates, who to a certain limited extent thought of himself as a pupil of Prodicus, is said to have described him as a man who had done much for the refinement of the speech and thinking of his disciples.

Protagoras's view is expressed in the famous statement, "Man is the measure of all things, of those that are, that they are; of those that are not, that they are not." In the sentiment underlying this statement the thought experience feels itself sovereign. It does not sense any connection with an objective world power. If Parmenides is of the opinion that the senses supply man with a world of deception, one could go further and add, "Why should not thinking, although one experiences it, also deceive?" Protagoras, however, would reply to this, "Why should it be man's concern if the world outside him is not as he perceives and thinks it? Does he imagine it for anyone else but himself? No matter how it may be for another being, this should be of no concern to man. The contents of his mind are only to serve him; with their aid he is to find his way through the world. Once he achieves complete clarity about himself, he cannot wish for any thought contents about the world except those that serve him." Protagoras means to be able to build on thinking. For this purpose he intends to have it rest exclusively on its own sovereign power.

With this step, however, Protagoras places himself in contradiction to the spirit that lives in the depths of Greek life. This spirit is distinctly perceptible in the Greek character. It manifests itself in the inscription, "Know Thyself," at the temple of Delphi. This ancient oracle wisdom speaks as if it contained the challenge for the progress of world conceptions that advances from the conception in images to the form of consciousness in which the secrets of the world are seized through thought. Through this challenge man is directed to his own soul. He is told that he can hear the language in his soul through which the world expresses its essence. He is thereby also directed toward something that produces uncertainties and insecurities for itself in its experience. The leading spirits of Greek civilization were to conquer the dangers of this self-supporting soul life. Thus, they were to develop thought in the soul into a world conception.

In the course of this development the sophists navigated in dangerous straits. In them the Greek spirit places itself at an abyss; it means to produce the strength of equilibrium through its own power. One should, as has been pointed out, consider the gravity and boldness of this attempt, rather than lightly condemn it even though condemnation is certainly justified for many of the sophists.

This attempt of the sophists takes place at a natural turning point of Greek life. Protagoras lived from 480 to 410 B.C. The Peloponnesian War, which occurred at this turning point of Greek civilization, lasted from 431 to 404 B.C. Before this war the individual member of Greek society had been firmly enclosed by his social connections. Commonwealth and tradition provided the measuring stick for his actions and thinking. The individual person had value and significance only as a member of the total structure. Under such circumstances the question, "What is the value of the individual human being?" could not be asked. The sophists, however, do ask this question, and in so doing introduce the era of Greek Enlightenment. Fundamentally, it is the question of how man arranges his life after he has become aware of his awakened thought life.

From Pherekydes (or Thales) to the sophists, one can observe how emaciated thought in Greece, which had already been born before these men, gradually finds its place in the stream of philosophical development. The effect thought has when it is placed in the service of world conception becomes apparent in them. The birth of thought, however, is to be observed in the entire Greek life. One could show much the same kind of development in the fields of art, poetry, public life, the various crafts and trades, and one would see everywhere how human activity changes under the influence of the form of human organization that introduces thought into the world conception. It is not correct to say that philosophy "discovers" thought. It comes into existence through the fact that the newly born thought life is used for the construction of a world picture that formerly had been formed out of experiences of a different kind.

* * *

While the sophists led the spirit of Greece, expressed in the motto, "Know Thyself," to the edge of a dangerous cliff, Socrates, who was born in Athens about 470 and was condemned to death through poison in 399 B.C., expressed this spirit with a high degree of perfection.

Historically, the picture of Socrates has come down to us through two channels of tradition. In one, we have the figure that his great disciple, Plato (427–347 B.C.), has drawn of him. Plato presents his philosophy in dialogue form, and Socrates appears in these dialogues as a teacher. He is shown as the "sage" who leads the persons around him through intellectual guidance to high stages of insight. A second picture has been drawn by Xenophon in his *Memorabilia of Socrates*. At first sight it seems as if Plato had idealized the character of Socrates and as if Xenophon had portrayed him more directly as he had been. But a more intimate inspection would likely show that both Plato and Xenophon each drew a picture of Socrates as they saw him from a special point of view. One is justified, therefore, in considering the question as to how these pictures supplement and illuminate each other.

The first thing that must appear significant here is that Socrates's philosophy has come down to posterity entirely as an expression of his personality, of the fundamental character of his soul life. Both Plato and Xenophon present Socrates in such a way that in him his personal opinion speaks everywhere. This personality carries in itself the awareness that, whoever expresses his personal opinion out of the true ground of the soul, expresses something that is more than just human opinion, something that is a manifestation of the purposes of the world order through human thinking. By those who think they know him, Socrates is taken as the living proof for the conviction that truth is revealed in the human soul through thinking if, as was the case with Socrates, this soul is grounded in its own substance. Looking on Socrates, Plato does not teach a doctrine that is asserted by contemplative thought, but the thought has a rightly developed human being speak, who then observes what he produces as truth. Thus, the manner in which Plato behaves toward Socrates becomes an expression for what man is in his relation to the world. What Plato has advanced about Socrates is significant and also the way in which he, in his activity as a writer, has placed Socrates in the world of Greek spiritual life.

With the birth of thought man was directed toward his "soul." The question now arises as to what this soul says when it begins to speak, expressing what the world forces have laid into it. Through the attitude Plato takes with respect to Socrates, the resulting answer is that in the human soul the reason of the world speaks what it intends to reveal to man. The foundation is laid with this step for the *confidence* expressed in the revelations of the human soul insofar as it develops *thought* in itself. The figure of Socrates appears in the sign of this confidence.

In ancient times the Greek consulted the oracles in the most important questions of life. He asked for prophecy, the revelation of the will and the opinion of the spiritual powers. Such an arrangement is in accord with the soul experience in images. Through the image man feels himself bound to the powers holding sway over the world. The oracle, then, is the institution by means of which somebody who is especially gifted in that direction finds his way to the spiritual powers better than other people. As long as one did not experience one's soul as separated from the outer world, the feeling was natural that this external world was able to express more through a special institution than through everyday experience. The picture spoke from without. Why should the outer world not be capable of speaking distinctly at a special place? Thought speaks to the inner soul. With thought, therefore, the soul is left *to its own resources*; it cannot feel united with another soul as with the revelations of a priestly oracle. To thought, one had to lend one's own soul. One felt of thought that it was a common possession of all men.

World reason shines into thought life without especially established institutions. Socrates felt that the force lives in the thinking soul that used to be sought in the *oracles*. He experienced the "daimonion" in himself, the spiritual force that leads the soul. Thought has brought the soul to the consciousness of itself. With his conception of the daimonion speaking in him that, always leading him, told him what to do, Socrates meant to say, "The soul that has found its way to the thought life is justified to feel as if it communicated in itself with the world reason. It is an expression of the high valuation of what the soul possesses in its thought experience."

"Virtue," under the influence of this view, is placed in a special light. Because Socrates values thought, he must presuppose that true virtue in human life reveals itself in the life of thought. True virtue must be found in thought life because it is from thought life that man derives his value. "Virtue is teachable." In this way is Socrates's conception most frequently expressed. It is teachable because whoever really seizes thought life must be in its possession. What Xenophon says about Socrates is significant in this respect. Socrates teaches a disciple about virtue and the following dialogue develops.

Socrates says:

> Do you believe there is a doctrine and science of justice, just as there is a doctrine of grammar?

The disciple:

> Yes, I do.

Socrates:

> Whom do you consider now as better versed in grammar, the one who intentionally writes and reads incorrectly, or the one who does so without intention?

The disciple:

> I should think the one who does it intentionally, for if he meant to, he could also do it correctly.

Socrates:

> Does it not seem to you that the one who intentionally writes incorrectly knows how to write, but the other one does not?

The disciple:

> Without doubt.

Socrates:

> Who now understands more of justice, he who intentionally lies or cheats, or he who does so inadvertently?

Socrates attempts to make clear to the disciple that what matters is to have the right thoughts about virtue. So also what Socrates says about virtue aims at the establishment of *confidence* in a soul that knows itself through thought experience. The right thoughts about virtue are to be trusted more than all other motivations. Virtue makes man more valuable when he experiences it in thought.

Thus, what the pre-Socratic age strove for becomes manifest in Socrates, that is, the appreciation of what humanity has been given through the awakened thought life. Socrates's method of teaching is under the influence of this conception. He approaches man with the presupposition that thought in life is in him; it only needs to be awakened. It is for this reason that he arranges his questions in such a way that the questioned person is stimulated to awaken his own thought life. This is the substance of the Socratic method.

Plato, who was born in Athens in 427 B.C., felt, as a disciple of Socrates, that his master had helped him to consolidate his confidence in the life of thought. What the entire previous development tended to bring into appearance reaches a climax in Plato. This is the conception that in thought life the world spirit reveals itself. The awareness of this conception sheds, to begin with, its light over all of Plato's soul life. Nothing that man knows through the senses or otherwise has any value as long as the soul has not exposed it to the light of thought. Philosophy becomes for Plato the science of *ideas* as the world of true being, and the *idea* is the manifestation of the world spirit through the revelation of thought. The light of the world spirit shines into the soul of man and reveals itself there in the form of *ideas*; the human soul, in seizing the idea, unites itself with the force of the world spirit. The world that is spread in space and time is like the mass of the ocean water in which the stars are reflected, but what is real is only reflected as idea. Thus, for Plato, the whole world changes into ideas that act upon each other. Their effect in the world is produced through the fact that the ideas are reflected in *hyle*, the original matter. What we see as the many individual things and events comes to pass through this reflection. We need not extend knowledge to hyle, the original matter, however, for in it is no truth. We reach truth only if we strip the world picture of everything that is not idea. For Plato, the human soul is living in the idea, but this life is so constituted that the soul is not a manifestation of its life in the ideas in all its utterances. Insofar as it is submerged in the life of ideas, it appears as the "rational soul" (thought-bearing soul), and as such, the soul appears to itself when it becomes aware of itself in thought perception. It must also manifest itself in such a way that it appears as the "non-rational soul" (not-thought-bearing soul). As such, it again appears in a twofold way as courage-developing, and as appetitive soul. Thus, Plato seems to distinguish three members or parts in the human soul: The rational soul, the courage-like (or will-exertive) soul and the appetitive soul. We shall, however, describe the spirit of his conceptional approach better if we express it in a different way. According to its nature, the soul is a member of the world of ideas, but it acts in such a way that it adds an activity to its life in reason through its courage life and its appetitive life. In this threefold mode of utterance it appears as earthbound soul. It descends as a rational soul through physical birth into a terrestrial existence, and with death again enters the world of ideas. Insofar as it is rational soul, it is *immortal*, for as such it shares with its life the eternal existence of the world of ideas.

Plato's doctrine of the soul emerges as a significant fact in the age of thought perception. The awakened thought directed man's attention toward the soul. A perception of the soul develops in Plato that is entirely the result of thought perception. Thought in Plato has become bold enough not only to point toward the soul but to express what the soul is, as it were, to describe it. What thought has to say about the soul gives it the force to know itself *in the eternal*. Indeed, thought in the soul even sheds light on the nature of the temporal by expanding its own being beyond this temporal existence. The soul perceives thought. As the soul appears in its terrestrial life, it could not produce in itself the pure form of thought. Where does the thought experience come from if it cannot be developed in the life on earth? It represents a *reminiscence* of a pre-terrestrial, purely spiritual state of being. Thought has seized the soul in such a way that it is not satisfied by the soul's terrestrial form of existence. It has been revealed to the soul in an earlier state of being (pre-existence) in the spirit world (world of ideas) and the soul recalls it during its terrestrial existence through the reminiscence of the life it has spent in the spirit.

What Plato has to say about the moral life follows from this soul conception. The soul is moral if it so arranges life that it exerts itself to the largest possible measure as rational soul. *Wisdom* is the virtue that stems from the rational soul; it ennobles human life. *Fortitude* is the virtue of the will-exertive soul; *Temperance* is that of the appetitive soul. These virtues come to pass when the rational soul becomes the ruler over the other manifestations of the soul. When all three virtues harmoniously act together, there emerges what Plato calls, *Justice*, the direction toward the Good, *Dikaiosyne*.

Plato's disciple, *Aristotle* (born 384 B.C. in Stageira, Thracia, died 321 B.C.), together with his teacher, represents a climax in Greek thinking. With him the process of the absorption of thought life into the world conception has been completed and come to rest. Thought takes its rightful possession of its function to comprehend, out of its own resources, the being and events of the world. Plato still uses his conceptual imagination to bring thought to its rightful authority and to lead it into the world of ideas. With Aristotle, this authority has become a matter of course. It is now a question of confirming it everywhere in the various fields of knowledge. Aristotle understands how to use thought as a tool that penetrates into the essence of things. For Plato, it had been the task to overcome the thing or being of the external world. When it has been overcome, the soul carries in itself the idea of which the external being had only been overshadowed, but which had been foreign to it, hovering over it in a spiritual world of truth. Aristotle intends to submerge into the beings and events, and what the soul finds in this submersion, it accepts as the essence of the thing itself. The soul feels as if it had only lifted this essence out of the thing and as if it had brought this essence for its own consumption into the thought form in order to be able to carry it in itself as a reminder of the thing. To Aristotle's mind, the ideas are in the things and events. They are the side of the things through which these things have a foundation of their own in the underlying material, matter (hyle).

Plato, like Aristotle, lets his conception of the soul shed its light on his entire world conception. In both thinkers we describe the fundamental constitution of their philosophy as a whole if we succeed in determining the basic characteristics of their soul conceptions. To be sure, for both of them many detailed studies would have to be considered that cannot be attempted in this sketch. But the direction their mode of conception took is, for both, indicated in their soul conceptions.

Plato is concerned with what lives in the soul and, as such, shares in the spirit world. What is important for Aristotle is the question of how the soul presents itself for man in his own knowledge. As it does with other things, the soul must also submerge into itself in order to find what constitutes its own essence. The idea, which, according to Aristotle, man finds in a thing outside his soul, is the essence of the thing, but the soul has brought this essence into the form of an idea in order to have it for itself. The idea does not have its reality in the cognitive soul but in the external thing in connection with its material (hyle). If the soul submerges into itself, however, it finds the idea as such in reality. The soul in this sense is idea, but active idea, an entity exerting action, and it behaves also in the life of man as such an active entity. In the process of germination of man it lays hold upon material existence.

While idea and matter constitute an inseparable unity in an external thing, this is not the case with the human soul and its body. Here the independent human soul seizes upon the corporeal part, renders the idea ineffective that has been active in the body before and inserts itself in its place. In Aristotle's view, a soul-like principle is active already in the bodily element with which the human soul unites itself, for he sees also in the bodies of the plants and of animals, soul-like entities of a subordinate kind at work. A body that carries in itself the soul elements of the plant and animal is, as it were, fructified by the human soul. Thus, for the terrestrial man, a body-soul entity is linked up with a spirit-soul entity. The spirit-soul entity suppresses the *independent* activity of the body-soul element during the earth life of man and uses the body-soul entity as an instrument. Five soul manifestations come into being through this process. These, in Aristotle, appear as five members of the soul: The plant-like soul (threptikon), the sentient soul (aisthetikon), the desire-developing soul (orektikon), the will-exerting soul (kinetikon) and the spirit-soul (dianoetikon). Man is spiritual soul through what belongs to the spiritual world and what, in the process of germination, links itself up with the body-soul entity. The other members of the soul come into being as the spiritual soul unfolds itself in the body and thereby leads its earth life.

With Aristotle's focus on a spiritual soul the perspective toward a spiritual world in general is naturally given. The world picture of Aristotle stands before our contemplative eye in such a way that we see below the life of things and events, thus presenting matter *and* idea; the higher we lift our eye, the more we see vanish whatever bears a material character. Pure spiritual essence appears, representing itself to man as idea, that is, the sphere of the world in which deity as pure spirituality that moves everything has its being. The spiritual soul of man belongs to this world sphere; before it is united with a body-soul entity, it does not exist as an individual being but only as a part of the world spirit. Through this connection it acquires its individual existence separated from the world spirit and continues to live after the separation from the body as a spiritual being. Thus, the individual soul entity has its beginning with the human earthly life and then lives on as immortal. A pre-existence of the soul before earth life is assumed by Plato but not by Aristotle. The denial of the soul's pre-existence is as natural to Aristotle, who has the idea exist in the thing, as the opposite view is natural to Plato, who conceives of the idea as hovering over the thing. Aristotle finds the idea in the thing, and the soul acquires in its body what it is to be in the spirit world as an individuality.

Aristotle is the thinker who has brought thought to the point where it unfolds to a world conception through its contact with the essence of the world. The age before Aristotle led to the experience of thought; Aristotle seizes the thoughts and applies them to whatever he finds in the world. The natural way, peculiar to Aristotle, in which he lives in thought as a matter of course, leads him also to investigate logic, the laws of thought itself. Such a science could only come into being after the awakened thought had reached a stage of great maturity and of such a harmonious relationship to the things of the outer world as we find it in Aristotle.

Compared with Aristotle, the other thinkers of antiquity who appear as his contemporaries or as his successors seem to be of much less significance. They give the impression that their abilities lack a certain energy that prevents them from attaining the stage of insight Aristotle had reached. One gets the feeling that they disagree with him because they are stating opinions about things they do not understand as well as he. One is inclined to explain their views by pointing to the deficiency that led them to utter opinions that have already been disproved essentially in Aristotle's work.

To begin with, one can receive such an impression from the *Stoics* and the *Epicureans*. *Zeno* of Kition (342–270 B.C.), *Kleanthes* (born 200 B.C.), *Chrysippus* (282–209 B.C.), and others belong to the Stoics, whose name was derived from the Hall of Columns in Athens, the Stoa. They accept what appears reasonable to them in earlier world conceptions, but they are mainly concerned with finding out what man's position is in the world by contemplation of it. They want to base on this, their decision as to how to arrange life in such a way that it is in agreement with the world order, and also in such a way that man can unfold his life in this world order according to his own nature. According to them, man dulls his natural being through desire, passion and covetousness. Through equanimity and freedom from desire, he feels best what he is meant to be and what he can be. The ideal man is the "sage" who does not hamper the process of the inner development of the human being by any vice.

As the thinkers before Aristotle were striving to obtain the knowledge that, after him, becomes accessible to man through the ability to perceive thoughts in the full consciousness of his soul, with the Stoics, reflection concentrates on the question as to what man is to do in order to express his nature as a human being in the best way.

Epicurus (born 324 B.C., died 270 B.C.) developed in his own way the elements that had already been latent in the earlier atomistic thinkers. He builds a view of life on this foundation that can be considered to be an answer to the question: As the human soul emerges as the blossom of world processes, how is it to live in order to shape its separate existence, its self-dependence in accordance with thinking guided by reason? Epicurus could answer this question only by a method that considered life only between birth and death, for nothing else can, with perfect intellectual honesty, be derived from the atomistic world conception. The fact of pain must appear to such a conception as a peculiar enigma of life. For pain is one of those facts that drive the soul out of the consciousness of its unity with the things of the world. One can consider the motion of the stars and the fall of rain to be like the motion of one's own hand, as was done in the world conception of more remote antiquity. That is to say, one can feel in both kinds of events the same uniform spirit-soul reality. The fact that events can produce pain in man but cannot do so in the external world, however, drives the soul to the recognition of its own special nature. A doctrine of virtues, which, like the one of Epicurus, endeavors to live in harmony with world reason, can, as may easily be conceived, appreciate an ideal of life that leads to the avoidance of pain and displeasure. Thus, everything that does away with displeasure becomes the highest Epicurean life value.

This view of life found numerous followers in later antiquity, especially among Roman gentlemen of cultural aspiration. The Roman poet, T. Lucretius Carus (95–52 B.C.), has expressed it in perfect artistic form in his poem, *De Rerum Natura*.

The process of perceiving thoughts leads the soul to the recognition of its own being, but it can also occur that the soul feels powerless to deepen its thought experience sufficiently to find a connection with the grounds of the world through this experience. The soul then finds itself torn loose from these grounds through its own thinking. It feels that thinking contains its own being, but it does not find a way to recognize in its thought life anything but its own statement. The soul can then only surrender to a complete renunciation of any kind of true knowledge. *Pyrrho* (360–270 B.C.) and his followers, whose philosophical belief is called scepticism, were in such a situation. Scepticism, the philosophy of doubt, attributes no other power to the thought experience than the formation of human opinions about the world. Whether or not these opinions have any significance for the world outside man is a question about which it is unwilling to make a decision.

In a certain sense, one can see a well-rounded picture in the series of Greek thinkers. One will have to admit, of course, that such an attempt to connect the views of the individual thinkers only too easily brings out irrelevant aspects of secondary significance. What remains most important is still the contemplation of the individual personalities and the impressions one can gain concerning the fact of how, in these personalities, the general human element is brought to manifestation in special cases. One can observe a process in this line of Greek thinkers that can be called the birth, growth and life of thought: In the pre-Socratic thinkers, the prelude; in Socrates, Plato and Aristotle, the culmination; after them, a decline and a kind of dissolution of thought life.

Whoever contemplates this development can arrive at the question as to whether thought life really has the power to give everything to the soul toward which it has led it by bringing it to the complete consciousness of itself. For the unbiased observer, Greek thought life has an element that makes it appear "perfect" in the best sense of the word. It is as if the energy of thought in the Greek thinkers had worked out everything that it contains in itself. Whoever judges differently will notice on closer inspection that somewhere in his judgment an error is involved. Later world conceptions have produced accomplishments through other forces of the soul. Of the later thoughts as such, it can always be shown that with respect to their real thought content they can already be found in some earlier Greek thinker. *What can be thought and how one can doubt about thinking and knowledge, all enters the field of consciousness in Greek civilization, and in the manifestation of thought the soul takes possession of its own being.*

Has Greek thought life, however, shown the soul that it has the power to supply it with everything that it has stimulated in it? The philosophical current called Neo-Platonism, which in a way forms an aftermath of Greek thought life, was confronted with this question. *Plotinus* (205–270 A.D.) was its chief representative. *Philo,* who lived at the beginning of the Christian era in Alexandria, could be considered a forerunner of this movement. He does not base his effort to construct a world conception on the creative energy of thought. Rather, he *applies* thought in order to understand the revelation of the Old Testament. He interprets what is told in this document as fact in an intellectual, allegorical manner. For him, the accounts of the Old Testament turn into symbols for soul events to which he attempts to gain access intellectually.

Plotinus does not regard thought experience as something that embraces the soul in its full life. Behind thought life another life of the soul must lie, a soul life that would be concealed rather than revealed by the action of thought. The soul must overcome the life in thought, must extinguish it in itself and only after this extinction can it arrive at a form of experience that unites it with the origin of the world. Thought leads the soul to itself; now it must seize something in itself that will again lead it out of the realm into which thought has brought it. What Plotinus strives for is an *illumination* that begins in the soul after it has left the realm to which it has been carried by thought. In this way he expects to rise up to a world being that does not enter into thought life. World reason, therefore, toward which Plato and Aristotle strive, is not, according to Plotinus, the last reality at which the soul arrives. It is rather the outgrowth of a still higher reality that lies beyond all thinking. From this reality beyond all thought, which cannot be compared with anything that could be a possible object of thought, all world processes emanate.

Thought, as it could manifest itself in Greek spiritual life, has, as it were, gone through a complete revolution and thereby all possible relationships of man to thought seem to be exhausted. Plotinus looks for sources other than those given in thought revelation. He leaves the continuing evolution of thought life and enters the realm of mysticism. It is not intended to give a description of the development of mysticism here, but only the development of thought life and what has its origin in this process is to be outlined. There are, however, at various points in the spiritual development of mankind connections between intellectual world conceptions and mysticism. We find such a point of contact in Plotinus. His soul life is not ruled only by thinking. He has a mystical experience that presents an inner awareness without the presence of thoughts in his soul. In this experience he finds his soul united with the world foundation. His way of presenting the connection of the world with its ground, however, is to be expressed in thoughts. The reality beyond thought is the most perfect; what proceeds from it is less perfect. In this way, the process continues down into the visible world, the most imperfect. Man finds himself in this world of imperfection. Through the act of perfecting his soul, he is to cast off what the world in which he finds himself can give him, and is thus to find a path of development through which he becomes a being that is of one accord with the perfect origin.

We see a personality in Plotinus who feels the impossibility to continue Greek thought life. He cannot find anything that would grow as a further branch of world conception out of thought itself. If one looks for the sense in which the evolution of philosophy proceeds, one is justified in saying that the formation of picture conception has turned into that of thought conceptions. In a similar way, the production of thought conception must change again into something else, but the evolution of the world conception is not ready for this in the age of Plotinus. He therefore abandons thought and searches outside thought experience. Greek thoughts, however, fructified by his mystical experiences, develop into the evolutionary ideas that present the world process as a sequence of stages proceeding in a descending order, from a highest most perfect being to imperfect beings. In the thinking of Plotinus, Greek thoughts continue to have their effect. They do not develop as an organic growth of the original forces, however, but are taken over into the mystical consciousness. They do not undergo a transformation through their own energies but through non-intellectual forces.

Ammonius Sakkas (175–242), *Porphyrius* (232–304), *Iamblichus* (who lived in the fourth century A.D.), *Proclus* (410–485), and others are followers and expounders of this philosophy.

In a way similar to that of Plotinus and his successors, Greek thinking in its more Platonic shade continued under the influence of a non-intellectual element. Greek thought in its Pythagorean nuance is treated by *Nigidius Figulus, Appolonius of Tyana, Moderatus of Gades,* and others.

Chapter III

*Thought Life from the Beginning
of the Christian Era to John Scotus Erigena*

In the age that follows the flowering of the Greek world conceptions, philosophy submerges into religious life. The philosophical trends vanish, so to speak, into the religious currents and emerge only later. It is not meant to imply by this statement that these religious movements have no connection with the development of the philosophical life. On the contrary, this connection exists in the most extensive measure. Here, however, no statement about the evolution of religious life is intended, but rather a characterization of the development of the world conceptions insofar as it results from thought experience as such.

After the exhaustion of Greek thought life, an age begins in the spiritual life of mankind in which the religious impulses become the driving forces of the intellectual world conceptions as well. For Plotinus, his own mystical experience was the source of inspiration of his ideas. A similar role for the spiritual development of mankind in its general life is played by the religious impulses in an age that begins with the exhaustion of Greek philosophy and lasts approximately until *John Scotus Erigena* (died 885 A.D.)

The development of thought does not completely cease in this age. We even witness the unfolding of magnificent and comprehensive thought structures. The thought energies, however, do not have their source within themselves but are derived from religious impulses.

The religious mode of conception in this period flows through the developing human souls and the resulting world pictures are derived from this stimulation. The thoughts that occur in this process are Greek thoughts that are still exerting their influence. They are adopted and transformed, but are not brought to new growth out of themselves. The world conceptions emerge out of the background of the religious life. What is alive in them is not self-unfolding thought, but the religious impulses that are striving to manifest themselves in the previously conquered thought forms.

We can study this development in several significant phenomena. We can see Platonic and older philosophies engaged on European soil in the endeavor to comprehend or to contradict what the religions spread as their doctrines. Important thinkers attempt to present the revelations of religion as fully justified before the forum of the old world conceptions.

What is historically known as *Gnosticism* develops in this way in a more Christian or a more pagan coloring. Personalities of significance of this movement are *Valentinus, Basilides* and *Marcion*. Their thought creation is a comprehensive conception of world evolution. Cognition, gnosis, when it rises from the intellectual to the trans-intellectual realm, leads into the conception of a higher world-creative entity. This being is infinitely superior to everything seen as the world by man, and so are the other lofty beings it produces out of itself—the *aeons*. They form a descending series of generations in such a way that a less perfect aeon always proceeds from a more perfect one. As such, in a later stage of evolution an aeon has to be considered to be also the creator of the world that is visible to man and to which man himself belongs. Into this world an aeon of the highest degree of perfection now can join. It is an aeon that has remained in a purely spiritual, perfect world and has there continued its development in the best possible way, while other aeons produced the imperfect and eventually the sensual world including man. In this manner, the connection of the two worlds that have gone through different paths of evolution is thinkable for the Gnostic. The imperfect world receives its stimulation at a certain point of evolution by the perfect one in order that it may begin to strive toward the perfect.

The Gnostics who were inclined toward Christianity saw in Christ Jesus the perfect aeon, which has united with the terrestrial world.

Personalities like *Clemens* of Alexandria (died ca. 211 A.D.) and *Origen* (born ca. 185 A.D.) stood more on a dogmatic Christian ground. Clemens accepts the Greek world conceptions as a preparation of the Christian revelation and uses them as instruments to express and defend the Christian impulses. Origen proceeds in a similar way.

We find a thought life inspired by religious impulses flowing together in a comprehensive stream of conceptions in the writings of *Dionysius the Areopagite*, which are mentioned from 533 A.D. on. They probably had not been composed much earlier, but they do go back, not in their details but in their characteristic features, to earlier thinking of this age. Their content can be sketched in the following way. When the soul liberates itself from everything that it can perceive and think as *being*, when it also transcends beyond what it is capable of thinking as *non-being*, then it can spiritually divine the realm of the *over-being*, the hidden Godhead. In this entity, primordial being is united with primordial goodness and primordial beauty. Starting from this primeval trinity, the soul witnesses a descending order of beings that lead down to man in hierarchical array.

In the ninth century Scotus Erigena adopts this conception of the world and develops it in his own way. The world for him presents itself as an evolution in four *forms of nature*. The first of these is the *creating and not created nature*. In it is contained the purely spiritual primordial cause of the world out of which evolves the *creating and created nature*. This is a sum of purely spiritual entities and energies, which through their activity produce the *created and not creating nature*, to which the sensual world and man belong. They develop in such a way that they are received into the *not created and not creating nature*, in which the facts of salvation, the religious means of grace, etc., unfold their effect.

In the world conceptions of the Gnostics, Dionysius and Scotus Erigena, the human soul feels its roots in a world ground on which it does not base its support through the forces of thought, but from which it wants to receive the world of thought as a gift. The soul does not feel secure in the native strength of thought. It strives, however, to experience its relation to the world ground in the form of thought. The soul has thought itself enlivened by another energy that derives from religious impulses, whereas in the Greek thinkers it lived out of its own strength. Thought in this age existed, so to speak, in a form in which its own energy was dormant. In the same way, we may also think of the energy of picture conception in the centuries that preceded the birth of thought. There must have been an ancient time when consciousness in the form of picture conception flourished, the same as did the later thought consciousness in Greece. It then drew its energy out of other impulses and only when it had gone through this intermediate state did it transform into thought experience. It is an intermediate state in the process of thought development that we witness in the first centuries of the Christian era.

In those parts of Asia where the conceptions of Aristotle had been spread, the tendency now arose to lend expression to the semitic religious impulses in the ideas of the Greek thinker. This tendency was then transplanted also to European soil and so entered into the European spiritual life through such thinkers as the great Aristotelians, *Averroës* (1126–1198), *Maimonides* (1135–1204), and others.

In Averroës, we find the view that it is an error to assume that a special thought world exists in the personality of man. There is only *one* homogeneous thought world in the divine primordial being. As light can be reflected in many mirrors, so also *one* thought world is revealed in many human beings. During human life on earth, to be sure, a further transformation of the thought world takes place, but this is, in reality, only a process in the spiritually homogeneous primordial ground. With man's death, the individual revelation through him simply comes to an end. His thought life now exists only in the *one thought life.*

This world conception allows the Greek thought experience to continue its effect, but does it in such a way that it is now anchored in the uniform divine world ground. It leaves us with the impression of being a manifestation of the fact that the developing human soul did not feel in itself the intrinsic energy of thought. It therefore projected this energy into an extra-human world power.

CHAPTER IV

*The World Conceptions
of the Middle Ages*

A foreshadowing of a new element produced by thought life itself emerges in St. Augustine (354–430). This element soon vanishes from the surface, however, to continue unnoticeably under the cover of religious conception, becoming distinctly discernible again only in the later Middle Ages. In St. Augustine, the new element appears as if it were a reminiscence of Greek thought life. He looks into the external world and into himself, and comes to the conclusion: May everything else the world reveals contain nothing but uncertainty and deception, one thing cannot be doubted, that is, the certainty of the soul's experience itself. I do not owe this inner experience to a perception that could deceive me; I am in it myself; it *is*, for I am present when its being is attributed to it.

One can see a new element in these conceptions as against Greek thought life, in spite of the fact that they seem at first like a reminiscence of it. Greek thinking points toward the soul; in St. Augustine, we are directed toward the center of the life of the soul. The Greek thinkers contemplated the soul in its relation to the world; in St. Augustine's approach, something *in* the soul life confronts this soul life and regards it as a special, self-contained world. One can call the center of the soul life the "ego" of man.

To the Greek thinkers, the relation of the soul to the world becomes problematic, to the thinkers of modern times, that of the "ego" to the soul. In St. Augustine, we have only the first indication of this situation. The ensuing philosophical currents are still too much occupied with the task of harmonizing world conception and religion to become distinctly aware of the new element that has not entered into spiritual life. But the tendency to contemplate the riddles of the world in accordance with the demand of this new element lives more or less unconsciously in the souls of the time that now follows. In thinkers like *Anselm of Canterbury* (1033–1109) and *Thomas Aquinas* (1227–1274), this tendency still shows itself in such a way that they attribute to self-supportive thinking the ability to investigate the processes of the world to a certain degree, but they limit this ability. There is for them a higher spiritual reality to which thinking, left to its own resources, can never attain, but that must be revealed to it in a religious way. Man is, according to Thomas Aquinas, rooted with his soul life in the reality of the world, but this soul life cannot know this reality in its full extent through itself alone. Man could not know how his own being stands in the course of the world if the spirit being, to which his knowledge does not penetrate, did not deign to reveal to him what must remain concealed to a knowledge relying on its own power alone. Thomas Aquinas constructs his world picture on this presupposition. It has two parts, one of which consists of the truths that are yielded to man's own thought experience about the natural course of things. This leads to a second part that contains what has come to the soul of man through the Bible and religious revelation. Something that the soul cannot reach by itself, if it is to feel itself in its full essence, must therefore penetrate into the soul.

Thomas Aquinas made himself thoroughly familiar with the world conception of Aristotle, who becomes, as it were, his master in the life of thought. In this respect, Aquinas is, to be sure, the most prominent, but nevertheless only one of the numerous personalities of the Middle Ages who erect their own thought structure entirely on that of Aristotle. For centuries, he is *il maestro di color che sanno*, the master of those who know, as Dante expresses the veneration for Aristotle in the Middle Ages. Thomas Aquinas strives to comprehend what is humanly comprehensible in Aristotelian method. In this way, Aristotle's world conception becomes the guide to the limit to which the soul life can advance through its own power for him. Beyond these boundaries lies the realm that the Greek world conception, according to Thomas, could not reach.

Therefore, human thinking for Thomas Aquinas is in need of another light by which it must be illuminated. He finds this light in revelation. Whatever was to be the attitude of the ensuing thinkers with respect to this revelation, they could no longer accept the life of thought in the manner of the Greeks. It is not sufficient to them that thinking comprehends the world; they make the presupposition that it should be possible to find a basic support for thinking itself. The tendency arises to fathom man's relation to his soul life. Thus, man considers himself a being *who* exists in his soul life. If one calls this *entity* the *ego*, one can say that in modern times the consciousness of the *ego* is stirred up in man's soul life in a way similar to that in which *thought* was born in the philosophical life of the Greeks. Whatever different forms the philosophical currents in this age assume, they all hinge on the search for the ego-entity. This fact, however, is not always brought clearly to the consciousness of the thinkers themselves. They mostly believe they are concerned with questions of a different nature. One could say that the *Riddle of the Ego* appears in a great variety of masks. At times it lives in the philosophy of the thinkers in such a concealed way that the statement that this riddle is at the bottom of some view or other might appear as an arbitrary or forced opinion. In the nineteenth century this struggle over the riddle of the ego comes to its most intensive manifestation, and the world conceptions of the present time are still profoundly engaged in this struggle.

This *world riddle* already lived in the conflict between the nominalists and the realists in the Middle Ages. One can call *Anselm of Canterbury* a representative of *realism*. For him, the general ideas that man forms when he contemplates the world are not mere nomenclatures that the soul produces for itself, but they have their roots in a real life. If one forms the general idea "lion" in order to designate all lions with it, it is certainly correct to say that, for sense perception, only the individual lions have reality. The general concept "lion" is not, however, only a summary designation with significance only for the human mind. It is rooted in a spiritual world, and the individual lions of the world of sense perception are the various embodiments of the one lion nature expressed in the "idea of lion."

Such a "reality of ideas" was opposed by Nominalists like *Roscellin* (also in the eleventh century). The "general ideas" are only summary designations for him, names that the mind forms for its own use for its orientation, but that do not correspond to any reality. According to this view, only the individual things are real. The quarrel is characteristic of the specific mentality of its participants. Both sides feel the necessity to search for the validity, the significance of the thoughts that the soul must produce. Their attitude to thoughts as such is different from what the attitudes of Plato and Aristotle were toward them. This is so because something has happened between the end of the development of Greek philosophy and the beginning of modern thought. Something has gone on under the surface of historical evolution that can, however, be observed in the attitude that the individual thinkers take with respect to their thought life.

To the Greek thinker, thought came as a perception. It arose in the soul as the red color appears when a man looks at a rose, and the thinker received it as a perception. As such the thought had the immediate power of conviction. The Greek thinker had the feeling, when he placed himself with his soul receptively before the spiritual world, that no incorrect thought could enter from this world into the soul just as no perception of a winged horse could come from the sense world as long as the sense organs were properly used. For the Greeks, it was a question of being able to garner thoughts from the world. They were then themselves the witnesses of their truth. The fact of this attitude is not contradicted by the Sophists, nor is it denied by ancient Scepticism. Both currents have an entirely different shade of meaning in antiquity from similar tendencies in modern times. They are not evidence against the fact that the Greek experienced thought in a much more elementary, content-saturated, vivid and real way than it can be experienced by the man of modern times. This vividness, which in ancient Greece *gave the character of perception to thought*, is no longer to be found in the Middle Ages.

What has happened is this. As in Greek times thought entered into the human soul, extinguishing the formerly prevalent picture consciousness, so, in a similar way, during the Middle Ages the consciousness of the "ego" penetrated the human soul, and this dampened the vividness of thought. The advent of the ego-consciousness deprived thought of the strength through which it had appeared as perception. We can only understand how the philosophical life advances when we realize how, for Plato and Aristotle, the thought, the idea, was something entirely different from what it was for the personalities of the Middle Ages and modern times. The thinker of antiquity had the feeling *that thought was given to him*; the thinker of the later time had the impression that *he was producing thought*. Thus, the question arises in him as to what significance what has been produced in the soul can have for reality. The Greek felt himself to be a soul separated from the world; he attempted to unite with the spiritual world in thought. The later thinker feels himself to be *alone with* his thought life. Thus, the inquiry into the nature of the "general ideas" begins. The thinker asks himself the questions, "What is it that I have really produced with them? Are they only rooted in me, or do they point toward a reality?"

In the period between the ancient current of philosophical life and that of modern philosophy, the source of Greek thought life is gradually exhausted. Under the surface, however, the human soul experiences the approaching ego-consciousness *as a fact*. Since the end of the first half of the Middle Ages, man is confronted with this process as an accomplished fact, and under the influence of this confrontation, new *Riddles of Life* emerge. Realism and Nominalism are symptoms of the fact that man realizes the situation. The manner in which both Realists and Nominalists speak about thought shows that, compared to its existence in the Greek soul, it has faded out, has been dampened as much as had been the old picture consciousness in the soul of the Greek thinker.

This points to the dominating element that lives in the modern world conceptions. An energy is active in them that strives beyond thought toward a new factor of reality. This tendency of modern times cannot be felt as the same that drove beyond thought in ancient times in Pythagoras and later in Plotinus. These thinkers also strove beyond thought but, according to their conception, the soul in its development, its perfection, would have to conquer the region that lies beyond thought. In modern times it is presupposed that the factor of reality lying beyond thought must approach the soul, must be given to it from without.

In the centuries that follow the age of Nominalism and Realism, philosophical evolution turns into a search for the new reality factor. One path among those discernible to the student of this search is the one the medieval Mystics—*Meister Eckhardt* (died 1327), *Johannes Tauler* (died 1361), *Heinrich Suso* (died 1366)—have chosen for themselves. We receive the clearest idea of this path if we inspect the so-called *German Theology* (Theologia, deutsch), written by an author historically unknown. The Mystics want to receive something into the ego-consciousness; they intend to fill it with something. They therefore strive for an inner life that is "completely composed," surrendered in tranquility, and that thus patiently waits to experience the soul to be filled with the "Divine Ego." In a later time, a similar soul mood with a greater spiritual momentum can be observed in *Angelus Silesius* (1624–1677).

A different path is chosen by *Nicolaus Cusanus* (Nicolaus Chrypffs, born at Kues on the Moselle, 1401, died 1464). He strives beyond intellectually attainable knowledge to a state of soul in which knowledge ceases and in which the soul meets its god in "knowing ignorance," *in docta ignorantia.* Examined superficially, this aspiration is similar to that of Plotinus, but the soul constitution of these two personalities is different. Plotinus is convinced that the human soul contains more than the world of thoughts. When it develops the energy that it possesses beyond the power of thought, the soul becomes conscious of the state in which it exists, and about which it is ignorant in ordinary life.

Paracelsus (1493–1541) already has the feeling with respect to nature, which becomes more and more pronounced in the modern world conception, that is an effect of the soul's feeling of desolation in its ego-consciousness. He turns his attention toward the processes of nature. As they present themselves they cannot be accepted by the soul, but neither can thought, which in Aristotle unfolded in peaceful communication with the events of nature, now be accepted as it appears in the soul. It is not perceived; it is formed in the soul. Paracelsus felt that one must not let thought itself speak; one must presuppose that something is behind the phenomena of nature that will reveal itself if one finds the right relationship to these phenomena. One must be capable of receiving something from nature that one does not create oneself as thought during the act of observation. One must be connected with one's "ego" by means of a factor of reality other than thought. A *higher nature behind nature* is what Paracelsus is looking for. His mood of soul is so constituted that he does not want to experience something in himself alone, but he means to penetrate nature's processes with his "ego" in order to have revealed to him the spirit of these processes that are under the surface of the world of the senses. The mystics of antiquity meant to delve into the depths of the soul; Paracelsus set out to take steps that would lead *to a contact with the roots of nature in the external world.*

Jakob Boehme (1575–1624) who, as a lonely, persecuted craftsman, formed a world picture as though out of an inner illumination, nevertheless implants into this world picture the fundamental character of modern times. In the solitude of his soul life he develops this fundamental trait most impressively because the inner dualism of the life of the soul, the contrast between the "ego" and the other soul experiences, stands clearly before the eye of his spirit. He experiences the "ego" as it creates an inner counterpart in its own soul life, reflecting itself in the mirror of his own soul. He then finds this inner experience again in the processes of the world. "In such a contemplation one finds two qualities, a good and an evil one, which are intertwined in this world in all forces, in stars and in elements as well as in all creatures." The evil in the world is opposed to the good as its counterpart; it is only in the evil that the good becomes aware of itself, as the "ego" becomes aware of itself in its inner soul experiences.

CHAPTER V

The World Conceptions of the Modern Age of Thought Evolution

The rise of natural science in modern times had as its fundamental cause the same search as the mysticism of Jakob Boehme. This becomes apparent in a thinker who grew directly out of the spiritual movement, which in *Copernicus* (1473–1543), *Kepler* (1571–1630), *Galileo* (1564–1642), and others, led to the first great accomplishments of natural science in modern times. This thinker is *Giordano Bruno* (1548–1600). When one sees how his world consists of infinitely small, animated, psychically self-aware, fundamental beings, the monads, which are uncreated and indestructible, producing in their combined activity the phenomena of nature, one could be tempted to group him with Anaxagoras, for whom the world consists of the "homoiomeries."

Yet, there is a significant difference between these two thinkers. For Anaxagoras, the thought of the homoiomeries unfolds while he is engaged in the contemplation of the world; the world suggests these thoughts to him. Giordano Bruno feels that what lies behind the phenomena of nature must be thought of as a world picture in such a way that the entity of the ego is possible in this world picture. The *ego* must be a *monad*; otherwise, it could not be real. Thus, the assumption of the monads becomes necessary. As only the monad can be real, therefore, the truly real entities are monads with different inner qualities.

In the depths of the soul of a personality like Giordano Bruno, something happens that is not raised into full consciousness; the effect of this inner process is then the formation of the world picture. What goes on in the depths is an unconscious soul process. The ego feels that it must form such a conception of itself that its reality is assured, and it must conceive the world in such a way that the ego can be real in it. Giordano Bruno has to form the conception of the monad in order to render possible the realization of both demands. In his thought the ego struggles for its existence in the world conception of the modern age, and the expression of this struggle is the view: I am a monad; such an entity is uncreated and indestructible.

A comparison shows how different the ways are in which Aristotle and Giordano Bruno arrive at the conception of God. Aristotle contemplates the world; he sees the evidence of reason in natural processes; he surrenders to the contemplation of this evidence; at the same time, the processes of nature are for him evidence of the *thought* of the "first mover" of these processes. Giordano Bruno fights his way through to the conception of the monads. The processes of nature are, as it were, extinguished in the picture in which innumerable monads are presented as acting on each other; God becomes the power entity that lives actively in all monads behind the processes of the perceptible world. In Giordano Bruno's passionate antagonism against Aristotle, the contrast between the thinker of ancient Greece and of the philosopher of modern times becomes manifest.

It becomes apparent in the modern philosophical development in a great variety of ways how the ego searches for means to experience its own reality in itself. What *Francis Bacon* of Verulam (1561–1626) represents in his writings has the same general character even if this does not at first sight become apparent in his endeavors in the field of philosophy. Bacon of Verulam demands that the investigation of world phenomena should begin with unbiased observation. One should then try to separate the essential from the non-essential in a phenomenon in order to arrive at a conception of whatever lies at the bottom of a thing or event. He is of the opinion that up to his time the fundamental thoughts, which were to explain the world phenomena, had been conceived first, and only thereafter were the description of the individual things and events arranged to fit these thoughts. He presupposed that the thoughts had not been taken out of the things themselves. Bacon wanted to combat this (deductive) method with his (inductive) method. The concepts are to be formed in direct contact with the things. One sees, so Bacon reasons, how an object is consumed by fire; one observes how a second object behaves with relation to fire and then observes the same process with many objects. In this fashion one arrives eventually at a conception of how things behave with respect to fire. The fact that the investigation in former times had not proceeded in this way had, according to Bacon's opinion, caused human conception to be dominated by so many *idols* instead of the true ideas about the things.

Goethe gives a significant description of this method of thought of Bacon of Verulam.

> Bacon is like a man who is well-aware of the irregularity, insufficiency and dilapidated condition of an old building, and knows how to make this clear to the inhabitants. He advises them to abandon it, to give up the land, the materials and all appurtenances, to look for another plot, and to erect a new building. He is an excellent and persuasive speaker. He shakes a few walls. They break down and some of the inhabitants are forced to move out. He points out new building grounds; people begin to level it off, and yet it is everywhere too narrow. He submits new plans; they are not clear, not inviting. Mainly, he speaks of new unknown materials and now the world seems to be well-served. The crowd disperses in all directions and brings back an infinite variety of single items while at home, new plans, new activities and settlements occupy the citizens and absorb their attention.

Goethe says this in his history of the theory of color where he speaks about Bacon. In a later part of the book dealing with Galileo, he says:

> If through Verulam's method of dispersion, natural science seemed to be forever broken up into fragments, it was soon brought to unity again by Galileo. He led natural philosophy back into the human being. When he developed the law of the pendulum and of falling bodies from the observation of swinging church lamps, he showed even in his early youth that, for the genius, one case stands for a thousand cases. In science, everything depends on what is called, *an aperçu*, that is, on the ability of becoming aware of what is really fundamental in the world of phenomena. The development of such an awareness is infinitely fruitful.

With these words Goethe indicated distinctly the point that is characteristic of Bacon. Bacon wants to find a secure path for science because he hopes that in this way man will find a dependable relationship to the world. The approach of Aristotle, so Bacon feels, can no longer be used in the modern age. He does not know that in different ages different energies of the soul are predominantly active in man. He is only aware of the fact that he must reject Aristotle. This he does passionately. He does it in such a way that Goethe is lead to say, "How can one listen to him with equanimity when he compares the works of Aristotle and of Plato with weightless tablets, which, just because they did not consist of a good solid substance, could so easily float down to us on the stream of time."

Bacon does not understand that he is aiming at the same objective that has been reached by Plato and Aristotle, and that he must use different means for the same aim because the means of antiquity can no longer be those of the modern age. He points toward a method that could appear fruitful for the investigation in the field of external nature, but as Goethe shows in the case of Galileo, even in this field something more is necessary than what Bacon demands.

The method of Bacon proves completely useless, however, when the soul searches not only for an access to the investigation of individual facts, but also to a world conception. What good is a groping search for isolated phenomena and a derivation of general ideas from them, if these general ideas do not, like strokes of lightning, flash up out of the ground of being in the soul of man, rendering account of their truth through themselves. In antiquity, thought appeared like a perception to the soul. This mode of appearance has been dampened through the brightness of the new ego-consciousness. What can lead to thoughts capable of forming a world conception in the soul must be so formed as if it were the soul's own invention, and the soul must search for the possibility of justifying the validity of its own creation. Bacon has no feeling for all this. He, therefore, points to the materials of the building for the construction of the new world conception, namely, the individual natural phenomena. It is, however, no more possible that one can ever build a house by merely observing the form of the building stones that are to be used, than that a fruitful world conception could ever arise in a soul that is exclusively concerned with the individual processes of nature.

Contrary to Bacon of Verulam, who pointed toward the bricks of the building, *Descartes* (Cartesius) and *Spinoza* turned their attention toward its plan. Descartes was born in 1596 and died in 1650. The starting point of his philosophical endeavor is significant with him. With an unbiased questioning mind he approaches the world, which offers him much of its riddles partly through revealed religion, partly through the observation of the senses. He now contemplates both sources in such a way that he does not simply accept and recognize as truth what either of them offers to him. Instead, he sets against the suggestions of both sources the "ego," which answers out of its own initiative with its *doubt* against all revelation and against all perception. In the development of modern philosophical life, this move is a fact of the most telling significance. Amidst the world the thinker allows nothing to make an impression on his soul, but sets *himself* against everything with a *doubt* that can derive its support only from the soul itself. Now the soul apprehends itself in its own action: I doubt, that is to say, I think. Therefore, no matter how things stand with the entire world, in my doubt-exerting thinking I come to the clear awareness that *I am*. In this manner, Cartesius arrives at his

Cogito ergo sum, I think, therefore I am. The ego in him conquers the right to recognize its own being through the radical doubt directed against the entire world.

Descartes derives the further development of his world conception out of this root. In the "ego" he had attempted to seize existence. Whatever can justify its existence together with the ego may be considered truth. The ego finds in itself, innate to it, the idea of God. This idea presents itself to the ego as true, as distinct as the ego itself, but it is so sublime, so powerful, that the ego cannot have it through its own power. Therefore, it comes from transcendent reality to which it corresponds. Descartes believes in the reality of the external world, not because this external world presents itself as real, but because the ego must believe in itself and then subsequently in God, and because God must be thought as truthful. For it would be untrue of God to suggest a real external world to man if the latter did not exist.

It is only possible to arrive at the recognition of the reality of the ego as Descartes does through a thinking that in the most direct manner aims at the ego in order to find a point of support for the act of cognition. That is to say, this possibility can be fulfilled only through an inner activity but never through a perception from without. Any perception that comes from without gives only the qualities of extension. In this manner, Descartes arrives at the recognition of two substances in the world: One to which extension, and the other to which thinking, is to be attributed and that has its roots in the human soul. The animals, which in Descartes's sense cannot apprehend themselves in inner self-supporting activity, are accordingly mere beings of extension, automata, machines. The human body, too, is nothing but a machine. The soul is linked up with this machine. When the body becomes useless through being worn out or destroyed in some way, the soul abandons it to continue to live in its own element.

Descartes lives in a time in which a new impulse in the philosophical life is already discernible. The period from the beginning of the Christian era until about the time of Scotus

Erigena develops in such a way that the inner experience of thought is enlivened by a force that enters the spiritual evolution as a powerful impulse. The energy of thought as it awakened in Greece is outshone by this power. Outwardly, the progress in the life of the human soul is expressed in the religious movements and by the fact that the forces of the youthful nations of Western and Central Europe become the recipients of the effects of the older forms of thought experience. They penetrate this experience with the younger, more elementary impulses and thereby transform it. In this process one forward step in the progress in human evolution becomes evident that is caused by the fact that older and subtle traces of spiritual currents that have exhausted their vitality, but not their spiritual possibilities, are continued by youthful energies emerging from the natural spring of mankind. In such processes one will be justified in recognizing the essential laws of the evolution of mankind. They are based on rejuvenating tendencies of the spiritual life. The acquired forces of the spirit can only then continue to unfold if they are transplanted into young, natural energies of mankind.

The first eight centuries of the Christian era present a continuation of the thought experience in the human soul in such a way that the new forces about to emerge are still dormant in hidden depths, but they tend to exert their formative effect on the evolution of world conception. In Descartes, these forces already show themselves at work in a high degree. In the age between Scotus Erigena and approximately the fifteenth century, thought, which in the preceding period did not openly unfold, comes again to the fore in its own force. Now, however, it emerges from a direction quite different from that of the Greek age. With the Greek thinkers, thought is experienced as a *perception*. From the eighth to the fifteenth centuries it comes from out of the depth of the soul so that man has the feeling: Thought generates itself within me. In the Greek thinkers, a relation between thought and the processes of nature was still immediately established; in the age just referred to, thought stands out as the product of self-consciousness. The thinker has the feeling that he must prove thought as justified. This is the feeling of the nominalists and the realists. This is also the feeling of Thomas Aquinas, who anchors the experience of thought in religious revelation.

The fifteenth and sixteenth centuries introduce a new impulse to the souls. This is slowly prepared and slowly absorbed in the life of the soul. A transformation takes place in the organization of the human soul. In the field of philosophical life, this transformation becomes manifest through the fact that thought cannot now be felt as a perception, but as a *product of self-consciousness*. This transformation in the organization of the human soul can be observed in all fields of the development of humanity. It becomes apparent in the renaissance of art and science, and of European life, as well as in the reformatory religious movements. One will be able to discover it if one investigates the art of Dante and Shakespeare with respect to their foundations in the human soul development. Here these possibilities can only be indicated, since this sketch is intended to deal only with the development of the intellectual world conception.

The advent of the mode of thought of modern natural science appears as another symptom of this transformation of the human soul organization. Just compare the state of the form of thinking about nature as it develops in Copernicus, Galileo and Kepler with what has preceded them. This natural scientific conception corresponds to the mood of the human soul at the beginning of the modern age in the sixteenth century. Nature is now looked at in such a way that the sense observation is to be the only witness of it. Bacon is one, Galileo another personality in whom this becomes apparent. The picture of nature is no longer drawn in a manner that allows thought to be felt in it as a power revealed by nature. Out of this picture of nature, every trait that could be felt as only a product of self-consciousness gradually vanishes. Thus, the creations of self-consciousness and the observation of nature are more and more abruptly contrasted, separated by a gulf. From Descartes on a transformation of the soul organization becomes discernible that tends to separate the picture of nature from the creations of the self-consciousness. With the sixteenth century a new tendency in the philosophical life begins to make itself felt. While in the preceding centuries thought had played the part of an element, which, as a product of self-consciousness, demanded its justification through the world picture, since the sixteenth century it proves to be clearly and distinctly resting solely on its own ground in the self-consciousness. Previously, thought had been felt in such a manner that the picture of nature could be considered a support for its justification; now it becomes the task of this element of thought to uphold the claim of its validity through its own strength. The thinkers of the time that now follows feel that in the thought experience itself something must be found that proves this experience to be the justified creator of a world conception.

The significance of the transformation of the soul life can be realized if one considers the way in which philosophers of nature, like *H. Cardanus* (1501–1576) and *Bernardinus Telesius* (1508–1588), still spoke of natural processes. In them a picture of nature still continued to show its effect and was to lose its power through the emergence of the mode of conception of natural science of Copernicus, Galileo and others. Something still lives in the mind of Cardanus of the processes of nature, which he conceives as similar to those of the human soul. Such an assertion would also have been possible to Greek thinking. Galileo is already compelled to say that what man has as the sensation of warmth within himself, for instance, exists no more in external nature than the sensation of tickling that a man feels when the sole of his foot is touched by a feather. Telesius still feels justified to say that warmth and coldness are the driving forces of the world processes, and Galileo must already make the statement that man knows warmth only as an inner experience. In the picture of nature he allows as thinkable only what contains nothing of this inner experience. Thus, the conceptions of mathematics and mechanics become the only ones that are allowed to form the picture of nature. In a personality like *Leonardo da Vinci* (1452–1519), who was just as great as a thinker as he was an artist, we can recognize the striving for a new law-determined picture of nature. Such spirits feel it necessary to find an access to nature not yet given to the Greek way of thinking and its after effects in the Middle Ages. Man now has to rid himself of whatever experiences he has about his own inner being if he is to find access to nature. He is permitted to depict nature only in conceptions that contain nothing of what he experiences as the *effects* of nature in himself.

Thus, the human soul dissociates itself from nature; it takes its stand on its own ground. As long as one could think that the stream of nature contained something that was the same as what was immediately experienced in man, one could, without hesitation, feel justified to have thought bear witness to the events of nature. The picture of nature of modern times forces the human consciousness to feel itself outside nature with its thought. This consciousness further establishes a validity for its thought, which is gained through its own power.

From the beginning of the Christian Era to Scotus Erigena, the experience of thought continues to be effective in such a way that its form is determined by the presupposition of a spiritual world, namely, the world of religious revelation. From the eighth to the sixteenth century, thought experience wrests itself free from the inner self-consciousness but allows, besides its own germinating power, the other power of consciousness, revelation, to continue in its existence. From the sixteenth century on, it is the picture of nature that eliminates the experience of thought itself; henceforth, the self-consciousness attempts to produce, out of its own energies, the resources through which it is possible to form a world conception with the help of thought. It is with this task that Descartes finds himself confronted. It is the task of the thinkers of the new period of world conception.

Benedict Spinoza (1632–1677) asks himself, "*What* must be assumed as a starting point from which the creation of a true world picture may proceed? This beginning is caused by the feeling that innumerable thoughts may present themselves in my soul as true; I can admit as the corner stone for a world conception only an element whose properties I must first determine." Spinoza finds that one can only begin with something that is in need of nothing else for its being. He gives the name, substance, to this being. He finds that there can be only one such substance, and that this substance is God. If one observes the method by which Spinoza arrives at this beginning of his philosophy, one finds that he has modeled it after the method of mathematics. Just as the mathematician takes his start from general truths, which the human ego forms itself in free creation, so Spinoza demands that philosophy should start from such spontaneously created conceptions. The one substance is as the ego must think it to be. Thought in this way, it does not tolerate anything existing outside itself as a peer, for then it would not be everything. It would need something other than itself for its existence. Everything else is, therefore, only *of* the substance, as one of its attributes, as Spinoza says. Two such attributes are recognizable to man. He sees the first when he looks at the outer world; the second, when he turns his attention inward. The first attribute is extension; the second, thinking. Man contains both attributes in his being. In his body he has extension; in his soul, thinking. When he thinks, it is the divine substance that thinks; when he acts, it is this substance that acts. Spinoza obtains the existence (*Dasein*) for the ego in anchoring it in the general all-embracing divine substance. Under such circumstances there can be no question of an absolute freedom of man, for man is no more to be credited with the initiative of his actions and thought than a stone with that of its motion; the agent in everything is the one substance. We can speak of a relative freedom in man only when he considers himself not as an individual entity, but knows himself as one with the one substance.

Spinoza's world conception, if consistently developed to its perfection, leads a person to the consciousness: I think of myself in the right way if I no longer consider myself, but know myself in my experience as one with the divine whole. This consciousness then, to follow Spinoza, endows the whole human personality with the impulse to do what is right, that is to say, god-filled action. This results as a matter of course for the one for whom the right world conception is realized as the full truth. For this reason Spinoza calls the book in which he presents his world conception, *Ethics*. For him, ethics, that is to say, moral behavior, is in the highest sense the result of the true knowledge of man's dwelling in the one substance. One feels inclined to say that the private life of Spinoza, of the man who was first persecuted by fanatics and then, out of his own free will give away his fortune and sought his subsistence in poverty as a craftsman, was in the rarest fashion the outer expression of his philosophical soul, which knew its ego in the divine whole and felt its inner experience, indeed, all experience, illumined by this consciousness.

Spinoza constructs a total world conception out of thoughts. These thoughts have to satisfy the requirement that they derive their justification for the construction of the picture out of the self-consciousness. In it their certainty must be rooted. Thoughts that are conceived by human consciousness in the same way as the self-supporting mathematical ideas are capable of shaping a world picture that is the expression of what, in truth, exists behind the phenomena of the world.

In a direction that is entirely different from that of Spinoza, *Gottfried Wilhelm von Leibniz* (1646–1716) seeks the justification of the ego-consciousness in the actual world. His point of departure is like that of Giordano Bruno insofar as he thinks of the soul or the "ego" as a monad. Leibniz finds the *self-consciousness* in the soul, that is, the knowledge of the soul of itself, a manifestation, therefore, of the ego. There cannot be anything else in the soul that thinks and feels except the soul itself, for how should the soul know of *itself* if the subject of the act of knowing were something other than itself? Furthermore, it can only be a simple entity, not a composite being, for the parts in it could and would have to know of each other. Thus, the soul is a simple entity, enclosed in itself and aware of its being, a monad. Nothing can come into this monad that is external to it, for nothing but itself can be active in it. All its experience, cognitive imagination, sensation, etc., is the result of its own activity. It could only perceive any other activity in itself through its defense against this activity, that is to say, it would at any rate perceive *only itself* in its defense. Thus, nothing external can enter this monad. Leibniz expresses this by saying that the monad has no windows. According to him, all real beings are monads, and only monads truly exist. These different monads are, however, differentiated with respect to the intensity of their inner life. There are monads of an extremely dull inner life that are as if in a continual state of sleep; there are monads that are, as it were, dreaming; there are, furthermore, the human monads in wake-consciousness, etc., up to the highest degree of intensity of the inner life of the divine principal monad. That man does not see monads in his sense perception is caused by the circumstance that the monads are perceived by him like the appearance of fog, for example, that is not really fog but a swarm of gnats. What is seen by the senses of man is like the appearance of a fog formed by the accumulated monads.

Thus, for Leibniz the world in reality is a sum of monads, which do not affect each other but constitute self-conscious beings, leading their lives independently of each other, that is, egos. Nevertheless, if the individual monad contains an after image of the general life of the world in its inner life, it would be wrong to assume that this is caused by an effect that the individual monads exert on each other. It is caused by the circumstance that in a given case one monad experiences inwardly by itself what is also independently experienced by another monad. The inner lives of the monads agree like clocks that indicate the same hours in spite of the fact that they do not affect each other. Just as the clocks agree because they have been originally matched, so the monads are attuned to each other through the pre-established harmony that issues from the divine principal monad.

This is the world picture to which Leibniz is driven because he has to form the picture in such a way that in it the *self-conscious* life of the soul, the ego, can be maintained as a reality. It is a world picture completely formed out of the "ego" itself. In Leibniz's view, this can, indeed, not be otherwise. In Leibniz, the struggle for a world conception leads to a point where, in order to find the truth, it does not accept anything as truth that is revealed in the outer world.

According to Leibniz, the life of man's senses is caused in such a way that the monad of the soul is brought into connection with other monads with a somnolent, sleeping and less acute self-consciousness. The body is a sum of such monads. The one waking soul monad is connected with it. This central monad parts from the others in death and continues its existence by itself.

Just as the world picture of Leibniz is one that is wholly formed out of the inner energy of the self-conscious soul, so the world picture of his contemporary *John Locke* (1632–1704), rests entirely on the feeling that such a productive construction out of the soul is not admissible. Locke recognizes only those parts of a world conception as justified that can be *observed* (experienced) and what can, on the basis of the observation, *be thought* about the observed objects. The soul for him is not a being that develops real experiences out of itself, but an empty slate on which the outer world writes its entries. Thus, for Locke, the human self-consciousness is a result of the experience; it is not an ego that is the cause of an experience. When a thing of the external world makes an impression on the soul, it can be said that the thing contains only extension, shape, motion in reality; through the contact with the senses, sounds, colors, warmth, etc., are produced. What thus comes into being through contact with the senses is only there as long as the senses are in touch with the things. Outside the perception there are only substances that are differently shaped and in various states of motion. Locke feels compelled to assume that, except shape and motion, nothing of what the senses perceive has anything to do with things themselves. With this assumption he makes the beginnings of a current of world conception that is unwilling to recognize the impressions of the external world experienced inwardly by man in his act of cognition, as belonging to the world "in itself."

It is a strange spectacle that Locke presents to the contemplative soul. Man is supposed to be capable of cognition only through the fact that he perceives, and that he thinks about the content of the perception, but what he perceives has only the least part to do with the properties pertaining to the world itself. Leibniz withdraws from what the world reveals and creates a world picture from within the soul; Locke insists on a world picture that is created by the soul in conjunction with the world, but no real picture of a world is accomplished through such a creation. As Locke cannot, like Leibniz, consider the *ego* itself as the fulcrum of a world conception, he arrives at conceptions that appear to be inappropriate to support a world conception because they do not allow the possession of the human ego to be counted as belonging to the center of existence. A world view like that of Locke loses the connection with every realm in which the *ego*, the self-conscious soul, could be rooted because it rejects from the outset any approaches to the world ground except those that disappear in the darkness of the senses.

In Locke, the evolution of philosophy produces a form of world conception in which the self-conscious soul struggles for its existence in the world picture but loses this fight because it believes that it gains its experiences exclusively in the intercourse with the external world represented in the picture of nature. The self-conscious soul must, therefore, renounce all knowledge concerning anything that could belong to the nature of the soul apart from this intercourse with the outside world.

Stimulated by Locke, *George Berkeley* (1685–1753) arrived at results that were entirely different from his. Berkeley finds that the impressions that the things and events of the world appear to produce on the human soul take place in reality *within this soul* itself. When I see "red," I must bring this "redness" into being within myself; when I feel "warm," the "warmth" lives within me. Thus it is with all things that I apparently receive from without. Except for those elements I produce within myself, I know nothing whatsoever about the external things. Thus, it is senseless to speak about things that consist of material substance, for I know only what appears in my mind as something spiritual. What I call a rose, for instance, is wholly spiritual, that is to say, a conception (an idea) experienced by my mind. There is, therefore, according to Berkeley, nothing to be perceived except what is spiritual, and when I notice that something is effected in me from without, then this effect can only be caused by spiritual entities, for obviously bodies cannot cause spiritual effects and my perceptions are entirely spiritual. There are, therefore, only spirits in the world that influence each other. This is Berkeley's view. It turns the conceptions of Locke into their contrary by construing everything as spiritual reality that had been considered as impression of the material things. Thus, Berkeley believes he recognizes himself with his self-consciousness immediately in a spiritual world.

Others have been led to different results by the thoughts of Locke. Condillac (1715–1780) is an example. He believes, like Locke, that all knowledge of the world must and, indeed, can only depend on the observation of the senses and on thinking. He develops this view to the extreme conclusion that thinking has in itself no self-dependent reality; it is nothing but a sublimated, transformed external sensation. Thus, only sense perceptions must be accepted in a world picture that is to correspond to the truth. His explanation in this direction is indeed telling. Imagine a human body that is still completely unawakened mentally, and then suppose one sense after another to be opened. What more do we have in the sentient body than we had before in the insensate organism? A body on which the surrounding world has made impressions. These impressions made by the environment have by no means produced what believes itself to be an "ego." This world conception does not arrive at the possibility of conceiving the "ego" as self-conscious "soul" and it does not accomplish a world picture in which this "ego" could occur. It is the world conception that tries to deliver itself of the task of dealing with the self-conscious soul by *proving its non-existence. Charles Bonnet* (1720–1793), *Claude Adrien Helvetius* (1715–1771), *Julien de la Mettrie* (1709–1751) and the system of nature (*système de la nature*) of *Holbach* that appeared in 1770 follow similar paths. In Holbach's work all traces of spiritual reality have been driven out of the world picture. Only matter and its forces operate in the world, and for this spirit-deprived picture of nature, Holbach finds the words, "O nature, mistress of all being, and you, her daughters, Virtue, Reason, and Truth, may you be forever our only divinities."

In de la Mettrie's *Man, a Machine*, a world conception appears that is so overwhelmed by the picture of nature that it can admit only nature as valid. What occurs in the self-consciousness must, therefore, be thought of in about the same way as a mirror picture that we compare with the mirror. The physical organism would be compared with the mirror, the self-consciousness with the picture. The latter has, apart from the former, no independent significance. In *Man, a Machine*, we read:

> If, however, all qualities of the soul depend so much on the specific organization of the brain and the body as a whole that they obviously *are* only this organization itself, then, in this case, we have to deal with a very enlightened machine. . . . 'Soul,' therefore, is only a meaningless expression of which one has no idea (thought picture), and that a clear head may only use in order to indicate by it the part in us that thinks. Just assume the simplest principle of motion and the animated bodies have everything they need in order to move, feel, repeat, in short, everything necessary to find their way in the physical and moral world. . . . If whatever thinks in my brain is not a part of this inner organ, why should my blood become heated when I make the plan for my works or pursue an abstract line of thought, calmly resting on my bed? (Compare de la Mettrie, *Man, a Machine*, Philosophische Bibliothek, Vol. 68.)

Voltaire (1694–1778) introduced the doctrines of Locke into the circles in which these thinkers had their effect (Diderot, Cabanis and others also belonged to them). Voltaire himself probably never went so far as to draw the last consequences of these philosophers. He allowed himself, however, to be stimulated by the thoughts of Locke and his sparkling and dazzling writings. Much can be felt of these influences, but he could not become a materialist in the sense of these thinkers. He lived in too comprehensive a thought horizon to deny the spirit. He awakened the need for philosophical questions in the widest circles because he linked these questions to the interest of them. Much would have to be said about him in an account that intended to trace philosophical investigation of current events, but that is not the purpose of this presentation. Only the higher problems of world conception in its specific sense are to be considered. For this reason, Voltaire, as well as Rousseau, the antagonist of the school of enlightenment, are not to be dealt with here.

Just as Locke loses his path in the darkness of the senses, so does *David Hume* (1711–1776) in the inward realm of the self-conscious soul, the experience of which appears to him to be ruled not by the forces of a world order, but by the power of human habit. Why does one say that one event in nature is a cause and another an effect? This is a question Hume asks. Man sees how the sun shines on a stone; he then notices that the stone has become warm. He observes that the first event often follows the second. Therefore, he becomes accustomed to think of them as belonging together. He makes the cause out of the sunshine, and the heating of the stone he turns into the effect. Thought habits tie our perceptions together, but there is nothing outside in a real world that manifests itself in such a connection. Man sees a thought in his mind followed by a motion of his body. He becomes accustomed to think of this thought as the cause and of the motion as the effect. Thought habits, nothing more, are, according to Hume, responsible for man's statements about the world processes. The self-conscious soul can arrive at a guiding direction for life through thought habits, but it cannot find anything in these habits out of which it could shape a world picture that would have any significance for the world event apart from the soul. Thus, for the philosophical view of Hume, every conception that man forms beyond the more external and internal observation remains only an object of belief; it can never become knowledge. Concerning the fate of the self-conscious human soul, there can be no reliable knowledge about its relation to any other world but that of the senses, only belief.

The picture of Leibniz's world conception underwent a drawn-out rationalistic elaboration through Christian Wolff (born in Breslau, 1679, professor in Halle). Wolff is of the opinion that a science could be founded that obtains a knowledge of what is possible through pure thinking, a knowledge of what has the potentiality for existence because it appears free from contradiction to our thinking and can be proven in this way. Thus, Wolff becomes the founder of a science of the world, the soul and God. This world conception rests on the presupposition that the self-conscious soul can produce thoughts in itself that are valid for what lies entirely and completely outside its own realm. This is the riddle with which Kant later feels himself confronted; how is knowledge that is produced in the soul and nevertheless supposed to have validity for world entities lying outside the soul, possible?

In the philosophical development since the fifteenth and sixteenth centuries, the tendency becomes manifest to rest the self-conscious soul on itself so that it feels justified to form valid conceptions about the riddles of the world. In the consciousness of the second half of the eighteenth century, *Lessing* (1729–1781) feels this tendency as the deepest impulse of human longing. As we listen to him, we hear many individuals who reveal the fundamental character of that age in this aspiration.

Lessing strives for the transformation of the religious truths of revelation into truths of reason. This aim is distinctly discernible in the various turns and aspects that his thinking has to take. Lessing feels himself with his self-conscious ego in a period of the evolution of mankind that is destined to acquire through the power of self-consciousness, what it had previously received from without through revelation. What has preceded this phase of history becomes for Lessing a process of preparation for the moment in which man's self-consciousness becomes autonomous. Thus, for Lessing, history becomes an "Education of the Human Race." This is also the title of his essay, written at the height of his life, in which he refuses to restrict the human soul to a single terrestrial life, but assumes repeated earth lives for it. The soul lives its lives separated by time intervals in the various periods of the evolution of mankind, absorbs from each period what such a time can yield and incarnates itself in a later period to continue its development. Thus, the soul carries the fruits of one age of humanity into the later ages and is "educated" by history. In Lessing's conception, the *"ego"* is, therefore, extended far beyond the individual life; it becomes rooted in a spiritually effective world that lies behind the world of the senses.

With this view Lessing stands on the ground of a world conception that means to stimulate the self-conscious ego to realize through its very nature how the active agent within itself is not completely manifested in the sense-perceptible individual life. In a different way, yet following the same impulse, *Herder* (1744–1803) attempts to arrive at a world picture. His attention turns toward the entire physical and spiritual universe. He searches, as it were, for the plan of this universe. The connection and harmony of the phenomena of nature, the first dawning and sunrise of language and poetry, the progress of historical evolution—with all this Herder allows his soul to be deeply impressed, and often penetrates it with inspired thought in order to reach a certain aim. According to Herder, something is striving for existence in the entire external world that finally appears in its manifested form in the human soul. The self-conscious soul, by feeling itself grounded in the universe, reveals to itself only the course its own forces took before it reached self-consciousness. The soul may, according to Herder's view, feel itself rooted in the cosmos, for it recognizes a process in the whole natural and spiritual connection that had to lead to the soul itself, just as childhood must lead to mature adulthood in man's personal existence. It is a comprehensive picture of this world thought of Herder that is expressed in his *Ideas Toward a Philosophy of the History of Mankind.* It represents an attempt to think the picture of nature in harmony with that of the spirit in such a way that there is in this nature picture a place also for the self-conscious human soul. We must not forget that Herder's world conception reflects his struggle to come to terms simultaneously with the conceptions of modern natural science and the needs of the self-conscious soul. Herder was confronted with the demands of modern world conception as was Aristotle with those of the Greek age. Their conceptions receive their characteristic coloring from the different way in which both thinkers had to take into account the pictures of nature provided by their respective ages.

Herder's attitude toward Spinoza, contrary to that of other contemporary thinkers, casts a light on his position in the evolution of world conception. This position becomes particularly distinct if one compares it to the attitude of *Friedrich Heinrich Jacobi* (1743–1819). Jacobi finds in Spinoza's world picture the elements that the human understanding must arrive at if it follows the paths predestined for it by its own forces. This picture of the world marks the limit of what man can know about the world. This knowledge, however, cannot decide anything about the nature of the soul, about the divine ground of the world or about the connection of the soul with the latter for this knowledge. These realms are disclosed to man only if he surrenders to an insight of belief that depends on a special ability of the soul. Knowledge in itself must, therefore, according to Jacobi, necessarily be atheistic. It can adhere strictly to logical order, but it cannot contain within itself divine world order. Thus, Spinozism becomes, for Jacobi, the only possible scientific mode of conception but, at the same time, he sees in it a proof of the fact that this mode of thinking cannot find the connection with the spiritual world. In 1787 Herder defends Spinoza against the accusation of atheism. He is in a position to do so, for he is not afraid to feel, in his own way but similar to that of Spinoza, man's experience with the divine being. Spinoza erects a pure thought structure; Herder tries to gain a world conception not merely through thinking but through the whole of the human soul life. For him, no abrupt contrast exists between belief and knowledge if the soul becomes clearly aware of the manner in which it experiences itself. We express Herder's intention if we describe the experience of the soul in the following way. When belief becomes aware of the reasons that move the soul, it arrives at conceptions that are no less certain than those obtained by mere thinking. Herder accepts everything that the soul can find within itself in a purified form as forces that can produce a world picture. Thus, his conception of the divine ground of the world is richer, more saturated, than that of Spinoza, but this conception allows the human ego to assume a relationship to the world ground, which in Spinoza appears merely as a result of thought.

We take our stand at a point where the various threads of the development of modern world conceptions intertwine, as it were, when we observe how the current of Spinoza's thought enters into it in the eighties of the eighteenth century. In 1785 F. H. Jacobi published his "Spinoza-Booklet." In it he relates a conversation between himself and Lessing that took place shortly before Lessing's death. According to this conversation, Lessing had confessed his adherence to Spinozism. For Jacobi, this also establishes Lessing's atheism. If one recognizes the "Conversation with Jacobi" as decisive for the intimate thoughts of Lessing, one must regard him as a person who acknowledges that man can only acquire a world conception adequate to his nature if he takes as his point of support the firm conviction with which the soul endows the thought living through its own strength. With such an idea Lessing appears as a person whose feeling prophetically anticipates the impulses of the world conceptions of the nineteenth century. That he expresses this idea only in a conversation shortly before his death, and that it is still scarcely noticeable in his writings, shows how hard, even for the freest minds, the struggle with the enigmatic questions that the modern age raised for the development of world conceptions became.

A world conception has to be expressed in thoughts. But the convincing strength of thought, which had found its climax in Platonism and which in Aristotelianism unfolded in an unquestioned way, had vanished from the impulses of man's soul. Only the spiritually bold nature of Spinoza was capable of deriving the energy from the mathematical mode of thinking to elaborate thought into a world conception that should point as far as the ground of the world. The thinkers of the eighteenth century could not yet feel the life-energy of thought that allows them to experience themselves as human beings securely placed into a spiritually real world. Lessing stands among them as a prophet in feeling the force of the self-conscious ego in such a way that he attributes to the soul the transition through repeated terrestrial lives.

The fact that thought no longer entered the field of consciousness as it did for Plato was unconsciously felt like a nightmare in questions of world conceptions. For Plato, it manifested itself with its supporting energy and its saturated content as an active entity of the world. Now, thought was felt as emerging from the substrata of self-consciousness. One was aware of the necessity to supply it with supporting strength through whatever powers one could summon. Time and again this supporting energy was looked for in the truth of belief or in the depth of the heart, forces that were considered to be stronger than thought, which was felt to be pale and abstract. This is what many souls continually experience with respect to thought. They feel it as a mere soul content out of which they are incapable of deriving the energy that could grant them the necessary security to be found in the knowledge that man may know himself rooted with his being in the spiritual ground of the world. Such souls are impressed with the logical nature of thought; they recognize such thought as a force that would be needed to construct a scientific world view, but they demand a force that has a stronger effect on them when they look for a world conception embracing the highest knowledge. Such souls lack the spiritual boldness of Spinoza needed to feel thought as the source of world creation, and thus to know themselves with thought at the world's foundation. As a result of this soul constitution, man often scorns thought while he constructs a world conception; he therefore feels his self-consciousness more securely supported in the darkness of the forces of feeling and emotion. There are people to whom a conception appears the less valuable for its relation to the riddles of the world, the more this conception tends to leave the darkness of the emotional sphere and enter into the light of thought. We find such a mood of soul in *I. G. Hamann* (died 1788). He was, like many a personality of this kind, a great stimulator, but with a genius like Hamann, ideas brought up from the dark depths of the soul have a more intense effect on others than thoughts expressed in rational form. In the tone of the oracles Hamann expressed himself on questions that fill the philosophical life of his time. He had a stimulating effect on Herder as on others. A mystic feeling, often of a poetistic coloring, pervades his oracular sayings. The urge of the time is manifested chaotically in them for an experience of a force of the self-conscious soul that can serve as supporting nucleus for everything that man means to lift into awareness about world and life.

It is characteristic of this age for its representative spirits to feel that one must submerge into the depth of the soul to find the point in which the soul is linked up with the eternal ground of the world; out of the insight into this connection, out of the source of self-consciousness, one must gain a world picture. A considerable gap exists, however, between what man actually was able to embrace with his spiritual energies and this inner root of the self-consciousness. In their spiritual exertion, the representative spirits do not penetrate to the point from which they dimly feel their task originates. They go in circles, as it were, around the cause of their world riddle without coming nearer to it. This is the feeling of many thinkers who are confronted with the question of world conception when, toward the end of the eighteenth century, Spinoza begins to have an effect. Ideas of Locke and Leibniz, also those of Leibniz in the attenuated form of Wolff, pervade their minds. Besides the striving for clarity of thought, the anxious mistrust against it is at work at the same time, with the result that conceptions derived from the depth of the heart are time and again inserted into the world picture for its completion. Such a picture is found reflected in Lessing's friend, *Mendelssohn*, who was hurt by the publication of Jacobi's conversation with Lessing. He was unwilling to admit that this conversation really had had the content that Jacobi reported. In that case, Mendelssohn argues, his friend would actually have confessed his adherence to a world conception that means to reach the root of the spiritual world by mere thoughts, but one could not arrive at a conception of the *life* of this root in this way. The world spirit would have to be approached differently to be felt in the soul as a life-endowed entity. This, Mendelssohn was sure, Lessing must have meant. Therefore, he could only have confessed to a "purified Spinozism," a Spinozism that would want to go beyond mere thinking while striving for the divine origin of existence. To feel the link with this origin in the manner it was made possible by Spinozism was a step Mendelssohn was reluctant to take.

Herder did not shy away from this step because he enriched the thought contours in the world picture of Spinoza with colorful, content-saturated conceptions that he derived from the contemplation of the panorama of nature and the world of the spirit. He could not have been satisfied with Spinoza's thoughts as they were. As given by their originator, they would have appeared to him as all painted gray on gray. He observed what went on in nature and in history and placed the human being into the world of his contemplation. What was revealed to him in this way showed him a connection between the human being and the origin of the world as well as the world itself, through the conception of which he felt himself in agreement with Spinoza's *frame of mind.* Herder was deeply and innately convinced that the contemplation of nature and of historical evolution should lead to a world picture through which man can feel his position in the world as a whole as satisfactory. Spinoza was of the opinion that he could arrive at such a world picture only in the light-flooded realm of a thought activity that was developed after the model of mathematics. If one compares Herder with Spinoza, remembering that Herder acknowledged the conviction of the latter, one is forced to recognize that in the evolution of modern world conception an impulse is at work that remains *hidden* behind the visible world pictures themselves. This impulse consists in the effort to *experience* in the soul what binds the self-consciousness to the totality of the world processes. It is the effort to gain a world picture in which the world appears in such a way that man can recognize himself *in* it as he must recognize himself when he allows the inner voice of his self-conscious soul to speak to him. Spinoza means to satisfy the desire for this kind of experience by having the power of *thought* enfold its own certainty. Leibniz fastens his attention on the *soul* and aims at a conception of the world as it must be thought if the soul, correctly conceived of, is to appear rightly placed in the world picture. Herder observes the world processes and is convinced from the outset that the right world picture will emerge in the soul if this soul approaches these processes in a healthy way and in its full strength. Herder is absolutely convinced of the later statement of Goethe that "every element of fact is already theory." He has also been stimulated by the thought world of Leibniz, but he would never have been capable of searching theoretically for an idea of the self-consciousness in the form of the monad first, and then constructing a world picture with this idea. The soul evolution of mankind presents itself in Herder in a way that enables him to point with special clarity and distinctiveness to the impulse underlying it in the modern age. What in Greece has been treated as thought (idea) as if it were a perception is now *felt* as an *inner experience of the soul,* and the thinker is confronted with the question: How must I penetrate into the depths of my soul to be able to reach the connection of the soul with the ground of the world in such a way that *my* thought will at the same time be the expression of the forces of world creation? The age of enlightenment as it appears in the eighteenth century is still convinced of finding its justification in thought itself. Herder develops beyond this viewpoint. He searches, not for the point of the soul where it reveals itself as thinking, but for the living source where the thought emerges out of the creative principle inherent in the soul. With this tendency Herder comes close to what one can call the mysterious experience of the soul with thought. A world conception must express itself in thoughts, but thought only then endows the soul with the power for which it searches by means of a world conception in the modern age, when it experiences this thought in its process of its birth in the soul. When thought is born, when it has turned into a philosophical system, it has already lost its magical power over the soul. For this reason, the power of thought and the philosophical world picture are so often underestimated. This is done by all those who know only the thought that is suggested to them from without, a thought that they are supposed to believe, to which they are supposed to pledge allegiance. The real power of thought is known only to one who *experiences* it in the process of its formation.

How this impulse lives in souls in the modern age becomes prominently apparent in a most significant figure in the history of philosophy—*Shaftesbury* (1671–1713). According to him, an "inner sense" lives in the soul; through this inner sense ideas enter into man that become the content of a world conception just as the external perceptions enter through the outer senses. Thus, Shaftesbury does not seek the justification of thought in thought itself, but by pointing toward a fact of the soul life that enables thought to enter from the foundation of the world into the interior of the soul. Thus, for Shaftesbury, man is confronted by a twofold outer world: The "external," material one, which enters the soul through the "outer" senses, and the spiritual outer world, which reveals itself to man through his "inner sense."

In this age a strong tendency can be felt toward a knowledge of the soul, for man strives to know how the essence of a world view is anchored in the soul's nature. We see such an effort in *Johann Nicolaus Tetens* (1736–1807). In his investigations of the soul he arrived at a distinction of the soul faculties that has been adopted into general usage at the present time: Thinking, feeling and willing. It was customary before him to distinguish just between the faculties of thinking and the appetitive faculty.

How the spirits of the eighteenth century attempt to watch the soul in the process of creatively forming its world picture can be observed in *Hemsterhuis* (1721–1790). In this philosopher, whom Herder considered to be one of the greatest thinkers since Plato, the struggle of the eighteenth century with the soul impulse of the modern age becomes demonstrably apparent. The thoughts of Hemsterhuis can be expressed approximately in the following way. If the human soul could, through its own power and without external senses, contemplate the world, the panorama of the world would lie displayed before it in a single moment. The soul would then be infinite in the infinite. If the soul, however, had *no* possibility to live in itself but depended entirely on the outer senses, then it would be confronted with a never ending temporal diffusion of the world. The soul would then live, unconscious of itself, in an ocean of sensual boundlessness. Between these two poles, which are never reached in reality but which mark the limits of the inner life as two possibilities, the soul lives its actual life; it permeates its own infinity with the boundlessness of the world.

In this chapter the attempt has been made to demonstrate, through the example of a few thinkers, how the soul impulse of the modern age flows through the evolution of world conception in the eighteenth century. In this current live the seeds from which the thought development of the "Age of Kant and Goethe" grew.

Chapter VI

The Age of Kant and Goethe

Those who struggled for clarity in the great problems of world and life conceptions at the end of the eighteenth century looked up to two men of great intellectual-spiritual power, *Kant* and *Goethe*. Another person who strove for such a clarity in the most forceful way was *Johann Gottlieb Fichte*. When he had become acquainted with Kant's *Critique of Practical Reason*, he wrote:

> *I am living in a new world.* . . . Things I had thought could never be proven to me, for instance, the concept of absolute freedom and duty, now have been proven to me and I feel much happier because of it. It is incomprehensible what a high degree of respect for humanity, what strength this philosophy gives us; what a blessing it is for an age in which morality had been destroyed in its foundation, and in which the concept of duty had been struck from all dictionaries.

And when, on the basis of Kant's conception, he had built his own *Groundwork of all Scientific Knowledge*, he sent the book to Goethe with the words:

> I consider you, and always have considered you, to be the representative of the purest spiritual force of feeling on the level of

development that mankind has reached at the present time. To you philosophy rightly turns. Your feeling is its touchstone.

A similar attitude to both representative spirits was taken by Schiller. He writes about Kant on October 28, 1794:

> I am not at all frightened by the prospect that the law of change, which shows no mercy to any human or divine work, will also destroy the form of the Kantian as well as every other philosophy. Its foundation, however, will not have to fear this destiny, for since the human race exists, and as long as there has been a reason, this philosophy has been silently acknowledged and mankind as a whole has acted in agreement with its principles.

Schiller describes Goethe's conception in a letter addressed to him on August 23, 1794:

> For a long time I have, although from a considerable distance, watched the course of your spirit, and with ever increasing admiration I have observed the path you have marked out for yourself. You are seeking the necessary in nature, but you are seeking it along the most difficult road, which any spirit weaker than yours would be most careful to avoid. You take hold of nature as a whole in order to obtain light in a particular point; in the totality of nature's various types of phenomena, you seek the explanation for the individual. . . . Had you been born a Greek, or even an Italian, and from the cradle been surrounded by an exquisite nature and an idealizing art, your path would have been infinitely shortened; perhaps it would have been made entirely unnecessary. With the first perception of things you would have caught the form of the Necessary, and from your first experiences the grand style would have developed in you. But now, having been born a German, your Greek spirit having thus been cast into a northern world, you had no choice but that of becoming a northern artist yourself, or of supplying your imagination with what it is refused by reality through the help of your power of thought and thus, to produce a second Greece, as it were, from *within* and by means of reason.

Seen from the present age, Kant and Goethe can be considered spirits in whom the evolution of world conception of modern times reveals itself as in an important moment of its development. These spirits experience intensely the enigmatic problems of existence, which have formerly, in a more preparatory stage, been latent in the substrata of the life of the soul.

To illustrate the effect that Kant exerted on his age, the statements of two men who stood at the full height of their time's culture may be quoted. Jean Paul wrote to a friend in 1788:

> For heaven's sake, do buy two books, Kant's *Foundation for a Metaphysics of Morals* and his *Critique of Practical Reason*. Kant is not a light of the world but a complete radiating solar system all at once.

Wilhelm von Humboldt makes the statement:

> Kant undertook the greatest work that philosophical reason has perhaps ever owed to a single man. . . . Three things remain unmistakably certain if one wants to determine the fame that Kant bestowed on his nation and the benefit that he brought to speculative thinking. Some of the things he destroyed will never be raised again, some of those to which he laid the foundation will never perish; most important of all, he brought about a reform that has no equal in the whole history of human thought.

This shows how Kant's contemporaries saw a revolutionary event in the development of world conception in his achievement. Kant himself considered it so important for this development that he judged its significance equal to that which Copernicus's discovery of the planetary motion holds for natural science.

Various currents of philosophical development of previous times continue their effect in Kant's thinking and are transformed in his thought into questions that determine the character of his world conception. The reader who feels the characteristic traits in those of Kant's writings that are most significant for his view is aware of a special appreciation of Kant for the mathematical mode of thinking as one of these traits. Kant feels that what is known in the way mathematical thinking knows, carries the certainty of its truth in itself. The fact that man is capable of mathematics proves that he is capable of truth. Whatever else one may doubt, the truth of mathematics cannot be doubted.

With this appreciation of mathematics the thought tendency of modern history of philosophy, which had put the characteristic stamp on Spinoza's realm of thoughts, appears in Kant's mind. Spinoza wants to construct his thought sequences in such a form that they develop strictly from one another as the propositions of mathematical science. Nothing but what is thought in the mode of thought of mathematics supplies the firm foundation on which, according to Spinoza, the human ego feels itself secure in the spirit of the modern age. Descartes had also thought in this way, and Spinoza had derived from him many stimulating suggestions. Out of the state of doubt he had to secure a fulcrum for a world conception for himself. In the mere passive reception of a thought into the soul, Descartes could not recognize such a support yielding force. This Greek attitude toward the world of thought is no longer possible for the man of the modern age. Within the self-conscious soul something must be found that lends its support to the thought. For Descartes, and again for Spinoza, this is supplied by the fulfillment of the postulate that the soul should deal with thought in general as it does in the mathematical mode of conception. As Descartes proceeded from his state of doubt to his conclusion, "I think, therefore I am," and the statements connected with it, he felt secure in these operations because they seemed to him to possess the *clarity* that is inherent in mathematics. The same general mental conviction leads Spinoza to elaborate a world picture for himself in which everything is unfolding its effect with strict necessity like the laws of mathematics. The one divine substance, which permeates all beings of the world with the determination of mathematical law, admits the human ego only if it surrenders itself completely to this substance, if it allows its self-consciousness to be absorbed by the world consciousness of the divine substance. This mathematical disposition of mind, which is caused by a longing of the "ego" for the security it needs, leads this "ego" to a world picture in which, through its striving for security, it has lost *itself,* its self-dependent, firm stand on a spiritual world ground, its freedom and its hope for an eternal self-dependent existence.

Leibniz's thoughts tended in the opposite direction. The human soul is, for him, the self dependent monad, strictly closed off in itself. But this monad experiences only what it contains *within itself;* the world order, which presents itself "from without, as it were," is only a delusion. Behind it lies the true world, which consists only of monads, the order of which is the pre-determined (pre-established) harmony that does *not* show itself to the outer observation. This world conception leaves its self-dependence to the human soul, the self-dependent existence in the universe, its freedom and hope for an eternal significance in the world's evolution. If, however, it means to remain consistent with its basic principle, it cannot avoid maintaining that everything known by the soul is *only* the soul itself, that it is incapable of going outside the self-conscious ego and that the universe cannot become revealed to the soul in its truth from without.

For Descartes and for Leibniz, the convictions they had acquired in their religious education were still effective enough that they adopted them in their philosophical world pictures, thereby following motivations that were not really derived from the basic principles of their world pictures. Into Descartes's world picture there crept the conception of a spiritual world that he had obtained through religious channels. It unconsciously permeated the rigid mathematical necessity of his world order and thus he did not feel that his world picture tended to extinguish his "ego." In Leibniz, religious impulses exerted their influence in a similar way, and it is for this reason that it escaped him that his world picture provided for no possibility to find anything except the content of the soul itself. Leibniz believed, nevertheless, that he could assume the existence of the spiritual world outside the "ego." Spinoza, through a certain courageous trait of his personality, actually drew the consequences of his world picture. To obtain the security for this world picture on which his self-consciousness insisted, he renounced the self-dependence of this self-consciousness and found his supreme happiness in feeling himself as a part of the one divine substance.

With regard to Kant we must raise the question of how he was compelled to feel with respect to the currents of world conception, which had produced its prominent representatives in Descartes, Spinoza and Leibniz. For all soul impulses that had been at work in these three were also active in him, and in his soul these impulses effected each other and caused the riddles of world and mankind with which Kant found himself confronted. A glance at the life of the spirit in the Age of Kant informs us of the general trend of Kant's feeling with respect to these riddles. Significantly, *Lessing's* (1729–1781) attitude toward the questions of world conception is symptomatic of this intellectual life. Lessing sums up his credo in the words, "The transformation of revealed truths into truths of reason is absolutely necessary if the human race is to derive any help from them." The eighteenth century has been called the century of the *Enlightenment.* The representative spirits of Germany understood enlightenment in the sense of Lessing's remark. Kant declared the enlightenment to be "man's departure from his self-caused bondage of mind," and as its motto he chose the words, "Have courage to use your *own* mind." Even thinkers as prominent as Lessing, however, at first had succeeded in no more than transforming rationally traditional doctrines of belief derived from the state of the "self-caused bondage of mind." They did not penetrate to a pure rational view as Spinoza did. It was inevitable that Spinoza's doctrine, when it became known in Germany, should make a deep impression on such spirits.

Spinoza really had undertaken the task of using his own mind, but in the course of this process he had arrived at results that were entirely different from those of the German philosophers of the enlightenment. His influence had to be so much the more significant since the lines of his reasoning, constructed according to mathematical methods, carried a much greater convincing power than the current of Leibniz's philosophy, which effected the spirits of that age in the form "developed" by Wolff. From Goethe's autobiography, *Poetry and Truth*, we receive an idea of how this school of thought impressed deeper spirits as it reached them through the channels of Wolff's conceptions. Goethe tells of the impressions the lectures of Professor Winckler in Leipzig, given in the spirit of Wolff, had made on him.

> At the beginning, I attended my classes industriously and faithfully, but the philosophy offered in no way succeeded in enlightening me. It seemed strange to me that in logic I was to tear apart, isolate and destroy, as it were, the intellectual operations I had been handling with the greatest ease since the days of my childhood, in order to gain an insight into their correct use. I thought I knew just about as much as the lecturer about the nature of things, the world and God, and on more than one occasion it seemed to me that there was a considerable hitch in the matter.

About his occupation with Spinoza's writings, however, the poet tells us, "I surrendered to this reading and, inspecting myself, I believed never to have seen the world so distinctly."

There were, however, only a few people who could surrender to Spinoza's mode of thought as frankly as Goethe. Most readers were led into deep conflicts of world conception by this philosophy. Goethe's friend, F. H. Jacobi, is typical of them. He believed that he had to admit that reason, left to its own resources, would not lead to the doctrines of belief, but to the view at which Spinoza had arrived—that the world is ruled by eternal, necessary laws. Thus, Jacobi found himself confronted with an important decision: Either to trust his reason and abandon the doctrines of his creed or to deny reason the possibility to lead to the highest insights in order to be able to retain his belief. He chose the latter. He maintained that man possessed a direct certainty in his innermost soul, a secure *belief* by virtue of which he was capable of feeling the truth of the conception of a personal God, of the freedom of will and of immortality, so that these convictions were entirely independent of the insights of reason that were leaning on logical conclusions, and had no reference to these things but only to the external things of nature. In this way, Jacobi deposed the *knowledge of reason* to make room for a *belief* that satisfied the needs of the heart. Goethe who was not at all pleased by this dethronement of reason, wrote to his friend, "God has punished you with metaphysics and placed a thorn in your flesh; he has blessed me with physics. I cling to the atheist's (Spinoza's) worship of God and leave everything to you that you call, and may continue to call, religion. Your trust rests in *belief* in God; mine in *seeing*." The philosophy of the enlightenment ended by confronting the spirits with the alternative, either to supplant the revealed truths by truths of reason in the sense of Spinoza, or to declare war on the knowledge of reason itself.

Kant also found himself confronted with this choice. The attitude he took and how he made his decision is apparent from the clear account in the preface to the second edition of his *Critique of Pure Reason.*

> Now let us assume that morality necessarily presupposes freedom (in its strictest sense) as a property of our will, pleading practical principles inherent in our reason that would be positively impossible without the presupposition of freedom. Speculative reason, however, having proven that this is not even thinkable, the former assumption, made on behalf of morality, would have to give way to the latter, whose opposite contains an obvious self-contradiction and therefore freedom, and with it morality, would have to give way to the *mechanism of nature.* But since, as the case lies, for the possibility of morality nothing more is required than that the idea of freedom be not contradictory in itself, and may at least be considered as thinkable *without the future necessity of being understood,* such that granting the freedom of a given action would not place any obstacle into the attempt of considering the same action (see in other relation) as a mechanism of nature. In this way, the doctrine of morality maintains its place . . . which could, however, not have happened if our critical philosophy had not previously enlightened us about *our inevitable ignorance with respect to things in themselves,*

restricting all that we can know theoretically to mere phenomena. In the same way, the positive value of the critical principles of pure reason can be brought to light with regard to the concepts of God and of the *simple nature of our soul,* which I do, however, leave undiscussed here for the sake of brevity. I cannot even *assume God, freedom and immortality* for the use of practical reason if I do not at the same time *deprive* speculative reason of its pretensions to excessive insight. . . . *I, therefore, had to suspend knowledge in order to make room for belief.* . . .

We see here how Kant stands on a similar ground as Jacobi in regard to knowledge and belief.

The way in which Kant had arrived at his results had led through the thought world of Hume. In Hume he had found the view that the things and events of the world in no way reveal connections of thought to the human soul, that the human mind imagined such connections only through habit while it is perceiving the things and events of the world simultaneously in space and successively in time. Kant was impressed by Hume's opinion according to which the human mind does not receive from the world what appears to it as knowledge. For Kant, the thought emerged as a possibility: What is knowledge for the human mind does *not* come from the reality of the world.

Through Hume's arguments, Kant was, according to his own confession, awakened out of the slumber into which he had fallen in following Wolff's train of ideas. How can reason produce judgments about God, freedom and immortality if its statement about the simplest events rests on such insecure foundation? The attack that Kant now had to undertake against the knowledge of reason was much more far-reaching than that of Jacobi. He had at least left to knowledge the possibility of comprehending nature in its necessary connection. Now Kant had produced an important accomplishment in the field of natural science with his *General Natural History and Theory of the Heavens,* which had appeared in 1755. He was satisfied to have shown that our whole planetary system could be thought to have developed out of a ball of gas, rotating around its axis.

Through strictly necessary mathematically measurable physical forces, he thought the sun and planets to have consolidated, and to have assumed the motions in which they proceed according to the teachings of Copernicus and Kepler. Kant thus believed he had proven, through a great discovery of his own, the fruitfulness of Spinoza's mode of thought, according to which everything happens with strict, mathematical necessity. He was so convinced of this fruitfulness that in the above-mentioned work he went so far as to exclaim, "Give me matter, and I will build you a universe!" The absolute certainty of all mathematical truths was so firmly established for him that he maintains in his *Basic Principles of Natural Science* that a *science in the proper sense of the word* is only one in which the application of mathematics is possible. If Hume were right, it would be out of the question to assume such a certainty for the knowledge of mathematical natural science, for, in that case, this knowledge would consist of nothing but thought habits that man had developed because he had seen the course of the world along certain lines. But there would not be the slightest guaranty that these thought habits had anything to do with the law-ordered connection of the things of the world. From his presupposition Hume draws the conclusion:

> The scenes of the universe are continually shifting, and one object follows another in an uninterrupteed succession, but the power of force which actuates the whole machine is entirely concealed from us and never discovers itself in any of the sensible qualities of body. . . . (*Enquiry Concerning Human Understanding*, Sec. VII, part 1.)

If we then place the world conception of Spinoza into the light of Hume's view, we must say, "In accordance with the perceived course of the processes of the world, man has formed the habit of thinking these processes in a necessary, law-ordered connection, but he is not entitled to maintain that this '*connection*' is anything but a mere thought habit." Now if this were the case, then it would be a mere deception of the human reason to imagine that it could, through itself, gain any insight into the nature of the world, and Hume could not be contradicted when he says about every world conception that is gained out of pure reason, "Throw it into the fire, for it is nothing but deception and illusion."

Kant could not possibly adopt this conclusion of Hume as his own. For him, the certainty of the knowledge of mathematical natural science was irrevocably established. He would not allow this certainty to be touched but was unable to deny that Hume was justified in saying that we gain all knowledge about real things only by observing them and by forming for ourselves thoughts about their connection that are based on this observation. If a law-ordered connection is inherent in things, then we must also extract this connection out of them, but what we really derive from the things is such that we know no more about it than that it has been so up to the present time. We do not know, however, whether such a connection is really so linked up with the nature of things that it cannot change in any moment. If we form for ourselves today a world conception based on our observations, events can happen tomorrow that compel us to form an entirely different one. If we received all our knowledge from things, there would be no certainty. Mathematics and natural sciences are a proof of this. That the world does not *give* its knowledge to the human mind was a view Kant was ready to adopt from Hume. That this knowledge does not contain certainty and truth, however, is a conclusion he was not willing to draw. Thus, Kant was confronted with the question that disturbed him deeply: How is it possible that man is in possession of true and certain knowledge and that he is, nevertheless, incapable of knowing anything of the reality of the world in itself?

Kant found an answer that saved the truth and certainty of human knowledge by sacrificing human insight into the grounds of the world. Our reason could never claim certainty about anything in a world lying spread out around us so that we would be affected by it through observation only. Therefore, our world can only be one that is constructed by ourselves: A world that lies within the limits of our minds. What is going on outside myself as a stone falls and causes a hole in the ground, I do not know. The law of this entire process is enacted within me, and it can proceed within me only in accordance with demands of my own mental organization. The nature of my mind requires that every effect should have a cause and that two times two is four. It is in accordance with this nature that the mind constructs a world for itself. No matter how the world outside ourselves might be constructed, today's world may not coincide in even a single trait with that of yesterday. This can never concern us for our mind produces its own world according to its own laws. As long as the human mind remains unchanged, it will proceed in the same way in the construction of the world. Mathematics and natural science do not contain the laws of the external world but those of our mental organization. It is, therefore, only necessary to investigate this organization if we want to know what is unconditionally true. "Reason does not derive its laws *from* nature but prescribes them *to* nature." Kant sums up his conviction in this sentence, but the mind does not produce its inner world without an impetus or impression from without. When I perceive the color red, the perception, "red," is, to be sure, a state, a process within me, but it is necessary for me to have an occasion to perceive "red." There are, therefore, "things in themselves," but we know nothing about them but the fact that they exist. Everything we observe belongs to the appearances within us. Therefore, in order to save the certainty of the mathematical and natural scientific truths, Kant has taken the whole world of observation in the human mind. In doing so, however, he has raised insurmountable barriers to the faculty of knowledge, for everything that we can know refers merely to processes within ourselves, to *appearances or phenomena*, not to things in themselves, as Kant expresses it. But the objects of the highest questions of reason—God, Freedom and Immortality—can never become phenomena. We see the appearances within ourselves; whether or not these have their origin in a divine being we cannot know. We can observe our own psychic conditions, but these are also only phenomena. Whether or not there is a free immortal soul behind them remains concealed to our knowledge. About the "things in themselves," our knowledge cannot produce any statement. It cannot determine whether the ideas concerning these "things in themselves" are true or false. If they are announced to us from another direction, there is no objection to assume their existence, but a *knowledge* concerning them is impossible for us. There is only one access to these highest truths. This access is given in the voice of duty, which speaks within us emphatically and distinctly, "You are *morally obliged* to do this and that." This "Categorical Imperative" imposes on us an obligation we are incapable of avoiding. But how could we comply with this obligation if we were not in the possession of a *free will?* We are, to be sure, incapable of *knowledge* concerning this quality of our soul, but we must *believe* that it is *free* in order to be capable of following its inner voice of duty. Concerning this freedom, we have, therefore, no certainty of knowledge as we possess it with respect to the objects of mathematics and natural science, but we have *moral certainty* for it instead. The observance of the categorical imperative leads to virtue. It is only through virtue that man can arrive at his destination. He becomes worthy of happiness. Without this possibility his virtue would be void of meaning and significance. In order that virtue may result from happiness, it is mandatory that a being exists who secures this happiness as an effect of virtue. This can only be an intelligent being, determining the highest value of things: God. Through the existence of virtue, its effect is guaranteed, and through this guarantee, in turn, the existence of God. Because man is a sensual being and cannot obtain perfect happiness in this imperfect world, his existence must transcend this sensual existence; that is to say, the soul must be immortal. The very thing about which we are denied *possible knowledge* is, therefore, magically produced by Kant out of the *moral belief* in the voice of duty. It was respect for the feeling of duty that restored a real world for Kant when, under the influence of Hume, the observable world withered away into a mere inner world. This respect for duty is beautifully expressed in his *Critique of Practical Reason:*

> Duty! Thou sublime, great name that containest nothing pleasurable to bid for our favor, but demandest submission, . . . proclaim-

ing a law in the presence of which all inclinations are silenced although they may secretly offer resistance. . . .

That the highest truths are not truths of knowledge but moral truths is what Kant considered as his discovery. Man has to renounce all insight into a supersensible world, but from his moral nature springs a compensation for this knowledge. No wonder Kant sees the highest demand on man in the unconditional surrender to duty. If it were not for duty to open a vista for him beyond the sensual world, man would be enclosed for his whole life in the world of the senses. No matter, therefore, what the sensual world demands; it has to give way before the peremptory claims of duty, and the sensual world cannot, out of its own initiative, agree with duty. Its own inclination is directed toward the agreeable, toward pleasure. These aims have to be opposed by duty in order to enable man to reach his destination. What man does for his pleasure is not virtuous; virtue is only what he does in selfless devotion to duty. Submit your desires to duty; this is the rigorous task that is taught by Kant's moral philosophy. Do not allow your will to be directed toward what satisfies you in your egotism, but so act that the principles of your action can become those of all men. In surrendering to the moral law, man attains his perfection. The belief that this moral law has its being above all other events of the world and is made real within the world by a divine being is, in Kant's opinion, true religion. It springs from the moral life. Man is to be good, not because of his belief in a God whose will demands the good; he is to be good only because of his feeling for duty. He is to believe in God, however, because duty without God would be meaningless. This is *religion within the Limits of Mere Reason.* It is thus that Kant entitles his book on religious world conception.

The course that the development of the natural sciences took since they began to flourish has produced in many people the feeling that every element that does not carry the character of strict necessity should be eliminated from our thought picture of nature. Kant had this feeling also. In his *Natural History of the Heavens*, he had even outlined such a picture for a certain realm of nature that was in accordance with this feeling. In a thought picture of this kind, there is no place for the conception of the self-conscious ego that the man of the eighteenth century felt necessary. The Platonic and the Aristotelian thought could be considered as the revelation of nature in the form in which that idea was accepted in the earlier age, and as that of the human soul as well. In thought life, nature and the soul met. From the picture of nature as it seems to be demanded by modern science, nothing leads to the conception of the self-conscious soul. Kant had the feeling that the conception of nature offered nothing to him on which he could base the certainty of self-consciousness. This certainty had to be created for the modern age had presented the self-conscious ego as a fact. The possibility had to be created to acknowledge this fact, but everything that can be recognized as knowledge by our understanding is devoured by the conception of nature. Thus, Kant feels himself compelled to provide for the self-conscious ego as well as for the spiritual world connected with it, something that is not knowledge but nevertheless supplies certainty.

Kant established selfless devotion to the voice of the spirit as the foundation of moral life. In the realm of virtuous action, such a devotion is not compatible with a surrender to the sensual world. There is, however, a field in which the sensual is elevated in such a way that it appears as the immediate expression of the spirit. That is the field of beauty and art. In our ordinary life we want the sensual because it excites our desire, our self-seeking interest. We desire what gives us pleasure, but it is also possible to take a selfless interest in an object. We can look at it in admiration, filled by a heavenly delight and this delight can be quite independent of the possession of the thing. Whether or not I should like to own a beautiful house that I pass has nothing to do with the "disinterested pleasure" that I may take in its beauty. If I eliminate all desire from my feeling, there may still be found as a remaining element a pleasure that is clearly and exclusively linked to the beautiful work of art. A pleasure of this kind is an "esthetic pleasure." The beautiful is to be distinguished from the agreeable and the good. The agreeable excites my interest because it arouses my desire; the good interests me because it is to be made real by me. In confronting the beautiful I have no such interest that is connected with my person. What is it then, by means of which my selfless delight is attracted? I can be pleased by a thing only when its purpose is fulfilled, when it is so organized that it serves an end. Fitness to purpose pleases; incongruity displeases, but as I have no interest in the reality of the beautiful thing, as the mere sight of it satisfies me, it is also not necessary that the beautiful object really serves a purpose. The purpose is of no importance to me; what I demand is only the appropriateness. For this reason, Kant calls an object "beautiful" in which we perceive fitness to purpose without thinking at the same time of a definite purpose.

What Kant gives in this exposition is not merely an explanation but also a justification of art. This is best seen if one remembers Kant's feeling in regard to his world conception. He expresses his feeling in profound, beautiful words:

> Two things fill the heart with ever new and always increasing admiration and awe: The starred heaven above me and the moral law within me. At first, the sight of an innumerable world quantity annihilates, as it were, my importance as a living creature, which must give back to the planet that is a mere dot in the universe the matter out of which it became what it is, after having been for a short while (one does not know how) provided with the energy of life. On second consideration, however, this spectacle infinitely raises my value as an intelligent being, through my (conscious and free) personality in which the moral law reveals to me a life that is independent of the whole world of the senses, at least insofar as this can be concluded from the purpose-directed destination of my existence, which is not hemmed in by the conditions and limitations of this life but extends into the infinite.

The artist now transplants this purpose-directed destination, which, in reality, rules in the realm of the moral world, into the world of the senses. Thus, the world of art stands between the realm of the world of observation that is dominated by the eternal stern laws of necessity, which the human mind itself has previously laid into this world, and the realm of free morality in which commands of duty, as the result of a wise, divine world-order, set out direction and aim. Between both realms the artist enters with his works. Out of the realm of the real he takes his material, but he reshapes this material at the same time in such a fashion that it becomes the bearer of a purpose-directed harmony as it is found in the realm of freedom. That is to say, the human spirit feels dissatisfied both with the realms of external reality, which Kant has in mind when he speaks of the starred heaven and the innumerable things of the world, and also with the realm of moral law. Man, therefore, creates a beautiful realm of "semblance," which combines the rigid necessity of nature with the element of a free purpose. The beautiful now is not only found in human works of art, but also in nature. There is nature-beauty as well as art-beauty. This beauty of nature is there without man's activity. It seems, therefore, as if there were observable in the world of reality, not merely the rigid law-ordered necessity, but a free wisdom-revealing activity as well. The phenomenon of the beautiful, nevertheless, does not force us to accept a conception of this kind, for what it offers is the form of a purpose-directed activity without implying also the thought of a real purpose. Furthermore, there is not only the phenomenon of integrated beauty but also that of integrated ugliness. It is, therefore, possible to assume that in the multitude of natural events, which are interconnected according to necessary laws, some happen to occur—accidentally, as it were—in which the human mind observes an analogy with man's own works of art. As it is not necessary to assume a real purpose, this element of free purpose, which appears as it were by accident, is quite sufficient for the esthetic contemplation of nature.

The situation is different when we meet the entities in nature to which the purpose concept is not merely to be attributed as accidental but that carry this purpose really within themselves. There are also entities of this kind according to Kant's opinion. They are the organic beings. The necessary law-determined connections are insufficient to explain them; these, in Spinoza's world conception are considered not only necessary but sufficient, and by Kant are considered as those of the human mind itself. For an "organism is a product of nature in which *everything* is, at the same time, purpose, just as it is cause and also effect." An organism, therefore, cannot be explained merely through rigid laws that operate with necessity, as is the case with inorganic nature. It is for this reason that, although Kant himself had, in his *General Natural History and Theory of the Heavens,* undertaken the attempt to "discuss the constitution and the mechanical origin of the entire world structure according to Newtonian principles," he is of the opinion that a similar attempt, applied to the world of organic beings, would necessarily fail. In his *Critique of Judgment,* he advances the following statement:

> It is, namely, absolutely certain that in following merely mechanical principles of nature we cannot even become sufficiently acquainted with organisms and their inner possibility, much less explain them. This is so certain that one can boldly say that it would be absurd for man to set out on any such attempt or to hope that at some future time a Newton could arise who would explain as much as the production of a blade of grass according to natural laws into which no purpose had brought order and direction. Such a knowledge must, on the contrary, be altogether denied to man.

Kant's view that it is the human mind itself that first projects the laws into nature that it then finds in it, is also irreconcilable with another opinion concerning a purpose-directed entity, for a purpose points to its originator through whom it was laid into such an entity, that is, to the rational originator of the world. If the human mind could explain a teleological being in the same way as an entity that is merely constituted according to natural necessity, it would also have to be capable of projecting laws of purpose out of itself into the things. Not merely would the human mind have to provide laws for the things that would be valid with regard to them insofar as they are appearances of his inner world, but it would have to be capable of prescribing their own destination to the things that are completely independent of the mind. The human mind would, therefore, have to be not merely a cognitive, but a creative, spirit; its reason would, like that of God, have to create the things.

Whoever calls to mind the structure of the Kantian world conception as it has been outlined here will understand its strong effect on Kant's contemporaries and also on the time after him, for he leaves intact all of the conceptions that had formed and impressed themselves on the human mind in the course of the development of western culture. This world conception leaves God, freedom and immortality, to the religious spirit. It satisfies the need for knowledge in delineating a territory for it inside the limits of which it recognizes unconditionally certain truths. It even allows for the opinion that the human reason is justified to employ, not merely the eternal rigorous natural laws for the explanation of living beings, but the purpose concept that suggests a designed order in the world.

But at what price did Kant obtain all this! He transferred all of nature into the human mind and transformed its laws into laws of this mind. He ejected the higher world order entirely from nature and placed this order on a purely moral foundation. He drew a sharp line of demarcation between the realm of the inorganic and that of the organic, explaining the former according to mechanical laws of natural necessity and the latter according to teleological ideas. Finally, he tore the realm of beauty and art completely out of its connection with the rest of reality, for the teleological form that is to be observed in the beautiful has nothing to do with *real* purposes. How a beautiful object comes into the world is of no importance; it is sufficient that it stimulates in us the conception of the purposeful and thereby produces our delight.

Kant not only presents the view that man's knowledge is possible so far as the law-structure of this knowledge has its origin in the self-conscious soul, and the certainty concerning this soul comes out of a source that is different from the one out of which our knowledge of nature springs. He also points out that our human knowledge has to resign before nature, where it meets the living organism in which thought itself seems to reign in nature. In taking this position, Kant confesses by implication that he cannot imagine thoughts that are conceived as active in the entities of nature themselves. The recognition of such thoughts presupposes that the human soul not merely thinks, but in thinking *shares* the life of nature in its inner experience. If somebody discovered that thoughts are capable not merely of being received as perceptions, as is the case with the Platonic and Aristotelian ideas, but that it is possible to *experience* thoughts by penetrating into the entities of nature, then this would mean that again a new element had been found that could enter the picture of nature as well as the conception of the self-conscious ego. The self-conscious ego by itself does not find a place in the nature picture of modern times. If the self-conscious ego, in filling itself with thought, is not merely aware that it forms this thought, but recognizes in thought a *life* of which it can know, "This life can realize itself also outside myself," then this self-conscious ego can arrive at the insight, "I hold within myself something that can also be found without." The evolution of modern world conception thus urges man on to the step: To find the thought in the self-conscious ego that is felt to be alive. *This step Kant did not take; Goethe did.*

* * *

In all essential points, Goethe arrived at the opposite to Kant's conception of the world. Approximately at the same time that Kant published his *Critique of Pure Reason*, Goethe laid down his creed in his prose hymn, *Nature*, in which he placed man completely into nature and in which he presented nature as bearing absolute sway, independent of man: Her own and man's law-giver as well. Kant drew all nature into the human mind. Goethe considered everything as belonging to this nature; he fitted the human spirit into the natural world order:

> Nature! We are surrounded and enveloped by her, incapable of leaving her domain, incapable of penetrating deeper into her. She draws us into the rounds of her dance, neither asking nor warning,

and whirls away with us until we fall exhausted from her arms. . . .
All men are in her and she is in them. . . . Even the most unnatural
is Nature; even the clumsiest pedantry has something of her genius.
. . . We obey her laws even when we resist them; we are working
with her even when we mean to work *against* her. . . . Nature is
everything. . . . She rewards and punishes, delights and tortures
herself. . . . She has placed me into life, she will also lead me out of
it. I trust myself into her care. She may hold sway over me. She will
not hate her work. It was not I who spoke of her. Nay, it was Nature
who spoke it all, true and false. Nature is the blame for all things;
hers is the merit.

This is the polar opposite to Kant's world conception. According to Kant, nature is entirely in the human spirit; according to Goethe, the human spirit is entirely in nature because nature itself is spirit. It is, therefore, easily understandable when Goethe tells us in his essay, *Influence of Modern Philosophy*:

> Kant's *Critique of Pure Reason* was completely outside my world. I attended many conversations concerning this book, and with some attention I could observe that the old main question of how much our own self contributed to our spiritual existence, and how much the outside world did, was renewed. I never separated them, and when I philosophized in my own way about objects, I did so with an unconscious naivety, really believing that I saw my opinion before my very eyes.

We need not waver in this estimate of Goethe's attitude toward Kant, in spite of the fact that Goethe uttered many a favorable judgment about the philosopher of Koenigsberg. This opposition between Kant and himself would only then have become quite clear to him if he had engaged himself in a thorough study of Kant, but this he did not do. In the above-mentioned essay he says, "It was the introductory passages that I liked; into the labyrinth itself, however, I could not venture to go; I was kept from it now by my poetic imagination, now by my common sense, and nowhere did I feel myself furthered."

Goethe has, nevertheless, expressed his opposition distinctly on one occasion in a passage that has been published only from the papers of the residuary estate in the Weimar Goethe Edition (Weimarische Ausgabe, 2; Abteilung, Band XI, page 377). The fundamental error of Kant was, as here expressed by Goethe, that he "considers the subjective faculty of knowledge as an object and discriminates the point where the subjective and the objective meet with great penetration but not *quite* correctly." Goethe just happens to be convinced that it is not only the spirit as such that speaks in the subjective human faculty of cognition, but that it is the spirit of nature that has created for itself an organ in man through which it reveals its secrets. It is not man at all who speaks about nature, but it is nature who speaks in man about itself. This is Goethe's conviction. Thus, he could say that whenever the controversy concerning Kant's world view "was brought up, I liked to take the side that gave most honor to man, and I completely agreed with all those friends who maintained with Kant that, although all our knowledge begins with experience, it nevertheless does not originate from experience." For Goethe believed that the eternal laws according to which nature proceeds are revealed in the human spirit, but for this reason, they were not merely the subjective laws of the spirit for him, but the objective laws of the order of nature itself.

It is for this reason also that Goethe could not agree when Schiller, under the influence of Kant, erected a forbidding wall of separation between the realms of natural necessity and of freedom. Goethe expressed himself on this point in his essay, *First Acquaintance with Schiller:*

> Schiller and some friends had absorbed the Kantian philosophy, which elevates the subject to such height while apparently narrowing it. It developed the extraordinary traits that nature had laid into his character and he, in his highest feeling of freedom and self determination, tended to be ungrateful to the great mother who had certainly not treated him stingily. Instead of considering nature as self-supporting, alive and productively spreading order and law from the lowest to the highest point, Schiller took notice of it only in the shape of a few empirical human natural inclinations.

In his essay, *Influence of Modern Philosophy*, Goethe points to his difference with Schiller in these words. "He preached the gospel of freedom; I was unwilling to see the rights of nature infringed upon." There was, indeed, an element of Kant's mode of conception in Schiller, but so far as Goethe is concerned, we are right in accepting what he himself said with regard to some conversations he had with the followers of Kant. "They heard what I had to say but they could not answer me or further me in any way. More than once it happened that one or the other of them admitted to me with a surprised smile that my conception was, to be sure, analogous to that of Kant, but in a curious fashion indeed."

Goethe did not consider art and beauty as a realm that was torn out of the interconnection of reality, but as a higher stage of nature's order. At the sight of artistic creations that especially interested him during his Italian journey he wrote, "Like the highest works of nature, the lofty works of art have been produced by men according to *true* and *natural* laws. Everything that is arbitrary and merely imagined fades away before them. *Here is necessity; here is God.*" When the artist proceeds as the Greeks did, namely, "according to the laws that Nature herself follows," then his works contain the same godly element that is to be found in nature itself. For Goethe, art is "a manifestation of secret natural laws." What the artist creates are works of nature on a higher level of perfection. Art is the continuation and human completion of nature, for "as man finds himself placed at the highest point of nature, he again considers himself a whole nature and as such has again to produce a peak in himself. For this purpose he raises his own existence by penetrating himself with all perfections and virtues, produces choice, order, harmony and meaning, and finally lifts himself as far as to the production of the work of art." Everything is nature, from the inorganic stone to the highest of man's works of art, and everything in this nature is ruled by the same "eternal, necessary and thereby divine laws," such that "the godhead itself could not change anything about it" (Poetry and Truth, Book XVI).

When, in 1811, Goethe read Jacobi's book, *On Things Divine*, it made him "uneasy."

> How could the book of a so warmly beloved friend, in which I was to see the thesis developed that nature conceals God, be welcome to me! My mode of world conception—purely felt, deeply-seated, inborn and practised daily as it was—had taught me inviolably to see *God in Nature, Nature in God,* and this to such an extent that this world view formed the basis of my entire existence. Under these circumstances, was not such a strange, one-sided and narrow-minded thesis to estrange me in spirit from this most noble man for whose heart I felt love and veneration? I did not, however, allow my painful vexation to linger with me but took refuge in my old asylum, finding my daily entertainment for several weeks in Spinoza's *Ethics*, and as my inner education had progressed in the meantime, to my astonishment I became aware of many things that revealed themselves to me in a new and different light and affected me with a peculiar freshness.

The realm of necessity in Spinoza's sense is a realm of inner necessity for Kant. For Goethe, it is the universe itself, and man with all his thinking, feeling, willing and actions is a link in this chain of necessities. In this realm there is only *one* order of law, of which the natural and the moral represent only the two sides of its essence. "The sun sheds its light over those good and evil, and to the guilty as to the best, the moon and the stars shine brightly." Out of one root, out of the eternal springs of nature, Goethe has everything pour forth: The inorganic and the organic beings, and man with all the fruits of his spirit, his knowledge, his moral order and his art.

> What God would just push the world from without,
> And let it run in circles on his finger?
> Him it behooves to move it in its core,
> Be close to nature, hug her to her breast
> So that what lives and weaves in him and is,
> Will never lack his power and his spirit.

In these words Goethe summed up his credo. Against Haller,

who had written the lines, "Into nature's sacred center, no created spirits enter," Goethe turns with his sharpest words:

> "Into nature's sacred center,"
> O, Philistine past compare
> "No created spirits enter"
> Wished you never would remind
> Me and all those of my kind
> Of this shallow verbal banter.
> We think we are everywhere
> With every step in Nature's care.
> "Happy he to whom she just
> Shows her dry external crust."
> I hear that repeated these sixty years
> Curse under my breath so no one hears,
> And to myself I a thousand times tell:
> Nature has neither core nor shell,
> Everything yields she gladly and well.
> Nature is at our beck and call
> Nature herself is one and all.
> Better search yourself once more
> Whether you be crust or core.

In following this world conception Goethe could also not recognize the difference between inorganic and organic nature, which Kant had ascertained in his *Critique of Judgment*. Goethe tended to explain living organisms according to the laws by which lifeless nature is explained. Concerning the various species in the plant world, the leading botanist of that time, Linné, states that there were as many species as there "have been created fundamentally different forms." A botanist who holds such an opinion can only attempt to study the quality of the individual forms and to differentiate them carefully from one another. Goethe could not consent to such a view of nature. "What Linnaeus wanted with might and main to separate, I felt in the very roots of my being as striving into union." Goethe searched for an entity that was common to all species of plants. On his Italian journey this general archetype in all plant forms becomes clearer to him step by step.

The many plants I have heretofore been used to see only in buckets and pots, here grow merrily and vigorously under the open sky, and while they thus fulfill their destination, they become clearer to us. At the sight of such a variety of new and renewed forms, my curious and favorite idea again occurred to me. Could I not discover in this crowd the archetypal plant (*Urpflanze*)? There really must be such a thing. How should I otherwise know that this or that given form is a plant if they had not all been designed after one model?

On another occasion Goethe expresses himself concerning this archetypal plant by saying, "It is going to become the strangest creature of the world for which nature herself shall envy me. With this model and the corresponding key, one is then capable of inventing plants to infinity, but they must be consistent in themselves, that is to say, plants that, even if they do not exist, at least *could* exist, and that are not *merely* shadows and schemes of a picturesque or poetic imagination, but have an inner truth and necessity." As Kant, in his *Natural History and Theory of the Heavens*, exclaims, "Give me matter and I will build you a world out of it," because he has gained insight into the law-determined interconnection of this world, so Goethe pronounces here that with the aid of the *archetypal plant* one could invent plants indefinitely that would be capable of existence because one would be in possession of the law of their origin and their development. What Kant was ready to acknowledge only for inorganic nature, that is, that its phenomena can be understood according to necessary laws, Goethe extends also to the world of organisms. In the letter in which he tells Herder about his discovery of the archetypal plant, he adds, "The same law will be applicable to all other living beings," and Goethe applies it, indeed. In 1795, his persevering studies of the animal world led him to "feel free to maintain boldly that all perfect organic beings, among which we see fishes, amphibia, birds, mammals, and at the top of the ladder, man, *were formed after one model*, which in its constant parts only varies in one or another direction and still develops and transforms daily through propagation."

In his conception of nature as well, therefore, Goethe stands in full opposition to Kant. Kant had called it a risky "adventure of reason," should reason attempt to explain the living with regard to its origin. He considered the human faculty of cognition as unfit for such an explanation.

> It is of infinite importance for reason not to eliminate the mechanism of nature in its productions, and not to pass by this idea in their explanation because without it no insight into the nature of things can be obtained. Even if it is admitted to us that the highest architect has created the forms of nature as they have been forever, or predetermined those that form according to the same model in the course of their development, our knowledge of nature would thereby nevertheless not be furthered in the slightest degree because *we do not know at all the mode of action and the ideas of this being* that are to contain the principles of the possibility of the natural beings and therefore *cannot explain nature by means of them from above.*

Against Kantian arguments of this kind, Goethe answers:

> If, in the moral realm through faith in God, virtue and immortality, we are to lift ourselves into the higher region and to approach the first Being, we should be in the same situation in the intellectual field, so that we, through the contemplation of an ever creative nature, should make ourselves worthy of a spiritual participation in its productions. As I had at first unconsciously and, following an inner instinct, insisted upon and relentlessly striven toward the archetypal, the typical, as I had even succeeded in constructing an appropriate picture, there was now nothing to keep me from courageously risking the *adventure of reason,* as the old man from Koenigsberg himself calls it.

In his archetypal plant, Goethe had seized upon an idea "with which one can . . . invent plants to infinity, but they must be consistent, that is to say, even if they do not exist, nevertheless they could exist and are not merely shadows and schemes of a picturesque or poetic imagination but have an inner truth and necessity." Thus, Goethe shows that he is about to find not merely the perceptible idea, the idea that is thought, in the self-conscious ego, but the *living idea.* The self-conscious ego *experiences* a realm in itself that manifests itself as both self-contained and at the same time appertaining to the external world, because the forms of the latter prove to be moulded after the models of the creative powers. With this step the self-conscious ego can appear as a real being. Goethe has developed a conception through which the self-conscious ego can feel itself enlivened because it feels itself *in union* with the creative entities of nature. The world conception of modern times attempted to master the riddle of the self-conscious ego; Goethe plants the *living idea* into this ego, and with this force of life pulsating in it, it proves to be a life-saturated reality. The Greek idea is akin to the picture; it is contemplated like a picture. The idea of modern times must be akin to life, to the living being; it is inwardly experienced. Goethe was aware of the fact that there is such an inward experience of the idea. In the self-conscious ego he perceived the breath of the living idea.

Goethe says of Kant's *Critique of Judgment* that he "owed a most happy period of his life to this book." "The great leading thoughts of this work were quite analogous to my previous creations, actions and thinking. The inner life of art and nature, the unfolding of the activity in both cases from within, was distinctly expressed in this book." Yet, this statement of Goethe must not deceive us concerning his opposition to Kant, for in the essay in which it occurs, we also read, "Passionately stimulated, I proceeded on my own paths so much the quicker because I, myself, did not know where they led, and because *I found little resonance with the Kantians* for *what* I had conquered for myself and for *the methods* in which I had arrived at my results. *For I expressed what had been stirred up in me and not what I had read.*"

A strictly *unitary (monastic) world conception* is peculiar to Goethe. He sets out to gain *one* viewpoint from which the whole universe reveals its law structure—"from the brick that falls from the roof to the brilliant flash of inspiration that dawns on you and that you convey." For "all effects of whatever kind they may be that we observe in experience are interconnected in the most continuous fashion and flow into one another."

> A brick is loosened from a roof. We ordinarily call this *accidental*. It hits the shoulder of a passerby, one would say *mechanically*, but not completely mechanically; it follows the laws of gravity and so its effect is *physical*. The torn vessels of living tissue immediately cease to function; at the same moment, the fluids act *chemically*, their elementary qualities emerge. But the disturbed *organic* life resists just as quickly and tries to restore itself. In the meantime, the whole human being is more or less unconscious and *psychically* shattered. Upon regaining consciousness the person feels *ethically* deeply hurt, deploring the interrupted activity of whatever kind it might have been, for man will only reluctantly yield to patience. *Religiously*, however, it will be easy for him to ascribe this incident to Providence, to consider it a prevention against a greater evil, as a preparation for a good of a higher order. This may be sufficient for the patient, but the recovered man arises *genially*, trusts in God and in himself and feels himself saved. He may well seize upon the accidental and turn it to his own advantage, thus beginning a new and eternally fresh cycle of life.

Thus, with the example of a fallen brick Goethe illustrates the interconnection of all kinds of natural effects. It would be an explanation in Goethe's sense if one could also derive their strictly law-determined interconnection out of *one* root.

Kant and Goethe appear as two spiritual antipodes at the most significant moment in the history of modern world conception, and the attitude of those who were interested in the highest questions was fundamentally different toward them. Kant constructed his world conception with all the technical means of a strict school philosophy; Goethe philosophized naively, depending trustfully on his healthy nature. For this reason, Fichte, as mentioned above, believed that in Goethe he could only turn "to the representative of the purest spirituality of *Feeling* as it appears on the stage of humanity that has been reached at the present time." But he had the opinion of Kant "that no human mind can advance further than to the limit at which Kant had stood, especially in his *Critique of Judgment.*" Whoever penetrates into the world conception of Goethe, however, which is presented in the cloak of naivete, will, nevertheless, find a firm foundation that can be expressed in the form of clear ideas. Goethe himself did not raise this foundation into the full light of consciousness. For this reason, his mode of conception finds entrance only slowly into the evolution of philosophy, and at the beginning of the nineteenth century it is Kant's position with which the spirits first attempt to come to clarity and with whom they begin to settle their account.

No matter how great Kant's influence was, his contemporaries could not help feeling that their deeper need for knowledge could not become satisfied by him. Such a demand for enlightenment urgently seeks after a unitary world conception as it is given in Goethe's case. With Kant, the individual realms of existence are standing side by side without transition. For this reason, Fichte, in spite of his unconditional veneration for Kant, could not conceal from himself the fact "that Kant had only hinted at the truth, but had neither presented nor proved it." And further:

> This wonderful, unique man had either a divination for the truth without being aware of the reasons for it, or he estimated his contemporaries as insufficient to have these reasons conveyed to them, or, again, he was reluctant during his lifetime to attract the superhuman veneration that sooner or later would have been bestowed upon him. No one has understood him as yet, and nobody will succeed in doing so who does not arrive at Kant's results in following his own ways; when it does happen, the world really will be astonished.
>
> But I know just as certainly that Kant had such a system in *mind,* that all statements that he actually did express are fragments and results of this system, and have meaning and consistence only under this presupposition.

For, if this were not the case, Fichte would "be more inclined to consider the *Critique of Pure Reason* the product of the strangest accident than as the work of a mind."

Other contemporaries also judged Kant's world of ideas to be insufficient. *Lichtenberg,* one of the most brilliant and at the same time most independent minds of the second half of the eighteenth century, who appreciated Kant, nevertheless could not suppress significant objections to his philosophy. On the one hand he says, "What does it mean to think in *Kant's spirit?* I believe it means to find the relation of our being, whatever that may be, toward the things we call external, that is to say, to define the relation of the subjective to the objective. This, to be sure, has always been the aim of all thorough natural scientists, but it is questionable if they ever proceeded so truly philosophically as did *Herr Kant.* What is and must be subjective was taken as objective."

On the other hand, however, Lichtenberg observes, "Should it really be an established fact that our reason cannot know anything about the supersensible? Should it not be possible for us to weave our ideas of God and immortality to as much purpose as the spider weaves his net to catch flies? In other words, should there not be beings who admire us because of our ideas of God and immortality just as we admire the spider and silkworm?"

One could, however, raise a much more significant objection. If it is correct that the law of human reason refers only to the inner worlds of the mind, how do we then manage even to speak of things outside ourselves at all? In that case, we should have to be completely caught in the cobweb of our inner world. An objection of this kind is raised by *G. E. Schulze* (1761–1833) in his book, *Aenesidemus,* which appeared anonymously in 1792. In it he maintains that all our knowledge is nothing but *mere* conceptions and we could in no way go beyond the world of our inner thought pictures. Kant's *moral truths* are also finally refuted with this step, for if not even the possibility to go beyond the inner world is thinkable, then it is also impossible that a moral voice could lead us into such a world that is impossible to think. In this way, a new doubt with regard to all truths develops out of Kant's view, and the philosophy of criticism is turned into scepticism.

One of the most consistent followers of scepticism is *S. Maimon* (1753–1800), who, from 1790 on, wrote several books that were under the influence of Kant and Schulze. In them he defended with complete determination the view that, because of the very nature of our cognitive faculty, we are not permitted to speak of the existence of external objects. Another disciple of Kant, *Jacob Sigismund Beck,* went even so far as to maintain that Kant himself had really not assumed things outside ourselves and that it was nothing but a misunderstanding if such a conception was ascribed to him.

One thing is certain; Kant offered his contemporaries innumerable points for attack and interpretations. Precisely through his unclarities and contradictions, he became the father of the classical German world conceptions of Fichte, Schelling, Schopenhauer, Hegel, Herbart and Schleiermacher. His unclarities became new questions for them. No matter how he endeavored to limit knowledge in order to make place for belief, the human spirit can confess to be satisfied in the true sense of the word only through knowledge, through cognition. So it came to pass that Kant's successors strove to restore knowledge to its full rights again, that they attempted to settle *through* knowledge the highest needs of man.

Johann Gottlieb Fichte (1762–1814) seemed to be chosen by nature to continue Kant's work in this direction. Fichte confessed, "The love of knowledge and especially speculative knowledge, when it has laid hold on man, occupies him to such an extent that no other wish is left in him but that to pursue it with complete calm and concentration." Fichte can be called an enthusiast of world conception. Through this enthusiasm he must have laid a charm on his contemporaries and especially on his students. Forberg, who was one of his disciples, tells us:

> In his public addresses his speech rushes powerfully on like a thunderstorm that unloads its fire in individual strokes of lightning; he lifts the soul up; he means to produce not only good men but great men; his eye is stern; his step bold; through his philosophy he intends to lead the spirit of the age; his imagination is not flowery,

but strong and powerful; his pictures are not graceful but bold and great. He penetrates into the innermost depths of his object and he moves in the realm of concepts with an ease that betrays that he not only lives in this invisible land, but rules there.

The most outstanding trait in Fichte's personality is the grand, *serious* style of his life conception. He measures everything by the highest standards. In describing the calling of the writer, for instance, he says:

> The idea itself must speak, not the writer. All his arbitrary traits, his whole individuality, all the manner and art peculiar to himself must have died in his utterances so that the manner and art of his idea alone may live, the highest life it can obtain in this language and this age. Since he is free from the obligations of the oral teacher, he is also free to conform to the receptivity of others without their excuses. He has not a given reader in mind but postulates the one who reads him, laying down the law as to how he must do so.
>
> But the work of the writer is a work for eternity. Let future ages swing up to a higher level in the science he has deposited in his work. What he has laid down in his book is not only the science, but the definite and perfect character of an age in regard to this science, and this will retain its interest as long as there are human beings in this world. Independent of all vicissitude, his writing speaks in all ages to all men who are capable of bringing his letters to life and who are stirred by his message, elevated and ennobled until the end of the world.

A man speaks in these words who is aware of his call as a spiritual leader of his age, and who seriously means what he says in the preface to his *Doctrine of Science:* "My person is of no importance at all, but Truth is of all importance for 'I am a priest of Truth'." We can understand that a man who, like him, lives "in the Kingdom of Truth" does not merely mean to *guide* others to an understanding, but that he intended to *force* them to it. Thus, he could give one of his writings the title, *A Radiantly Clear Report to the Larger Public Concerning the Real Essence of the Newest Philosophy. An Attempt to Force the Readers to Understand.* Fichte is a personality who believes that, in order to walk life's course, he has no need of the real world and its facts; rather, he keeps his eyes riveted on the world of idea. He holds those in low esteem who do not understand such an idealistic attitude of spirit.

While in the narrow horizon that is given through ordinary experience, people think and judge more objectively and correctly than perhaps ever before, most are, nevertheless, completely confused and dazzled as soon as they are to go even one step further. Where it is impossible to rekindle the once extinguished spark of the higher genius, one has to leave them within the circle of their horizon and, insofar as they are useful and necessary in this circle, one can grant them their value in and for it without curtailment. But when they now demand of us to bring down to their level everything they, themselves, cannot reach up to, when they, for instance, demand that everything printed should be useful as a cookbook, or as a textbook of arithmetic, or as a book of general regulations and orders, and then decry everything that cannot be used in such a fashion, then they are very wrong indeed.

We know as well, and possibly better than they, that ideals cannot be presented in the real world. What we maintain, however, is that the reality has to be judged by them, to be modified through those who feel the necessary strength for it within themselves. Suppose they could not convince themselves of this necessity. Then they would lose very little of what they are by nature anyway, and humanity would lose nothing at all. Their decision would merely make clear that they alone are not counted on in the scheme of providence for mankind's perfection. Providence will doubtless continue to pursue its course; we commend those people, however, to the care of a kind nature, to supply them in due time with rain and sunshine, with wholesome food and an undisturbed circulation of their gastric juices, at the same time endowing them with clever thoughts!

Fichte wrote these words in the preface to the publication of the lectures in which he had spoken to the students of Jena on the *Destination of the Scholar*. Views like those of Fichte have their origin in a great energy of the soul, giving sureness for knowledge of world and life. Fichte had blunt words for all those who did not feel the strength in themselves for such a sureness. When the philosopher, Reinhold, ventured the statement that the inner voice of man could also be in error, Fichte replied, "You say the philosopher should entertain the thought that he, as an individual, could also be mistaken and that he, therefore, could and should learn from others. Do you know whose thought mood you are describing with these words? That of a man who has never in his whole life been really *convinced* of something." To this vigorous personality, whose eyes were entirely directed to the inner life, it was repugnant to search anywhere else for a world conception, the highest aim man can obtain, except in his inner life. "All culture should be the exercise of all faculties toward the *one* purpose of complete freedom, that is to say, of the complete independence from everything that is not we, ourselves, our pure Self (reason, moral law), *for only this is ours.* . . ."

This is Fichte's judgment in his *Contributions Toward the Corrections of the Public Judgments Concerning the French Revolution,* which appeared in 1793. Should not the most valuable energy in man, his power of knowledge, be directed toward this *one* purpose of complete independence from everything that is not we, ourselves? Could we ever arrive at a complete independence if we were dependent in our world conception on any kind of being? If it had been predetermined by such a being outside ourselves of what nature our soul and our duties *are,* and that we thereby procured a knowledge *afterwards* out of such an accomplished fact? If we are independent, then we must be independent also with regard to the knowledge of truth. If we receive something that has come into existence without our help, then we are dependent on this something. For this reason, we cannot *receive* the highest truths. We must create them, they must come into being through us. Thus, Fichte can only place something at the summit of his world conception that obtains its existence through ourselves. When we say about a thing of the external world, "It *is,*" we are doing so because we perceive it. We know that we are recognizing the existence of *another* being. What this other being is does not depend on us. We can know its qualities only when we direct our faculty of perception toward it. We should never know what "red," "warm," "cold" is, if we did not know it through perception. We cannot add anything to these qualities of the thing, nor can we subtract anything from them. We say, *"They are."* What they are is what *they* tell us. This is entirely different in regard to our own existence. Man does not say to himself, "It is," but, "I am." He says, thereby, not only *that* he is, but also *what* he is, namely, an "I." Only *another* being could say concerning me, "It is." This is, in fact, what another being would *have* to say, for even in the case that this other being should have created me, it could not say concerning *my* existence, "I am." The statement, "I am," loses all meaning if it is not uttered by the being itself that speaks about its own existence. There is, therefore, nothing in the world that can address me as "I" except myself. This recognition of myself as an "I," therefore, must be my own original action. No being outside myself can have influence on this.

At this point Fichte found something with respect to which he saw himself completely independent of every "foreign" entity. A God could *create* me, but he would have to leave it to myself to recognize myself as an "I." I give my ego-consciousness to myself. In this way, Fichte obtained a firm point for his world conception, something in which there is certainty. How do matters stand now concerning the existence of other beings? I ascribe this existence to them, but to do so I have not the same right as with myself. They must become part of my "I" if I am to recognize an existence in them with the same right, and they do become a part of myself as I perceive them, for as soon as this is the case, they are there *for me.* What I can say is only, my "self" feels "red," my "self" feels "warm." Just as truly as I ascribe to myself an existence, I can also ascribe it to my feeling, to my sensation. Therefore, if I understand myself rightly, I can only say, I am, and I myself ascribe existence also to an external world.

For Fichte, the external world lost its independent existence in this way: It has an existence that is only ascribed to it by the ego, projected by the ego's imagination. In his endeavor to give to his own "self" the highest possible independence, Fichte deprived the outer world of all self-dependence. Now, where such an independent external world is not supposed to exist, it is also quite understandable if the interest in a knowledge concerning this external world ceases. Thereby, the interest in what is properly called knowledge is altogether extinguished, for the ego learns nothing through *its* knowledge but what it produces for itself. In all such knowledge the human ego holds soliloquies, as it were, with itself. It does not transcend its own being. It can do so only through what can be called living action. When the ego acts, when it accomplishes something in the world, then it is no longer alone by itself, talking to itself. Then its actions flow out into the world. They obtain a self-dependent existence. I accomplish something and when I have done so, this something will continue to have its effect, even if I no longer participate in its action. What I know has being only through myself, what I do, is part and parcel of a *moral world order* independent of myself. But what does all certainty that we derive from our own ego mean compared to this highest truth of a moral world order, which must surely be independent of ourselves if existence is to have any significance at all? All knowledge is something only for the ego, but this world order *must* be something outside the ego. It must be, in spite of the fact that we cannot know anything of it. We must, therefore, *believe* it.

In this manner Fichte also goes beyond *knowledge* and arrives at a *belief*. Compared to this belief, all knowledge is as dream to reality. The ego itself has only such a dream existence as long as it contemplates itself. It makes itself a *picture* of itself, which does not have to be anything but a passing picture; it is *action* alone that remains. Fichte describes this dream life of the world with significant words in his *Vocation of Man:*

> There is nowhere anything permanent, neither within myself nor outside, but there is only a never ceasing change. Nowhere do I know of any *being,* not even of my own being. *I, myself,* do not know at all, and I am not. *Pictures* are; they are the only thing that is, and

they know of themselves after the fashion of pictures; hovering pictures that pass by, without anything *that* they pass: interconnected through pictures of pictures, pictures without anything that is depicted in them, without meaning and purpose. I, myself, am one of these pictures; in fact, I am not even that but only a confused picture of pictures. All reality is changed into a strange dream without a life of which to dream, without a spirit to do the dreaming; it changes into a dream, which is held together by a dream of itself. *Seeing*—this is the dream; *thinking*—the source of all beings, of all reality, which I imagine, of *my* being, my strength of my purposes. *This is the dream of that dream.*

In what a different light the moral world order, the world of belief, appears to Fichte:

My will is to exert its effect absolutely through itself, without any tool that would only weaken its expression, in a completely homogeneous sphere, as reason upon reason, as spirit upon what is also spirit; in a sphere to which, however, my will is not to *give* the law of life, of activity, of progression, but which contains this in itself. My will, then, is to exert itself upon self-active reason, but self-active reason is will. The law of the supersensible world accordingly would be a *will*. . . . This sublime will, therefore, does not pursue its course separated from the rest of the world of reason in a detached fashion. There is a spiritual bond between the sublime will and all finite rational beings, and the sublime will itself *is* this spiritual bond within the world of reason. . . . I hide my face before you and I lay my hands on my lips. What you are for yourself and how you appear to yourself, I can never know as surely as I can never become you. After having lived through a thousand spirit worlds a thousand times, I shall be able to understand you as little as now in this house of clay. What I understand becomes finite merely through my understanding it, and the finite can never be changed into the infinite, not even through an infinite growth and elevation. You are separated from the finite not by a difference in degree but in kind. Through that gradation they will make you into a greater and greater man, but never into God, into the infinite that is capable of no measure.

Because knowledge is a dream and the moral world order is

the only true reality for Fichte, he places the life through which man participates in the moral world order higher than knowledge, the contemplation of things. "Nothing," so Fichte maintains, "has unconditional value and significance except life; everything else, for instance thinking, poetic imagination and knowledge, has value only insofar as it refers in some way to the living, insofar as it proceeds from it or means to turn back into it."

This is the fundamental ethical trait in Fichte's personality, which extinguished or reduced in significance everything in his world conception that does not directly tend toward the moral destination of man. He meant to establish the highest, the purest aims and standards for life, and for this purpose he refused to be distracted by any process of knowledge that might discover contradictions with the natural world order in these aims. Goethe made the statement, "The active person is always without conscience; no one has conscience except the onlooker." He means to say that the contemplative man estimates everything in its true, real value, understanding and recognizing everything in its own proper place. The active man, however, is, above everything else, bent on seeing his demands fulfilled; he is not concerned with the question of whether or not he thereby encroaches upon the rights of things. Fichte was, above all, concerned with action; he was, however, unwilling to be charged by contemplation with lack of conscience. He, therefore, denied the value of contemplation.

To effect life immediately—this was Fichte's continuous endeavor. He felt most satisfied when he believed that his words could become action in others. It is under the influence of this ardent desire that he composed the following works. *Demand to the Princess of Europe to Return the Freedom of Thought, Which They Have Heretofore Suppressed. Heliopolis in the Last Year of the Old Darkness 1792; Contributions Toward the Correction of the Public Judgment Concerning the French Revolution 1793.* This ardent desire also caused him to give his powerful speeches, *Outline of the Present Age* Presented in Lectures in Berlin in 1804–5; *Direction Toward the Beatific Life or Doctrine of*

Religion, Lectures given in Berlin in 1806; finally, his *Speeches to the German Nation, 1808.*

Unconditional surrender to the moral world order, action that springs out of the deepest core of man's nature: These are the demands through which life obtains value and meaning. This view runs through all of Fichte's speeches and writings as the basic theme. In his *Outline of the Present Age,* he reprimands this age with flaming words for its egotism. He claims that everybody is only following the path prescribed by his lower desires, but these desires lead him away from the great totality that comprises the human community in moral harmony. Such an age must needs lead those who live in its tendency into decline and destruction. What Fichte meant to enliven in the human soul was the sense of duty and obligation.

In this fashion, Fichte attempted to exert a formative influence on the life of his time with his ideas because he saw these ideas as vigorously enlivened by the consciousness that man derives the highest content of his soul life from a world to which he can obtain access by settling his account with his "ego" all by himself. In so doing man feels himself in his true vocation. From such a conviction, Fichte coins the words, "I, myself, and my necessary purpose are the supersensible."

To be aware of himself as consciously living in the supersensible is, according to Fichte, an experience of which man is capable. When he arrives at this experience, he then knows the "I" within himself, and it is only through this act that he becomes a philosopher. This experience, to be sure, cannot be "proven" to somebody who is *unwilling* to undergo it himself. How little Fichte considers such a "proof" possible is documented by expressions like, "The gift of a philosopher is inborn, furthered through education and then obtained by self-education, but there is no human art to *make* philosophers. For this reason, philosophy expects few proselytes among those men who are *already formed, polished and perfected.* . . ."

Fichte is intent on finding a soul constitution through which the human "ego" can experience itself. The knowledge of nature seems unsuitable to him to reveal anything of the essence of the "ego." From the fifteenth to the eighteenth century, thinkers arose who were concerned with the question: What element could be found in the picture of nature by means of which the human being could become explainable in this picture? Goethe did not see the question in this way. He felt a spiritual nature behind the externally manifested one. For him, the human soul is capable of experiences through which it lives not only in the externally manifested, but within the creative forces. Goethe was in quest of the idea, as were the Greeks, but he did not look for it as perceptible idea. He meant to find it in *participating* in the world processes through inner experience where these can no longer be perceived. Goethe searched *in the soul* for *the life of nature*. Fichte also searched in the soul itself, but he did not focus his search where nature lives in the soul but immediately where the soul feels its own life kindled without regard to any other world processes and world entities with which this life might be connected. With Fichte, a world conception arose that exhausted all its endeavor in the attempt to find an inner soul life that compared to the thought life of the Greeks, as did their thought life to the picture conception of the age before them. In Fichte, thought becomes an experience of the ego as the picture had become thought with the Greek thinkers. With Fichte, world conception is ready to *experience self-consciousness;* with Plato and Aristotle, it had arrived at the point to *think soul consciousness*.

* * *

Just as Kant dethroned knowledge in order to make place for belief, so Fichte declared knowledge to be mere appearance in order to open the gates for living action, for moral activity. A similar attempt was also made by *Schiller*. Only in his case, the part that was claimed by belief in Kant's philosophy, and by action in that of Fichte, was now occupied by *beauty*. Schiller's significance in the development of world conception is usually underestimated. Goethe had to complain that he was not recognized as a natural scientist just because people had become accustomed to take him as a poet, and those who penetrate into

Schiller's philosophical ideas must regret that he is appreciated so little by the scholars who deal with the history of world conception, because Schiller's field is considered to be limited to the realm of poetry.

As a thoroughly self-dependent thinker, Schiller takes his attitude toward Kant, who had been so stimulating and thought-provoking to him. The loftiness of the moral belief to which Kant meant to lift man was highly appreciated by the poet who, in his *Robbers*, and *Cabal and Love*, had held a mirror to the corruption of his time. But he asked himself the question: Should it indeed be a necessary truth that man can be lifted to the height of "the categorical imperative" only through the struggle against his desires and urges? Kant wanted to ascribe to the sensual nature of man only the inclination toward the low, the self-seeking, the gratification of the senses, and only he who lifted himself above the sensual nature, who mortified the flesh and who alone allowed the pure spiritual voice of duty to speak within him: Only he could be virtuous. Thus, Kant debased the natural man in order to be able to elevate the moral man so much the higher. To Schiller this judgment seemed to contain something that was unworthy of man. Should it not be possible to ennoble the impulses of man to become in themselves inclined toward the life of duty and morality? They would then not have to be suppressed to become morally effective. Schiller, therefore, opposes Kant's rigorous demand of duty in the epigram:

Scruples of Conscience.
  Gladly I serve my friends, but, alas, I do so with pleasure
  And so I oftentimes grieve that I lack virtue indeed.
Decision.
  There is no better advice; you must try to despise them
  And with disgust you must do strictly as duty commands.

Schiller attempted to dissolve these "scruples of conscience" in his own fashion. There are actually two impulses ruling in man: The impulses of the sensual desire and the impulse of reason. If man surrenders to the sensual impulse, he is a plaything of his desires and passions, in short, of his egoism. If he gives himself completely up to the impulses of reason, he is a slave of its rigorous commands, its inexorable logic, its categorical imperative. A man who wants to live *exclusively* for the sensual impulse must silence reason; a man who wants to serve reason *only* must mortify sensuality. If the former, nevertheless, listens to the voice of reason, he will yield to it only reluctantly against his own will; if the latter observes the call of his desires, he feels them as a burden on his path of virtue. The physical nature of man and his spiritual character then seem to live in a fateful discord. Is there no state in man in which both the impulses, the sensual and the spiritual, live in harmony? Schiller's answer to this question is positive. There is, indeed, such a state in man. It is the state in which the *beautiful* is created and enjoyed. He who creates a work of art follows a free impulse of nature. He follows an inclination in doing so, but it is not physical passion that drives him. It is imagination; it is the spirit. This also holds for a man who surrenders to the enjoyment of a work of art. The work of art, while it affects his sensuality, satisfies his spirit at the same time. Man can yield to his desires without observing the higher laws of the spirit; he can comply with his duties without paying attention to sensuality. A beautiful work of art affects his delight without awakening his desires, and it transports him into a world in which he abides by virtue of his own disposition. Man is comparable to a child in this state, following his inclinations in his actions without asking if they run counter to the laws of reason. "The sensual man is led through beauty . . . into thinking; through beauty, the spiritual man is led back to matter, returned to the world of the senses" (*Letters on the Esthetic Education of Man*; Letter 18).

> The lofty freedom and equanimity of the spirit, combined with strength and vigor is the mood in which we should part from a genuine work of art; there is no surer test of its true esthetic quality. If, after an enjoyment of this kind, we find ourselves inclined to some particular sentiment or course of action, but awkward and ill

at ease for another, then this can serve as infallible proof that we have not experienced a *pure esthetic* effect; this may be caused by the object or our mode of approach, or (as is almost always the case) by both causes simultaneously. (Letter 22.)

As man is, through beauty, neither the slave of sensuality nor of reason, but because through its mediation both factors contribute their effect in a balanced cooperation in man's soul, Schiller compares the instinct for beauty with the child's impulse who, in his play, does not submit his spirit to the laws of reason, but employs it freely according to his inclination. It is for this reason that Schiller calls the impulse for beauty, play-impulse:

> In relation to the agreeable, to the good, to the perfect, man is *only* serious, but he plays with beauty. In this respect, to be sure, we must not think of the games that go on in real life and that ordinarily are concerned with material objects, but in real life we should also search in vain for the beauty that is meant here. The beauty existing in reality is on the same level as the play-impulse in the real world, but through the ideal of beauty, which is upheld by reason, an ideal is also demanded of the play-impulse that man is to consider wherever he plays. (Letter 15.)

In the realization of this ideal play-impulse, man finds the reality of *freedom*. Now, he no longer *obeys* reason, nor does he follow sensual inclinations any longer. He now acts from inclination as if the spring of his action were reason. "Man shall only play with beauty and it is *only with beauty* that he shall play. . . . To state it without further reserve, man plays only when he is human in the full sense of the word and *he is only wholly human when he is playing.*" Schiller could also have said: In play man is *free;* in following the command of duty, and in yielding to sensuality, he is *unfree.* If man wants to be human in the full meaning of the word, and also with regard to his moral actions, that is to say, if he really wants to be free, then he must live in the same relation to his virtues as he does to beauty. He must ennoble his inclinations into virtues and must be so permeated by his virtues that he feels no other inclination than that of following them. A man who has established this harmony between inclination and duty can, in every moment, count on the morality of his actions as a matter of course.

From this viewpoint, one can also look at man's social life. A man who follows his sensual desires is self-seeking. He would always be bent on his own well-being if the state did not regulate the social intercourse through laws of reason. The free man accomplishes through his own impulse what the state must demand of the self-seeking. In a community of free men no compulsory laws are necessary.

> In the midst of the fearful world of forces, and in the awe-demanding sanctuary of laws, the esthetic formative impulse is imperceptibly building a third delightful realm of play and appearances in which man is released from the fetters of all circumstances and freed from everything that is called compulsion, both in the physical and in the moral world. (Letter 27.)
>
> This realm extends upward as far as the region where reason rules with unconditional necessity and where all matter ceases; it stretches below as far as the world in which the force of nature holds sway with blind compulsion.

Thus, Schiller considers a moral realm as an ideal in which the temper of virtue rules with the same ease and freedom as the esthetic taste governs in the realm of beauty. He makes life in the realm of beauty the model of a perfect moral social order in which man is liberated in every direction. Schiller closes the beautiful essay in which he proclaims this ideal with the question of whether such an order had anywhere been realized. He answers with the words:

> As a need, it exists in every delicately attuned soul; as an actuality it can probably only be found, like the pure church and the pure republic, in a few select circles where, not the thoughtless imitation of heterogeneous customs, but the inherent beautiful nature guides the demeanor, where man goes with undismayed simplicity and undisturbed innocence through the most complicated situations without the need of offending the freedom of others nor of defending

his own, without need of offending his dignity in order to show charm and grace.

In this virtue refined into beauty, Schiller found a mediation between the world conceptions of Kant and Goethe. No matter how great the attraction that Schiller had found in Kant when the latter had defended the ideal of a pure humanity against the prevailing moral order, when Schiller became more intimately acquainted with Goethe, he became an admirer of Goethe's view of world and life. Schiller's mind, always relentlessly striving for the purest clarity of thought, was not satisfied before he had succeeded in penetrating also conceptually into this wisdom of Goethe. The high satisfaction Goethe derived from his view of beauty and art, and also for his conduct of life, attracted Schiller more and more to the mode of Goethe's conception. In the letter in which Schiller thanks Goethe for sending him his *Wilhelm Meister,* he says:

> I cannot express to you how painfully I am impressed when I turn from a product of this kind to the bustle of philosophy. In the one world everything is so serene, so alive, so harmoniously dissolved, so truly human; in the other, everything is so rigorous, so rigid and abstract, so unnatural, because nature is always nothing but synthesis and philosophy is antithesis. I may claim, to be sure, to have in all my speculations remained as faithful to nature as is compatible with the concept of analysis; I may, indeed, have remained more faithful to her than *our Kantians considered permissible and possible.* I feel, nevertheless, the infinite distance between life and reflection, and in such a melancholy moment I cannot help considering as a defect in my nature what, in a more cheerful hour, I must regard as merely a trait inherent in the nature of things. In the meantime, I am certain of this at least: The poet is the only *true man* and, compared to him, the best philosopher is merely a caricature.

This judgment of Schiller can only refer to the Kantian philosophy with which he had had his experiences. In many respects, it estranges man from nature. It approaches nature with no confidence in it but recognizes as valid truth only what is derived from man's own mental organization. Through this trait all judgments of that philosophy seem to lack the lively content and color so characteristic of everything that has its source in the immediate experience of nature's events and things themselves. This philosophy moves in bloodless, gray and cold abstractions. It has sacrificed the warmth we derive from the immediate touch with things and beings and has exchanged the frigidity of its abstract concepts for it. In the field of morality, also, Kant's world conception presents the same antagonism to nature. The duty-concept of pure reason is regarded as its highest aims. What man loves, what his inclinations tend to, everything in man's being that is immediately rooted in man's nature, must be subordinated to this ideal of duty. Kant goes even as far as the realm of beauty to extinguish the share that man must have in it according to his original sensations and feelings. The beautiful is to produce a delight that is completely "free from interest." Compare that with how devoted, how really *interested* Schiller approaches a work in which he admires the highest stage of artistic production. He says concerning *Wilhelm Meister:*

> I can express the feeling that permeates me and takes possession of me as I read this book no better than as a sweet well-being, as a feeling of spiritual and bodily health, and I am firmly convinced that this must be the feeling with all readers in general. . . . I explain this well-being with the quiet clarity, smoothness and transparence that prevails throughout the book, leaving the reader without the slightest dissatisfaction and disturbance, and producing no more emotion than is necessary to kindle and support a cheerful life in his soul.

These are not the words of somebody who believes in delight without interest, but of a man who is convinced that the pleasure in the beautiful is capable of being so refined that a complete surrender to this pleasure does not involve degradation. Interest is not to be extinguished as we approach the work of art; rather are we to become capable of including in our interest what has its source in the spirit. The "true" man is to develop this kind of interest for the beautiful also with respect to his moral conceptions. Schiller writes in a letter to Goethe, "It is really worth observing that the slackness with regard to esthetic things appears always to be connected with moral slackness, and that a pure rigorous striving for high beauty with the highest degree of liberality concerning everything that is nature will contain in itself rigorism in moral life."

The estrangement from nature in the world conception and in all of the culture of the time in which he lived was felt so strongly by Schiller that he made it the subject of his essay, *On Naive and Sentimental Poetry*. He compares the life conception of his time with that of the Greeks and raises the question, "How is it that we, who are infinitely surpassed by the ancients in everything that is nature, can render homage to nature to a higher degree, cling to her with fervour and can embrace even the lifeless world with the warmest sentiments." He answers this question by saying:

> This is caused by the fact that, with us, nature has vanished out of humanity and we therefore find her in reality only outside humanity in the inanimate world. It is not our greater *naturalness,* but, quite to the contrary, the *unnaturalness* of our lives, state of affairs and customs that drives us to give satisfaction in the physical to the awakening sense for truth and simplicity, which, like the moral faculty from which it springs, lies without corruption and inextinguishably in all men's hearts because we no longer can hope to find it in the moral world. It is for this reason that the feeling with which we cling to nature is so closely related to the sentiment with which we lament the loss of the age of childhood and of the child's innocence. Our childhood is the only unspoiled nature that we still find in civilized humanity, and it is, therefore, no wonder that every footstep of nature leads us back to our own childhood.

This was entirely different with the Greeks. They lived their lives within the bounds of the natural. Everything they did sprang from their *natural* conception, feeling and sentiment. They were intimately bound to nature. Modern man feels himself in his own being placed in contrast to nature. As the urge toward this primeval mother of being cannot be extinguished, it transforms itself in the modern soul into a yearning for nature, into a search for it. The Greek *had* nature; modern man *searches* for nature.

As long as man is still pure nature and, to be sure, not brutal, he acts as an undivided sensual unity and as a harmonizing whole. His senses and his reason, his receptive and his self-active faculties, have not as yet separated in their function and certainly do not act in contradiction to each other. His sentiments are not the formless play of chance; his thoughts, not the empty play of his imagination. These thoughts have their origin in the *law of necessity;* the sentiments, in *reality*. As soon as man comes into the state of civilization, and as soon as art enters into his sphere of life, the *sensual* harmony is dissolved and he can now only act as a *moral* unity, that is to say, as striving for unity. The agreement between his perception and his thought, which in his former state was *actual,* is now merely *ideal;* it is no longer *in* him, but *beyond* him; as a thought whose realization is demanded, it is no longer a fact of his life.

The fundamental mood of the Greek spirit was *naive,* that of modern man is *sentimental.* The Greeks' world conception could, for this reason, be rightly realistic, for he had not yet separated the spiritual from the natural; for him, nature included the spirit. If he surrendered to nature, it was to a *spirit-saturated nature.* This is not so with modern man. He has detached the spirit from nature; he has lifted the spirit into the realm of gray abstractions. If he were to surrender to *his* nature, he would yield to a nature deprived of all spirit. Therefore, his loftiest striving must be directed toward the *ideal;* through the striving for this goal, spirit and nature are to be reconciled again. In Goethe's mode of spirit, however, Schiller found something that was akin to the Greek spirit. Goethe felt that he saw his ideas and thoughts with his eyes because he felt reality as an undivided unity of spirit and nature. According to Schiller, Goethe had preserved something in himself that will be attained again by the "sentimental man" when he has reached the climax of his striving. Modern man arrives at such a summit in the esthetic mood as Schiller describes it in the state of soul in which sensuality and reason are harmonized again.

The nature of the development of modern world conception is significantly characterized in the observation Schiller made to Goethe in his letter of August 23, 1794:

> Had you been born a Greek and been surrounded since birth by exquisite nature and idealizing art, your road would have been infinitely shortened; perhaps it would have been made entirely unnecessary. With the very first perception of things, you would have absorbed the form of the necessary, and with your first experience, the grand style would have developed within you. As it is now . . . since your Greek spirit was cast into this nordic creation, you had no other choice than either to become a nordic artist yourself or to supplement your imagination by means of thought for what reality fails to supply, and thus to give birth from within to another Greece.

Schiller, as these sentences show, is aware of the course that the development of soul life has taken from the age of the ancient Greeks until his own time, for the Greek soul life disclosed itself in the life of thought and he could accept this unveiling because thought was for him a perception like the perception of color and sounds. *This* kind of thought life has faded away for modern man. The powers that weave creatively through the world must be experienced by him as an inner soul experience, and in order to render this imperceptible thought life inwardly visible, it nevertheless must be filled by imagination. This imagination must be such that it is felt as one with the creative powers of nature.

Because *soul consciousness* has been transformed into *self-consciousness* in modern man, the question of world conception arises: How can self-consciousness experience itself so vividly that it feels its conscious process as permeating the creative process of the living world forces? Schiller answered this question for himself in his own fashion when he claimed the life in the artistic experience as his ideal. In this experience the human self-consciousness feels its kinship with an element that transcends the mere nature picture. In it, man feels himself *seized by the spirit* as he surrenders as a natural and sensual being to the world. Leibniz had attempted to *understand* the human soul as a monad. Fichte had not proceeded from a mere idea to gain clarity of the nature of the human soul; he searched for a form of *experience* in which this soul lays hold on its own being. Schiller raises the question: Is there a form of experience for the human soul in which it can feel how it has its roots in spiritual reality? Goethe experiences ideas in himself that present themselves to him at the same time as *ideas of nature*.

In Goethe, Fichte and Schiller, the *experienced idea*—one could also say, the *idea-experience*—forces its way into the soul. Such a process had previously happened in the world of the Greeks with the *perceived idea,* the *idea-perception*.

The world and life conception that lived in Goethe in a natural (naive) way, and toward which Schiller strove on all detours of his thought development, does not feel the need for the kind of universally valid truth that sees its ideal in the mathematical form. It is satisfied by another truth, which our spirit derives from the immediate intercourse with the real world. The insights Goethe derived from the contemplation of the works of art in Italy were, to be sure, not of the unconditional certainty as are the theorems of mathematics, but they also were less abstract. Goethe approached them with the feeling, "Here is necessity, here is God." A truth that could not also be revealed in a perfect work of art did not exist for Goethe. What art makes manifest with its technical means of tone, marble, color, rhythm, etc., springs from the same source from which the philosopher also draws who does not avail himself of visual means of presentation but who uses as his means of expression only thought, the idea itself. "*Poetry* points at the mysteries of nature and attempts to solve them through the picture," says Goethe. "*Philosophy* points at the mysteries of reason and attempts to solve them through the word." In the final analysis, however, reason and nature are, for him, inseparably one; the same truth is the foundation of both. An endeavor for knowledge, which lives in detachment from things in an abstract world, does not seem to him to be the highest form of cognitive life. "It would be the highest attainment to understand that all factual knowledge is already theory." The blueness of the sky reveals the fundamental law of color phenomena to us. "One should not search for anything behind the phenomena; they, themselves, are the message."

The psychologist, Heinroth, in his *Anthology,* called the mode of thinking through which Goethe arrived at his insights into the natural formation of plants and animals, an "object-related thinking" (*Gegenstaendliches Denken*). What he means is that this mode of thinking does not detach itself from its objects, but that the objects of observation are intimately permeated with this thinking, that Goethe's mode of thinking is at the same time a form of observation, and his mode of observation a form of thinking. Schiller becomes a subtle observer as he describes this mode of spirit. He writes on this subject in a letter to Goethe:

> Your observing eye, which so calmly and clearly rests on things, keeps you from being ever exposed to the danger of going astray in the direction where speculation and an arbitrary, merely introspective imagination so easily lose their way. Your correct intuition contains everything, and in a far greater completeness, for which an analytical mind searches laboriously; only because everything is at your disposal as a complete whole are you unaware of your own riches, for unfortunately we know only what we dissect. Spirits of your kind, therefore, rarely know how far advanced they are and how little cause they have to borrow from philosophy, which in turn can only learn from them.

For the world conception of Goethe and Schiller, truth is not only contained in science, but also in art. Goethe expresses his opinion as follows, "I think science could be called the knowledge of the general art. Art would be science turned into action. Science would be reason, and art its mechanism, wherefore one could also call it practical science. Thus, finally, science would be the *theorem* and art the *problem.*" Goethe describes the interdependence of scientific cognition and artistic expression of knowledge thus:

> It is obvious that an . . . artist must become greater and more erudite if he not only has his talent but is also a well-informed botanist; if he knows, starting from the root, all the influences of the various parts of a plant on its thriving and growth, their function and mutual effect; if he has an insight into the successive development of the leaves, the flowers, the fertilization, the fruit and the new germ, and if he contemplates this process. Such an artist will not merely show his taste through his power of selection from the realm of appearances, but he will also surprise us with his correct presentation of the characteristic qualities.

Thus, *truth* rules in the process of artistic creation for the artistic style depends, according to this view, ". . . on the deepest foundations of knowledge, on the essence of things insofar as it is permissible to know it in visible and touchable forms." The fact that creative imagination is granted a share in the process of knowledge and that the abstract intellect is no longer considered to be the only cognitive faculty is a consequence of this view concerning truth. The conceptions on which Goethe based his contemplations on plant and animal formations were not gray and abstract thoughts but *sensual-supersensual pictures*, created by spontaneous imagination. Only observation combined with imagination can really lead into the essence of things, not bloodless abstraction; this is Goethe's conviction. For this reason, Goethe said about Galileo that he made his observations as a genius "for whom *one* case represents a thousand cases . . . when he developed the doctrine of the pendulum and the fall of bodies from swinging church lamps." Imagination uses the one case in order to produce a content-saturated picture of what is essential in the appearances; the intellect that operates by means of abstractions can, through combination, comparison and calculation of the appearances, gain no more than a general rule of their course. This belief in the possible cognitive function of an imagination that rises into a conscious participation in the creative world process is supported by Goethe's entire world conception. Whoever, like him, sees nature's activity in everything, can also see in the spiritual content of the human imagination nothing but higher products of nature. The pictures of fantasy are products of nature and, as they represent nature, they can only contain truth, for otherwise nature would lie to herself in these afterimages that she creates of herself. Only men with imagination can attain to the highest stages of knowledge. Goethe calls these men the "comprehensive" and the "contemplative" in contrast to the merely "intellectual-inquisitive," who have remained on a lower stage of cognitive life.

> The intellectual inquisitive need a calm, unselfish power of observation, the excitement of curiosity, a clear intellect . . . ; they only digest scientifically what they find ready-made.
> The contemplative are already creative in their attitude, and knowledge in them, as it reaches a higher level, demands contemplation unconsciously and changes over into that form; much as they may shun the word "imagination," they will, nevertheless, before they are aware of it, call upon the support of *creative imagination.* . . . The comprehensive thinkers who, with a prouder name, could be called creative thinkers, are, in their attitude, productive in the highest sense, for, as they start from ideas, they express from the outset the unity of the whole. From then on, it is the task of nature, as it were, to submit to these ideas.

It cannot occur to the believer in such a form of cognition to speak of limitations of human knowledge in a Kantian fashion, for he *experiences* within himself what man needs as his truth. The core of nature is in the inner life of man. The world conception of Goethe and Schiller does not *demand* of its truth that it should be a repetition of the world phenomena in conceptual form. It does not demand that its conception should literally *correspond* to something outside man. What appears in man's inner life as an ideal element, as something spiritual, is as such not to be found in any external world; it appears as the climax of the whole development. For this reason, it does not, according to this philosophy, have to appear in all human beings in the same shape. It can take on an individual form in any individual. Whoever expects to find the truth in the agreement with something external can acknowledge only *one form of it*, and he will look for it, with Kant, in the type of metaphysics that *alone* "will be able to present itself as science." Whoever sees the element in which, as Goethe states in his essay on Winckelmann, "the universe, if it could feel itself, would rejoice as having arrived at its aim in which it could admire the climax of its own becoming and being," such a thinker can say with Goethe, "If I know my relation to myself and to the external world, I call this truth; in this way everybody can have his own truth and it is yet the same." For "man in himself, insofar as he uses his healthy senses, is the greatest and most exact apparatus of physics that is possible. Yet, that the experiments separated, as it were, from man, and that one wants to know nature only according to the indications of artificial instruments, even intending to limit and prove in this way what nature is capable of, is the greatest misfortune of modern physics." Man, however, "stands so high that in him is represented what cannot be represented otherwise. What is the string and all mechanical division of it compared to the ear of the musician? One can even say, 'What are all elementary phenomena of nature themselves compared to man who must master and modify them all in order to be able to assimilate them to himself to a tolerable degree.'"

Concerning his world picture, Goethe speaks neither of a mere knowledge of intellectual concepts nor of belief; he speaks of a *contemplative perception in the spirit*. He writes to Jacobi, "You trust in belief in God; I, in seeing." This seeing in the spirit as it is meant here thus enters into the development of world conception as the soul force that is appropriate to an age to which thought is no longer what it had been to the Greek thinkers, but in which thought had revealed itself as a product of self-consciousness, a product, however, that is arrived at through the fact that this self-consciousness is aware of itself as having its being *within* the spiritually creative forces of nature. Goethe is the representative of an epoch of world conception in which the need is felt to make the transition from mere thinking to spiritual seeing. Schiller strives to justify this transition against Kant's position.

* * *

The close alliance that was formed by Goethe, Schiller and their contemporaries between poetic imagination and world conception has freed this conception from the lifeless expression that it must take on when it exclusively moves in the region of the abstract intellect. This alliance has resulted in the belief that there is a personal element in world conception. It is possible for man to work out an approach to the world for himself that is in accordance with his own specific nature and enter thereby into the world of reality, not merely into a world of fantastic schemes. His ideal no longer needs to be that of Kant, which is formed after the model of mathematics and arrives at a world picture that is once and for all finished and completed. Only from a spiritual atmosphere of such a conviction that has an inspiring effect on the human individuality can a conception like that of *Jean Paul* (1763–1825) arise. "The heart of a genius, to whom all other splendor and help-giving energies are subordinated, has *one* genuine symptom, namely, a new outlook on world and life." How could it be the mark of the highest developed man, of genius, to create a new world and life conception if the conceived world consisted only in *one* form? Jean Paul is, in his own way, a defender of Goethe's view that man experiences inside his own self the ultimate existence. He writes to Jacobi:

> Properly speaking, we do not merely *believe* in divine freedom, God and virtue, but we really *see* them manifested or in the process of manifestation; this very seeing is a *knowing* and a higher form of knowing, while the knowledge of intellect merely refers to a seeing of a lower order. One could call *reason* the consciousness of the only positive, for everything positive experienced by sense perception does finally dissolve into the spiritual, and *understanding* carries on its bustle only with the relative, which in itself is nothing, so that before God all conditions of "more or less," and all stages of comparison cease to be.

Jean Paul will not allow anything to deprive him of the right to experience truth inwardly and to employ all forces of the soul for this purpose. He will not be restricted to the use of logical intellect.

> Transcendental philosophy (Jean Paul has in mind here the world view following Kant) is not to tear the heart, man's living root, out of his breast to replace it with a pure impulse of selfhood; I shall not consent to be liberated from the dependence of Love, to be blessed by pride only.

With these words he rejects the world-estranged moral order of Kant.

> I remain firmly with my conviction that there are four last, and four first things: Beauty, Truth, Morality and Salvation, and their synthesis is not only necessary but also already a fact, but only in a subtle *spiritual-organic* unity (and for just this reason it *is* a unity), without which we could not find any understanding of these four evangelists or world continents, nor any transition between them.

The critical analysis of the intellect, which proceeded with an extreme logical rigor, had, in Kant and Fichte, come to the point of reducing the self-dependent significance of the real life-saturated world to a mere shadow, to a dream picture. This view was unbearable to men gifted with spontaneous imagination, who enriched life by the creation of their imaginative power. These men *felt* the reality; it was there in their perception, present in their souls, and now it was attempted to prove to them its mere dreamlike quality. "The windows of the philosophical academic halls are too high to allow a view into the alleys of real life," was the answer of Jean Paul.

Fichte strove for the purest, highest experienced truth. He renounced all knowledge that does not spring from our own inner source. The counter movement to his world conception is formed by the *Romantic Movement*. Fichte acknowledges only the truth, and the inner life of man only insofar as it reveals the truth; the world conception of the romanticists acknowledges only the inner life, and it declares as valuable everything that springs from this inner life. The ego is not to be chained by anything external. Whatever it produces is justified.

One may say about the romantic movement that it carries Schiller's statement to its extreme consequence, "Man plays only where he is human in the full sense of the word, and he is only wholly human when he is playing." Romanticism wants to make the whole world into a realm of the artistic. The fully developed man knows no other norms than the laws he creates through his freely ruling imaginative power, in the same way as the artist creates those laws he impresses into his works. He rises above everything that determines him from without and lives entirely through the springs of his own self. The whole world is for him nothing but a material for his esthetic play. The seriousness of man in his everyday life is not rooted in truth. The soul that arrives at true knowledge cannot take seriously the things by themselves; for such a soul they are not in themselves valuable. They are endowed with value only by the soul. The mood of a spirit that is aware of his sovereignty over things is called by the romanticists, the *ironical* mood of spirit.

Karl Wilhelm Ferdinand Solger (1780–1819) gave the following explanation of the term "romantic irony": The spirit of the artist must comprise all directions in one sweepimg glance and this glance, hovering above everything, looking down on everything and annihilating it, we call *"irony." Friedrich Schlegel* (1772–1829), one of the leading spokesmen for the romantic turn of spirit, states concerning this mood of irony that it takes everything in at a glance and rises infinitely above everything that is limited, also above some form of art, virtue or genius. Whoever lives in this mood feels bound by nothing; nothing determines the direction of his activity for him. He can "at his own pleasure tune himself to be either philosophical or philological, critical or poetical, historical or rhetorical, antique or modern." The ironical spirit rises above an eternal moral world order, for this spirit is not told what to do by anything except himself. The ironist is to do what he pleases, for his morality can only be an esthetic morality. The romanticists are the heirs of

Fichte's thought of the uniqueness of the ego. They were, however, unwilling to fill this ego with a moral belief, as Fichte did, but stood above all on the right of fantasy and of the unrestrained power of the soul. With them, thinking was entirely absorbed by poetic imagination. Novalis says, "It is quite bad that poetry has a special name and that the poet represents a special profession. *It is not anything special by itself. It is the mode of activity proper to the human spirit.* Are not the imaginations of man's heart at work every minute?" The ego, exclusively concerned with itself, can arrive at the highest truth: "It seems to man that he is engaged in a conversation, and some unknown spiritual being causes him to develop the most *evident thoughts* in a miraculous fashion.

Fundamentally, what the romanticists aimed at did not differ from what Goethe and Schiller had also made their credo: A conception of man through which he appeared as perfect and as free as possible. *Novalis* experiences his poems and contemplations in a soul mood that had a relationship toward the world picture similar to that of Fichte. Fichte's spirit, however, works the sharp contours of pure concepts, while that of Novalis springs from a richness of soul, feeling where others think, living in the element of love where others aim to embrace what is and what goes on in the world with ideas. It is the tendency of this age, as can be seen in its representative thinkers, to search for the higher spirit nature in which the self-conscious soul is rooted because it cannot have its roots in the world of sense reality. Novalis feels and experiences himself as having his being within the higher spirit nature. What he expresses he feels through his innate genius as the revelations of this very spirit nature. He writes:

> One man succeeded; he lifted the veil of the goddess at Saïs. What did he see then? He saw—wonder of wonders—himself.

Novalis expresses his own intimate feeling of the spiritual mystery behind the world of the senses and of the human self consciousness as the organ through which this mystery reveals itself, in these words:

The spirit world is indeed already unlocked for us; it is always revealed. If we suddenly became as elastic as we should be, we should see ourselves in the midst of it.

CHAPTER VII

*The Classics of World
and Life Conception*

A sentence in Friedrich Wilhelm Joseph Schelling's *Philosophy of Nature* strikes us like a flash of lightning illuminating the past and future path of the evolution of philosophy. It reads, "To philosophize about nature means to create nature." What had been a deep conviction of Goethe and Schiller, namely, that creative imagination must have a share in the creation of a world conception, is monumentally expressed in this sentence. What nature yields voluntarily when we focus our attention on it in observation and perception does not contain its deepest meaning. Man cannot conceive this meaning from without. He must produce it.

Schelling was especially gifted for this kind of creation. With him, all spiritual energies tended toward the imagination. His mind was inventive without compare. His imagination did not produce pictures as the artistic imagination does, but rather concepts and ideas. Through this disposition of mind he was well-suited to continue along Fichte's path of thought. Fichte did not have this productive imagination. In his search for truth he had penetrated as far as to the center of man's soul, the "ego." If this center is to become the nucleus for the world conception, then a thinker who holds this view must also be capable of arriving at thoughts whose content are saturated with world and life as he proceeds from the "ego" as a vantage point. This can only be done by means of the power of imagination, and this power was not at Fichte's disposal. For this reason, he was really limited in his philosophical position all his life to directing attention to the "ego" and to pointing out that it has to gain a content in thoughts. He, himself, had been unable to supply it with such a content, which can be learned clearly from the lectures he gave in 1813 at the University of Berlin on the *Doctrine of Science* (Posthumous Works, Vol. 1). For those who want to arrive at a world conception, he there demands "a completely new inner sense organ, which for the ordinary man does not exist at all." But Fichte does not go beyond this postulate. He fails to develop what such an organ is to perceive. Schelling saw the result of this higher sense in the thoughts that his imagination produced in his soul, and he calls this "intellectual imagination" (*intellectuelle Anschauung*). For him, then, who saw a *product* created by the spirit in the spirit's statement about nature, the following question became urgent. How can what springs from the spirit be the pattern of the law that rules in the real world, holding sway in real nature? With sharp words Schelling turns against those who believe that we "merely *project* our ideas into nature," because "they have no inkling of what nature is and must be for us. . . . For we are not satisfied to have nature accidentally (through the intermediary function of a third element, for instance) correspond to the laws of our spirit. We insist that nature itself necessarily and fundamentally should not only express, but realize, the laws of our spirit and that it should only then be, and be called, nature if it did just this. . . . *Nature is to be the visible spirit: spirit the invisible nature.* At this point then, at the point of the absolute identity of the spirit *in* us and of nature *outside* us, the problem must be solved as to how a nature outside ourselves should be possible."

Nature and spirit, then, are not two different entities at all but one and the same being in two different forms. The real meaning of Schelling concerning this unity of nature and spirit has rarely been correctly grasped. It is necessary to immerse oneself completely into his mode of conception if one wants to avoid seeing in it nothing but a triviality or an absurdity. To clarify this mode of conception one can point to a sentence in Schelling's book, *On the World Soul*, in which he expresses himself on the nature of gravity. Many people find a difficulty in understanding this concept because it implies a so-called "action in distance." The sun attracts the earth in spite of the fact that there is nothing between the sun and earth to act as intermediary. One is to think that the sun extends its sphere of activity through space to places where it is not present. Those who live in coarse, sensual perceptions see a difficulty in such a thought. How can a body *act* in a place where *it is not*? Schelling reverses this thought process. He says, "It is true that a body *acts* only where *it is*, but it is just as true that *it is only* where it *acts*." If we see that the sun affects the earth through the force of attraction, then it follows from this fact that it extends its being as far as our earth and that we have no right to limit its existence exclusively to the place in which it acts through its being visible. The sun transcends the limits where it is visible with its being. Only a part of it can be seen; the other part reveals itself through the attraction. We must also think of the relation of spirit and nature in approximately this manner. The spirit is not merely where it is perceived; it is also where it perceives. Its being extends as far as to the most distant places where objects can still be observed. It embraces and permeates all nature that it knows. When the spirit thinks the law of an external process, this process does not remain outside the spirit. The latter does not merely receive a mirror picture, but extends its essence into a process. The spirit permeates the process and, in finding the law of the process, it is not the spirit in its isolated brain corner that proclaims this law; it is the law of the process that expresses itself. The spirit has moved to the place where the law is active. Without the spirit's attention the law would also have been active but it would not have been expressed. When the spirit submerges into the process, as it were, the law is then, in addition to being active in nature, expressed in conceptual form. It is only when the spirit withdraws its attention from nature and contemplates its own being that the impression arises that the spirit exists in separation from nature, in the same way that the sun's existence appears to the eye as being limited within a certain space when one disregards the fact that it also has its being where it works through attraction. Therefore, if I, within my spirit, cause ideas to arise in which laws of nature are expressed, the two statements, "I produce nature," and "nature *produces itself* within me," are equally true.

Now there are two possible ways to describe the one being that is spirit and nature at the same time. First, I can point out the natural laws that are at work in reality; second, I can show how the spirit proceeds to arrive at these laws. In both cases I am directed by the same object. In the first instance, the law shows me its activity in nature; in the second, the spirit shows me the procedure used to represent the same law in the imagination. In the one case, I am engaged in natural science; in the other, in spiritual science. How these two belong together is described by Schelling in an attractive fashion:

> The necessary trend of all natural science is to proceed from nature toward intelligence. This, and nothing else, is at the bottom of the tendency to bring theory into natural phenomena. The highest perfection of natural science would be the perfect transfiguration of all laws of nature into laws of imagination and thinking. The phenomena (the material element) must completely vanish and only the laws (the formal element) must remain. This is the reason for the fact that the more the law-structure in nature, itself, emerges, as if it were breaking the crust, the more the covering element vanishes. The phenomena themselves become more spiritual and finally disappear. The phenomena of optics are nothing but a geometry, the lines of which are drawn by the light, and this light, itself, is already of an ambiguous materiality. In the phenomena of magnetism, all material traces have already vanished. Of the phenomena of gravity, which, even according to natural scientists, can only be understood as a direct spiritual effect of action into distance, nothing is left but their law, the application of which is the mechanism of the celestial motions on a large scale. The completed theory of nature would be the one through which the whole of nature would dissolve into

intelligence. The inanimate and consciousless products of nature are only unsuccessful attempts of nature to reflect itself, and the so-called dead nature is, in general, an immature intelligence, so that the intelligent character shines through unconsciously in its phenomena. The highest aim of nature—to become completely objective to itself—can be reached by it only through the highest and last reflection, which is man, or, more generally speaking, what we call reason, through which nature returns in its own track and whereby it becomes evident that nature originally is identical with what is known in us as the intelligent and conscious element.

Schelling spun the facts of nature into an artful network of thought in such a fashion that all of its phenomena stood as in an ideal, harmonious organism before his creative imagination. He was inspired by the feeling that the ideas that appear in his imagination are also the creative forces of nature's process. Spiritual forces, then, are the basis of nature, and what appears dead and lifeless to our eyes has its origin in the spiritual. In turning our spirit to this, we discover the ideas, the spiritual, in nature. Thus, for man, according to Schelling, the things of nature are manifestations of the spirit. The spirit conceals itself behind these manifestations as behind a cover, so to speak. It shows itself in our own inner life in its right form. In this way, man knows what is spirit, and he is therefore able to find the spirit that is hidden in nature. The manner in which Schelling has nature return as spirit in himself reminds one of what Goethe believes is to be found in the perfect artist. The artist, in Goethe's opinion, proceeds in the production of a work of art as nature does in its creations. Therefore, we should observe in the artist's creation the same process through which everything has come into being that is spread out before man in nature. What nature conceals from the outer eye is presented in perceptible form to man in the process of artistic creation. Nature shows man only the finished works; man must decipher from these works how it proceeded to produce them. He is confronted with the creatures, not with the creator. In the case of the artist, creation and creator are observed at the same time. Schelling wants to penetrate through the products of nature to nature's creative process. He places himself in the position of creative nature and brings it into being within his soul as an artist produces his work of art. What are, then, according to Schelling, the thoughts that are contained in his world conception? They are the ideas of the creative spirit of nature. What preceded the things and what created them is what emerges in an individual human spirit as thought. This thought is to its original real existence as a memory picture of an experience is to the experience itself. Thereby, human science becomes for Schelling a reminiscence of the spiritual prototypes that were creatively active before the things existed. A divine spirit created the world and at the end of the process it also creates men in order to form in their souls as many tools through which the spirit can, in recollection, become aware of its creative activity. Schelling does not feel himself as an individual being at all as he surrenders himself to the contemplation of the world phenomena. He appears to himself as a part, a member of the creative world forces. Not *he* thinks, but the spirit of the world forces thinks in him. This spirit contemplates his own creative activity in him.

Schelling sees a world creation on a small scale in the production of a work of art. In the thinking contemplation of things, he sees a reminiscence of the world creation on a large scale. In the panorama of the world conception, the very ideas, which are the basis of things and have produced them, appear in our spirit. Man disregards everything in the world that the senses perceive in it and preserves only what pure thinking provides. In the creation and enjoyment of a work of art, the idea appears intimately permeated with elements that are revealed through the senses. According to Schelling's view, then, nature, art and world conception (philosophy) stand in the following relation to one another. Nature presents the finished products; world conception, the productive ideas; art combines both elements in harmonious interaction. On the one side, artistic activity stands halfway between creative nature, which produces without being aware of the ideas on the basis of which it creates, and, on the other, the thinking spirit, which knows these ideas without being able at the same time to create things with their help. Schelling expesses this with the words:

> The ideal world of art and the real world of objects are therefore products of one and the same activity. The concurrence of both (the conscious and the unconscious) *without* consciousness leads to the real world, *with* consciousness to the esthetic world. The objective world is only the more primitive, still unconscious poem of the spirit, the general organon of philosophy, and the *philosophy* of art is the crowning piece of its entire structure.

The spiritual activities of man, his thinking contemplation and his artistic creation, appear to Schelling not merely as the separate accomplishments of the individual person, but, if they are understood in their highest significance, they are at the same time the achievement of the supreme being, the world spirit. In truly dithyrambic words, Schelling depicts the feeling that emerges in the soul when it becomes aware of the fact that its life is not merely an individual life limited to a point of the universe, but that its activity is one of general spirituality. When the soul says, "I know; I am aware," then, in a higher sense, this means that the world spirit remembers its action before the existence of things; when the soul produces a work of art, it means that the world spirit repeats, on a small scale, what that spirit accomplished on a large scale at the creation of all nature.

> The soul in man is not the principle of individuality, then, but that through which he lifts himself above all selfhood, through which he becomes capable of self-sacrifice, of selfless love, and, to crown it all, of the contemplation and knowledge of the essence of things and thereby of art. The soul is no longer occupied with matter, nor is it engaged in any direct intercourse with matter, but it is alone with spirit as the life of things. Even when appearing in the body, the soul is nevertheless free from the body, the consciousness of which—in its most perfect formation—merely hovers like a light dream by which it is not disturbed. The soul is not a quality, nor faculty, nor anything of that kind in particular. *The soul does not know, but is knowledge. The soul is not good, not beautiful* in the way that bodies

also can be beautiful, *but it is beauty itself.* (*On the Relation of Fine Arts to Nature.*)

Such a mode of conception is reminiscent of the German mysticism that had a representative in Jakob Boehme (1575–1624). In Munich, where Schelling lived with short interruptions from 1806–1842, he enjoyed the stimulating association with Franz Benedict Baader, whose philosophical ideas moved completely in the direction of this older doctrine. This association gave Schelling the occasion to penetrate deeply into the thought world that depended entirely on a point of view at which he had arrived in his own thinking. If one reads the above quoted passage from the address, *On the Relation of the Fine Arts to Nature*, which he gave at the Royal Academy of Science in Munich in 1807, one is reminded of Jakob Boehme's view, "As thou beholdest the depth and the stars and the earth, thou seest thy God, *and in the same thou also livest and hast thy being*, and the same God ruleth thee also . . . thou art created out of *this* God and thou livest in Him; all thy knowledge also standeth in this God and when thou diest thou wilt be buried in this God."

As Schelling's thinking developed, his contemplation of the world turned into the contemplation of God, or theosophy. In 1809, when he published his *Philosophical Inquiries Concerning the Nature of Human Freedom and Topics Pertinent to This Question*, he had already taken his stand on the basis of such a theosophy. All questions of world conception are now seen by him in a new light. If all things are divine, how can there be evil in the world since God can only be perfect goodness? If the soul is in God, how can it still follow its selfish interests? If God is and acts within me, how can I then still be called free, as I, in that case, do not at all act as a self-dependent being?

Thus does Schelling attempt to answer these questions through contemplation of God rather than through world contemplation. It would be entirely incongruous to God if a world of beings were created that he would continually have to lead and direct as helpless creatures. God is perfect only if he can create a world that is equal to himself in perfection. A god who can produce only what is less perfect than he, himself, is imperfect himself. Therefore, God has created beings in men who do not need his guidance, but are themselves free and independent as he is. A being that has its origin in another being does not have to be dependent on its originator, for it is not a contradiction that the son of man is also a man. As the eye, which is possible only in the whole structure of the organism, has nevertheless an independent life of its own, so also the individual soul is, to be sure, comprised in God, yet not directly activated by him as a part in a machine.

> God is not a God of the dead, but of the living. How he could find his satisfaction in the most perfect machine is quite unintelligible. No matter in what form one might think the succession of created beings out of God, it can never be a mechanical succession, not a mere causation or production so that the products would not be anything in themselves. Nor could it be an emanation such that the emanating entity would remain merely a part of the being it sprang from and therefore would have no being of its own, nothing that would be self-dependent. The sequence of things out of God is a self-revelation of God. God, however, can only become revealed to himself in an element similar to him, in beings that are free and act out of their own initiative, for whose existence there is no ground but God but who are themselves like God.

If God were a God of the dead and all world phenomena merely like a mechanism, the individual processes of which could be derived from him as their cause and mover, then it would only be necessary to describe God and everything would be comprehended thereby. Out of God one would be able to understand all things and their activity, but this is not the case. The divine world has self-dependence. God created it, but it has its own being. Thus, it is indeed divine, but the divine appears in an entity that is independent of God; it appears in a non-divine element. As light is born out of darkness, so the divine world is born out of non-divine existence, and from this non-divine element springs evil, selfishness. God thus has not all beings in his power. He can give them the light, but they, themselves, emerge from the dark night. They are the sons of this night, and God has no power over whatever is darkness in them. They must work their way through the night into the light. This is their freedom. One can also say that the world is God's creation out of the ungodly. The ungodly, therefore, is the first, and the godly the second.

Schelling started out by searching for the ideas in all things, that is to say, by searching for what is divine in them. In this way, the whole world was transformed into a manifestation of God for him. He then had to proceed from God to the ungodly in order to comprehend the imperfect, the evil, the selfish. Now the whole process of world evolution became a continuous conquest of the ungodly by the godly for him. The individual man has his origin in the ungodly. He works his way out of this element into the divine. This process from the ungodly to the godly was originally the dominating element in the world. In antiquity men surrendered to their natures. They acted naively out of selfishness. The Greek civilization stands on this ground. It was the age in which man lived in harmony with nature, or, as Schiller expresses it in his essay, *On Naive and Sentimental Poetry*, man, himself, was nature and therefore did not seek nature. With the rise of Christianity, this state of innocence of humanity vanishes. Mere nature is considered as ungodly, as evil, and is seen as the opposite of the divine, the good. Christ appears to let the light of the divine shine in the darkness of the ungodly. This is the moment when "the earth becomes waste and void for the second time," the moment of "birth of the higher light of the spirit, which was from the beginning of the world, but was not comprehended by the darkness that operated by and for itself, and was then still in its concealed and limited manifestation. It appears in order to oppose the personal and spiritual evil, also in personal and human shape, and as mediator in order to restore again the connection of creation and God on the highest level. For only the personal can heal the personal, and God must become man to enable man to come to God."

Spinozism is a world conception that seeks the *ground* of all world events in God, and derives all processes according to external necessary laws from this ground, just as the mathematical truths are derived from the axioms. Schelling considers such a world conception insufficient. Like Spinoza, he also believes that all things are in God, but according to his opinion, they are not determined only by "the lifelessness of his system, the soullessness of its form, the poverty of its concepts and expressions, the inexorable harshness of its statements that tallies perfectly with its abstract mode of contemplation." Schelling, therefore, does find Spinoza's "mechanical view of nature" perfectly consistent, but nature, itself, does not show us this consistency.

> All that nature tells us is that it does not exist as a result of a geometric necessity. There is in it, not clear, pure reason, but personality and spirit; otherwise, the geometric intellect, which has ruled so long, ought to have penetrated it long ago. Intellect would necessarily have realized its idol of general and eternal laws of nature to a far greater extent, whereas it has everyday to acknowledge nature's irrational relation to itself more and more.

As man is not merely intellect and reason but unites still other faculties and forces within himself, so, according to Schelling, is this also the case with the divine supreme being. A God who is clear, pure reason seems like personified mathematics. A God, however, who cannot proceed according to pure reason with his world creation but continuously has to struggle against the ungodly, can be regarded as "a wholly personal living being." His life has the greatest analogy with the human life. As man attempts to overcome the imperfect within himself as he strives toward his ideal of perfection, so such a God is conceived as an eternally struggling God whose activity is the progressive conquest of the ungodly. Schelling compares Spinoza's God to the "oldest pictures of divinities, who appeared the more mysterious the less individually-living features spoke out of them." Schelling endows his God with more and more individualized traits. He depicts him as a human being when he says, "If we consider what is horrible in nature and the spirit-world, and how much more a benevolent hand seems to cover it up for us, then we cannot doubt that the deity is reigning over a world of horror, and that God could be called the horrible, the terrible God, not merely figuratively but literally."

Schelling could no longer look upon a God like this in the same way in which Spinoza had regarded his God. A God who orders everything according to the laws of reason can also be understood through reason. A personal God, as Schelling conceived him in his later life, is incalculable, for he does not act according to reason alone. In a mathematical problem we can pre-determine the result through mere thinking; with an acting human being this is not possible. With him, we have to wait and see what action he will decide upon in a given moment. Experience must be added to reason. A pure rational science is, therefore, insufficient for Schelling for a conception of world and God. In the later period of his world conception, he calls all knowledge that is derived from reason a negative knowledge that has to be supplemented by a positive knowledge. Whoever wants to know the living God must not merely depend on the necessary conclusions of reason; he must plunge into the life of God with his whole personal being. He will then *experience* what no conclusion, no pure reason can give him. The world is not a necessary effect of the divine cause, but a free action of the personal God. What Schelling believed he had reached, not by the cognitive process of the *method of reason,* but by *intuition* as the free incalculable acts of God, he has presented in his *Philosophy of Revelation* and *Philosophy of Mythology.* He used the content of these two works as the basis of the lectures he gave at the University of Berlin after he had been called to the Prussian capital by Frederic Wilhelm IV. They were published only after Schelling's death in 1854.

With views of this kind, Schelling shows himself to be the boldest and most courageous of the group of philosophers who were stimulated to develop an idealistic world conception by Kant. Under Kant's influence, the attempt to philosophize about things that transcended thinking and observation was abandoned. One tried to be satisfied with staying within the limits of observation and thinking. Where Kant, however, had concluded from the necessity of such a resignation that no knowledge of transcendent things was possible, the post-Kantians declared that as observation and thinking do not *point at* a transcendent divine element, they *are* this divine element themselves. Among those who took this position, Schelling was the most forceful. Fichte had taken everything into the ego; Schelling had spread this ego over everything. What he meant to show was not, as Fichte did, that the ego was everything, but that everything was ego. Schelling had the courage to declare not only the ego's content of ideas as divine, but the whole human spirit-personality. He not only elevated the human reason into a godly reason, but he made the human life content into the godly personal entity. A world explanation that proceeds from man and thinks of the course of the whole world as having as its ground an entity that directs its course in the same way as man directs his actions, is called *anthropomorphism*. Anyone who considers events as being dependent on a general world reason, explains the world anthropomorphically, for this *general* world reason is nothing but the human reason made into this general reason. When Goethe says, "Man never understands how anthropomorphic he is," he has in mind the fact that our simplest statements concerning nature contain hidden anthropomorphisms. When we say a body rolls on because another body pushed it, we form such a conception from our *own* experience. *We* push a body and it rolls on. When we now see that a ball moves against another ball that thereupon rolls on, we form the conception that the first ball *pushed* the second, using the analogy of the effect we ourselves exert. Haeckel observes that the anthropomorphic dogma "compares God's creation and rule of the world with the artful creation of an ingenious technician or engineer, or with the government of a wise ruler. God, the Lord, as creator, preserver and ruler of the world is, in all his thinking and doing, always conceived as similar to a human being."

Schelling had the courage of the most consistent anthropomorphism. He finally declared man, with all his life-content, as divinity, and since a part of this life-content is not only the reasonable but the unreasonable as well, he had the possibility of explaining also the unreasonable in the world. To this end, however, he had to supplement the view of reason by another view that does not have its source in thinking. This higher view, according to his opinion, he called "positive philosophy."

> It "is the free philosophy in the proper sense of the word; whoever does not want it, may leave it. I put it to the free choice of everybody. I only say that if, for instance, somebody wants to get at the real process, a free world creation, etc., he can have all this only by means of such a philosophy. If he is satisfied with a rational philosophy and has no need beyond it, he may continue holding this position, only he must give up his claim to possess with and in a rational philosophy what the latter simply cannot supply because of its very nature, namely, the real God, the real process and a free relation between God and world."
>
> The negative philosophy "will remain the preferred philosophy for the school, the positive philosophy, that for life. Only if both of them are united will the complete consecration be obtained that can be demanded of philosophy. As is well-known in the Eleusinian mysteries, the minor mysteries were distinguished from the major ones and the former were considered as a prerequisite stage of the latter . . . The positive philosophy is the necessary consequence of the correctly understood negative one and thus one may indeed say that in the negative philosophy are celebrated the minor mysteries of philosophy, in the positive philosophy, the major ones."

If the inner life is declared to be the divine life, then it appears to be an inconsistency to limit this distinction to a part of this inner life. Schelling is not guilty of this inconsistency. The moment he declared that to explain nature is to create nature, he set the direction for all his life conception. If thinking contemplation of nature is a repetition of nature's creation, then the fundamental character of this creation must also correspond to that of human action; it must be an act of freedom, not one of geometric necessity. We cannot know a free creation through the laws of reason; it must *reveal* itself through other means.

* * *

The individual human personality lives and has its being in and through the ground of the world, which is spirit. Nevertheless, man is in possession of his full freedom and self-dependence. Schelling considered this conception as one of the most important in his whole philosophy. Because of it, he thought he could consider *his* idealistic trend of ideas as a progress from earlier views since those earlier views thought the individual to be completely determined by the world spirit when they considered it rooted in it, and thereby robbed it of its freedom and self-dependence.

> For until the discovery of idealism, the real concept of freedom was lacking in all systems, in that of Leibniz as well as in that of Spinoza. A freedom that many of us had conceived and even boasted of because of the vivid inner experience it touched on, namely, one that is to consist merely in the domination of the intelligent principle over the forces of sensuality and desire, such a freedom could be derived from Spinoza's presupposition, not merely as a last resort, but with clarity and the greatest of ease.

A man who had only this kind of freedom in mind and who, with the aid of thoughts that had been borrowed from Spinozism, attempted a reconciliation of the religious consciousness with a thoughtful world contemplation, of theology and philosophy, was Schelling's contemporary, *Friedrich Daniel Ernst Schleiermacher* (1768–1834). In his speeches on *Religion Addressed to the Educated Among Its Scorners* (1799), he exclaimed, "Sacrifice with me in reverence to the spirit of the saintly departed Spinoza! The lofty world spirit filled him; the infinite was his beginning and end; the universe his only and eternal love. He reflected himself in holy innocence and deep humility in the eternal world, and could observe how he, in turn, was the world's most graceful mirror."

Freedom for Schleiermacher is not the ability of a being to decide itself, in complete independence, on its life's own aim and direction. It is, for him, only a "development out of oneself." But a being can very well develop out of itself and yet be unfree in a higher sense. If the supreme being of the world has planted a definite seed into the separate individuality that is brought to maturity by him, then the course of life of the individual is precisely predetermined but nevertheless develops out of itself. A freedom of this kind, as Schleiermacher thinks of it, is readily thinkable in a necessary world order in which everything occurs according to a strict mathematical necessity. For this reason, it is possible for him to maintain that *"the plant also has its freedom."* Because Schleiermacher knew of a freedom only in this sense, he could also seek the origin of religion in the most unfree feeling, in the *"feeling of absolute dependence."* Man feels that he must rest his existence on a being other than himself, on God. His religious consciousness is rooted in this feeling. A feeling is always something that must be linked to something else. It has only a derived existence. The thought, the idea, have so distinctly a self-dependent existence that Schelling can say of them, "Thus thoughts, to be sure, are produced by the soul, but the produced thought is an independent power continuing its own action by itself, and indeed growing within the soul to the extent that it conquers and subdues its own mother." Whoever, therefore, attempts to grasp the supreme being in the form of thoughts, receives this being and holds it as a self-dependent power within himself. This power can then be *followed* by a feeling, just as the conception of a beautiful work of art is followed by a certain feeling of satisfaction. Schleiermacher, however, does not mean to seize the object of religion, but *only* the religious feeling. He leaves the object, God, entirely indefinite. Man feels himself as dependent, but he does not know the being on which he depends. All concepts that we form of the deity are inadequate to the lofty character of this being. For this reason, Schleiermacher avoids going into any definite concepts concerning the deity. The most indefinite, the emptiest conception, is the one he likes best. "The ancients experienced religion when they considered every characteristic form of life throughout the world to be the work of a deity. They had absorbed the peculiar form of activity of the universe as a definite feeling and designated it as such." This is why the subtle words that Schleiermacher uttered concerning the essence of immortality are indefinite:

> The aim and character of a religious life is not an immortality that is outside of time, or behind time, or else merely after *this* time, but one that is still *in* time. It is the immortality that we can already have here in this temporal life and that is a problem, the solution of which continually engages us. To become one with the infinite in the midst of the finite, and to be eternal in every moment, is the immortality of religion.

Had Schelling said this, it would have been possible to connect it with a definite conception. It would then mean, "Man produces the thought of God. This would then be God's memory of his own being. The infinite would be brought to life in the individual person. It would be present in the finite." But as Schleiermacher writes those sentences without Schelling's foundations, they do no more than create a nebulous atmosphere. What they express is the dim feeling that man depends on something infinite. It is the theology in Schleiermacher that prevents him from proceeding to definite conceptions concerning the ground of the world. He would like to lift religious feeling, piety, to a higher level, for he is a personality with rare depth of soul. He demands dignity for true religious devotion. Everything that he said about this feeling is of noble character. He defended the moral attitude that is taken in Schlegel's *Lucinde,* which springs purely out of the individual's own arbitrary free choice and goes beyond all limits of traditional social conceptions. He could do so because he was convinced that a man can be genuinely religious even if he is venturesome in the field of morality. He could say, "There is no healthy feeling that is not pious." Schleiermacher did understand religious feeling. He was well-acquainted with the feeling that Goethe, in his later age, expressed in his poem, *Trilogy of Passion*:

> From our heart's pureness springs a yearning tender
> Unto an unknown Being, lofty, blameless,
> In gratefulness unchallenged to surrender,
> Unriddling for ourselves the Ever-Nameless
> *In pious awe—*

Because he felt this religious feeling deeply, he also knew how to describe *the inner religious life*. He did not attempt to know the object of this devotion but left it to be done by the various kinds of theology, each in its own fashion. What he intended to delineate was the realm of religious experience that is independent of a knowledge of God. In this sense, Schleiermacher was a peace-maker between belief and knowledge.

* * *

"In most recent times religion has increasingly contracted the developed extent of its content and withdrawn into the intensive life of *religious fervor* or *feeling* and often, indeed, in a fashion that manifests a thin and meager content." Hegel wrote these words in the preface of the second edition of his *Encyclopedia of the Philosophical Sciences* (1827). He continued by saying:

> As long as religion still has a creed, a doctrine, a dogmatic system, it has something that philosophy can make its concern and use to join hands with religion. This fact, however, must not be approached by the inferior, dividing intellect through which modern religion is blinded. It considers the realms of philosophy and religion as being mutually exclusive and in separating them in this way assumes that they can only be linked together externally. The real relation, and this is implied also in the previous statement, is such that religion can, to be sure, be without philosophy. Philosophy, however, cannot be without religion, but comprises it within its own realm. The true religion, the religion of the spirit, must have such a credo, must have a *content*. The spirit is essentially consciousness of content that has become objective. As feeling, it is the non-objective content *itself* and only the lowest stage of consciousness, and, indeed, of the very form of soul life that man has in common with the animals. It is thinking only that makes the spirit out of the soul, the soul with which the animal also is gifted. Philosophy is only a consciousness of

this content, of the spirit and of its truth. It is consciousness of man's essential nature that distinguishes him from the animal and *makes him capable of religion.*

The whole spiritual physiognomy of *Georg Wilhelm Friedrich Hegel* (1770–1831) becomes apparent when we hear words like these from him, through which he wanted to express clearly and poignantly that he regarded *thinking* that is conscious of itself as the highest activity of man, as the force through which alone man can gain a position with respect to the ultimate questions. The feeling of dependence, which was considered by Schleiermacher as the originator of religious experience, was declared to be characteristically the function of the animal's life by Hegel. He stated paradoxically that if the feeling of dependence were to constitute the essence of Christianity, then the dog would be the best Christian. Hegel is a personality who lives completely in the element of thought.

> Because man is a thinking being, common sense, no more than philosophy, will ever relinquish its prerogative to rise from the empirical world conception to God. This elevation has as its prerequisite the world contemplation of *thinking, not merely that of the sensual, animal consciousness.*

Hegel makes into the content of his world conception what can be obtained by self-conscious thinking. For what man finds in any other way can be nothing but a preparatory stage of a world conception.

> The *elevation* of thinking above the sensual, its transcendence from the finite to the infinite, the *leap* into the supersensible that is taken with an abrupt termination of sensual content—all this is thinking itself; this transition itself is *thinking.* When such a transition is not to be made, it means that no thinking is taking place. In fact, animals do not go beyond sensual perception and immediate impression, and do not make this leap. For this reason, they have no religion.

What man can extract from things through thinking is the highest element that exists in them and for him. Only this element can he recognize as their essence. Thought is, therefore, the essence of things for Hegel. All perceptual imagination, all scientific observation of the world and its events do, finally, result in man's production of *thoughts* concerning the connection of things. Hegel's work now proceeds from the point where perceptual imagination and scientific observation have reached their destination: With thought as it *lives* in self-consciousness. The scientific observer looks at nature; Hegel observes what the scientific observer states about nature. The observer attempts to reduce the variety of natural phenomena to a unity. He explains one process through the other. He strives for order, for organic systematic simplicity in the totality of the things that are presented to the senses in chaotic multiplicity. Hegel searches for systematic order and harmonious simplicity in the results of the scientific investigator. He adds to the science of nature a science of the thoughts about nature. All thoughts that can be produced about the world form, in a natural way, a uniform totality. The scientific observer gains his thoughts from being confronted with the individual things. This is why the thoughts themselves appear in his mind also, at first individually, one beside another. If we consider them now side by side, they become joined together into a totality in which every individual thought forms an organic link. Hegel means to give this totality of thoughts in his philosophy. No more than the natural scientist, who wants to determine the laws of the astronomical universe, believes that he can construct the starry heavens out of these laws, does Hegel, who seeks the law-ordered connections within the thought world, believe he can derive from these thoughts any laws of natural science that can only be determined through empirical observation. The statement, repeated time and again, that it was Hegel's intention to exhaust the full and unlimited knowledge of the whole universe through pure thinking is based on nothing more than a naive misunderstanding of his view. He has expressed it distinctly enough: "To comprehend what *is,* is the task of philosophy, for what is reasonable is real, and what is real is reasonable. . . . *When philosophy paints its picture gray on gray, a figure of life has become old. . . . Minerva's owl begins its flight only as the twilight of nightfall sets in.*"

From these words it should be apparent that the factual knowledge must already be there when the thinker arrives to see them in a new light from his viewpoint. One should not demand of Hegel that he derive new natural laws from pure thought, for he had not intended to do this at all. What he had set out to do was to spread philosophical light over the sum total of natural laws that existed in his time. Nobody demands of a natural scientist that he create the starry sky, although in his research he is concerned with the firmament. Hegel's views, however, are declared to be fruitless because he thought about the laws of nature and did not create these laws at the same time.

What man finally arrives at as he ponders over things is their essence. It is the foundation of things. What man receives as his highest insight is at the same time the deepest nature of things. The thought that *lives* in man is, therefore, also the objective content of the world. One can say that the thought is at first in the world in an unconscious form. It is then received by the human spirit. It becomes apparent to itself in the human spirit. Just as man, in directing his attention into nature, finally finds the thought that makes the phenomena comprehensible, so he also finds thought within himself, as he turns his attention inward. As the essence of nature is thought, so also man's own essence is thought. In the human self-consciousness, therefore, thought contemplates itself. The essence of the world arrives at its own awareness. In the other creatures of nature thought is active, but this activity is not directed toward itself but toward something other than itself. Nature, then, does contain thought, but in thinking, man's thought is not merely contained; it is here not merely active, but is directed toward itself. In external nature, thought, to be sure, also unfolds life, but there it only flows into something else; in man, it lives in itself. In this manner the whole process of the world appears to Hegel as thought process, and all occurrences in this process are represented as preparatory phases for the highest event that there is: The thoughtful comprehension of thought itself. This event takes place in the human self-consciousness. Thought then works its way progressively through until it reaches its highest form of manifestation in which it comprehends itself.

Thus, in observing any thing or process of reality, one always sees a definite phase of development of thought *in* this thing or process. The world process is the progressive evolution of thought. All phases except the highest contain within themselves a self-contradiction. *Thought* is in them, but they contain more than it reveals at such a lower stage. For this reason, it overcomes the contradictory form of its manifestation and speeds on toward a higher one that is more appropriate. The contradiction then is the motor that drives the thought development ahead. As the natural scientist thoughtfully observes things, he forms concepts of them that have this contradiction within themselves. When the philosophical thinker thereupon takes up these thoughts that are gained from the observation of nature, he finds them to be self-contradictory forms. But it is this very contradiction that makes it possible to develop a complete thought structure out of the individual thoughts. The thinker looks for the contradictory element in a thought; this element is contradictory because it points toward a higher stage of its development. Through the contradiction contained in it, every thought points to another thought toward which it presses on in the course of its development. Thus, the philosopher can begin with the simplest thought that is bare of all content, that is, with the abstract thought of being. From this thought he is driven by the contradiction contained therein toward a second phase that is higher and less contradictory, etc., until he arrives at the highest stage, at thought living within itself, which is the highest manifestation of the spirit.

Hegel lends expression to the fundamental character of the evolution of modern world conception. The Greek spirit knows thought as perception; the modern spirit knows it as the self-engendered product of the soul. In presenting his world conception, Hegel turns to the creations of self-consciousness.

He starts out by dealing only with the self-consciousness and its products, but then he proceeds to follow the activity of the self-consciousness into the phase in which it is aware of being united with the world spirit. The Greek thinker *contemplates* the world, and his *contemplation* gives him an insight *into the nature of the world*. The modern thinker, as represented by Hegel, means to live with his inner experience in the world's creative process. He wants to insert himself into it. He is then convinced that he discovers himself in the world, and he listens to what the spirit of the world reveals as its being while this very being is present and alive in his self-consciousness. Hegel is in the modern world what Plato was in the world of the Greeks. Plato lifted his spirit-eye contemplatively to the world of ideas so as to catch the mystery of the soul in this contemplation. Hegel has the soul immerse itself in the world-spirit and unfold its inner life after this immersion. So the soul lives as its own life what has its ground in the world spirit into which it submerged.

Hegel thus seized the human spirit in its highest activity, that is, in thinking, and then attempted to show the significance of this highest activity within the entirety of the world. This activity represents the event through which the universal essence, which is poured out into the whole world, finds itself again. The highest activities through which this self-finding is accomplished are art, religion and philosophy. In the work of nature, thought is contained, but here it is estranged from itself. It appears not in its own original form. A real lion that we see is, indeed, nothing but the incarnation of the thought, "lion." We are, however, not confronted here with the thought, lion, but with the corporeal being. This being, itself, is not concerned with the thought. Only I, when I want to comprehend it, search for the thought. A work of art that depicts a lion represents outwardly the form that, in being confronted with a real lion, I can only have as a *thought-image*. The corporeal element is there in the work of art for the sole purpose of allowing the thought to appear. Man creates works of art in order to make outwardly visible that element of things that he can otherwise only grasp in thoughts. In reality, thought can appear to itself in its appropriate form only in the human self-consciousness. What really appears only inwardly, man has imprinted into sense-perceived matter in the work of art to give it an external expression. When Goethe stood before the monuments of art of the Greeks, he felt impelled to confess that here is necessity, here is *God.* In Hegel's language, according to which God expresses himself in the thought content of the world manifested in human self-consciousness, this would mean: In the works of art man sees reflected the highest revelations of the world in which he can really participate only within his own spirit. Philosophy contains thought in its perfectly pure form, in its original nature. The highest form of manifestation of which the divine substance is capable, the world of thought, is contained in philosophy. In Hegel's sense, one can say the whole world is divine, that is to say, permeated by thought, but in philosophy the divine *appears directly* in its godliness while in other manifestations it takes on the form of the ungodly. Religion stands halfway between art and philosophy. In it, thought does not as yet live as pure thought but in the form of the picture, the symbol. This is also the case with art, but there the picture is such that it is borrowed from the external perception. The pictures of religion, however, are spiritualized symbols.

Compared to these highest manifestations of thought, all other human life expressions are merely imperfect preparatory stages. The entire historical life of mankind is composed of such stages. In following the external course of the events of history one will, therefore, find much that does not correspond to pure thought, the object of reason. In looking deeper, however, we see that in historical evolution the thought of reason is nevertheless in the process of being realized. This realization just proceeds in a manner that appears as ungodly on the surface. On the whole, one can maintain the statement, *"Everything real is reasonable."* This is exactly the decisive point, that thought, the historical world spirit, realizes itself in the entirety of history. The individual person is merely a tool for the realization of the purpose of this world spirit. Because Hegel recognizes the highest essence of the world in *thought,* he also demands of the individual that he subordinate himself to the general thoughts that rule the world evolution.

> The great men in history are those whose special personal purposes contain the substantial element that is the will of the world spirit. This content is their true power. It is also contained in the general unconscious instincts of the people. They are inwardly driven to it and have nothing further to fall back upon that would enable them to resist the individual who has made the execution of such a purpose his own interest. The people gather around his colors. He shows them and brings into reality their own immanent purposes. If we appraise the fate of these world-historical individuals, we must say that they have had the good fortune to be the executive agent of a purpose that represented a step in the progress of the general spirit. We can call a 'strategem or reason,' the way in which *reason* employs individuals as its tools, for it has them execute their own purposes with all fury of passion, and in so doing, it not only remains unharmed, but actually realizes itself. The particular is mostly negligible in comparison with the general; the individuals are sacrificed and abandoned. World history thus presents the spectacle of struggling individuals and, in the field of the particular, everything happens in an entirely natural fashion. Just as in the animal nature the preservation of life is purpose and instinct of the individual specimen, and just as general reason holds sway while the individual drops out, in the same way things also happen in the spiritual world. The passions work mutual destruction on each other. Reason alone wakes, follows its purpose and prevails.

Man as an individual can seize the comprehensive spirit only in his thinking. Only in the contemplation of the world is God entirely present. When man acts, when he enters the active life, he becomes a link and therefore can also participate only as a link in the complete chain of reason.

Hegel's doctrine of state is also derived from thoughts of this kind. Man is alone with his thinking; with his actions he is a link of the community. The reasonable order of community, the thought by which it is permeated, is the *state*. The individual person, according to Hegel, is valuable only insofar as the general reason, thought, appears within such a person, for thought is the essence of things. A product of nature does not possess the power to bring thought in its highest form into appearance; man has this power. He will, therefore, fulfill his destination only if he makes himself a carrier of thought. As the state is realized thought, and as the individual man is only a member within its structure, it follows that man has to serve the state and not the state, man.

> If the state is confused with society, and if its end is then defined as the security and protection of property and individual freedom, then it follows that the interest of the individual as such is the last purpose for which the two are associated, and from this again it would follow that it is merely a matter of an arbitrary choice of the individual to become a member of the state or not. The state has, however, an entirely different relation toward the individual. As it is objective spirit, the individual man himself has objectivity, truth and morality only insofar as he is a member of it. The union as such is the true content and purpose, and it is the destination of the individuals to lead a generally valid life. Their subsequent satisfaction, activity and behavior has this substantial element of general validity as its basis and as its result.

What place is there for *freedom* in such a life-conception? The concept of freedom through which the individual human being is granted an absolute to determine aim and purpose of his own activity is not admitted as valid by Hegel. For what could be the advantage if the individual did not derive his aim from the reasonable world of thoughts but made his decision in a completely arbitrary fashion? This, according to Hegel, would really be absence of freedom. An individual of this kind would not be in agreement with his own essence; he would be imperfect. A perfect individual can only want to realize his essential nature, and the ability to do this is his freedom. This essential nature now is embodied in the state. Therefore, if man acts according to the state, he acts in freedom.

> The state, in and by itself, is the moral universe, the realization of freedom, and it is reason's absolute purpose that freedom be real.

The state is the spirit that has a foothold in the world, whereas in nature it realizes itself only in a self-estranged form as dormant spirit. . . . The fact that the state exists testifies to God's walk through the world. It has its ground in the power of reason that causes its self-realization through the force of will.

Hegel is never concerned with things as such, but always with their reasonable, thoughtful content. As he always *searched* for thoughts in the field of world contemplation, so he also wanted to see life *directed* from the viewpoint of thought. It is for this reason that he fought against indefinite ideals of state and society and made himself the champion of the order existing in reality. Whoever dreams of an indefinite ideal for the future believes, in Hegel's opinion, that the general reason has been waiting for him to make his appearance. To such a person it is necessary to explain particularly that reason is already contained in everything that is real. He called Professor Fries, whose colleague he was in Jena and whose successor he became later in Heidelberg, the "General Field Marshal of all shallowness" because he had intended to form such an ideal for the future "out of the mush of his heart."

The comprehensive defense of the real and existing order has earned Hegel strong reproaches even from those who were favorably inclined toward the general trend of his ideas. One of Hegel's followers, Johann Eduard Erdmann, writes in regard to this point:

> The decided preponderance that Hegel's philosophy is granted in the middle of the 1820's over all other contemporary systems has its cause in the fact that the momentary calm that it established in the wake of the wild struggles in the field of politics, religion and church policy, correspond appropriately to a philosophy that has been called—in reprehension by its antagonists, and in praise by its friends—the 'philosophy of the restoration'.

This name is justified to a much greater extent than its coiners had realized.

One should not overlook the fact also that Hegel created,

through his sense of reality, a view that is in a high degree close and favorable to life. Schelling had meant to provide a view of life in his "Philosophy of Revelation," but how foreign are the conceptions of his contemplation of God to the immediately experienced real life! A view of this kind can have its value, at most, in festive moments of solitary contemplation when man withdraws from the bustle of everyday life to surrender to the mood of profound meditation; when he is engaged, so to speak, not in the service of the world, but of God. Hegel, however, had meant to impart to man the all-pervading feeling that he serves the general divine principle also in his everyday activities. For him, this principle extends, as it were, down to the last detail of reality, while with Schelling it withdraws to the highest regions of existence. Because Hegel *loved* reality and life, he attempted to conceive it in its most reasonable form. He wanted man to be guided by reason every step of his life. In the last analysis he did not have a low estimation of the individual's value. This can be seen from utterances like the following.

> The richest and most concrete is the *most subjective*, and the element that withdraws the most into profundity is the most powerful and all-comprehensive. The highest and most pointed peak is the *pure personality*, which alone through the absolute dialectic, which is nature, encompasses everything within itself and at the same time, because it develops to the highest stage of freedom and insists on simplicity, which is the first immediacy and generality.

But in order to become "pure personality" the individual has to permeate himself with the whole element of reason and to absorb it into his self, for the "pure personality," to be sure, is the highest point that man can reach in his development, but man cannot claim this stage as a mere gift of nature. If he has lifted himself to this point, however, the following words of Hegel become true:

> That man knows of God is a communal knowledge in the meaning of the ideal community, for man knows of God only insofar as God knows of himself in man. This knowledge is

self-consciousness of God, but also a knowledge that God has of man; *this knowledge that God has of man is the knowledge that man has of God. The spirit of man, to know of God, is only the spirit of God himself.*

According to Hegel, only a man in whom this is realized deserves the name of "personality," for with him reason and individuality coincide. He realizes God within himself for whom he supplies in his consciousness the organ to contemplate himself. All thoughts would remain abstract, unconscious, ideal forms if they did not obtain living reality in man. Without man, God would not be there in his highest perfection. He would be the incomplete basic substance of the world. He would not know of himself. Hegel has presented this God before his realization in life. The content of the presentation is Hegel's *Logic*. It is a structure of lifeless, rigid, mute thoughts. Hegel, himself, calls it the "realm of shadows." It is, as it were, to show God in his innermost, eternal essence before the creation of nature and of the finite spirit. But as self-contemplation necessarily belongs to the nature of God, the content of the "Logic" is only the dead God who demands existence. In reality, this realm of the pure abstract truth does not occur anywhere. It is only our intellect that is capable of separating it from living reality. According to Hegel, there is nowhere in existence a completed first being, but there is only one in eternal motion, in the process of continual *becoming*. This eternal being is the "eternally real truth in which the eternally active reason is free for itself, and for which necessity, nature and history only serve as forms of manifestation and as vessels of its glory."

Hegel wanted to show how, in man, the world of thoughts comprehends itself. He expressed in another form Goethe's conception:

> When a man's healthy nature acts in its entirety, when he feels himself in the world as in a great, beautiful, worthy and cherished whole, when inner harmony fills him with pure and free delight, then the universe, if it could become aware of itself, would rejoice as

having reached its destination and would admire the peak of its own becoming and being.

Translated into Hegel's language, this means that when man experiences his own being in his thinking, then this act has not merely an individual personal significance, but a universal one. The nature of the universe reaches its peak in man's self-knowledge; it arrives at its completion without which it would remain a fragment.

In Hegel's conception of knowledge this is not understood as the seizing of a content that, without the cognitive process, exists somewhere ready-made in the world; it is not an activity that produces *copies* of the real events. What is created in the act of thinking cognition exists, according to Hegel, nowhere else in the world but only in the act of cognition. As the plant produces a blossom at a certain stage of development, so the universe produces the content of human knowledge. Just as the blossom is not there *before* its development, so the thought content of the world does not exist before it appears in the human spirit. A world conception in which the opinion is held that in the process of knowledge only copies of an already existing content come into being, makes man into a lazy spectator of the world, which would also be completely there without him. Hegel, however, makes man into the active co-agent of the world process, which would be lacking its peak without him.

Grillparzer, in his way, characterized Hegel's opinion concerning the relation of thinking and world in a significant epigram:

It may be that you teach us prophetically God's form of thinking. But it's human form, friend, you have decidedly spoiled.

What the poet has in mind here in regard to human thinking is just the thinking that presupposes that its content exists ready-made in the world and means to do nothing more than to supply a copy of it. For Hegel, this epigram contains no rebuke, for this thinking about something else is, according to his view, not the highest, most perfect thinking. In thinking about a thing of nature one searches for a concept that *agrees* with an external object. One then comprehends through the thought that is thus formed what the external object is. One is then confronted with two different elements, that is, with the thought and with the object. But if one intends to ascend to the highest viewpoint, one must not hesitate to ask the question: What is thought itself? For the solution of this problem, however, there is again nothing but thought at our disposal. In the highest form of cognition, then, thought comprehends itself. No longer does the question of an agreement with something outside arise. Thought deals exclusively with itself. This form of thinking that has no support in any external object appears to Grillparzer as destructive for the mode of thinking that supplies information concerning the variety of things spread out in time and space, and belonging to both the sensual and spiritual world of reality. But no more than the painter destroys nature in reproducing its lines and color on canvas, does the thinker destroy the ideas of nature as he expresses them in their spiritually pure form. It is strange that one is inclined to see in thinking an element that would be hostile to reality because it abstracts from the profusion of the sensually presented content. Does not the painter, in presenting in color, shade and line, abstract from all other qualities of an object? Hegel suitably characterized all such objections with his nice sense of humor. If the primal substance whose activity pervades the world "slips, and from the ground on which it walks, falls into the water, it becomes a fish, an organic entity, a living being. If it now slips and falls into the element of *pure thinking*—for even pure thinking they will not allow as its proper element—then it suddenly becomes something bad and finite; of this one really ought to be ashamed to speak, and would be if it were not officially necessary and because there is simply no use denying that there is some such thing as logic. Water is such a cold and miserable element; yet life nevertheless feels comfortably at home in it. Should thinking be so much worse an element? Should the absolute feel so uncomfortable and behave so badly in it?"

It is entirely in Hegel's sense if one maintains that the first being created the lower strata of nature and the human being as well. Having arrived at this point, it has resigned and left to man the task to create, as an addition to the external world and to himself, the thoughts about the things. Thus, the original being, *together with the human being as a co-agent, create the entire content of the world.* Man is a fellow-creator of the world, not merely a lazy spectator or cognitive ruminator of what would have its being just as well without him.

What man is in regard to his innermost existence he is through nothing else but himself. For this reason, Hegel considers freedom, not as a divine gift that is laid into man's cradle to be held by him forever after, but as a result toward which he progresses gradually in the course of his development. From life in the external world, from the stage in which he is satisfied in a purely sensual existence, he rises to the comprehension of his spiritual nature, of his own inner world. He thereby makes himself independent of the external world; he follows his inner being. The spirit of a people contains natural necessity and feels entirely dependent on what is moral public opinion in regard to custom and tradition, quite apart from the individual human being. But gradually the individual wrests himself loose from *this* world of moral convictions that is thus laid down in the external world and penetrates into his own inner life, recognizing that he can develop moral convictions and standards out of his own spirit. Man lifts himself up to the vantage point of the supreme being that rules within him and is the source of his morality. For his moral commandment, he no longer looks to the external world but within his own soul. He makes himself dependent only on himself (paragraph 552 of Hegel's *Encyclopedia of the Philosophical Sciences*). This independence, this freedom then is nothing that man possesses from the outset, but it is *acquired* in the course of historical evolution. *World history is the progress of humanity in the consciousness of freedom.*

Since Hegel regards the highest manifestations of the human spirit as processes in which the primal being of the world finds the completion of its development, of its *becoming,* all other phenomena appear to him as the preparatory stages of this highest peak; the final stage appears as the aim and purpose toward which everything tends. This conception of a purposiveness in the universe is different from the one in which world creation and world government are thought to be like the work of an ingenious technician or constructor of machines, who has arranged all things according to useful purposes. A utility doctrine of this kind was rigorously rejected by Goethe. On February 20th, 1831, he said to Eckermann (compare *Conversations of Goethe with Eckermann*, Part II):

> Man is inclined to carry his usual views from life also into science and, in observing the various parts of an organic being, to inquire after their purpose and use. This may go on for awhile and he may also make progress in science for the time being, but he will come across phenomena soon enough where such a narrow view will prove insufficient and he will be entangled in nothing but contradictions if he does not acquire a higher orientation. Such utilitarian teachers will say that the bull has horns to defend itself with, but there I ask why the sheep have none. Even when they have horns, why are they twisted around the sheep's ears so that they cannot be of any use at all. It is a different thing to say that the bull defends himself with his horns because they are there. The question *why* is not scientific at all. We fare a little better with the question *how*, for if I ask the question, 'How does the bull have horns?' I am immediately led to the observation of his organization, and this shows me at the same time why the lion has no horns and cannot have any.

Nevertheless, Goethe recognizes, in another sense, a purposeful arrangement in all nature that finally reaches its aim in man and has all its works so ordered, as it were, that he will fulfill his destination in the end. In his essay on Winckelmann, he writes, "For to what avail is all expenditure and labor of suns and planets and moons, of stars and galaxies, of comets and of nebulae, and of completed and still growing worlds, if not at last a happy man rejoices in his existence?" Goethe is also convinced that the nature of all world phenomena is brought to light as truth in and through man (compare what is said on pp. 110ff). To comprehend how everything in the world is so laid out that man has a worthy task and is capable of carrying it out is the aim of this world conception. What Hegel expresses at the end of his *Philosophy of Nature* sounds like a philosophical justification of Goethe's words:

> In the element of life nature has completed her course and has made her peace as she turns into a higher phase of being. The spirit has thus emerged from nature. The aim of nature is her own death, to break through the crust of immediate sensual existence, to burn as a phoenix in order to emerge from this external garment, rejuvenated as spirit. Nature thus becomes estranged from herself in order that she may recognize her own being, thereby bringing about a reconciliation with herself. . . . The spirit therefore exists *before* nature as its real purpose; nature originates from the spirit.

This world conception succeeded in placing man so high because it saw realized in man what is the basis of the whole world, as the fundamental force, the primal being. It prepares its realization through the whole gradual progression of all other phenomena but is fulfilled only in man. Goethe and Hegel agree perfectly in this conception. What Goethe had derived from his *contemplative observation* of nature and spirit, Hegel expresses through his lucid *pure thinking unfolding its life in self-consciousness*. The method by which Goethe explained certain natural processes through the stages of their growth and development is applied by Hegel to the whole cosmos. For an understanding of the plant organism Goethe demanded:

> Watch how the plant *in its growth* changes step by step and, gradually led on, transforms from blossoms to fruits.

Hegel wants to comprehend all world phenomena in the gradual progress of their development from the simplest dull activity of inert matter to the height of the self-conscious spirit. In the self-conscious spirit he sees the revelation of the primal substance of the world.

Chapter VIII

Reactionary World Conceptions

"The bud vanishes in the breaking of the blossom, and one could say that the former is contradicted by the latter. In the same way, the fruit declares the blossom to be a false existence and replaces it as its truth. These forms are not merely different from one another but they crowd each other out as they are incompatible. Their fluid nature makes them at once into moments of the organic whole in which they not only do not contradict each other, but in which the one is as necessary as the other, and it is only this equal necessity that constitutes the life of the whole."

In these words of Hegel, the most significant traits of his mode of conception are expressed. He believes that the things of reality carry within themselves their own contradiction and that the incentive for their growth, for the living process of their development, is given by the fact that they continually attempt to overcome this contradiction. The blossom would never become fruit if it were without contradiction. It would have no reason to go beyond its unquestioned existence.

An exactly opposite intellectual conviction forms the point of departure of *Johann Friedrich Herbart* (1776–1841). Hegel is a sharp thinker, but at the same time a spirit with a great thirst for reality. He would like to have only things that have absorbed the rich, saturated content of the world into themselves. For this reason, Hegel's thoughts must also be in an eternal flux, in a continuous state of becoming, in a forward motion as full of contradictions as reality itself. Herbart is a completely abstract thinker. He does not attempt to penetrate into things but looks at them from the corner into which he has withdrawn as an isolated thinker. The purely logical thinker is disturbed by a contradiction. He demands clear concepts that can exist side by side. One concept must not interfere with another. The thinker sees himself in a strange situation because he is confronted with reality that is full of contradictions, no matter what he may undertake. The concepts that he can derive from this reality are unsatisfactory to him. They offend his logical sense. This feeling of dissatisfaction becomes the point of departure. Herbart feels that if the reality that is spread out before his senses and before his mind supplies him with contradictory concepts, then it cannot be the true reality for which his thinking is striving. He derives his task from this situation. The contradictory reality is not real being but only appearance. In this view he follows Kant to a certain degree, but while Kant declares true being unattainable to thinking cognition, Herbart believes one penetrates from appearance to being by transforming the contradictory concepts of appearance and changing them into concepts that are free from contradictions. As smoke indicates fire, so appearance points at a form of being as its ground. If, through our logical thinking, we elaborate out of a contradictory world picture given to us by our senses and our mind, one that is not contradictory, then we gain from this uncontradictory world picture what we are looking for. This world picture, to be sure, does not *appear* in this form that is free from contradictions, but it lies behind the apparent one as true reality. Herbart does not set out to comprehend the directly given reality, but creates another reality through which the former is to become explainable. He arrives in this fashion at an abstract thought system that looks rather meager as compared to the rich, full reality. The true reality cannot be a unity, for a unity would have to contain within itself the infinite variety of the real things and events. It must be a plurality of simple entities, eternally equal to themselves, incapable of change and development. Only a simple entity that unchangeably preserves its qualities is free from contradictions. An entity in development is something different in one moment from what it is in another, that is, its qualities are contradictory at various times. The true world is, therefore, a plurality of simple, never-changing entities, and what we perceive are not these simple entities but their relations to one another. These relations have nothing to do with the real being. If one simple entity enters into a relationship with another, the two entities are not changed thereby, but I do perceive the result of their relationship. The reality we perceive directly is a sum of relations between real entities. When one entity abandons its relation to another and replaces it by a relationship with a third entity, something happens without touching the being of the entities themselves. It is this event that we perceive, namely, our apparent contradictory reality. It is interesting to note how Herbart, on the basis of this conception, forms his thoughts concerning the life of the soul. The soul is, as are all other real entities, simple and unchangeable in itself. This entity is now engaged in relations with other beings. The expression of these relations is life in thought-pictures. Everything that happens within us—imagination, feeling, will—is an interplay between the soul and the rest of the world of real entities. Thus, for Herbart, the soul life becomes the appearance of relations into which the simple soul-entity enters with the world. Herbart has a mathematical mind, and his whole world conception is derived fundamentally from mathematical conceptions. A number does not change when it becomes the link of an arithmetical operation. Three remains three, whether it is added to four or subtracted from seven. As the numbers have their place within the mathematical operations, so do the individual entities within the relationships that develop between them. For this reason, psychology becomes an arithmetical operation for Herbart. He attempts to apply mathematics to psychology. How the thought-images condition each other, how they effect one another, what results they produce through their co-existence are things calculated by Herbart. The "ego" is not the spiritual entity that we lay hold of in our self-conciousness, but it is the result of the cooperation of all thought-pictures and thereby also nothing more than a sum, a last expression of relationships. Of the simple entity, which is the basis of our soul life, we know nothing, but its continual relation to other entities is apparent to us. In this play of relations *one* entity is entangled. This condition is expressed by the fact that all these relationships are tending toward a center, and this tendency expresses itself in the thought of the ego.

Herbart is, in another sense than Goethe, Schiller, Schelling, Fichte and Hegel, a representative of the development of modern world conception. Those thinkers attempt a representation of the self-conscious soul in a world picture capable of containing this self-conscious soul as an element. In so doing they become the spokesmen for the spiritual impulse of their age. Herbart is confronted with this impulse and he must admit the feeling that this impulse is there. He attempts to understand it, but in the form of thinking that he imagines to be the correct one, he finds no possibility of penetrating into the life of the self-conscious being of the soul. He remains outside of it. One can see in Herbart's world conception what difficulties man's thinking encounters when it tries to comprehend what it has essentially become in the course of mankind's evolution. Compared to Hegel, Herbart appears like a thinker who strives in vain for an aim at which Hegel believes actually to have arrived. Herbart's thought constructions are an attempt to outline as an external spectator what Hegel means to present through the inner participation of thought. Thinkers like Herbart are also significant for the characterization of the modern form of world conception. They indicate the aim that is to be reached by the very display of their insufficient means for the attainment of this aim. The spiritual aim of the age motivates Herbart's struggle; his intellectual energy is inadequate to understand and to express this struggle sufficiently. The course of the philosophical evolution shows that, besides the thinkers who move on the crest of the time-impulses, there are also always some active ones who form world conceptions through their failure to understand these impulses. Such world conceptions may well be called reactionary.

Herbart reverts to the view of Leibniz. His simple soul entity is unchangeable; it neither grows nor decays. It existed when this apparent life contained within man's ego began, and will again withdraw from these relations when this life ceases to continue independently. Herbart arrives at his conception of God through his world picture, which contains many simple entities that produce the events through their relations. Within these processes we observe purpose-directed order. But the relations could only be accidental and chaotic if the entities, which, according to their own nature, would have nothing in common, were left entirely to themselves. The fact that they are teleologically ordered, therefore, points toward a wise world ruler who directs their relations. "No one is capable of giving a close definition of deity," says Herbart. He condemns "the pretensions of the systems that speak of God as of an object to be comprehended in sharply drawn contours by means of which we would rise to a knowledge for which we are simply denied the data."

Man's actions and artistic creations are completely without foundation in this world picture. All possibility to fit them into this system is lacking. For what could a relationship of simple entities that are completely indifferent to all processes mean to the actions of man? So Herbart is forced to look for independent tools both for ethics and for esthetics. He believes he finds them in human feeling. When man perceives things or events, he can associate the feeling of pleasure or displeasure with them. We are pleased when we see man's will going in a direction that is in agreement with his convictions. When we make the opposite observation, the feeling of displeasure overcomes us. Because of this feeling we call the agreement of conviction and will good; the discord, we call morally reprehensible. A feeling of this kind can be attached only to a *relationship* between moral elements. The will as such is morally indifferent, as is also the conviction.

Only when the two *meet* does ethical pleasure or displeasure emerge. Herbart calls a relation of moral elements a practical idea. He enumerates five such practical-ethical ideas: The idea of moral freedom, consisting of the agreement of will and moral conviction; the idea of perfection that has its basis in the fact that the strong pleases rather than the weak; the idea of right, which springs from displeasure with antagonism; the idea of benevolence, which expresses the pleasure that one feels as one furthers the will of another person; the idea of retribution, which demands that all good and evil that has originated in a person is to be compensated again in the same person.

Herbart bases his ethics on a human feeling, on moral sentiment. He separates it from the world conception that has to do with *what is*, and transforms it into a number of postulates of what *should be*. He combines it with esthetics and, indeed, makes it a part of them. For the science of esthetics also contains postulates concerning what is to be. It, too, deals with relations that are associated with feelings. The individual color leaves us esthetically indifferent. When one color is joined to another, this combination can be either satisfactory or displeasing to us. What pleases in a combination is beautiful; what displeases, is ugly. *Robert Zimmermann* (1824–1898) has ingeniously constructed a science of art on these principles. Only a part of it, the part that considers those relations of beauty that are concerned with the realm of action, is to be the ethics or the science of the good. The significant writings of Robert Zimmermann in the field of esthetics (science of art) show that even attempts at philosophical formulations that do not reach the summit of cultural impulses of a time can produce important stimulations for the development of the spirit.

Because of his mathematically inclined mind, Herbart successfully investigated those processes of human soul life that really do go on with a certain regularity in the same way with all human beings. These processes will, of course, not prove to be the more intimate and individually characteristic ones. What is original and characteristic in each personality will be overlooked by such a mathematical intellect, but a person of such a mentality will obtain a certain insight into the average processes of the mind and, at the same time, through his sure skill in handling the arithmetical calculations, will control the measurement of the mental development. As the laws of mechanics enable us to develop technical skills, so the laws of the psychological processes make it possible for us to devise a technique in education for the development of mental abilities. For this reason, Herbart's work has become fruitful in the field of pedagogy. He has found many followers among pedagogues, but not among them alone. This seems at first sight hard to understand with regard to a world conception offering a picture of meager, colorless generalities, but it can be explained from the fact that it is just the people who feel a certain need for a world conception who are easily attracted by such general concepts that are rigidly linked together like terms of an arithmetical operation. It is something fascinating to experience how one thought is linked to the next as if it were through a self-operative mechanical process, because this process awakens in the observer a feeling of security. The mathematical sciences are so highly appreciated because of this assurance. They unfold their structure, so to speak, through their own force. They only have to be supplied with the thought material and everything else can be left to their logical necessity, which works automatically. In the progress of Hegel's thinking, which is saturated with reality, the thinker continually has to take the initiative. There is more warmth, more direct life in this mode of thinking, but it also requires the constant support of the soul forces. This is because it is reality in this case that the thinker catches in his thoughts, an ever-flowing reality that at every point shows its individual character and fights against every logical rigidity. Hegel also had a great number of pupils and followers, but they were much less faithful than those of Herbart. As long as Hegel's powerful personality enlivened his thoughts, they exerted their charm, and as long as his words were heard under its spell, they carried great conviction. After Hegel's death many of his pupils went their own paths. This is only natural, for whoever is self-dependent will also shape his own attitude toward reality in his own fashion. We observe a different process with Herbart's pupils. They elaborate the master's doctrine, but they continue the fundamental stock of his thoughts without change. A thinker who finds his way into Hegel's mode of thinking penetrates into the course of the world's development that is manifested in innumerable evolutionary phases. The individual thinker, of course, can be stimulated to follow this course of evolution, but he is free to shape the various stages according to his own individual mode of conception. In Herbart's case, however, we deal with a firmly constructed thought system that commands confidence through the solidity of its structure. One may reject it, but if one accepts it, one will have to accept it in its original form. For the individual personal element, which challenges and forces us to face the self of another thinker with our own self, is lacking here.

* * *

"Life is a miserable affair; I have decided to spend mine by thinking about it." *Arthur Schopenhauer* (1788–1861) spoke these words in a conversation with Wieland at the beginning of his university years, and his world conception sprang from this mood. Schopenhauer had experienced personal hardship and had observed the sad lives of others when he decided upon concentrating on philosophical thought as a new aim of life. The sudden death of his father, caused by a fall from a storehouse, his bad experiences in his career as a merchant, the sight of scenes of human miseries that he witnessed as a young man while travelling, and many other things of similar kind had produced in him the wish, not so much to know the world, but rather to procure for himself a means to endure it through contemplation. He needed a world conception in order to calm his gloomy disposition. When he began his university studies, the thoughts that Kant, Fichte and Schelling introduced to the German philosophical life were in full swing. Hegel's star was just then rising. In 1806 he had published his first larger work, *The Phenomenology of the Spirit.* In Goettingen, Schopenhauer heard the teachings of *Gottlob Ernst Schulze*, the author of the book, *Aenesidemus*, who was, to be sure, in a certain respect an opponent of Kant, but who nevertheless drew the student's attention to Kant and Plato as the two great spirits toward whom he would have to look. With fiery enthusiasm Schopenhauer plunged into Kant's mode of conception. He called the revolution that his study caused in his head a spiritual rebirth. He found it even more satisfactory because he considered it to be in agreement with the views of Plato, the other philosopher Schulze had pointed out to him.

Plato had said, "As long as we approach the things and events merely through sensual perceptions, we are like men who are chained in a dark cave in such a way that they cannot turn their heads; therefore, they can only see, by means of the light of a fire burning behind them, the shadows upon the opposite wall, the shadows of real things that are carried between the fire and their backs, the shadows of each other and of themselves. These shadows are to the real things what the things of sensual perception are to the *ideas,* which are the true reality. The things of the sensually perceptible world come into existence and pass again, the ideas are eternal."

Did not Kant teach this, too? Is not the perceptible world only a world of appearances for him also? To be sure, the sage from Koenigsberg did not attribute this eternal reality to the ideas, but with respect to the perception of the reality spread out in space and time, Schopenhauer thought Plato and Kant to be in complete agreement. Soon he also accepted this view as an irrevocable truth. He argued, "I have a knowledge of the things insofar as I see, hear, feel them, etc., that is to say, insofar as I have them as a thought picture in my mind's eye. An object then can be there for me *only by being represented to my mind as a thought image.* Heaven, earth, etc., are therefore *my mind's imaginations,* for the "thing in itself" that corresponds to them has become my mind's object only by taking on the character of a thought representation."

Although Schopenhauer found everything that Kant stated concerning the subjective character of the world of perception absolutely correct, he was not at all satisfied with regard to

Kant's remarks concerning the thing in itself. Schulze had also been an opponent of Kant's view in this respect. How can we know anything at all of a "thing in itself"? How can we even express a word about it if our knowledge is completely limited to *thought pictures of our mind,* if the "thing in itself" lies completely outside their realm? Schopenhauer had to search for another path in order to come to the "thing in itself." In his search he was influenced by the contemporary world conceptions more than he ever admitted. The element that Schopenhauer added to the conviction that he had from Kant and Plato as the "thing in itself," we find also in Fichte, whose lectures he had heard in 1811 in Berlin. We also find this element in Schelling. Schopenhauer could hear the most mature form of Fichte's views in Berlin. This last form is preserved in Fichte's posthumous works. Fichte declared with great emphasis, while Schopenhauer, according to his own admission, "listened attentively," that all being has its last roots in a *universal will.* As soon as man discovers will in himself, he gains the conviction that there is a world independent of himself as an individual. Will is not a knowledge of the individual but a form of real *being.* Fichte could also have called his world conception, *The World as Knowledge and Will.* In Schelling's book, *Concerning the Nature of Human Freedom and Matters Connected with This Problem,* we actually find the sentences, "In the last and deepest analysis there is no other being than *will.* Will is fundamental being and will alone can claim all its predicates: To be without cause, eternal, independent of time, self-assertive. All philosophy is striving for just this aim, to find this highest expression."

That will is fundamental being becomes Schopenhauer's view also. When knowledge is extinguished, will remains, for will also precedes knowledge. "Knowledge has its origin in my brain," says Schopenhauer, "but my brain must have been produced through an active, creative force. Man is aware of such a creative energy in his own will." Schopenhauer now attempts to prove that what is active in all other things is also *will.* The will, therefore, is, as the "thing in itself," at the root of all reality that is merely *represented* in the thought pictures of our mental life, and we can have a knowledge of this "thing in itself." It is not, as Kant's "thing in itself," beyond our perceptive imagination but we experience its actuality within our own organism.

The development of modern world conception is progressive in Schopenhauer insofar as he is the first thinker to make the attempt to elevate *one* of the fundamental forces of the self-consciousness to the general principle of the world. The active self-consciousness contains the riddle of the age. Schopenhauer is incapable of finding a world picture that contains the *roots* of self-consciousness. Fichte, Schelling and Hegel had attempted to do that. Schopenhauer takes *one* force of the self-consciousness, *will*, and claims that this element is not merely in the human soul but in the whole world. Thus, for him, man is not rooted with his full self-consciousness in the world's foundation, but at least with a part of it, with his will. Schopenhauer thus shows himself to be one of those representatives of the evolution of modern world conception who can only partially encompass the fundamental riddle of the time within their consciousness.

Goethe also had a profound influence on Schopenhauer. From the autumn of 1813 until the following spring, the young Schopenhauer enjoyed the company of the poet. Goethe introduced him personally to his doctrine of colors. Goethe's mode of conception agreed completely with the view that Schopenhauer had developed concerning the behavior of our sense organs and our mind in the process of perception of things and events. Goethe had undertaken careful and intensive investigations concerning the perceptions of the eye and phenomena of light and colors, and had elaborated their results in his work, *Concerning the Doctrine of Colors*. He had arrived at results that differed from those of Newton, the founder of the modern theory of color. The antagonism that exists in this field between Newton and Goethe cannot be judged properly if one does not start by pointing to the difference between the world conceptions of these two personalities. Goethe considered the sense organs of man as the highest physical apparatuses. For the world of colors, he therefore had to estimate the eye as his highest judge for the observation of law-determined connections. Newton and the physicists investigated the phenomena that are pertinent to this question in a fashion that Goethe called "the greatest misfortune of modern physics," and that consisted in the fact that the experiments have been separated, as it were, from man.

> One wants to know nature only according to the indications of artificial instruments and thereby even intends to limit and to prove what nature is capable of.

The eye perceives light and darkness and, within the light-dark field of observation, the colors. Goethe takes his stand within this field and attempts to prove how light, darkness and the colors are connected. Newton and his followers meant to observe the processes of light and colors as they would go on if there were no human eye. But the stipulation of such an external sphere is, according to Goethe's world conception, without justification. We do not obtain an insight into the nature of a thing by disregarding the effects we observe, but this nature is given to us through the mind's exact observation of the regularity of these effects. The effects that the eye perceives, taken in their totality and represented according to the law of their connection *are* the essence of the phenomena of light and color, not a separated world of external processes that are to be determined by means of artificial instruments.

> It is really of no avail that we attempt to express directly the nature of a thing. What we are aware of are effects, *and a complete account of these effects might possibly encompass the essence of that thing.* Vainly do we endeavor to describe the character of a man; we put his deeds and actions together, however, and a picture of his character arises before our eyes. Colors are the actions of light; they are what light does and suffers. In this sense we can expect information from them concerning the nature of light. Color and light are indeed in close relation but we must think of them both as belonging to nature as a whole; *for it is nature as a whole that is ready to manifest itself in special ways to the sense of the eye.*

Here we find Goethe's world view applied to a special case. In the human organism, through its senses, through the soul of man, there is revealed what is concealed in the rest of nature. In man, nature reaches its climax. Whoever, therefore, like Newton, looks for the truth of nature outside man, will not find it, according to Goethe's fundamental conviction.

Schopenhauer sees in the world that the mind perceives in space and time only an idea of this mind. The essence of this world of thought pictures is revealed to us in our will, by which we see our own organism permeated. Schopenhauer, therefore, cannot agree with a physical doctrine that sees the nature of light, not in the mental content of the eye, but in a world that is supposed to exist separated from the eye. Goethe's mode of conception was, for this reason, more agreeable to Schopenhauer because Goethe did not go beyond the world of the perceptual content of the eye. He considered Goethe's view to be a confirmation of his own opinion concerning this world. The antagonism between Goethe and Newton is not merely a question of physics but concerns the world conception as a whole. Whoever is of the opinion that a valid statement about nature can be arrived at through experiments that can be detached from the human being must take his stand with Newton's theory of color and remain on that ground. Modern physics is of this opinion. It can only agree with the judgment concerning Goethe's theory of colors that Helmholtz expressed in his essay, *Goethe's Anticipations of Future Ideas in Natural Science*:

> Wherever it is a question of problems that can be solved through poetic divination producing imaginative pictures, the poet has shown himself capable of the most excellent work; wherever only a consciously applied inductive method could have helped, Goethe has failed.

If one sees in the pictures of human imagination only products that are added to an already complete nature, then it is of course necessary to determine what goes on in nature apart from these pictures. But if one sees in them manifestations of the essence contained in nature as Goethe did, then one will consult them in investigating the truth. Schopenhauer, to be sure, shares neither the first nor the second standpoint. He is not at all ready to recognize sense perceptions as containing the essence of things. He rejects the method of modern physics because physics does not limit itself to the element that alone is directly given, namely, that of perceptions as mental pictures. But Schopenhauer also transformed this question from a problem of physics into one of world conception. As he also begins his world conception with man and not with an external world apart from man, he had to side with Goethe, who had consistently drawn the conclusion for the theory of colors that necessarily follows if one sees in man with his healthy sense organs "the greatest and most exact physical apparatus." Hegel, who as a philosopher stands completely on this foundation, had for this reason forcefully defended Goethe's theory of colors. He says in his *Philosophy of Nature*:

> For the description of the color phenomenon that is adequate to its concept, we are indebted to Goethe, who was attracted early by the phenomena of color and light and who was drawn to their contemplation especially in painting; his pure and simple sense of nature had to revolt against such barbarism of reflected thought as is found in Newton. Goethe took up everything about light and color that had been stated and experimentally demonstrated since Plato. He conceived the phenomenon as simple, and the truest instinct of reason does consist in the ability of approaching a phenomenon from that side that allows its simplest representation.

For Schopenhauer, the essential ground for all world processes is the *will*. It is an eternal dark urge for existence. It contains no reason because reason comes into existence only in the human brain, which in turn is created by the will. Hegel sees the spirit as the root of the world in self-conscious reason, and in human reason, only as individual realization of the general world reason. Schopenhauer, by contrast, recognizes reason only as a product of the brain, as a mere bubble that comes into being at the end of the process in which will, the unreasoning blind urge, has created everything else first. In Hegel, all things and processes are permeated by reason; in Schopenhauer, everything is without reason, for everything is the product of the will without reason. The personality of Schopenhauer exemplifies unequivocally a statement of Fichte, "The kind of world conception a man chooses depends on the kind of man he is."

Schopenhauer had bad experiences and had become acquainted with the worst side of the world before he decided to spend his life in contemplation of it. It is for this reason that he is satisfied to depict the world as essentially deprived of reason as a result of blind will. Reason, according to his mode of thinking, has no power over un-reason, for it is itself the result of un-reason; it is illusion and dream, produced out of will. Schopenhauer's world conception is the dark, melancholy mood of his soul translated into thought. His eye was not prepared to follow the manifestations of reason in the world with pleasure. This eye saw only un-reason that was manifest in sorrow and pain. Thus, his doctrine of ethics could only be based on the observation of suffering. An action is moral only if it has its foundation in such an observation. *Sympathy, pity,* must be the source of human actions. What better course could be taken by a man who has gained the insight that all beings suffer than to let his actions be guided by pity. As everything unreasonable and evil has its roots in will, man will stand morally the higher the more he mortifies his unruly will in himself. The manifestation of this will in the individual person is selfishness, egotism. Whoever surrenders to pity and thereby wills not for himself but for others, has become master of the will.

One method of freeing oneself from the will consists in surrendering to artistic creations and to the impressions that are derived from works of art. The artist does not produce to satisfy a desire for something; he does not produce his works because of a will that is selfishly directed toward things and events. His production proceeds out of unegotistic joy. He plunges into the essence of things in pure contemplation. This is also true of the enjoyment of art. As long as we approach a work of art with the desire stirring in us to own it, we are still entangled in the lower appetites of the will. Only when we admire beauty without desiring it have we raised ourselves to the lofty stage where we no longer are dependent on the blind force of will. Then art has become for us a means to free ourselves for the moment from the unreasoning force of the blind will to exist. The deliverance takes place in its purest form in the enjoyment of the *musical work of art,* for music does not speak to us through the medium of representative imagination as do the other arts. Music copies nothing in nature. As all things and events are only mental pictures, so also the arts that take these things as models can only make impressions on us as manifestations of imaginations. Man produces tone out of himself without a natural model. Because man has will as his own essence within himself, it can only be the will through which the world of music is directly released. It is for this reason that music so deeply moves the human soul. It does this because music is the manifestation of man's inner nature, his true being, his will, and it is a triumph of man that he is in possession of an art in which he enjoys selflessly, freed from the fetters of the will, what is the root of all desire, of all unreason. This view of Schopenhauer concerning music is again the result of his most personal nature. Even before his university years, when he was apprenticed to a merchant in Hamburg, he wrote to his mother:

> How did the heavenly seed find a place on the hard ground on which necessity and poverty struggle for every little spot? We have been banished from the primordial spirit and are not to reach up to him. Yet, a pitiful angel has begged the heavenly flower for us and it blossoms in full glory rooted in this soil of misery. The pulsations of the *divine art of music* have not ceased to beat through the centuries of barbarism, and a *direct resonance of the eternal* is preserved in this art for us, understandable to every soul and exalted above even vice and virtue.

From the attitude that is taken toward art by the two antipodes of world conception, Hegel and Schopenhauer, one can learn how a world conception deeply affects the personal relation of man toward the various realms of life. Hegel, who saw in man's world of conceptions and ideas the climax toward which all external nature strives as its perfection, can recognize as the most perfect art only the one in which the spirit appears in its most perfect form, and in which this spirit at the same time clings to the element that continuously strives toward the spirit. Every formation of external nature *tends* to be spirit, but it does not reach this aim. When a man now creates such an external spatial form, endowing it as an artist with the spirit for which material itself strives without being capable of reaching it, then he has produced a perfect work of art. This is the case in the art of *sculpture*. What otherwise appears only in the inward life of the soul as formless spirit, as idea, is shaped by the artist out of matter. The soul, the inner life that we perceive in our consciousness as being without shape, is what speaks out of a statue, out of a formation of space. This marriage of the sensual world with the world of the spirit represents the artistic ideal of a world conception that sees the purpose of nature in the creation of the spirit, and therefore can also recognize the beautiful only in a work that appears as immediate expression of the spirit emerging in the form of nature. Whoever, like Schopenhauer, however, sees in all nature only mental pictures, cannot possibly recognize the ideal of art in a work that imitates nature. He must choose an art as his ideal that is free of all nature, that is to say, *music*.

Schopenhauer considered everything that leads toward the extirpation, the mortification of the will quite consistently as desirable, for an extirpation of the will means an extinction of the unreasonable in the world. Man is to give up will. He is to kill all desire within himself. *Asceticism* is, for this reason, Schopenhauer's moral ideal. The wise man will extinguish within himself all wishes; he will annihilate his will completely. He will reach the point where no motivation forces him to exert his will. All striving consists merely in *quietistic* yearning for deliverance from all life. In the world-renouncing life-views in Buddhism,

Schopenhauer acknowledged a doctrine of profound wisdom. Compared to Hegel's, one can thus call Schopenhauer's world view reactionary. Hegel attempted everywhere to affect a reconciliation of man with life; he always strove to present all action as a cooperation with a reason-directed order of the world. Schopenhauer regarded enmity to life, withdrawal from reality and world flight as the ideal of the wise man.

* * *

Hegel's mode of world and life conception contains an element that can produce doubts and questions. Hegel's point of departure is pure thinking, the abstract idea, which he himself once called "an oysterlike, gray or entirely black" being (in a letter to Goethe on February 20, 1821), of which he maintained at the same time should be considered the "representation of God as he is in his eternal essence before the creation of nature and a finite spirit." The aim that he reaches is the individual human spirit endowed with a content of its own, through whom first comes to light what led only a shadow-like existence in a gray, oyster-like element. This can easily be understood to mean that a *personality* as a living self-conscious being does not exist outside the human spirit. Hegel derives the content-saturated element that we *experience* within ourselves from the ideal element that we *obtain through thinking*. It is quite comprehensible that a spirit of a certain inner disposition felt repulsed by this view of world and life. Only thinkers of such a selfless devotion as that of *Karl Rosenkranz* (1805–1879) could so completely find their way into Hegel's movement of thought and, in such perfect agreement with Hegel, create for themselves structures of ideas that appear like a rebirth of Hegel's own thought structure in a less impressive medium. Others could not understand how man is to be enlightened through pure idea with respect to the infinity and variety of the impressions that pour in on him as he directs his observations toward nature, crowded as it is with colors and forms, and how he is to profit if he lifts his soul from experiences in the world of sensation, feeling and perception-guided imagination to the frosty heights of pure thought. To interpret Hegel in this fashion is to misunderstand him, but it is quite comprehensible that he should have been misunderstood in this way.

This mood that was dissatisfied with Hegel's mode of thinking found expression in the current thought that had representatives in *Franz Xaver von Baader* (1765–1841), *Karl Christian Friedrich Krause* (1781–1832), *Immanuel Hermann Fichte* (1797–1879), *Christian Hermann Weisse* (1801–1866), *Anthon Guenther* (1783–1863), *Karl Friedrich Eusebius Thrahndorff (1782–1863) Martin Deutinger* (1815–1864), and *Hermann Ulrici* (1806–1884). They attempted to replace the gray, oyster-like pure thought of Hegel by a life-filled, personal, primal entity, an individual God. Baader called it an "atheistic conception" to believe that God attained a perfect existence only in man. God must be a personality and the world must not, as Hegel thought, proceed from him like a logical process in which one concept always necessarily produces the next. On the contrary, the world must be God's free creation, the product of his almighty will. These thinkers approach the Christian doctrine of revelation. To justify and fortify this doctrine scientifically becomes the more-or-less conscious purpose of their thinking. Baader plunged into the mysticism of *Jakob Boehme* (1757–1624), *Meister Eckhart* (1250–1329), *Tauler* (1290–1361) and *Paracelsus* (1494–1541), whose language, so rich in pictures, he considered a much more appropriate means to express the most profound truths than the pure thoughts of Hegel's doctrine. That Baader also caused Schelling to enrich his thoughts with a deeper and warmer content through the assimilations of conceptions from Jakob Boehme has already been mentioned.

In the course of the development of the modern world conception personalities like Krause will always be remarkable. He was a mathematician who allowed himself to be swayed by the proud, logically perfect character of this science, and attempted a solution of the problems of world conception after the model of the method he was used to as a mathematician. Typical of this kind of thinker is the great mathematician, Newton, who treated the phenomena of the visible universe as if it were an arithmetical problem but, at the same time, satisfied his own need concerning the fundamental questions of world conception in a fashion that approached the belief to be found in revealed religion. Krause finds it impossible to accept a conception that seeks the primal being of the world *in* the things and processes. Whoever, like Hegel, looks for God in the world cannot find him, for the world, to be sure, is in God, but God is not in the world. He is a self-dependent being resting within himself in blissful serenity. Krause's world of ideas rests on "thoughts of an infinite, self-dependent being, outside of which there is nothing; this being comprises everything by itself and in itself as the *one* ground, and that we have to think of as the ground of reason, nature and humanity." He does not want to have anything in common with a view "that takes the finite or the world as the sum total of everything finite to be God itself, idolizing and confusing it with God." No matter how deep one may penetrate into the reality given to the senses and the mind, one will never arrive in this way at the fundamental ground of all being. To obtain a conception of this being is possible only if one accompanies all finite observation with a divinatory vision of an over-worldly reality.

Immanuel Hermann Fichte settled his account with Hegelianism poignantly in his essay, *Propositions for the Prolegomena of Theology* (1826), and *Contributions Toward a Characterization of Modern Philosophy* (1829). Then, in numerous works, he tried to prove and elaborate his view that a conscious personal being must be recognized as the basis of all world phenomena. In order to procure an emphatic effect for the opposition to Hegel's conception, which proceeded from pure thought, Immanuel Hermann Fichte joined hands with friends who were of the same opinion. In 1837, together with Weisse, Sengler, K. Ph. Fischer, Chalybaeus, Fr. Hoffmann, Ulrici, Wirth and others, he began the publication of the *Journal for Philosophy and Speculative Theology*. It is Fichte's conviction that we have risen to the highest knowledge only if we have understood that "the highest thought that truly solves the world problem is the idea of a primal subject or *absolute personality,* which knows and fathoms itself in its ideal as well as real infinity."

> The world creation and preservation that comprises the *world reality,* consists solely in the uninterrupted consciousness-permeated will-direction of God, such that he is only consciousness and will, but both in a highest union, therefore, only *person,* or person in the most eminent sense of the word.

Chr. Hermann Weisse believed that it was necessary to proceed from Hegel's world conception to a completely theological mode of conception. In the Christian idea of the three personalities in the *one* deity, he saw the aim of his thinking. He attempted to represent this idea as the result of a natural and unsophisticated common sense and did so with an uncommon array of ingenuity. In his triune, Weisse believed that in a personal deity possessing a living will he had something *infinitely richer* than Hegel with his gray idea. This living will is to "give to the inner godly nature with one breath the one definite form and no other that is implied at all places in the Holy Writ of the Old and New Testaments. In it, God is shown prior to the creation of the world as well as during and after that event in the shining element of his glory as surrounded by an interminable heavenly host of serving spirits in a fluid immaterial body, which enables him to fully communicate with the created world."

Anton Guenther, the "Viennese Philosopher," and Martin Deutinger, who was under his influence, move with the thoughts of their world conception completely within the framework of the catholic theological mode of conception. Guenther attempts to free man from the natural world order by dividing him into two parts—a natural being that belongs to the world of necessary law, and a spirit being that constitutes a self-dependent part of a higher spirit world and has an existence comparable to an "entity" as described by Herbart. He believes that he overcomes Hegelianism in this manner and that he supplies the foundation for a Christian world conception. The Church itself was not of this opinion, for in Rome Guenther's writings were included in the Prohibitory Index. Deutinger fought vehemently against Hegel's "pure thinking," which, in his opinion, ought to be prevented from devouring life-filled reality. He ranks the living will higher than pure thought. It can, as creative will, produce something; thought is powerless and abstract. Thrahndorff also takes living will as his point of departure. The world cannot be explained from the shadowy realm of ideas, but a vigorous will must seize these ideas in order to create real being. The world's deepest content does not unfold itself to man in thoughtful comprehension, but in an emotional reaction, in *love* through which the individual surrenders to the world, to the will that rules in the universe. It is quite apparent that all these thinkers endeavor to overcome thinking and its object, the pure idea. They are unwilling to acknowledge thinking as the highest manifestation of the spirit of man. In order to comprehend the ultimate substance of the world, Thrahndorff wants to approach it, not with the power of *knowledge, but of love*. It is to become an object of emotion, not of reason. It is the belief of these philosophers that through clear, pure thinking the ardent, religious devotion to the primordial forces of existence are destroyed.

This opinion has its root in a misconception of Hegel's thought world. Its misunderstanding becomes especially apparent in the views concerning Hegel's attitude toward religion that spread after his death. The lack of clarity that began to prevail regarding this attitude resulted in a split among Hegel's followers into one party that considered his world conception to be a firm pillar of revealed Christianity, and another that used his doctrine to dissolve the Christian conceptions and to replace them by a radically liberal view.

Neither party could have based its opinion on Hegel if they had understood him correctly, for Hegel's world conception contains nothing that can be used for support of a religion or for its destruction. He had meant to do this with respect to any religion as little as he had intended to create any natural phenomena through his pure thought. As he had set out to extract the pure thought from the processes of nature in order to comprehend them in that way, so he had also, in the case of religion, merely the intention to bring its thought content to the surface. As he considered everything that is real in the world as reasonable just because it is real, so he held this view also in regard to religion. It must come into existence by soul forces quite beyond those that are at the disposal of the thinker when he approaches them in order to comprehend them.

It was also an error of such thinkers as Fichte, Weisse, Deutinger and others that they fought against Hegel because he had not proceeded from the realm of pure thought to the religious experience of the personal deity. Hegel had never set himself a task of this kind. He considered that to be the task of the religious consciousness. The younger Fichte, Weisse, Krause, Deutinger and the rest wanted to *create* a new religion through their world conception. Hegel would have considered such a task to be as absurd as the wish to illuminate the world through the *idea* of light, or to create a magnet out of the thought of magnetism. To be sure, in Hegel's opinion, religion has its root in the idea, just as the whole world of nature and the spirit. For this reason, it is possible that the human spirit can rediscover this idea in religion, but as the magnet was created out of the thought of magnetism *before* the human mind came into being, and as the latter only afterwards has to *comprehend* the magnet's creation, so also religion has become what it is before its thought emerged in the human soul as an illuminating part of world conception. If Hegel had lived to experience the religious criticism of his pupils, he would have felt compelled to say, "Take your hands off all foundation of religion, off all *creation* of religious conceptions, as long as you want to remain thinkers and do not intend to become messiahs." The world conception of Hegel, if it is correctly understood, cannot have a retroactive effect on the religious consciousness. The philosopher who reflects on the realm of art has the same relation to his object as the thinker who wants to fathom the nature of religion.

* * *

The *Halle Yearbooks,* published from 1838 to 1843 by Arnold Ruge and Theodor Echtermeyer, served as a forum for the philosophical controversies of the time. Starting with a defense and explanation of Hegel, they soon proceeded to develop his ideas independently, and thus made the transition to the views that are called "radical world conceptions" in the next chapter. After 1841, the editors called their journal, *The German Yearbook*, and, as one of their aims, they considered "the fight against political illiberality, against theories of feudalism and landed property." In the historical development of the time they became active as radical politicians, demanding a state in which perfect freedom prevails. Thus, they abandoned the spirit of Hegel, who wanted to understand history, not to make it.

CHAPTER IX

The Radical World Conceptions

At the beginning of the forties of the last century a man who had previously thoroughly and intimately penetrated the world conceptions of Hegel, now forcefully attacked them. This man was *Ludwig Feuerbach* (1804–1872). The declaration of war against the philosophy in which he had grown up is given in a radical form in his essay, *Preliminary Theses for the Reformation of Philosophy* (1842), and *Principle of the Philosophy of the Future* (1843). The further development of his thoughts can be followed in his other writings, *The Essence of Christianity* (1841), *The Nature of Religion* (1845), and *Theogony* (1857).

In the activity of Ludwig Feuerbach a process is repeated in the field of the science of the spirit that had happened almost a century earlier (1759) in the realm of natural science through the activity of *Caspar Friedrich Wolff*. Wolff's work had meant a reform of the idea of evolution in the field of biology. How the idea of evolution was understood before Wolff can be most distinctly learned from the views of *Albrecht von Haller*, a man who opposed the reform of this conception most vehemently. Haller, who is quite rightly respected by physiologists as one of the most significant spirits of this science, could not conceive the development of a living being in any other form than that in which the germ already contains all parts that appear in the course of life, but on a small scale and perfectly preformed. Evolution, then, is supposed to be an unfolding of something that was there in the first place but was hidden from perception because of its smallness, or for other reasons. If this view is consistently upheld, there is no development of anything new. What happens is merely that something that is concealed, encased, is continuously brought to the light of day. Haller stood quite rigorously for this view. In the first mother, Eve, the whole human race was contained, concealed on a small scale. The human germs have only been unfolded in the course of world history. The same conception is also expressed by the philosopher Leibniz (1646–1716):

> So I should think that the souls, which some day will be human souls, have been in the seed stage, as it is also with those of other species; that they have existed in the form of organized things in our forefathers as far back as Adam, that is to say, since the beginning of things.

Wolff opposed this idea of evolution with one of his own in *Theoria Generationis*, which appeared in 1759. He proceeded from the supposition that the members of an organism that appear in the course of life have not existed previously but come into being at the moment they become perceptible as real new formations. Wolff showed that the egg contains nothing of the form of the developed organism but that its development constitutes a series of new formations. This view made the conception of a real *becoming* possible, for it showed how something comes into being that had not previously existed and that therefore "comes to be" in the true sense of the word.

Haller's view really denies *becoming* as it admits only a continuous process of *becoming visible* of something that had previously existed. This scientist had opposed the idea of Wolff with the peremptory decree, "There is no becoming" (*Nulla est epigenesis*). He had, thereby, actually brought about a situation in which Wolff's view remained unconsidered for decades.

Goethe blames this encasement theory for the resistance with which his endeavors to explain living beings was met. He had attempted to comprehend the formations in organic nature through the study of the process of their development, which he understood entirely in the sense of a true evolution, according to which the newly appearing parts of an organism have not already had a previously concealed existence, but do indeed *come into being* when they appear. He writes in 1817 that this attempt, which was a fundamental pre-supposition of his essay on the metamorphosis of plants written in 1790, "was received in a cold, almost hostile manner, but such reluctance was quite natural. The *encasement theory,* the concept of preformation, of a successive development of what had existed since Adam's times, had in general taken possession even of the best minds."

One could see a remnant of the old encasement theory even in Hegel's world conception. The pure thought that appears in the human mind was to have been encased in all phenomena before it came to its perceptible form of existence in man. Before nature and the individual spirit, Hegel places his pure thought that should be, as it were, "the representation of God as he was according to his eternal essence before the creation" of the world. The development of the world is, therefore, presented as an unwrapping of pure thought. The protest of Ludwig Feuerbach against Hegel's world conception was caused by the fact that Feuerbach was unable to acknowledge the existence of the spirit *before* its real appearance in man, just as Caspar Friedrich Wolff had been unable to admit that the parts of the living organism should have been preformed in the egg. Just as Wolff saw *spontaneous formations* in the organs of the developed organism, so did Feuerbach with respect to the individual spirit of man. This spirit is in no way there before its perceptible existence; it *comes into being* only in the moment it appears. According to Feuerbach, it is unjustified to speak of an all-embracing spirit, of a being in which the individual spirit has its roots. No reason-endowed being exists prior to its appearance in the world that would shape matter and the perceptible world, and in this way cause the appearance of man as its visible after-image. What exists before the development of the human spirit consists of mere matter and blind forces that form a nervous system out of themselves concentrated in the brain. In the brain something *comes into existence* that is a completely *new formation,* something that has never been before: the human soul, endowed with reason. For such a world conception there is no possibility to derive the processes and things from a spiritual originator because, according to this view, a spiritual being is a new formation through the organization of the brain. If man projects a spiritual element into the external world, then he imagines arbitrarily that a being like the one that is the cause of his own actions exists outside of himself and rules the world. Any spiritual primal being must first be created by man through his fantasy; the things and processes of the world give us no reason to assume its original existence. It is not the original spirit being that has created man after his image, but man has formed a fantasy of such a primal entity after his own image. This is Feuerbach's conviction. "Man's knowledge of God is man's knowledge of himself, of his own nature. Only the unity of being and consciousness is truth. Where God's consciousness is, there is also God's being: *it is, therefore, in man*" (*The Essence of Christianity*, 1841). Man does not feel strong enough to rest within himself; he therefore created an infinite being after his own image to revere and to worship. Hegel's world conception had eliminated all other qualities from the supreme being, but it had retained the element of reason. Feuerbach removes this element also and with this step he removes the supreme being itself. He replaces the wisdom of God completely by the wisdom of the world. As a necessary turning point in the development of world conception, Feuerbach declares the "open confession and admission that the consciousness of God is nothing but the consciousness of humanity," and that man is "incapable of thinking, divining, imagining, feeling, believing, willing, loving and worshipping as an absolute divine being any other being *than the human being.*" There is an observation of nature and an observation of the spirit, but there is no observation of the nature of God. Nothing is real but the factual.

> The real in its reality, or as real, is the real as the object of the senses, the *sensual.* Truth, reality and sensuality are identical. Only a sensual being is a true, a real being. Only through the senses is an object given in the true sense of the word, not through thinking by itself. The object that is given in thinking, or identical with it, is only thought.

Indeed, this can be summed up as follows. The phenomenon of thinking appears in the human organism as a new formation, but we are not justified to imagine that this thought had existed before its appearance in any form invisibly encased in the world. One should not attempt to explain the condition of something actually given by deriving it from something that is assumed as previously existing. Only the factual is true and divine, "what is immediately sure of itself, that which directly speaks for and convinces of itself, that which immediately effects the assertion of its existence, what is absolutely decided, incapable of doubt, clear as sunlight. But only the sensual is of such a clarity. Only where the sensual begins does all doubt and quarrel cease. The secret of immediate knowledge is sensuality." Feuerbach's credo has its climax in the words, "To make philosophy the concern of humanity was my first endeavor, but whoever decides upon a path in this direction will finally be led with necessity to *make man the concern of philosophy.*" "The new philosophy makes man, and with him nature as the basis of man, the only universal and ultimate object of philosophy; it makes an anthropology that includes physiology in it—the universal science."

Feuerbach demands that reason is not made the basis of departure at the beginning of a world conception but that it should be considered the product of evolution, as a new formation in the human organism in which it makes its actual appearance. He has an aversion to any separation of the spiritual from the physical because it can be understood in no other way than as a result of the development of the physical.

> When the psychologist says, "I distinguish myself from my body," he says as much as when the philosopher in logic or metaphysics

says, "I leave human nature unconsidered." Is it possible to leave your own nature out of consideration? Are you not doing so as a human being? Do you think without a head? Thoughts are departed souls. All right, but is not even a departed soul still a faithful picture of a human being who was once in the flesh? Do not even the most general metaphysical concepts of being and essence change as the real being and essence of man changes? What does "I leave human nature out of consideration," then mean? Nothing more than this: I leave man unconsidered so far as he is the object of my consciousness and of my thinking, but not the man who lies behind my consciousness; that is to say, not my own nature to which my process of abstraction also is bound whether I like it or not. So, as a psychologist, you may disregard your body, but in your nature you are intimately linked to it, that is, you think yourself as distinguishable from your body but you *are* not at all really different from it because of this thought. . . . Was Lichtenberg not right when he maintained that one really should not say, "I think," but, "It thinks"? If, indeed, the "I think" now distinguishes itself from the body, does that force us to conclude that the process that is expressed in the words, "It thinks," the involuntary element of our thinking, the root and the basis of the "I think," is also distinct from the body? How is it, then, that we cannot think at all times, that the thoughts are not at our disposal whenever we choose? Why do we often fail to make headway with some intellectual work in spite of the greatest exertion of our will until some external occasion, often no more than a change in the weather, sets our thoughts afloat again? *This is caused by the fact that our thought process is also an organic activity.* Why must we often carry some thoughts with us for years before they become clear and distinct to us? *For the reason that our thoughts also are subject to an organic development, that our thoughts also must have their time to mature as well as the fruits in the field or the child in the mother's womb.*

* * *

Feuerbach drew attention to *Georg Christoph Lichtenberg,* a thinker who died in 1799 and who must be considered a precursor of a world conception that found expression in thinkers like Feuerbach. Lichtenberg's stimulating and thought-provoking conceptions were less fruitful for the nineteenth century probably because the powerful thought structures of Fichte, Schelling and Hegel over-shadowed everything. They over-shadowed the spiritual development to such a degree that ideas that were expressed aphoristically as strokes of lightning, even if they were as brilliant as Lichtenberg's, could be overlooked. We only have to be reminded of a few statements of this important person to see that in the thought movement introduced by Feuerbach the spirit of Lichtenberg experiences a revival.

> God created man after his image, which probably means that man created God after his own image.
> Our world is going to be so sophisticated one day that it will be as ridiculous to believe in God as it is nowadays to believe in ghosts.
> Is our concept of God really anything but a personified mystery?
> The conception that we form of a soul is very much like that of a magnet in the earth. It is merely a picture. It is an innate trick in man to think everything in this form.
> Rather than to claim that the world is reflected in us, we should say that our reason is reflected in the world. We just cannot help discovering order and wisdom in the world; it follows from the nature of our thought faculty. But it does not necessarily follow that what we must think should really be so. . . . In this way, then, no God can be proven.
> We become aware of certain conceptions that do not depend on us; then there are others of which we at least think that they depend on us. Where is the boundary line between them? We only know *that* our perceptions, conceptions and thoughts are *there*. *It thinks,* one should say, just as one says, *It rains,* or, *Thought strikes* as one says, *Lightning strikes.*

If Lichtenberg had combined such original flashes of thought with the ability to develop a harmoniously rounded world conception, he could not have remained unnoticed to the degree that he did. In order to form a world conception, it is not only necessary to show superiority of mind, as Lichtenberg did, but also the ability to form ideas in their interconnection in all directions and to round them plastically. This faculty he lacked. His superiority is expressed in an excellent judgment concerning the relation of Kant to his contemporaries:

> I believe that just as the followers of Mr. Kant always charge their opponents with not understanding him, there are also some among them who believe that Mr. Kant must be right because they understand him. His mode of conception is new and different from the usual one, and, if one now suddenly has begun to understand it, one is inclined to accept it as truth, especially since he has so many ardent followers. But one should always consider that this understanding is not as yet a reason to believe it to be true. I believe that most of Kant's followers, overwhelmed by the joy of having understood an abstract and obscurely presented system, were also convinced that this system had been proven.

How akin in spirit Feuerbach could feel to Lichtenberg becomes especially clear if one compares the views of both thinkers with respect to the relation of their world conceptions to practical life. The lectures Feuerbach gave to a number of students during the winter of 1848 on *The Nature of Religion* closed with these words:

> I only wish that I have not failed in the task that I set for myself as I expressed it in the first hours, namely, to convert you from friends of God to friends of men, from believers into thinkers, from praying men to working men, from adherants to a supersensible realm to students of this world, from being Christians, who according to their own confession and admission are half animal and half angel, into human beings, into entirely human beings.

Whoever, like Feuerbach, bases all world conception on the knowledge of nature and man, must also reject all direction and duties in the field of morality that are derived from a realm other than man's natural inclinations and abilities, or that set aims that do not entirely refer to the sensually perceptible world. "My *right* is my lawfully recognized desire for happiness; my *duty* is the desire for happiness of others that I am compelled to recognize." Not in looking with expectation toward a world beyond do I learn what I am to do, but through the contemplation of this one. Whatever energy I spend to fulfill any task that refers to the next world, I have robbed from this world for which I am exclusively meant. "Concentration on *this world*" is, therefore, what Feuerbach demands. We can read similar expressions in Lichtenberg's writings. But just such passages in Lichtenberg are always mixed with elements that show how rarely a thinker who lacks the ability to develop his ideas in himself harmoniously succeeds in following an idea into its last consequences. Lichtenberg does, indeed, demand concentration on this world, but he mixes conceptions that refer to the next even into the formulation of this demand.

> I believe that many people, in their eagerness for an education for heaven, forget the one that is necessary for the earth. *I should think that man would act wisest if he left the former entirely to itself.* For if we have been placed into this position by a wise being, which cannot be doubted, then we should do the best we can and not allow ourselves to be dazzled by revelations. What man needs to know for his happiness he certainly does know without any more revelations than he possesses according to his own nature.

Comparisons like this one between Lichtenberg and Feuerbach are significantly instructive for the historical evolution of man's world conception. They show most distinctly the direction in which these personalities advance because one can learn from them the change that has been wrought by the time interval that lies between them. Feuerbach went through Hegel's philosophy. He derived the strength from this experience to develop his own opposing view. He no longer felt disturbed by Kant's question of whether we are in fact entitled to attribute reality to the world that we perceive, or whether this world merely existed in our minds. Whoever upholds the second possibility can project into the true world behind the perceptual representations all sorts of motivating forces for man's actions. He can admit a supernatural world order as Kant had done. But whoever, like Feuerbach, declares that the sensually perceptible alone is real must reject every supernatural world order. For him there is no categorical imperative that could somehow have its origin in a transcendent world; for him there are only duties that result from the natural drives and aims of man.

To develop a world conception that was as much the opposite of Hegel's as that of Feuerbach, a personality was necessary that was as different from Hegel as was Feuerbach. Hegel felt at home in the midst of the full activity of his contemporary life. To influence the actual life of the world with his philosophical spirit appeared to him a most attractive task. When he asked for his release from his professorship at Heidelberg in order to accept another chair in Prussia, he confessed that he was attracted by the expectation of finding a sphere of activity where he was not entirely limited to mere teaching, but where it would also be possible for him to affect the practical life. "It would be important for him to have the expectation of moving, with advancing age, from the precarious function of teaching philosophy at a university to another activity and to become useful in such a capacity."

A man who has the inclinations and convictions of a thinker must live in peace with the shape that the practical life of his time has taken on. He must find the ideas reasonable by which this life is permeated. Only from such a conviction can he derive the enthusiasm that makes him want to contribute to the consolidation of its structure. Feuerbach was not kindly inclined toward the life of his time. He preferred the restfulness of a secluded place to the bustle of what was for him "modern life." He expresses himself distinctly on this point:

> I shall never, at any rate, be reconciled with the life in the city. To go from time to time into the city to teach there, that I consider, after the impressions I have already stated here, to be good and indeed my duty, but then I must go back again into the solitude of the country to study and rest there in the arms of nature. My next task is to prepare my lectures as my audience wants them, or to prepare my father's papers for print.

From his seclusion Feuerbach believed himself to be best able to judge what was not natural with regard to the shape that the actual human life assumed. To cleanse life from these illusions, and what was carried into it by human illusions, was what Feuerbach considered to be his task. To do this he had to keep his distance from life as much as possible. He searched for the true life but he could not find it in the form that life had taken through the civilization of the time. How sincere he was with his "concentration on this world" is shown by a statement he made concerning the March revolution. This revolution seemed to him a fruitless enterprise because the conceptions that were behind it still contained the old belief in a world beyond.

> The March revolution was a child of the Christian belief, even if it was an illegitimate one. The constitutionalists believed that the Lord only had to say, "Let there be freedom! Let there be right!" and right and freedom would be there. The republicans believed that all they had to do was to *will* a republic to call it to life. They believed, therefore, in the creation of a republic out of *nothing*. The constitutionalists transplanted the idea of the Christian world-miracles to the field of politics; the republicans, that of the Christian miracle of action.

Only a personality who is convinced that he carries within him the harmony of life that man needs can, in the face of the deep hostility that existed between him and the real world, utter the hymns in praise of reality that Feuerbach expressed. Such a conviction rings out of words like these:

> Lacking any expectation for the next world, I can hold myself in this one in the vale of tears of German politics and European political life in general, alive and in mental sanity, only by making the present age into an object of Aristophanic laughter.

Only a personality like this could search for all those forces in man himself that the others wanted to derive from external powers.

The birth of thought in the Greek world conception had had

the effect that man could no longer feel himself as deeply rooted in the world as had been possible with the old consciousness in the form of picture conceptions. This was the first step in the process that led to the formation of an abyss between man and the world. A further stage in this process consisted in the development of the mode of thinking of modern natural science. This development tore nature and the human soul completely apart. On the one side, a nature picture had to arise in which man in his spiritual-psychical essence was not to be found, and on the other, an idea of the human soul from which no bridge led into nature. In nature one found law-ordered necessity. Within its realm there was no place for the elements that the human soul finds within: The impulse for freedom, the sense for a life that is rooted in a spiritual world and is not exhausted within the realm of sensual existence. Philosophers like Kant escaped the dilemma only by separating both worlds completely, finding a knowledge in the one, and in the other, belief. Goethe, Schiller, Fichte, Schelling and Hegel conceived the idea of the self-conscious soul to be so comprehensive that it seemed to have its root in a higher spirit nature. In Feuerbach, a thinker arises who, through the world picture that can be derived from the modern mode of conception of natural science, feels compelled to deprive the human soul of every trait contradictory to the nature picture. He views the human soul as a part of nature. He can only do so because, in his thoughts, he has first removed everything in the soul that disturbed him in his attempt to acknowledge it as a part of nature. Fichte, Schelling and Hegel took the self-conscious soul for what it was; Feuerbach changes it into something he needs for his world picture. In him, a mode of conception makes its appearance that is over-powered by the nature picture. This mode of thinking cannot master both parts of the modern world picture, the picture of nature and that of the soul. For this reason, it leaves one of them, the soul picture, completely unconsidered. Wolff's idea of "new formation" introduces fruitful thought impulses to the nature picture. Feuerbach utilizes these impulses for the spirit-science that can only exist, however, by not admitting the spirit at all. Feuerbach initiates a trend of modern philosophy that is helpless in regard to the most powerful impulse of the modern soul life, namely, man's active self-consciousness. In this current of thought, that impulse is dealt with, not merely as an incomprehensible element, but in a way that avoids the necessity of facing it in its true form, changing it into a factor of nature, which, to an unbiased observation, it really is not.

* * *

"God was my first thought, reason my second and *man* my third and last one." With these words Feuerbach describes the path along which he had gone, from a religious believer to a follower of Hegel's philosophy, and then to his own world conception. Another thinker, who, in 1834, published one of the most influential books of the century, *The Life of Jesus*, could have said the same thing of himself. This thinker was *David Friedrich Strauss* (1808–1874). Feuerbach started with an investigation of the human soul and found that the soul had the tendency to project its own nature into the world and to worship it as a divine primordial being. He attempted a psychological explanation for the genesis of the concept of God. The views of Strauss were caused by a similar aim. Unlike Feuerbach, however, he did not follow the path of the psychologist but that of the historian. He did not, like Feuerbach, choose the concept of God in general in its all-embracing sense for the center of his contemplation, but the Christian concept of the "God incarnate," Jesus. Strauss wanted to show how humanity arrived at this conception in the course of history. That the supreme divine being reveals itself to the human spirit was the conviction of Hegel's world conception. Strauss had accepted this, too. But, in his opinion, the divine idea, in all its perfection, cannot realize itself in an individual human being. The individual person is always merely an imperfect imprint of the divine spirit. What one human being lacks in perfection is presented by another. In examining the whole human race one will find in it, distributed over innumerable individuals, all perfections belonging to the deity. The human race as a whole, then, is God made flesh, God incarnate. This is, according to Strauss, the true thinker's concept of Jesus. With this viewpoint Strauss sets out to criticize the Christian concept of the God incarnate. What, according to this idea, is distributed over the whole human race, Christianity attributes to one personality who is supposed to have existed *once* in the course of history.

> The quality and function, which the doctrine of the Church attributes to Christ, are contradictory to each other if applied to one individual, one God incarnate; *in the idea of the human race,* they harmonize with one another.

Supported by careful investigations concerning the historical foundation of the Gospels, Strauss attempts to prove that the conceptions of Christianity are a result of religious fantasy. Through this faculty the religious truth that the human race is God incarnate was dimly felt, but it was not comprehended in clear concepts but merely expressed in poetic form, in a myth. For Strauss, the story of the Son of God thus becomes a myth in which the idea of humanity was poetically treated long before it was recognized by thinkers in the form of pure thought. Seen from this viewpoint, all miraculous elements of the history of Christianity become explainable without forcing the historian to take refuge in the trivial interpretation that had previously often been accepted. Earlier interpretations had often seen in those miracles intentional deceptions and fraudulent tricks to which either the founder of the religion himself had allegedly resorted in order to achieve the greatest possible effect of his doctrine, or which the apostles were supposed to have invented for this purpose. Another view, which wanted to see all sorts of natural events in the miracles, was also thereby eliminated. The miracles are now seen as the poetic dress for real truths. The story of humanity rising above its finite interests and everyday life to the knowledge of divine truth and reason is represented in the picture of the dying and resurrected saviour. The finite dies to be resurrected as the infinite.

We have to see in the myths of ancient peoples a manifestation of the picture consciousness of primeval times out of which the consciousness of thought experience developed. A feeling for this fact arises in the nineteenth century in a personality like Strauss. He wants to gain an orientation concerning the development and significance of the life of thought by concentrating on the connection of world conception with the mythical thinking of historical times. He wants to know in what way the myth-making imagination still affects modern world conception. At the same time, he aspires to see the human self-consciousness rooted in an entity that lies beyond the individual personality by thinking of all humanity as a manifestation of the deity. In this manner, he gains a support for the individual human soul in the general soul of humanity that unfolds in the course of historical evolution.

Strauss becomes even more radical in his book, *The Christian Doctrine in the Course of Its Historical Development and Its Struggle with Modern Science*, which appeared in the years 1840 and 1841. Here he intends to dissolve the Christian dogmas in their poetic form so as to obtain the thought content of the truths contained in them. He now points out that the modern consciousness is incompatible with the consciousness that clings to the old mythological picture representation of the truth.

> May, then, the believers allow the knowers to go their own way unmolested and vice versa; we do not deprive them of their belief; let them grant us our philosophy, and, if the super-pious should succeed in ejecting us from their church, we shall consider that as a gain. Enough wrong compromises have now been attempted; only the separation of the opposite camps can now lead us ahead.

These views of Strauss produced an enormous uproar. It was deeply resented that those representing the modern world conception were no longer satisfied in attacking only the basic religious conceptions in general, but, equipped with all scientific means of historical research, attempted to eliminate the irrelevancy about which Lichtenberg had once said that it consisted of the fact that "human nature had submitted even to the yoke of a *book*." He continued:

> One cannot imagine anything more horrible, and this example alone shows what a helpless creature man really is *in concreto,* enclosed as he really is in this two-legged vessel of earth, water and salt. If it were ever possible that reason could have a despotic throne erected, a man who seriously wanted to contradict the Copernican system through the authority of a book would have to be hanged. To read in a book that it originates from God is not a proof as yet that it really does. It is certain, however, that our reason has its origin in God no matter in what sense one takes the word God. Reason punishes, where it rules, only through the natural consequences of a transgression or through instruction, if instruction can be called punishment.

Strauss was discharged from his position as a tutor at the Seminary of Tuebingen because of his book, *The Life of Jesus,* and when he then accepted a professorship in theology at the University of Zurich, the peasants came to meet him with threshing flails in order to make the position of the dissolver of the myth impossible and to force his retirement.

Another thinker, *Bruno Bauer* (1809–1882), in his criticism of the old world conception from the standpoint of the new, went far beyond the aim that Strauss had set for himself. He held the same view as Feuerbach, that man's nature is also his supreme being and any other kind of a supreme being is only an illusion created after man's image and set above himself. But Bauer goes further and expresses this opinion in a grotesque form. He describes how he thinks the human ego came to create for itself an illusory counter-image, and he uses expressions that show they are not inspired by the wish for an intimate understanding of the religious consciousness as was the case with Strauss. They have their origin in the pleasure of destruction. Bauer says:

> The all-devouring ego became frightened of itself; it did not dare to consider itself as everything and as the most general power, that is to say, it still kept the form of the religious spirit and thus completed its self-alienation in setting its own general power against itself in fear and trembling for its own preservation and salvation.

Bruno Bauer is a personality who sets out to test his

impetuous thinking critically against everything in existence. That thinking is destined to penetrate to the essence of things is a conviction he adopted from Hegel's world conception, but he does not, like Hegel, tend to let thinking lead to results and a thought structure. His thinking is not productive, but critical. He would have felt a definite thought or a positive idea as a limitation. He is unwilling to limit the power of critical thought by taking his departure from a definite point of view as Hegel had done.

> Critique is, on the one hand, the last act of a definite philosophy, which through this act frees itself from the limitation of a positive determination, still curtailed in its generality. It is, therefore, on the other hand, the presupposition without which philosophy cannot be raised to the last level of generality of the self-consciousness.

This is the credo of the *Critique of World Conception* to which Bruno Bauer confesses. This "critique" does not believe in thoughts and ideas but in thinking alone. "Only now has man been discovered," announces Bauer triumphantly, for now man is bound by nothing except his thinking. It is not human to surrender to a non-human element, but to work everything out in the melting pot of thinking. Man is not to be the after-image of another being, but above all, he is to be "a human being," and he can become human only through his thinking. The thinking man is the true man. Nothing external, neither religion nor right, neither state nor law, etc., can make him into a human being, but only his thinking. The weakness of a thinking that strives to reach the self-consciousness but cannot do so is demonstrated in Bauer.

* * *

Feuerbach had declared the "human being to be man's supreme being; Bruno Bauer maintained that he had discovered it for the first time through his critique of world conception; *Max Stirner* (1806–1856) set himself the task of approaching this *"human being"* completely without bias and without presupposition in his book, *The Only One and His Possession*, which appeared in 1845. This is Stirner's judgment:

> With the power of desperation, Feuerbach grasps at the entire content of Christianity, not in order to throw it away, but, on the contrary, in order to seize it, to draw upon this content for so long and so ardently desired and yet always so remote, with a last effort down from heaven, to have and to hold onto it forever. Is this not the clutch of last despair, a matter of life and death, and is it not at the same time the Christian yearning and passionate desire for the beyond? The hero does not mean to depart into the beyond, but to draw the *beyond* down to himself so that it should turn into *this world*. Has not all the world since then been screaming more or less consciously, "This world is all that matters; heaven must come down to earth and must be felt here already?"

Stirner opposes the view of Feuerbach with his violent contradiction:

> The highest being, to be sure, is man's being, but exactly because it is his *being* and not he, himself, is it a matter of complete indifference whether we contemplate it outside man, considering it as God, or whether we find it in him and call it "the nature of man," or the "human being." I am neither God nor the human being, neither the highest being *nor my own* being, and for this reason, it is fundamentally of no importance whether I think this nature within myself or without. We do, indeed, always think the supreme being in both forms of beyondness, in the inward one as well as in the outward one at the same time, for the "spirit of God" is, according to Christian conception, also "our spirit" and "dwelleth within us." This spirit dwells in heaven and within us. We, poor things, are nothing but his "dwelling place" and if Feuerbach now goes about and destroys his heavenly habitations and forces him bag and baggage to move into us, then we, as his terrestrial quarters, will become very badly overcrowded.

The individual human ego does not consider itself from its own standpoint but from the standpoint of a foreign power. A religious man claims that there is a divine supreme being whose after-image is man. He is possessed by this supreme being. The Hegelian says that there is a general world reason and it realizes itself to reach its climax in the human ego. The ego is therefore possessed by this world reason. Feuerbach maintains that there is a nature of the human being and every particular person is an individualized after-image of this nature. Every individual is thereby *possessed* by the idea of the "nature of humanity." For only the individual man is really existing, not the "generic concept of humanity" by which Feuerbach replaces the divine being. If, then, the individual man places the "genus man" above himself, he abandons himself to an illusion, just as much as when he feels himself dependent on a personal God. For Feuerbach, therefore, the commandments the Christian considers as given by God, and which for this reason he accepts as valid, change into commandments that have their validity because they are in accordance with the general idea of humanity. Man now judges himself morally by asking the question: Do my actions as an individual correspond to what is adequate to the nature of humanity in general? For Feuerbach says:

> If the essence of humanity is man's supreme being, then the highest and first law of his practical life must also be the love of man to man. *Homo homini deus est,* man is God to man. *Ethics is in itself a divine power.* Moral relationships are by themselves truly religious relationships. Life in general is, in its substantial connections, of a thoroughly divine nature. Everything that is right, true and good carries the ground of its salvation in its own qualities. Friendship is and shall be sacred, as shall be property and marriage, and sacred shall be the well-being of every man, but sacred in and for itself.

There are, then, general human powers, and ethics is one of them. It is sacred in and for itself; the individual has to submit to it. The individual is not to will what it decides out of its own initiative, but what follows from the direction of the sacred ethics. The individual is *possessed* by this ethics. Stirner characterizes this view as follows:

The God of all, namely, the human being, has now been elevated to be the God of the individual, for it is the highest aim of all of us to be a human being. As no one can entirely become what the idea of humanity expresses, however, the "human being" remains for every individual a sublime beyond, an unattainable supreme being, a God.

But such a supreme being is also *thinking,* which has been elevated to be God by the critique of world conception. Stirner cannot accept this either.

The critical thinker is afraid of becoming *dogmatic,* or of making positive statements. Of course, he would in doing so become the opposite of a critic, a dogmatist; he would then be as bad as a dogmatist as he is now good as a critic. . . . There must by no means be any dogma! This is his dogma. For the critic stays on the same ground with the dogmatist, namely, on the ground of *thought.* Like the dogmatist, he always proceeds from a thought, but he differs insofar as he abandons the practice of preserving the principal thought in the *process of thinking;* he does not allow this process to become stabilized. He only emphasizes the process of thinking against the belief in thoughts, the process of the former against the stagnation of the latter. No thought is safe against criticism because it is thinking or the thinking spirit itself. . . . I am no antagonist of criticism, that is to say, I am no dogmatist and feel that the teeth of the critic that tear the flesh of the dogmatist do not touch me. If I were a dogmatist, I should place a dogma, a thought, an idea, a principle, at the beginning, and I should begin this process as a systematic thinker by spinning it out into a system that is a thought structure. If, on the other hand, I were a critical thinker, that is, an opponent of the dogmatist, then I should lead the fight of free thinking against the enslaved thought. I should defend thinking against the result of this activity. But I am neither the champion of thought nor of thinking.

Every thought is also produced by the individual ego of an individual, even the thought of one's own being, and when man means to know his own ego and wants to describe it according to its nature, he immediately brings it into dependence on this nature. No matter what I may invent in my thinking, as soon as

I determine and define myself conceptually, I make myself the slave of the result of the definition, the concept. Hegel made the ego into a manifestation of reason, that is to say, he made it dependent on reason. But all such generalities cannot be valid with regard to the ego because they all have their source in the ego. They are caused by the fact that the ego is deceived by itself. It is really not dependent, for everything on which it could depend must first be produced by the ego. The ego must produce something out of itself, set it above itself and allow it to turn into a spectre that haunts its own originator.

> Man, you have bats in your belfry; there is a screw loose in your head! You imagine big things; you invent a whole world of Gods that is supposed to be there for your benefit, a realm of spirit for which you are destined, an ideal that is becoming you. You have an *idée fixe!*

In reality, no thinking can approach what lives within me as "I." I can reach everything with my thinking; only my ego is an exception in this respect. I cannot think it; I can only *experience* it. I am not will; I am not idea; I am that no more than the image of a deity. I make all other things comprehensible to myself through thinking. The ego I *am*. I have no need to define and to describe myself because I experience myself in every moment. I need to describe only what I do not immediately experience, what is outside myself. It is absurd that I should also have to conceive myself as a thought, as an idea, since I always *have* myself as something. If I face a stone, I may attempt to explain to myself what this stone is. What I *am* myself, I need not explain; it is given in my life.

Stirner answers to an attack against his book:

> The "only one" is a word and with a word it should be possible to *think* something; a word should have a thought content. But the "only one" is a *thoughtless* word; it does not have a thought content. What then is its content if it is not thought? It is a content that cannot be there a second time and therefore is also incapable of being *expressed;* for if it could be expressed, really and completely

pressed out, then it would be there a second time; it would be there in the expression. Because the content of the "only one" is not a thought content, it is also unthinkable and ineffable, but because it is ineffable, this perfectly empty phrase is at the same time *not a phrase*. Only when nothing is said of you, when you are simply called, are you recognized as you. As long as *something* is said of you, you are recognized only as this something (human being, spirit, Christian, etc.). The "only one" does not contain a statement because it is only *name*, saying nothing more than that you are you and nothing but you; that you are a unique "you" and you yourself. Through this, you are without a predicate, and thereby without quality, calling, legal standing and restriction, and so forth. (Compare Stirner's *Kleine Schriften*, edited by J. H. Mackay, pp. 116.)

Stirner, in an essay written in 1842, *The Untrue Principle of Our Education, or Humanism and Realism*, had already expressed his conviction that thinking cannot penetrate as far as the core of the personality. He therefore considers it an untrue educational principle if this core of the personality is not made the objective of education, but when knowledge as such assumes this position in a one-sided way.

A knowledge that does not so purge and concentrate itself that it inspires the will, or in other words, that only weighs me down with possession and property instead of having become entirely one with me so that the freely moving ego, unhampered by any cumbersome belongings travels through the world with an open mind; a knowledge, then, that has not become *personal* will make a miserable preparation for life. . . . If it is the cry of our time, after the *freedom of thought* has been obtained, to continue this freedom to its end through which it turns into the *freedom of will* so that the latter can be realized as the aim of a new epoch, then the last aim of education can no longer be *knowledge* but a *will* that is born out of *knowledge*, and the revealing expression of the educational aim is the *personal* or *free man*. . . . As in certain other spheres, so also in that of education, freedom is not allowed to break forth; the power of *opposition* is not yielded the floor: *subordination* is insisted upon. Only formal and material drill is the aim of this education; in the menagerie of the humanists nothing but "scholars" are produced and in that of the realists, nothing but "useful citizens." Both then produce nothing but *submissive* human beings. *Knowledge* must die to be resurrected as *will* and to restore itself daily in free *personalities.*

The personality of the individual human being can alone contain the source of his actions. The moral duties cannot be commandments that are given to man from somewhere, but they must be aims that man sets for himself. Man is mistaken if he believes that he does something because he follows a commandment of a general code of sacred ethics. He does it because the life of his ego drives him to it. I do not love my neighbor because I follow a sacred commandment of neighborly love, but because my ego draws me to my neighbor. It is not that I *am* to love him; I *want* to love him. What men have *wanted* to do they have placed as commandments above themselves. On this point Stirner can be most easily understood. He does not deny *moral action.* What he does deny is the *moral commandment.* If man only understands himself rightly, then a moral world order will be the result of his actions. Moral *prescriptions* are a spectre, an *idée fixe,* for Stirner. They prescribe something at which man arrives all by himself if he follows entirely his own nature. The abstract thinkers will, of course, raise the objection, "Are there not criminals?" These abstract thinkers anticipate general chaos if moral prescriptions are not sacred to man. Stirner could reply to them, "Are there not also diseases in nature? Are they not produced in accordance with eternal unbreakable laws just as everything that is healthy?"

As little as it will ever occur to any reasonable person to reckon the sick with the healthy because the former is, like the latter, produced through natural laws, just as little would Stirner count the immoral with the moral because they both come into being when the individual is left to himself. What distinguishes Stirner from the abstract thinkers, however, is his conviction that in human life morality will be dominating as much as health is in nature, when the decision is left to the discretion of individuals. He believes in the moral nobility of human nature, in the free development of morality out of the individuals. It seems to him that the abstract thinkers do not believe in this nobility, and he is, therefore, of the opinion that they debase the nature of the individual to become the slave of general commandments, the corrective scourges of human action. There must be much evil depravity at the bottom of the souls of these "moral persons," according to Stirner, because they are so insistent in their demands for moral prescriptions. They must indeed be lacking love because they want love to be ordered to them as a commandment that should really spring from them as spontaneous impulse.

Only twenty years ago it was possible that the following criticism could be made in a serious book:

> Max Stirner's book, *The Only One and His Possession*, destroyed spirit and humanity, right and state, truth and virtue as if they were idols of the bondage of thought, and confessed without reluctance, "I place nothing above myself!" (Heinrich von Treitschke, *Deutsche Geschichte*, Part V, pp. 416; 1927.)

This only proves how easily Stirner can be misunderstood as a result of his radical mode of expression because, to him, the human individual was considered to be so noble, so elevated, unique and free that not even the loftiest thought world was supposed to reach up to it. Thanks to the endeavors of John Henry Mackay, we have today a picture of his life and his character. In his book, *Max Stirner, His Life and His Work* (Berlin, 1898), he has summed up the complete result of his research extending over many years to arrive at a characterization of Stirner who was, in Mackay's opinion, "The boldest and most consistent of all thinkers."

Stirner, like other thinkers of modern times, is confronted with the self-conscious ego, challenging comprehension. Others search for means to comprehend this ego. The comprehension meets with difficulties because a wide gulf has opened up between the picture of nature and that of the life of the spirit. Stirner leaves all that without consideration. He faces the fact of the self-conscious ego and uses every means at his disposal to express this fact. He wants to speak of the ego in a way that forces everyone to look at the ego for himself, so that nobody can evade this challenge by claiming that the ego is this or the ego is that. Stirner does not want to point out an idea or a thought of the ego, but the living ego itself that the personality finds in itself.

Stirner's mode of conception, as the opposite pole to that of Goethe, Schiller, Fichte, Schelling and Hegel, is a phenomenon that had to appear with a certain necessity in the course of the development of modern world conception. Stirner became aware of the self-conscious ego with an inescapable, piercing intensity. Every thought production appeared to him in the same way in which the mythical world of pictures is experienced by a thinker who wants to seize the world in thought alone. Against this intensely experienced fact, every other world content that appeared in connection with the self-conscious ego faded away for Stirner. He presented the self-conscious ego in complete isolation.

Stirner does not feel that there could be difficulties in presenting the ego in this manner. The following decades could not establish any relationship to this isolated position of the ego. For these decades are occupied above all with the task of forming the nature picture under the influence of the mode of thought of natural science. After Stirner had presented the one side of modern consciousness, the fact of the self-conscious ego, the age at first withdraws all attention from this ego and turns to the picture of nature where this "ego" is not to be found.

The first half of the nineteenth century had born its world conception out of the spirit of idealism. Where a bridge is laid to lead to natural science, as it is done by Schelling, Lorenz Oken (1779–1851) and Henrik Steffens (1773–1845), it is done from the viewpoint of the idealistic world conception and in its interest. So little was the time ready to make thoughts of natural science fruitful for world conceptions that the ingenious conception of Jean Lamarck pertaining to the evolution of the most perfect organisms out of the simple one, which was published in

1809, drew no attention at all. When in 1830 Geoffroy de St. Hilaire presented the idea of a general natural relationship of all forms of organisms in his controversy with Couvier, it took the genius of Goethe to see the significance of this idea. The numerous results of natural science that were contributed in the first half of the century became new world riddles for the development of world conception when Charles Darwin in 1859, opened up new aspects for an understanding of nature with his treatment of the world of living organisms.

THE RIDDLES OF PHILOSOPHY
Part II

*Introductory Remarks
to the 1914 Edition*

The description of the life of the philosophical spirit from the middle of the nineteenth century to the present time, which has been attempted in this second volume of The Riddles of Philosophy, cannot be of the same character as the survey of the works of the preceding thinkers. This survey had to remain within the most restricted circle of the philosophical problems. The last sixty years represent the age in which the mode of conception of natural science attempted, from different points of view, to shake the foundation on which philosophy formerly stood. During this time, the view arose that maintained that the results of natural science shed the necessary light on the question of man's nature, his relation to the world and other riddles of existence, which the intellectual work of philosophy had formerly sought to supply. Many thinkers who wanted to serve philosophy now tried to imitate the mode of investigation of natural science. Others laid the foundation for their world conception, not in the fashion of the old philosophical mode of thinking, but simply by taking over that basis from the mode of conception of natural science, biology or physiology. Those who meant to preserve the independence of philosophy believed it best to examine thoroughly the results of natural science in order to prevent them from invading the philosophical sphere. It is for this reason necessary, in presenting the philosophical life of this period, to pay attention to the views that, derived from natural science, have been introduced into world conceptions. The significance of these views for philosophy becomes apparent only if one examines the scientific foundations from which they are derived, and if one realizes for oneself the tendencies of scientific thinking according to which they were developed. This situation is given expression in this book by the fact that some parts of it are formulated almost as if a presentation of general natural scientific ideas, and not one of philosophical works, had been intended. The opinion appears to be justified that this method of presentation shows distinctly how thoroughly natural science has influenced the philosophical life of the present time.

A reader who finds it reconcilable to his mode of thinking to conceive the evolution of the philosophical life along the lines indicated in the introduction of the first volume of this book, and for which the more detailed account of the book has attempted to supply the foundation, will also find it possible to accept the indicated relation between philosophy and natural science in the present age as a necessary phase of its evolution. Through the centuries since the beginning of Greek philosophy this evolution tended to lead the human soul toward the experience of its inner essential forces. With this inner experience the soul became more and more estranged in the world that the knowledge of external nature had erected for itself. A conception of nature arose that is so exclusively concerned with the observation of the external world that it does not show any inclination to include in its world picture what the soul experiences in its inner world. This conception considers it as unjustified to paint the world picture in a way that it would show these inner experiences of the human soul as well as the results of the research of natural science. It characterizes the situation in which philosophy found itself in the second half of the nineteenth century, and in which many currents of thought can still be found in the present time. Such a judgment does not have to be artificially introduced to the study of the philosophy of this age. It can be arrived at by simply observing the facts. The second volume of this book attempts to record this new development, but it has also made it necessary to add to the second edition a final chapter that contains "A Brief Outline of an Approach to Anthroposophy."

One can be of the opinion that this account does not belong in the framework of the whole book but, in the preface to the first volume, it was announced that the purpose of this presentation "is not only to give a short outline of the history of philosophical problems, but also to discuss these problems and the attempts at their solution through their historical treatment." The view expressed in this book tries to show that many situations arising from the attempted solutions in the philosophy of the present tend to recognize an element in the inner experience of the human soul that manifests itself in such a way that the exclusive claim of natural science can no longer deny that element a place in the modern world picture. As it is the philosophical conviction of the author of this book that the account of the final chapter deals with soul experiences that are adequate to bring fulfillment to the search of modern philosophy, he feels he was justified in adding this chapter to his presentation. As a result of observation of these philosophies, it seems to the author to be basically characteristic of them and of their historical manifestation that they do not consistently continue their direction toward the goal they are seeking. This direction must lead toward the world conception that is outlined at the end of the book, which aims at a real *science of the spirit.* The reader who can agree with this can find in this conception something that supplies the solutions to problems that the philosophy of the present time poses without giving answers. If this is true, the content of the last chapter will also throw light on the *historical* position of modern philosophy.

The author of this book does not imagine that everyone who can accept the content of the final chapter must necessarily also seek a world conception that replaces philosophy by a view that can no longer be recognized as a philosophy by traditional philosophers. What this book means to show is that philosophy, if it arrives at the point where it understands itself, must lead the spirit to a soul experience that is, to be sure, the fruit of its work, but also grows beyond it. In this way, philosophy retains its significance for everyone who, according to his mode of thinking, must demand a secure intellectual foundation for the results of this soul experience. Whoever can accept these results through a natural sense for truth, is justified in feeling himself on secure ground even if he pays no special attention to a philosophical foundation of these results. But whoever seeks the *scientific* justification of the world conception that is presented at the end of the book, must follow the path of the philosophical foundation.

That this path, if it is followed through to its end, leads to the experience of a spiritual world, and that the soul through this experience can become aware of its own spiritual essence through a method that is independent of its experience and knowledge through the sense world, is what the presentation of this book attempts to prove. It was not the author's intention to project this thought as a preconceived idea into his observation of philosophical life. He wanted to search without bias for the conception expressed in this life itself. He has at least endeavored to proceed in this way. He believes that this thought could be best presented by speaking the language of a natural scientist, as it were, in some parts of the book. Only if one is capable of temporarily identifying oneself completely with a certain point of view is it possible to do full justice to it. By this method of deliberately taking the position of a world view, the human soul can most safely obtain the ability to withdraw from it again and enter into modes of conception that have their source in realms that are not comprised by this view of the world.

* * *

The printing of this second volume of The Riddles of Philosophy was about half finished before the great war that mankind is now experiencing broke out. It was finished just as this event began. This is only to indicate what outer events stirred and occupied my soul as the last thoughts included in this book passed before my inner eye.

Rudolf Steiner

September 1, 1914
Berlin

Chapter I

The Struggle Over the Spirit

Hegel felt that with his thought structure he had arrived at the goal for which the evolution of world conception had been striving since man had attempted to conquer the enigmatic problems of existence within the realm of thought experiences. With this feeling he wrote, toward the end of his *Encyclopedia of the Philosophical Sciences*, the following words. "The concept of philosophy is the idea *that thinks itself*; it is knowing truth. . . . Philosophical knowledge has in this manner gone back to its beginning, and the *content of logic* thus becomes its result as the *spiritual element* that has revealed itself as truth, as it is in itself and for itself."

The experience of itself in thought, according to Hegel, is to give to the human soul the consciousness of being at its true original source. In drinking from this source, filling itself with thoughts from it, the soul is supposed to live in its own true essence and in that of nature at the same time, for both nature and the soul are manifestations of thought. Through the phenomena of nature the thought world looks at the soul, which seizes in itself the creative power of thought so that it knows itself in union with all world processes. The soul thus sees its own narrow circle of self-consciousness enlarged through the fact that the world observes itself consciously in it. The soul thereby ceases to consider itself merely as something that is aware of itself in the transitory sensual body between birth and death. The imperishable spirit, which is not bound to any sensual existence, knows itself in the soul, and the soul is aware of being bound to this spirit in an inseparable union.

Let us place ourselves in the position of the soul of a personality who could follow Hegel's trend of ideas to the extent that he believed that he experienced the presence of thought in his consciousness in the same way as Hegel himself. We can then feel how, for such a soul, age-old enigmatic questions appear to be placed in a light that can be highly satisfactory to such an inquirer. Such satisfaction is indeed apparent, for instance, in the numerous writings of the Hegelian thinker, *Karl Rosenkranz*. As we absorb these writings with concentrated attention (*System of Philosophy*, 1850; *Psychology*, 1844; *Critical Explanations of the Hegelian Philosophy*, 1851), we feel ourselves confronted with a personality who is convinced he has found in Hegel's ideas what can provide a satisfactory cognitive relation to the world for the human soul. Rosenkranz can be mentioned in this respect as a significant example because he is not at all blindly following Hegel every step, but shows that he is a spirit motivated by the consciousness that Hegel's position toward world and man contains the possibility of giving a healthy foundation to a world conception.

What could a thinker like Rosenkranz experience with regard to this foundation? Since the birth of thought in ancient Greece, and during centuries of philosophical investigation of the riddles of existence with which every soul was fundamentally confronted, a number of major problems have crystallized. In modern times the problem of the significance, the value and the limits of knowledge has moved, as the fundamental problem, into the center of philosophical reflection. What relation has man's perception, conception and thought to the real world? Can this process of perception and thinking result in a knowledge that is capable of enlightening man concerning the questions about which he wants to be enlightened? For a person who thinks like Hegel, this question answers itself through the implication in Hegel's thought concept. As he gains hold of thought, he is convinced he experiences the creative spirit of the world. In this union with creative thought he feels the value and true significance of cognition. He cannot ask, "What is the meaning of knowledge?" for he experiences this significance as he is engaged in the act of knowing. Through this fact the Hegelian is directly opposed to all Kantianism. Witness what Hegel himself has to say against the Kantian method of investigating cognition before the act of knowledge has taken place.

> A main point of the critical philosophy consists in the fact that before it sets out to develop a knowledge of God, the essence of things, etc., it is demanded that the faculty of knowledge must be investigated as to whether it is capable of doing such things. One must know the *instrument* before one undertakes the work that is to be achieved by means of it. If this instrument should prove insufficient, all endeavor would be wasted. This thought has appeared so *plausible* that it aroused the greatest admiration and agreement, and led knowledge, motivated by an interest in the objects of knowledge, back to itself. If, however, one does not want to deceive oneself with words, it is quite easy to see that other instruments can be investigated and judged in some other way than by undertaking the work with them for which they are meant. But knowledge can be investigated in no other way than *in the act of knowledge*; in the case of this so-called instrument, the process to test it is nothing but knowledge itself. To know before one knows is as absurd as the wise intention of the scholastic thinker who wanted to *learn to swim before he dared go into the water.*

For Hegel, the main point was that the soul should experience itself as filled with the living world thought. Thus, it grows beyond its ordinary existence; it becomes, as it were, the vessel in which world thought, living in thinking, seizes itself in full consciousness. The soul is not merely felt as a vessel of this world spirit but as an entity conscious of its union with that spirit. Thus it is, according to Hegel, not possible to investigate the essence of knowledge. We must immediately raise ourselves into participation in this essence through its experience and, with that step, we are directly inside the process of knowledge. If one stands inside that process, one is *in possession of* that knowledge and feels no longer the need to inquire after its significance. If one cannot take this stand, one lacks also the ability to investigate it. The Kantian philosophy is an impossibility for Hegel's world conception because, in order to answer the question, "How is knowledge possible," the soul would first have to produce knowledge. In that case, the question of its existence could not be raised beforehand.

In a certain sense Hegel's philosophy amounts to this: He allows the soul to lift itself to a certain height at which point it grows into unity with the world. With the birth of thought in Greek philosophy the soul separated from the world. The soul is felt as in solitude as opposed to the world. In this seclusion the soul finds itself holding sway within itself. It is Hegel's intention to bring this experience of thought to its climax. At the same time he finds the creative world principle in the highest thought experience. The soul has thus completed the course of a perfect circle in separating itself at first from the world in order to search for thought. It feels itself separated from the world only as long as it recognizes in thought *nothing but thought*. It feels united with the world again as it discovers in thought the original source of the world. Thus, the circle is closed. Hegel can say, "In this manner science has returned to its beginning."

Seen from such a viewpoint, the other main problems of human knowledge are set in such a light that one can believe one sees all existence in one coherent world conception. As a second major problem, one can consider the question of *deity as the ground of the world.* The elevation of the soul that enables the world thought to awaken to self-knowledge as it lives within the soul is, for Hegel, at the same time the soul's union with the divine world ground. According to him, one therefore cannot ask the question, "*What* is the divine ground of the world?" or, "What is man's relation toward it?" One can only say, "When the soul really experiences truth in the act of knowledge, it penetrates into this ground of the world."

A third major question in the above-mentioned sense is the cosmological problem, that is to say, the problem of the inner essence of the outer world. This essence can, according to Hegel, be sought only in thought itself. When the soul arrives at the point of experiencing thought in itself, it also finds in its self-experience the form of thought it can recognize as it observes the processes and entities of the external world. Thus, it can, for instance, find something in its thought experience of which it knows immediately that this is the essence of light. As it then turns its eye to nature, it sees in the external light the manifestation of the thought essence of light.

In this way, for Hegel, the whole world dissolves into thought entity. Nature swims, as it were, as a frozen part in the cosmos of thought, and the human soul becomes thought in the thought world.

The fourth major problem of philosophy, the question of the nature and destiny of the soul, seems to Hegel's mind satisfactorily answered through the true progress of thought experience. At first, the soul finds itself bound to nature. In this connection it does not know itself in its true entity. It divorces itself from this nature existence and finds itself then separated in thought, arriving at last at the insight that it possesses in thought both the true essence of nature and its own true being as that of the living spirit as it lives and weaves as a member of this spirit.

All materialism seems to be overcome with this philosophy. Matter itself appears merely as a *manifestation of the spirit.* The human soul may feel itself as becoming and having its being in the spiritual universe.

In the treatment of the problem of the soul the Hegelian world conception shows probably most distinctly what is unsatisfactory about it. Looking at this world conception, the human soul must ask, "Can I really find myself in the comprehensive thought construction of the world erected by Hegel?" We have seen that all modern world conception must look for a world picture in which the entity of the human soul finds an adequate place. To Hegel, the whole world is thought; within this thought the soul also has its supersensible thought existence. But can the soul be satisfied to be contained as world thought in the general thought world? This question arises in thinkers who had been stimulated by Hegel's philosophy in the middle of the nineteenth century.

What are really the most urgent riddles of the soul? They are the ones for the answers of which the soul must feel a yearning, expecting from them the feeling of security and a firm hold in life. There is, to begin with, the question, "What is the human soul essentially?" Is the soul identical with the corporeal existence and do its manifestations cease with the decay of the body as the motion of the hands of a clock stop when the clock is taken apart? Or, is the soul an entity independent of the body, possessing life and significance in a world apart from that in which the body comes into being and dissolves into nothing? Connected with these questions is another problem. How does man obtain knowledge of such a world? Only in answering *this* question can man hope to receive light for the problems of life: Why am I subjected to this or that destiny? What is the source of suffering? What is the origin of morality?

Satisfaction can be given only by a world conception that offers answers to the above-mentioned questions and at the same time proves its right to give such answers.

Hegel offered a world of thoughts. If this world is to be the all inclusive universe, then the soul is forced to regard itself in its inner substance as thought. If one seriously accepts this cosmos of thought, one will find that the individual soul life of man dissolves in it. One must give up the attempt to explain and to understand this individual soul life and is forced to say that the significance of the soul does *not* rest in its individual experience but in the fact that it is contained in the general thought world. This is what the Hegelian world conception fundamentally does say. One should contrast it with what Lessing had in mind when he conceived the ideas of his *Education of the Human Race.* He asked the question of the significance for the *individual* human soul beyond the life that is enclosed between birth and death. In pursuing this thought of Lessing one can say that the soul after physical death goes through a form of existence in a world that lies outside the one in which man lives, perceives and thinks in his body; after an appropriate time, such a purely spiritual form of experience is followed again by a new earth life. In this process a world is implied with which the human soul, as a particular, individual entity, is bound up. Toward *this* world the soul feels directed in searching for its own true being. As soon as one conceives the soul as separated from the connection with its physical form of existence, one must think of it as belonging to that same world. For Hegel, however, the life of the soul, in shedding all individual traits, is absorbed first into the general thought process of the historical evolution, then into that of the general spiritual-intellectual world processes. In Hegel's sense, one solves the riddle of the soul in leaving all individual traits of that soul out of consideration. The individual is not real, but the historical process. This is illustrated by the passage toward the end of Hegel's *Philosophy of History*:

> We have exclusively considered the progress of the concept and had to renounce the tempting pleasure to depict the fortune, the flourishing periods of the peoples, the greatness and the beauty of the individuals, the interest of their destiny in sorrow and joy. Philosophy has to deal only with the lustre of the idea that is reflected in world history. Weary of the immediate passions in the world of reality, philosophy emancipates into contemplation; it is the interest of philosophy to recognize the course of development of the self-realization of the idea.

Let us look at Hegel's doctrine of the soul. We find here the description of the process of the soul's evolution within the body as "natural soul," the development of consciousness of self and of reason. We then find the soul realizing the ideas of right, morality and the state in the external world. It is then described how the soul *sees* in world history, as a continuous life, what it thinks as ideas. It is shown how it *lives* these ideas as art and religion, and how the soul unites with the truth that thinks itself, seeing itself in the living creative spirit of the universe.

Every thinker who feels like Hegel must be convinced that the world in which he finds himself is entirely spirit, that all material existence is also nothing but a manifestation of the spirit. If such a thinker searches for the spirit, he will find it essentially as active *thought, as living, creative idea.* This is what the soul is confronted with. It must ask itself if it *can* really consider itself as a being that is nothing but thought essence. It can be felt as the real greatness, the irrefutable element of Hegel's world conception that the soul, in rising to true thought, feels elevated to the creative principle of existence. To feel man's relation to the world in this way was an experience of deep satisfaction to those personalities who could follow Hegel's thought development.

How can one live with this thought? That was the great riddle confronting modern world conception. It had resulted from the continuation of the process begun in Greek philosophy when thought had emerged and when the soul had thereupon become detached from external existence. Hegel now has attempted to place the whole range of thought experience before the soul, to present to the soul, as it were, everything it can produce as thought out of its depths. In the face of this thought experience Hegel now demands of the soul that it recognize itself according to its deepest nature in this experience, that it feel itself in this element as in its deepest ground.

With this demand of Hegel the human soul has been brought to a decisive point in the attempt to obtain a knowledge of its own being. Where is the soul to turn when it has arrived at the element of pure thought but does not want to remain stationary at this point? From the experience of perception, feeling and will, it proceeds to the activity of thinking and asks, "What will result if I think about perception, feeling and will?" Having arrived at thinking, it is at first not possible to proceed any further. The soul's attempt in this direction can only lead to *thinking* again. Whoever follows the modern development of philosophy as far as the age of Hegel can have the impression that Hegel pursues the impulses of this development to a point beyond which it becomes impossible to go so long as this process retains the general character exhibited up to that time. The observation of this fact can lead to the question: If thinking up to this stage brings philosophy in Hegel's sense to the construction of a world picture that is spread out before the soul, has this energy of thinking then really developed *everything* that is potentially contained within it? It could be, after all, that thinking contains more possibilities than that of mere thinking. Consider a plant, which develops from the root through its stem and leaves into blossom and fruit. The life of this plant can now be brought to an end by taking the seed from the fruit and using it as human food, for instance. But one can also expose the seed of the plant to the appropriate conditions with the effect that it will develop into a new plant.

In concentrating one's attention on the significance of Hegel's philosophy, one can see how the thought picture that man develops of the world unfolds before him like a plant; one can observe that the development is brought to the point where the seed, thought, is produced. But then this process is brought to an end, just as in the life of the plant whose seed is not developed further in its own organic function, but is used for a purpose that is as extraneous to this life as the purpose of human nutrition is to the seed of the reproductive organs. Indeed, as soon as Hegel has arrived at the point where thought is developed as an element, he does not continue the process that brought him to this point. He proceeds from sense perception and develops everything in the human soul in a process that finally leads to thought. At this stage he stops and shows how this element can provide an explanation of the world processes and world entities. This purpose can indeed be served by thought, just as the seed of a plant may be used as human food. But should it not be possible to develop a *living element* out of thought? Is it not possible that this element is deprived of its own life through the use that Hegel makes of it, as the seed of a plant is deprived of its life when it is used as human food? In what light would Hegel's philosophy have to appear if it were possibly true that thought can be used for the enlightenment, for the explanation of the world processes, as a plant seed can be used for food but only by sacrificing its continued growth? The seed of a plant, to be sure, can produce only a plant of the same kind. Thought, however, as a seed of knowledge, could, if left to its living development, produce something of an entirely new kind, compared to the world picture from which its evolution would proceed. As the plant life is ruled by the *law of repetition,* so the life of knowledge could be under the *law of enhancement and elevation.* It is unthinkable that thought as we employ it for the explanation of external science should be merely a by-product of evolution, just as the use of plant seeds for food is a side-track in the plant's continuous development. One can dismiss ideas of this kind on the ground that they have their origin in an arbitrary imagination and that they represent mere possibilities without any value. It is just as easily understood that the objection can be raised that at the point at which this idea would be developed we would enter the realm of arbitrary fantasy. To the observer of the historical development of the philosophies of the nineteenth century this question can nevertheless appear in a different light. The way in which Hegel conceives the element of thought does indeed lead the evolution of world conception to a dead end. One feels that thought has reached an extreme; yet, if one wants to introduce this thought in the form in which it is conceived in the immediate life of knowledge, it becomes a disappointing failure. There arises a longing for a life that should spring from the world conception that one has accomplished.

Friedrich Theodor Vischer begins to write his *Esthetics* in Hegel's manner in the middle of the nineteenth century. When finished, it is a work of monumental importance. After its completion he becomes the most penetrating critic of his own work. If one searches for the deeper reason for this strange process, one finds that Vischer has become aware of the fact that, as he had permeated his work with Hegelian thoughts, he had introduced an element that had become dead, since it had been taken out of the ground that had provided its life conditions, just as a plant seed dies when its growth is cut off. A peculiar perspective is opening before us as we see Hegel's world conception in this light. The nature of the thought element could demand to be received as a living seed and, under certain conditions, to be developed in the soul. It could unfold its possibility by leading beyond the world picture of Hegel to a world conception in which the soul could come to a knowledge of its own being with which it could truly hold its own position in the external world. Hegel has brought the soul to the point where it can live with the element of thought; the progress beyond Hegel would lead to the *thought's growth in the soul* beyond itself *and into a spiritual world.* Hegel understood how the soul magically produces thought within itself and experiences itself in thought. He left to posterity the task of discovering by means of living thoughts, which are active in a truly spiritual world, the real being of the soul that cannot fully experience itself in the element of mere thought.

It has been shown in the preceding exposition how the development of modern world conception strives from the *perception* of thought toward the *experience* of thought. In Hegel's world conception the world seems to stand before the soul as a self-produced thought experience, but the trend of evolution seems to indicate further progress. Thought must not become stationary as thought; it must not be *merely* thought, not *be experienced merely through thinking*; it must awaken to a still higher life.

As arbitrary as all this may appear at first, it is nevertheless the view that prevails when a more penetrating observation of the development of modern world conception in the nineteenth century is made. Such an observation shows how the demands of an age exert their effect in the deeper strata of the evolution of history. It shows the aims that men set for themselves as *attempts* to do justice to these demands. Men of modern times were confronted with the world picture of natural science. It was necessary to find conceptions concerning the life of the soul that could be maintained while this world picture was sustained. The whole development from Descartes, Spinoza, Leibniz, Locke, to Hegel, appears as a struggle for such conceptions. Hegel brings this struggle to a certain conclusion. His mode of thinking, as he presents the world as thought, appears to be latent everywhere with his predecessors. He takes the bold step as a thinker to bring all world conceptions to a climax by uniting them in a comprehensive thought picture. With him the age has, for the time being, exhausted the energy of its advancing impulses. What was formulated above, that is, the demand to experience the life of thought inwardly, is *unconsciously* felt. This demand is felt as a burden on the souls at the time of the middle of the nineteenth century. People despair of the impossibility of fulfilling this demand, but they are not fully aware of their despair. Thus, a stagnation in the philosophical field sets in. The productivity with respect to philosophical ideas ceases. It would have had to develop in the indicated direction, but first it seems to be necessary to pause in deliberation about the achievement that has been attained. Attempts are made to start from one point or another of the philosophical predecessors, but the force to continue the world picture of Hegel fruitfully is lacking.

Witness Karl Rosenkranz's description of the situation in the preface to his *Life of Hegel* (1844):

> It is not without regret that I part from this work, but it is necessary to proceed at some time from *becoming* to *existence.* Does it not seem, however, that we are nowadays only the grave-diggers and survivors to set monuments to the philosophers who were born in the second half of the eighteenth century, and who died in the first of the nineteenth century? Kant began this march of death of the German philosophers in 1804. He was followed by Fichte, Jacobi, Solger, Reinhold, Krause, Schleiermacher, William von Humboldt, Friedrich Schlegel, Herbart, Baader, Wagner, Windischmann, Fries, and so many others. . . . Do we see a succeeding generation for this harvest of death? Are we capable also of sending into the second half of our century a venerable group of thinkers? Are there living among our young men those who are inspired to immortal exertion for speculative contemplation, by Platonic enthusiasm and Aristotelian joy of painstaking industry? . . . Strangely enough, in our day the talents seem to be not *quite* able to hold onto their task. They are quickly used up and after a few promising flowers, they become barren and begin to copy and repeat themselves at the very moment when, after having overcome their still immature, imperfect, one-

sided and stormy youthful attempts, periods of forceful and concentrated activity should begin. Some of them, full of exaggerated eagerness, go too far in their quest and must, like Constantin Frantz, take back partly in later books what they said in earlier ones . . .

It can often be seen that, after the middle of the nineteenth century, people found themselves forced to subscribe to such a judgment of the philosophical situation of the time. The excellent thinker, Franz Brentano, made the following statement in the inaugural speech for his professorship, *Concerning the Reasons for Discouragement in the Philosophical Field*, in 1874:

> In the first decades of our century the lecture halls of the German philosophers were overcrowded; in more recent times, this flood has been followed by an ebb tide. One often hears that gifted men accuse the younger generation of lacking the sense for the highest branches of knowledge. That would be a sad but also an incomprehensible fact. How could it be that the entire new generation should be inferior to the earlier one in spiritual momentum and mobility? It was in reality not a lack of talent but . . . lack of confidence that had the effect of decreasing philosophical studies. If the hope for success had come back, the highest honors in this field would be waiting in vain to be conquered . . .

In Hegel's lifetime, and for a short time after, there already were people who felt that his world picture showed its weakness in the very point that contained its greatness. His world conception leads toward thought but also forces the soul to consider its nature to be exhausted in the thought element. If this world conception would bring thought in the above-mentioned sense to a life of its own, then this could only happen within the individual soul life; the soul would thereby find its relation toward the whole cosmos. This was felt, for instance, by Troxler, but he did not develop the conviction beyond the state of a dim feeling. In lectures that he gave at the University of Bern in 1835 he expressed himself as follows:

> Not only now but also twenty years ago, we have been living with the most intimate conviction, and we have tried to show this in

writing and speech, that a philosophy and an anthropology that was to embrace man in his entirety, God and the world, can only be founded on the idea and the reality of man's individuality and immortality. For this fact, the whole book, *Insight into Man's Nature*, which appeared in 1811, is an undeniable proof. It is also borne out in the last chapter of our *Anthropology* entitled, "The Absolute Personality," which had a wide circulation in the form of a booklet. We therefore take the liberty to quote from the beginning of that chapter. "The whole inner nature of man has been constructed on *divine misproportions*, which are dissolved in the glory of a superterrestrial destination, as all motivating springs have their origin in the spirit and only the weights are from the world. We have now traced these misproportions with their manifestations from their dark earthly root, and have followed the spiral of the heavenly plant, which appears to wind only around a great and noble stem from all sides and in all directions. We approach the top, which continues to rise, unattainable and continuously beyond our grasp, into the upper, brighter realms of another world whose light is only softly dawning on us and the breath of which we may feel . . ."

Such words sound to a man of the present sentimental and not very scientific, but one only needs to observe the goal toward which Troxler steers. He does not want to dissolve the nature of man into a world of ideas but attempts to lay hold on *man in man* as the *individual and immortal personality*. Troxler wants to see the nature of man anchored in a world that is not merely thought. For this reason, he calls attention to the fact that one can distinguish something in the human being that binds man to a world beyond the sensual world and that is *not* merely thought.

> Philosophers of earlier times have already distinguished a subtle, noble soul body from the coarser material body, or, in this sense, assumed a kind of sheath of the spirit, a soul that was endowed with the picture of the body they called *model* (Schema) and that was the inner higher man for them.

Troxler, himself, divided man into material body (*Koerper*), soul body (*Leib*), soul (*Seele*) and spirit (*Geist*). He thereby distinguished the entity of the soul in a manner that allowed him to see the latter enter the sense world with its material body and soul body, and extend into a supersensible world with its soul and spirit. This entity spreads its individual activity not merely into the sense world but also into the spiritual world. It does not lose its individuality in the mere generality of thought, but Troxler does not arrive at the point of conceiving thought as a living seed of knowledge in the soul. He does not succeed in justifying the individual members of soul and spirit by letting this germ of knowledge live within the soul. He does not suspect that thought could grow into something during his life that could be considered as the individual life of the soul, but he can speak of this individual existence of the soul only from a dimly experienced feeling, as it were. Troxler could not come to more than such a feeling concerning these connections because he was too dependent on positive dogmatic religious conceptions. Since he was in possession of a far-reaching comprehensive knowledge of the evolution of world conception, his rejection of Hegelian philosophy can nevertheless be seen as of greater significance than one that springs from mere personal antipathy. It can be seen as an expression of the objection against Hegel that arises from the intellectual mood of the Hegelian age itself. In this light we have to understand Troxler's verdict:

> Hegel has brought speculation to the highest stage of its perfection and in the very act of doing so he has destroyed it. His system has become for this intellectual current the last word; its indirect verdict is: Up to this point and not a step further!

In this form Troxler asks the question, which, if developed from a dim feeling into a clear idea, would probably have to be expressed as follows: How does the philosophical world conception develop beyond the phase of the mere thought experience in Hegel's sense to an inner participation in thought that has come to life?

A book that is characteristic of the relation of Hegel's world conception toward the mood of the time was published by *C. H.*

Weisse in 1834 with the title, *The Philosophical Secret Doctrine of the Immortality of the Human Individual.* In this book is to be found the following passage:

> Whoever has studied Hegel's philosophy in its entire inner connection, is acquainted with the manner in which this philosophy, as it is constructed with perfect consistency in its dialectic method, shows the subjective spirit of the finite individual as *absorbed* into the objective spirit of law, state and morality. The subjective spirit thus becomes subordinated. It is simultaneously accepted and rejected until it finally changes into a dependent element of this higher spirit. In this fashion, the finite individual, as it has long been noted both in and outside Hegel's school, is made into a transitory phenomenon. . . . What purpose, what significance could there be for the continued existence of such an individual after the world spirit *has passed through it* . . . ?

Weisse attempts to contrast this meaninglessness of the individual soul with his own description of its imperishable existence. That he, too, could not really progress beyond Hegel can be easily understood from his line of thought that has been briefly outlined in an earlier chapter of this book.

The powerlessness of Hegel's thought picture could be felt when it was confronted with the individual entity of the soul, and it showed up again in the rising demand to penetrate deeper into nature than is possible by mere sense perception. That everything presented to the senses in reality represents thought and as such is *spirit* was seen clearly by Hegel, but whether one had gained an insight into *all* spirit in nature by knowing this *spirit of nature* was a new question. If the soul cannot grasp its own being by means of thought, could it not still be the case that with another form of experience of its own being the soul could nevertheless experience deeper forces and entities in nature? Whether such questions are formulated in completely distinct awareness or not is not the point in question. What matters is *whether or not they can be asked* with regard to a world conception. If this is possible, then such a world conception leaves us with the impression of being unsatisfactory. Because this was the case with Hegel's philosophy, it was not accepted as one that gives the right picture of the world, that is, one to which the highest problems and world riddles could be referred. This must be distinctly observed if the picture that is presented by the development of world conception in the middle of the nineteenth century is to be seen in its proper light. In this time further progress was made with respect to the picture of external nature, which, even more powerfully than before, weighed on the general human outlook on the world. It should be understandable that the philosophical conceptions of this time were engaged in a hard struggle since they had, as described above, arrived at a critical point. To begin with it is noteworthy to observe how Hegel's followers attempted to defend his philosophy.

Carl Ludwig Michelet (1801–93), the editor of Hegel's *Philosophy of Nature*, wrote in his preface to this work in 1841:

> Will people continue to consider it a limitation of philosophy to create only thoughts and not even a leaf of grass? That is to say that it can create only the general, lasting, truly valuable, and not the particular, sensual transitory? But if one should see the limitation of philosophy not only in the fact that philosophy cannot produce the particular, but also in the fact that it does not even know *how* it is made, then the answer is: This "how" does not stand higher than knowledge but rather lower than knowledge; therefore, knowledge cannot have its limitation in this respect. As the question is asked "how" this change of the idea into the reality takes place, knowledge is lost for the reason that nature is the unconscious idea and the leaf of grass grows without any knowledge. But true creation of general values is the one element of which philosophical inquiry cannot be deprived. . . . And now we maintain that the purest thought development of speculation will be in the most perfect agreement with the results of experience, and its sense for nature will discover nothing in nature but embodied ideas.

In the same preface Michelet also expresses a hope:

> Thus Goethe and Hegel are the two geniuses who, in my opinion, are destined to blaze the trail for a speculative physics of the future,

as they prepare the reconciliation of speculation and experience.
. . . Especially these Hegelian lectures could best of all have the effect of paving the way for a recognition in this respect, for as they show a comprehensive empirical knowledge, they represent the surest test for Hegel's speculation.

The subsequent time did not lead to such a reconciliation. A certain animosity against Hegel took possession of ever widening circles. The spread of this feeling against him in the course of the fifties of the last century can be seen from the words that Friedrich Albert Lange uses in his *History of Materialism* in 1865:

His (Hegel's) whole system moves within the realm of our thoughts and fantasies about things that are given high-sounding names with complete disregard as to the validity that the phenomena and the concepts derived from them can have. . . . Through Schelling and Hegel, pantheism became the dominant mode of thinking in natural philosophy, a world conception that with a certain mystical depth implies at the same time, almost as a matter of principle, the danger of fantastic extravagance. Instead of separating experience and the world of the senses strictly from the ideal element, and instead of trying to find the reconciliation of these realms in the nature of man, the pantheist undertakes the unification of spirit and nature through the verdict of poetic reason without any critical intervention.

This view concerning Hegel's mode of thinking is, to be sure, as inadequate to Hegel's world conception as possible. (See Hegel's philosophy as described in the chapter, *The Classics of World Conception.*) It does dominate numerous spirits as early as the middle of the nineteenth century, however, and it gains progressively more ground. A man who, from 1833 to 1872, was in an influential position with the German intellectual life as a professor of philosophy in Berlin, *Friedrich Adolf Trendelenburg* (1802–72), could be sure of meeting strong public approval when he pronounced the judgment that Hegel wanted "to teach without learning" through his method because he was under the impression "that he was in possession of the divine concept, which is hampered by the process of laborious research work." It was in vain that Michelet attempted to correct such a judgment by quoting Hegel's own words: "To experience we owe the development of philosophy. The empirical sciences prepare the content of the particular to the point where they can be admitted into the realm of philosophy. They also imply thereby the need of thinking itself to come up with concrete definitions."

Characteristic of the course of development of the world conceptions of the middle decades of the nineteenth century is an observation made by an important but unfortunately little known thinker, *K. Ch. Planck.* In the preface of an excellent book published in 1850 and entitled, *The World Ages*, he says:

> To realize consciously that everything is under the condition of a purely natural order of law, and at the same time to produce the full self-conscious freedom of the spirit, the self-dependent inner law of its nature, this twofold tendency, which is the distinguishing fundamental signature of modern history, presents in its most direct and pure form also the task of the present book. The first tendency becomes apparent on all sides since the revival of the sciences in the rebirth of independent and comprehensive natural research and its liberation from the purely religious life. It can be seen in the change of the whole physical world conception caused by this, as well as in the ever increasing matter of factness of the view of things in general. It appears finally, in its highest form, in the philosophical tendency to comprehend the laws of nature according to their inner necessity, but it also shows its practical aspect in the gradual development of this immediate present life with respect to its natural conditions.

The growing influence of the natural sciences is expressed in words like this. The confidence in these sciences was becoming greater. The belief became predominant that through the means and the results of the natural sciences one could obtain a world conception that is free from the unsatisfactory elements of the Hegelian one.

A picture of the total change that took place in this direction can be derived from a book that can be considered as representative of this period in the fullest sense of the word, Alexander von Humboldt's, *Cosmos, Sketch of a Physical World Description*. The author, who represents the pinnacle of education in the field of physical science of his time, speaks of his confidence in a world conception of natural science:

> My confidence is based on the splendid state of the natural sciences themselves, whose wealth consists no longer in the abundance of their facts but in the interconnections of the observations. The general results that impress every educated mind as interesting have wonderfully multiplied since the end of the eighteenth century. The individual facts stand less isolated by themselves; the gaps between the formations are closed. What remained for a long time obscure to the inquiring mind when seen in a narrower horizon becomes explained through the observations that have been obtained on an expedition into the most distant regions. Forms of plants and animals, which seemed to be isolated for a long time, are now falling in line through the discovery of connecting links or through forms of transition. A general interconnection, not in a simple linear direction, but in a net-like, woven texture according to a higher development, or the stunted growth of certain organisms, is what gradually unfolds before the eye of the inquiring natural observer. . . . The general study of nature awakens in us, as it were, organs that have long been dormant. We enter into a more intimate relation with the outer world.

In his *Cosmos*, Humboldt leads the description of nature only to the gateway of a world conception. He does not make the attempt to connect the wealth of the phenomena by means of general ideas of nature, but links the things and facts in a natural way to each other as can be expected from "the entirely objective turn of his mind."

Soon other thinkers emerged who were bold enough to make combinations and who tried to penetrate into the nature of things on the basis of natural science. What they intended to produce was nothing less than a radical transformation of all former philosophical world and life conceptions by means of modern science and knowledge of nature. In the most forceful way the natural science of the nineteenth century had paved the way for them. What they intended to do is radically expressed by Feuerbach:

> To assume God before nature is about the same as to assume the church before you have the stone out of which it is built, or to assume that the art of architecture has put the stones together to make a building before the chemical compounds that make up the stone, in short, before the natural genesis and formation of the stone.

The first half of the century produced many results of natural science that are bricks for the architecture of a new structure of world conception. It is, to be sure, correct that a building cannot be erected if there are no bricks to do it with, but it is no less true that one cannot do anything with these bricks if, *independent of them*, a picture of the building to be erected does not exist. Just as no structure can come into existence if one puts these bricks together at random, one upon the other and side by side, joining them with mortar as they come, so can no world conception come from the individual known truths of natural science if there is not, *independent of these and of physical research*, a power in the human soul to form the world conception. This fact was left out of consideration by the antagonists of an independent philosophy.

In examining the personalities who in the eighteen-fifties took part in the erection of a structure of world conception, the features of three men are particularly prominent: *Ludwig Buechner* (1824–99), *Carl Vogt* (1817–95) and *Jacob Moleschott* (1822–93). If one wants to characterize the fundamental feeling that inspires these three men, one need only repeat Moleschott's words:

> If man has investigated all properties of the materials that make an impression on his developed sense organs, he has thereby grasped the essence of things. With this accomplishment he arrives at his—that is to say, humanity's—absolute knowledge. Another knowledge does not exist for man.

All philosophy that has been so far advanced has, according to these men, yielded only knowledge without lasting meaning. The idealistic philosophers believe, according to Buechner and those who shared his views, that they derive their knowledge from reason. Through this method, however, one cannot, as Buechner maintains, come to a meaningful structure of conceptions. "But truth can only be gained by listening to nature and her rule," says Moleschott. At that time and during the following years, the protagonists for such a world conception, directly derived from nature, were collectively called materialists. It was emphatically declared that this materialism was an age-old world conception, concerning which enlightened spirits had long recognized how unsatisfactory it was for a higher thinker. Buechner attacked that opinion. He pointed out that:

> In the first place materialism, or the whole philosophical current moving in its direction, has never been disproved. It is not only the oldest form of philosophical contemplation in existence but also one that emerged anew with new energies at every revival of philosophy in the course of history. Furthermore, the materialism of our day is no longer the same as it was formerly with Epicurus or the Encyclopedists, but an entirely different thought current or methods, which is supported by the results of the positive sciences. This is a method that is distinguished from its preceding form by the fact that it is no more like the older materialism, a system, but a simple realistic philosophical contemplation of existence that, above all, traces the uniform principle in the world of nature and of the spirit, striving to show everywhere a natural and law-determined connection of all phenomena of that world.

Goethe's attitude toward Holbach, one of the most prominent materialists of the eighteenth century French Encyclopedists, illustrates the position a spirit, who strives in a most pronounced way for a thinking in accordance with nature and does full justice to the mode of conception of natural science, can nevertheless take toward materialism. *Paul Heinrich Dietrich von Holbach* (1723–1789) published his *Système de la Nature* in 1770. Goethe, who came across this book in Strassburg, in *Poetry and Truth* describes the repulsive impression that he received from it.

Matter was to be there from eternity, and it was to have been in motion from eternity. Through this motion, now to the right, now to the left in all directions, it was to have produced without further difficulty all the infinite phenomena of existence. This we might even have accepted as satisfactory if the author had really constructed before our eyes the world out of his matter in motion. But he might have known as little about nature as we did, for after postulating a few general concepts, he again turns away from nature in order to transform what appears higher than nature, or what appears as a higher nature in nature, into the material, heavy nature, to be sure, in motion, but without direction and shape, and he thinks that he gained a great deal in so doing.

Goethe was deeply convinced that "theory in itself and by itself has no value except to make us believe in the connection of the phenomena." (*Sprueche in Prosa*, Deutsche Nationalliteratur, Goethe's Werke, Vol. 36, 2, pp. 357.)

The results of natural science gained in the first half of the nineteenth century were, to be sure, as knowledge of facts, well-suited to supply a foundation to the materialists of the fifties for their world conception. Science has penetrated deeper and deeper into the connections of the material processes insofar as they can be reached by sense observation and by the form of thinking that is based on that sense observation. If one now wants to deny to oneself and to others that there is spirit active in matter, one nevertheless unconsciously reveals this spirit. For what Friedrich Theodor Vischer says in the third volume of his essay, *On Old and New Things*, is in a certain sense quite correct. "That the so-called matter can produce something, the function of which is spirit, is in itself the complete proof against materialism." In this sense, Buechner unconsciously disproves materialism by attempting to prove that the spiritual processes spring from the depths of the material facts presented to sense observation.

An example that shows how the results of natural science took on forms that could be of a deeply penetrating influence on the conception of the world is given in *Woehler's* discovery of 1828. This scientist succeeded in producing a substance synthetically outside the living organism that had previously only been known to be formed within. This experiment seemed to supply the proof that the former belief, which assumed that certain material compounds could be formed only under the influence of a special life force contained in the organism, was incorrect. If it was possible to produce such compounds outside the living body, then one could draw the conclusion that the organism was also working only with the forces with which chemistry deals. The thought arose for the materialists that, if the living organism does not need a special life force to produce what formerly had been attributed to such a force, why should this organism then need special spiritual energies in order to produce the processes to which mental experiences are bound? Matter in all its qualities now became for the materialists what generates all things and processes from its core. From the fact that carbon, hydrogen, oxygen and nitrogen combine in an organic compound, it did not seem far to go to Buechner's statement, "The words soul, spirit, thought, feeling, will, life, do not stand for any real things but only for properties, qualifications, functions of the living substance, or results of entities that have their basis in the material forms of existence." A divine being or the human soul were no longer called immortal by Buechner, but rather matter and energy. Moleschott expressed the same conviction with the words:

> Energy is not a creative God; no essence of things is detachable from the material basis. It is a quality of matter, inseparable from it, eternally inherent in it. Carbon, hydrogen and oxygen are the powers that split the firmest rock and transform it into fluid processes in which life is generated. Change of matter and form in the individual parts while the fundamental structure remains the same is the mystery of animal life.

The research done in the first half of the nineteenth century in natural science enabled Ludwig Buechner to express the view, "In a way similar to that in which the steam engine produces motion, the intricate organic complication of energy endowed materials in the animal body produces a sum total of certain effects, which, combined in a unity, are called spirit, soul, thought by us." And *Karl Gustav Reuschle* declared in his book, *Philosophy and Natural Science, in Memory of David Friedrich Strauss* (1874), that the results of natural science themselves implied a philosophical element. The affinities that one discovered between the natural forces were thought to lead into the mysteries of existence.

Such an important relation was found by *Oersted* in 1819 in Copenhagen. He saw that a magnetic needle is deflected by an electric current. *Faraday* discovered the corresponding phenomenon in 1831, that by moving a magnet toward a spirally twisted copper wire, electricity can be generated in the latter. Electricity and magnetism thereby were shown to be related natural phenomena. Both energies were no longer isolated facts; it was now apparent that they had a common basis in their material existence. *Julius Robert Mayer* penetrated deeper into the nature of matter and energy in the eighteen-forties when he became aware of the fact that there exists a definite relation that can be expressed numerically between mechanical work and heat. Out of pressure, impact and friction, etc., that is to say, out of work, heat is generated. In the steam engine, heat is again changed into work. The quantity of heat produced by a given amount of work can be calculated from the quantity of this work. If one changes the quantity of heat that is necessary to heat a kilogram of water by one degree centigrade into work, one can with this work lift 424 kilograms to a height of one meter. It cannot be surprising that the discovery of such facts was considered to be a vast progress away from such explanations concerning matter as Hegel had offered: "The transition from ideality to reality, from abstraction to concrete existence, in this case, from space and time to the reality that appears as matter, is incomprehensible for the intellect and therefore appears to it always as something external and merely given." The significance of a remark of this kind is recognized only if *thought* as such can be seen as something valuable. This consideration, however, would not occur to the above-mentioned thinkers.

To discoveries such as these concerning the unity of the organic forces of nature, others were added that threw light on the problem of the composition of the world of organisms. In 1838 the botanist, *Schleiden,* recognized the significance of the simple cell for the plant organism. He showed that every texture of the plant, and therefore the plant itself, is made up of these "elementary organisms." Schleiden had recognized this "elementary organism" as a little drop of mucilaginous fluid surrounded by a cellular membrane. These cells are so multiplied and joined to one another that they form the structure of the plant. Soon after this, *Schwann* discovered the same general structure for the world of animal organisms. Then, in 1827, the brilliant naturalist, *Karl Ernst von Baer,* discovered the human egg. He also described the process of the development of higher animals and of man from the egg.

In this way one had everywhere given up the attempt to look for ideas that could be considered fundamental for the things of nature. Instead, one had observed the facts that show in which way the higher, more complicated processes and entities of nature develop from the simpler and lower ones. The men who were in search of an idealistic interpretation of the phenomena of the world became ever more rare. It was still the spirit of idealistic world conception that in 1837 inspired the anthropologist, Burdach, with the view that life did not have its origin in matter but rather a higher force transformed matter according to its own design. Moleschott had already said, "The force of life, as life itself, is nothing more than the result of the complicated interacting and interweaving physical and chemical forces."

The consciousness of the time tended to explain the universe through no other phenomena than those that are displayed before the eyes of men. Charles Lyell's work, *Principles of Geology*, which was published in 1830, brought the whole older geology to an end with this principle of explanation. Up to Lyell's epoch-making work it was believed that the evolution of the earth had taken place in abrupt revolutions. Everything that had come into being on earth was supposed to have been destroyed repeatedly by complete catastrophies. Over the graves of the victims new creations were supposed to have risen. In this manner, one explained the presence of the remnants of plants and animals in the various strata of the earth. Cuvier was the principal representative who believed in such repeated periods of creation. Lyell was convinced that it was unnecessary to assume such interruptions of the steady course of evolution of the earth. If one only presupposed sufficiently long periods of time, one could say that forces today still at work on earth caused the entire development. In Germany, Goethe and Karl von Hoff had already professed such a view. Von Hoff maintained it in his *History of the Natural Changes of the Surface of the Earth, Documented by Traditional Sources*, which appeared in 1822. With great boldness of thought, enthusiasts Vogt, Buechner and Moleschott set out to explain all phenomena from material processes as they take place before the senses of man.

The situation that arose when the physiologist, Rudolf Wagner, found himself opposed by Carl Vogt was typical of the intellectual warfare that the materialists had to wage. In 1852, in the paper, *Allgemeine Zeitung*, Wagner had declared himself in favor of accepting an independent soul entity, thereby opposing the view of materialism. He said "that the soul could divide itself because the child inherited much from his father and much also from his mother." Vogt answered this statement for the first time in his *Pictures from Animal Life*. His position in this controversy is clearly exposed in the following:

> The soul, which is to be the substance, the very essence of the individuality of the individual, indivisable entity, is to be capable of dividing itself. Theologists, be sure you catch this heretic. He has been up to now one of your people! Divided souls! If the soul can be divided in the act of conception as Mr. Rudolf Wagner thinks, then it could also be possible that this soul could be divided in death, the portion that was burdened with sins going into purgatory, while the other part would go directly into paradise. Mr. Wagner also promises at the end of his physiological letters some excursions into the field of the physiology of the divided souls.

The controversy became intense when Wagner, at the assembly of natural scientists in Goettingen in 1854, read a paper against materialism entitled, *Man's Creation and the Substance of the Soul.* He meant to prove two things. In the first place, he set out to show that the results of modern physical science were not a contradiction of the biblical belief in the descent of the human race from one couple. In the second instance, he wanted to demonstrate that these results did not imply anything concerning the soul. Vogt wrote a polemical treatise, *Bigoted Faith and Science* (*Koehlerglaube und Wissenschaft*), against Wagner in 1855, which showed him to be equipped with the full insight of the natural science of his time. At the same time, he appeared to be a sharp thinker who, without reserve, disclosed his opponents' conclusions as illusions. Vogt's contradiction of Wagner's first statement comes to a climax in the passage, "All investigations of history and of natural history lead to the positive proof of the origin of the human races from a plurality of roots. The doctrines of the Scripture concerning Adam and Noah, and the twice occurring descent of man from a single couple are scientifically untenable legends."

Against Wagner's doctrine of the soul, Vogt maintained that we see the psychical activities of man develop gradually as part of the development of the physical organs. From childhood to the maturity of life we observe that the spiritual activities become more perfect. With the shrinking of the senses and the brain, the "spirit" shrinks proportionally. "A development of this kind is not consistent with the assumption of an immortal soul substance that has been planted into the brain as its organ."

That the materialists, as they fought their opponents, were not merely confronted with intellectual reasons but also with emotions, becomes perfectly clear in the controversy between Vogt and Wagner. For Wagner had appealed, in a paper at Goettingen, for the moral need that could not endure the thought that "mechanical machines walking about with two arms and legs" should finally be dissolved into indifferent material substances, without leaving us the hope that the good they are doing should be rewarded and the evil punished. Vogt's answer was, "The existence of an immortal soul is, for Mr. Wagner, not the result of investigation and thought. . . . He needs an immortal soul in order to see it tortured and punished after the death of man."

Heinrich Czolbe (1819–73) attempted to show that there is a point of view from which the moral world order can be in agreement with the views of materialism. In his book, *The Limits and Origin of Knowledge Seen in Opposition to Kant and Hegel,* which appeared in 1865, he explained that every theology had its origin in a dissatisfaction with this world.

> The exclusion of the supersensible, or those incomprehensible things that lead to the assumption of a second world, that is, to naturalism, is in no way forced upon us through the power of the facts of natural science—not even through philosophy that means to know everything—but in the last analysis through morality, namely, through that particular kind of moral behavior in man toward the world that we can call satisfaction with the natural world.

Czolbe considers the longing for a supernatural world actually a result of an ingratitude against the natural world. The basic causes of a philosophy that looks toward a world beyond this one are, for him, moral shortcomings, sins against the spirit of the natural world order. For these sins distract us "from the striving toward the highest possible happiness of every individual" and from fulfilling the duty that follows from such a striving "against ourselves and others without regard for supernatural reward and punishment." According to Czolbe, every human being is to be filled with a "grateful acceptance of his share of earthly happiness, which may be possibly small, and with a humble acceptance of its limits and its necessary sorrow." Here we meet a rejection of a supernatural world order for moral reasons.

In Czolbe's world conception one also sees clearly what qualities made materialism so acceptable to human thinking, for there is no doubt that Buechner, Vogt and Moleschott were not philosophers to a sufficient degree to demonstrate the foundations of their views logically. Without losing their way in heights of idealistic thoughts, in their capacity as naturalists they drew their conclusions more from sense observations. To render an account of their method by justifying it from the nature of human knowledge was no enterprise to their liking. Czolbe, however, did undertake just that. In his *New Presentation of Sensualism* (1855), we find the reasons given why he considers a knowledge built on the basis of sensual perceptions valuable. Only a knowledge of this kind supplies concepts, judgments and conclusions that can be distinctly conceived and envisaged. Every conclusion that leads to something sensually inconceivable, and every indistinct concept is to be rejected. The soul element is not clearly conceivable, according to Czolbe, but the material on which the spiritual appears as a quality. He therefore attempts to reduce self-consciousness to visible material processes in the essay he published in 1856, *The Genesis of Self-consciousness, an Answer to Professor Lotze*. Here he assumes a circular movement of the parts of the brain. Through such a motion returning in its own track, the impression that a thing causes in the senses is made into a conscious sensation. It is strange that this physical explanation of consciousness became, at the same time, the occasion for him to abandon his materialism. This is the point where one of the weaknesses inherent in materialism becomes apparent in him. If he had remained faithful to his principle, he would never have gone further than the facts that are accessible to the senses allow. He would speak of no other processes in the brain than those that can positively be asserted through the means of natural science. What Czolbe sets out to establish is, however, an aim in an infinite distance. Spirits like Czolbe are not satisfied with what *is* investigated, they hypothetically assume facts that have not as yet been investigated. Such an alleged fact is the circular motion of the parts of the brain. A complete investigation of the brain will most likely lead to the discovery of processes of a kind that do not occur anywhere else in the world. From them, one will be able to draw the conclusion that the psychical processes conditioned by brain processes do occur *only* in connection with a brain. Concerning his hypothetical circular movements, Czolbe could not claim that they were limited to the brain. They could occur also outside the animal organism, but in that case, they would have to lead to psychical phenomena also in inanimate objects. Czolbe, who is so insistent on perceptual clarity, actually does not consider an animation of all nature as impossible. He asks, "Should not my view be a realization of the world soul, which Plato defended in his Timaeus? Should we not be able to find here the point where the Leibnizian idealism, which has the whole world consist of animated entities (monads), unites with modern naturalism?"

On a larger scale the mistake that Czolbe made with circular brain motion occurred again in the brilliant thinker, *Carl Christian Planck* (1819–80). The writings of this man have been completely forgotten, in spite of the fact that they belong to the most interesting works of modern philosophy. Planck strives as intensely as any materialist for a world conception that is completely derived from perceptible reality. He criticizes the German idealism of Fichte, Schelling and Hegel for seeking the essence of things onesidedly in the idea. "To explain things really out of themselves is to recognize them in their original conditioned state and in their finiteness." (Compare Planck, *The World Ages*.) "There is only the one and truly pure nature, so that mere nature in the narrower sense of the word and spirit are opposites only within the one nature in the higher and more comprehensive sense."

Now the strange thing happens in Planck's philosophy that he declares the real, the world extending before him, to be the element that the explanation of the world has to seek. He nevertheless does not proceed with the observation of the facts in order to reach this element of the real world extending before him, for he believes that human reason is capable of penetrating through its own power to the real. Hegel had, according to Planck, made the mistake of having reason contemplate its own being so that it saw itself again in all things. Planck, however, intended to have reason no longer withheld within its own limits, but to have it go beyond itself into the element of extension, the truly real. Planck blames Hegel because Hegel had reason spin its own cobweb out of itself, whereas he, himself, is bold enough to have reason spin real objective existence. Hegel maintained that the spirit is capable of comprehending the essence of things because reason *is* the essence of things and because it comes into being in the human spirit. Planck declares that the essence of things is not reason, but he uses reason merely to represent this essence. A bold world construction, brilliantly conceived, but conceived far from real observation, far from real things, yet constructed in the belief that it was entirely permeated with genuine reality—such is Planck's structure of ideas. He considers the world process a living interplay of expansion and contraction. Gravity is for him the tendency of the bodies, spread in space, to contract. Heat and light are the tendency of a body to bring its contracted matter into activity at a distance, and therefore the tendency of expansion.

Planck's relation toward his contemporaries is most interesting. Feuerbach said of himself, "Hegel maintains the standpoint that he wants to construct the world; my standpoint is to know the world as being; he descends, I ascend. Hegel stands man on his head; I place him on his feet, which are resting on geology." With these words the materialists could also have characterized their credo, but Planck proceeds in his method exactly like Hegel. He believes, however, that he proceeds like Feuerbach and the materialists. The materialists, if they had interpreted his method in their own way, would have had to say to him, "From your standpoint you attempt to construct the world. Nevertheless, you believe you proceed by recognizing the world as being; you descend, but you take this descent to be an ascent. You stand the world on its head and you are of the opinion that that head is a foot." The will toward natural, factual reality could probably not be expressed more poignantly than through the world conception of a man who wanted to produce not merely ideas but reality out of reason.

The personality of Planck appears no less interesting when he is compared with his contemporary, Max Stirner. It is significant here to consider Planck's ideas concerning the motivations of human action and community life. As the materialist proceeded from the materials and forces actually presented to the senses to arrive at their explanation of nature, so Stirner started from the real individual personality as a guide line for human behavior. Reason is only with the individual. What reason decides on as a guide line for action can therefore also have validity only for the individual. Life in community will naturally result from the natural interaction of the individual personalities. If everyone acts according to his reason, the most desirable state of affairs will come to pass through the most free cooperation of all. The natural community life comes into being as a matter of course if everyone has reason rule his own individuality since, according to the materialists, the natural view of worldly phenomena comes to pass if one has the things express their nature and if one limits the activity of reason to a mere combination and interpretation of the statements of the senses. As Planck does not explain the world by allowing things to speak for themselves, but decides by his reason what the things allegedly say, so he also does not, in regard to community life, depend on a real interaction of personalities but dreams of an association of peoples with a supreme judicial power serving the general welfare and ordered by reason. Here also, then, he considers it possible that reason should master what lies beyond the personality.

> The original general law of right demands necessarily its external existence in a general power of right, for it would itself not be real as a general element in an external form if it were left to the individuals themselves to execute it, as the individuals by themselves are, according to their legal positions, only representatives of their personal right, not as the general right as such.

Planck constructs the general power of right because he can realize the idea of right for himself only in this manner. Five years earlier, Max Stirner had written, "My own master and the creator of my own right—I recognize no other source of right than myself. Neither God, nor state, nor nature, nor man himself with his 'eternal human rights,' neither a divine nor a human right." It is his opinion that the real right of the individual cannot exist within a general right. It is thirst for reality that drives Stirner to take his negative attitude toward an unreal general right. It is the same thirst for reality that, in turn, motivates Planck in his attempt to crystallize out of an idea a real state of right.

In reading Planck's books one feels that he was deeply disturbed by the thought of a twofold world order. He considered the belief in such an interaction of two world orders—a natural order and a purely spiritual one—as something contrary to nature and intolerable.

There have been thinkers before Planck's time, of course, who strove for a purely natural-scientific mode of conception. Leaving aside several other more or less clear attempts in this direction, Lamarck, for instance, in 1809 outlined a picture of the genesis and development of living organisms, which, according to the state of knowledge of his time, should have had a great deal of attraction for a contemporary world conception. He thought of the simplest organisms as having come into existence through inorganic processes under certain conditions. Once an organism is formed in this way, it develops, through adjustment to given conditions of the external world, new formations that serve its life. It grows new organs because it needs them. The organisms then are capable of transformation and thereby also of perfection. Lamarck imagines this transformation in the following way. Consider an animal that gets its food from high trees. It is therefore compelled to stretch its neck. In the course of time its neck then becomes longer under the influence of this need. A short-necked animal is transformed into the giraffe with its long neck. The animals, then, have not come into existence in their variety, but this variety has developed in the course of time under the influence of changing conditions. Lamarck is of the opinion that man is included in this evolution. Man has developed in the course of time out of related forms similar to monkeys into forms that allowed him to satisfy higher physical and spiritual needs. Lamarck in this way linked up the whole world of organisms, including man, to the realm of the inorganic.

Lamarck's attempt at an explanation of the varieties of the forms of life was met with little attention by his contemporaries. Two decades later a controversy arose in the French Academy between Geoffroy St. Hilaire and George Cuvier. Geoffroy St. Hilaire believed he recognized a common structural design in the world of animal organisms in spite of its great variety. Such a general plan was a necessary prerequisite for an explanation of their development from one another. If they had developed from one another, they must have had some fundamental common element in spite of their variety. In the lowest animal something must be recognizable that only needs perfection in order to change this lower form in the course of time into that of a higher animal. Cuvier turned strongly against the consequences of this view. He was a cautious man who pointed out that the facts did not uphold such far-reaching conclusions. As soon as Goethe heard of this conflict, he considered it the most important event of the time. Compared to this controversy, the interest that he took in the July Revolution, a political event that took place at the same time, appears insignificant. Goethe expressed himself on this point clearly enough in a conversation that he had with Soret in August, 1830. He saw clearly that the adequate conception of the organic world depended on this controversial point. In an essay Goethe supported St. Hilaire with great intensity. (Compare Goethe's writings on natural science, Vol. 36, Goethe Edition, Deutsche National Literatur.) He told Johannes von Mueller that he considered Geoffroy St. Hilaire to be moving in the same direction he himself had taken up fifty years earlier. This shows clearly what Goethe meant to do when he began, shortly after his arrival in Weimar, to take up his studies on animal and plant formations. Even then he had an explanation of the variety of living forms in mind that was more adequate to nature, but he was also a cautious man. He never maintained more than what the facts entitled him to state, and he tells in his introduction to his *Metamorphosis of the Plant* that the time was then in considerable confusion with respect to these facts. The opinion prevailed, as Goethe expressed it, that it was only necessary for the monkey to stand up and to walk on his hind legs in order to become a human being.

The thinkers of natural science maintained a mode of conception that was completely different from that of the Hegelians. For the Hegelians, it was possible to remain within their ideal world. They could develop their idea of man from their idea of the monkey without being concerned with the question of how nature could manage to bring man into being in the real world side by side with the monkey. Michelet had simply pronounced that it was no concern of the idea to explain the specific "how" of the processes in the real world. The thinker who forms an idealistic world conception is, in this respect, in the same position as the mathematician who only has to say through what thought operation a circle is changed into an ellipse and an ellipse into a parabola or hyperbola. A thinker, however, who strives for an explanation through facts would have to point at the actual processes through which such a transformation can come to pass. He is then forming a realistic world conception. Such a thinker will not take the position that Hegel describes:

> It has been a clumsy conception of the older and also of the more recent philosophy of nature to consider the development and transition of one form and realm of nature into a higher one as an external and real production that one has dated back into the darkness of the past for the sake of clarification. It is characteristic of nature to be so external in its structure that its forms fall apart in differentiated manifestations and that these forms exist indifferently side by side; the idea, which guides the stages in their succession, *is* the inner nature of these separated manifestations. Such nebulous conceptions, which are really just sensual conceptions, as, for instance, the alleged progression of plants and animals from water, and then again, the evolution of the more developed animal formations from the lower ones, and so forth, must be given up by a thoughtful contemplation. (Hegel's Werke, 1847, Vol. 7, p. 33.)

In opposition to such a statement of an idealistic thinker, we hear that of the realistic Lamarck:

> In the primal beginning only the simplest and lowest animals and plants developed, and only lastly those of a highly complicated organization. The course of the evolution of the earth and its organic population was quite gradual and not interrupted by violent revolutions. The simplest animals and the simplest plants that occupy the lowest stages on the scale of organisms have come into existence, and do so even today, through spontaneous generation (*generatio spontanea*).

There was in Germany also a man of the same conviction as Lamarck. *Lorenz Oken* (1779–1859) presented a natural evolution of organic beings that was based on "sensual conceptions." To quote him, "Everything organic has originated from a slimy substance (*Urschleim*), is merely slime formed in various ways. This original slime has come into being in the ocean in the course of the planetary evolution out of inorganic matter."

In spite of such deeply provocative turns of thought there had to be, especially with thinkers who were too cautious to leave the thread of factual knowledge, a doubt against a naturalistic mode of thinking of this kind as long as the question of the teleology of living beings had not been cleared. Even Johannes Mueller, who was a pioneer as a thinker and as a research scientist, was, because of his consideration of the idea of teleology, prompted to say:

> The organic bodies are distinguished from the inorganic not merely by the composition of elements that they represent, but also by the continuous activity that is at work in living organic matter, which creates also teleologically and in a reason-directed plan, by arranging the parts for the purpose of the whole. It is this that is the distinguishing mark of an organism. (Johannes Mueller, *Handbuch der Physiologie des Menschen*, 3, 1838; Vol. 1, p. 19.)

With a man like Johannes Mueller, who remained strictly within the limits of natural scientific research, and for whom the thought of purpose-conformity remained as a private conviction in the background of his factual research work, this view was not likely to produce any particular consequences. He investigated the laws of the organisms in strict objectivity regardless of the purpose connection, and became a reformer of modern natural science through his comprehensive mind; he knew how to make use of the physical, chemical, anatomical, zoological, microscopical and embryological knowledge in an unlimited way. His view did not keep him from basing psychological qualities of the objects of his studies on their physical characteristics. It was one of his fundamental convictions that no one could be a psychologist without being a physiologist. But if a thinker went beyond the field of research in natural science and entered the realm of a general world conception, he was not in the fortunate position easily to discard an idea like that of teleological structure. For this reason, it is easy to understand why a thinker of the importance of *Gustave Theodor Fechner* (1801–87) would make the statement in his book, *Zend-Avesta, or Concerning the Nature of Heaven and the World Beyond* (1852), that it seems strange how anyone can believe that no consciousness would be necessary to create conscious beings as the human beings are, since even unconscious machines can be created only by conscious human beings. Also, *Karl Ernst von Baer,* who followed the evolution of the animals from their initial state, could not resist the thought that the processes in living organisms were striving toward certain goals and that the full concept of purpose was, indeed, to be applied for all of nature. (Karl Ernst von Baer, *Studies from the Field of Natural Science,* 1876, pp. 73 & 82.)

Difficulties of this kind, which confront certain thinkers as they intend to build up a world picture, the elements of which are supposed to be taken entirely from the sensually perceptible nature, were not even noticed by materialistic thinkers. They attempted to oppose the idealistic world picture of the first half of the century with one that receives all explanation exclusively from the facts of nature. Only in a knowledge that had been gained from these facts did they have any confidence.

There is nothing more enlightening concerning the inner conviction of the materialists than this confidence. They have been accused of taking the soul out of things and thereby depriving them of what speaks to man's heart, his feelings. Does it not seem that they do take all qualities out of nature that lift man's spirit and that they debase nature into a dead object that satisfies only the intellect that looks for causes but deprives us of any inner involvement? Does it not seem that they undermine morality that rises above mere natural appetites and looks for motivations, merely advocating the cause of animal desires, subscribing to the motto: Let us eat and drink and follow our physical instincts for tomorrow we die? Lotze (1817–81) indeed makes the statement with respect to the materialistic thinkers of the time in question that the followers of this movement value the truth of the drab empirical knowledge in proportion to the degree in which it offends everything that man's inner feelings hold sacred.

When one becomes acquainted, however, with Carl Vogt, one finds in him a man who had a deep understanding for the beauty of nature and who attempted to express this as an amateur painter. He was a person who was not at all blind to the creations of human imagination but felt at home with painters and poets. Quite a number of materialists were inspired by the esthetic enjoyment of the wonderful structure of organisms to a point where they felt that the soul must have its origin in the body. The magnificent structure of the human brain impressed them much more than the abstract concepts with which philosophy was concerned. How much more claim to be considered as the causes of the spirit, therefore, did the former seem to present than the latter.

Nor can the reproach that the materialists debased morality be accepted without reserve. Their knowledge of nature was deeply bound up with ethical motivations. Czolbe's endeavor to stress the moral foundation of naturalism was shared by other materialists. They all meant to instill in man the joy of natural existence; they intended to direct him toward his duties and his tasks on earth. They felt that human dignity could be enhanced if man could be conscious of having developed from a lower being to his present state of perfection. They believed that only a man who knows the material necessities that underlie his actions is capable of properly judging them. They argued that only *he* knows how to judge a man according to his value who is aware that matter is the basis for life in the universe, that with natural necessity life is connected with thought and thought in turn gives rise to good and ill will. To those who see moral freedom endangered by materialism, Moleschott answers:

> Everybody is free who is joyfully aware of the natural necessity of his existence, his circumstances, claims and demands, and of the limits and extent of his sphere of activity. A man who understands this natural necessity knows also his right to fight his way through for demands that are in accordance with the needs of the human race. More than that, because only that freedom that is in harmony with the genuinely human will be defended with natural necessity by the species. We can be assured of the final victory over all suppressors in any struggle for human ends.

With attitudes of this kind, with a devotion to the wonders of nature, with moral sentiments as described above, the materialists were ready to receive the man who overcame the great obstacle for a naturalistic world conception. This man appeared to them in *Charles Darwin*. His work, through which the teleological idea was placed on the solid ground of natural science, was published in 1859 with the title, *The Origin of the Species by Means of Natural Selection, or the Preservation of Favored Races in the Struggle for Life.*

For an understanding of the impulses that are at work in the evolution of philosophical world conception, the examples of the advances in natural science mentioned (to which many others could be added) are *not significant in themselves.* What is important is the fact that advances of this kind coincided in time with the development of the Hegelian world picture. The presentation of the course of evolution of philosophy in the previous chapters has shown that the modern world picture, since the days of Copernicus, Galileo, etc., stood under the influence of the mode of conception of natural science. This influence, however, could not be as significant as that of the accomplishment of the natural sciences of the nineteenth century. There were also important advances of natural science at the turn of the eighteenth to the nineteenth centuries. We only need to be reminded of the discovery of oxygen by Lavoisier, and of the findings in the field of electricity by Volta and many others. In spite of these discoveries spirits like Fichte, Schelling and Goethe could, while they fully recognized these advances, nevertheless, arrive at a world picture that started from the spirit. They could not be so powerfully impressed by the mode of conception of natural science as were the materialistic thinkers in the middle of the nineteenth century. It was still possible to recognize on the *one* side of the world picture the conceptions of natural science, and on the *other* side of it, certain conceptions that contained *more* than "mere thought." Such a conception was, for instance, that of the "force of life," or of the "teleological structure" of an organism. Conceptions of this kind made it possible to say that there is something at work in the world that does not come under the ordinary natural law, something that is more spiritual. In this fashion one obtained a conception of the spirit that had, as it were, "a factual content." Hegel had then proceeded to deprive the spirit of all factual elements. He had diluted it into "mere thought." For those for whom "mere thoughts" could be nothing but *pictures* of factual elements, this step appeared as the philosophical proof of the unreality of the spirit. These thinkers felt that they had to find something that possessed a real content for them to take the place of Hegel's "mere thought things." For this reason, they sought the origin of the "spiritual phenomena" in material processes that could be sensually observed "as facts." The world conception was pressed toward the thought of the material origin of the spirit through the transformation of the spirit that Hegel had brought about.

If one understands that there are deeper forces at work in the historical course of human evolution than those appearing on the surface, one will recognize the significance for the development of world conception that lies in the characteristic attitude that the materialism of the nineteenth century takes toward the formation of the Hegelian philosophy. Goethe's thoughts contained the seeds for a continuation of a philosophy that was taken up by Hegel, but insufficiently. If Goethe attempted to obtain a conception with his "archetypal plant" that allowed him to experience this thought inwardly so that he could intellectually derive from it such a specific plant formation as would be capable of life, he showed thereby that he was striving to bring thought to life within his soul. Goethe had reached the point where thought was about to begin a life-like evolution, while Hegel did not go beyond thought as such. In communion with a thought that had come to life within the soul, as Goethe attempted, one would have had a spiritual experience that could have recognized the spirit also in matter. In "mere thought" one had no such experience. Thus, the evolution of world conception was put to a hard test. According to the deeper historical impulses, the modern time tended to experience *not thought alone,* but to find a conception for the self-conscious ego through which one could be aware that this ego is firmly rooted in the structure of the world. In conceiving this ego as a product of material processes, one had pursued this tendency by simply following the trend in a form easily understandable at that time. Even the *denial* of the spiritual entity of the self-conscious ego by the materialism of the nineteenth century still contains the impulse of the search for this ego. For this reason, the impulse with which natural science affected philosophy in this age was quite different from the influences it had had on previous materialistic currents. These earlier currents had not as yet been so hard pressed by something comparable to Hegel's thought philosophy to seek for a safe ground in the natural sciences. This pressure, to be sure, does not affect the leading personalities to a point where they are clearly aware of it, but as an impulse of the time, it exerts its effect in the subconscious currents of the soul.

Chapter II

Darwinism and World Conception

If the thought of the teleological structure of nature was to be reformed in the sense of a naturalistic world conception, the purpose-adjusted formation of the organic world had to be explained in the same fashion as the physicist or the chemist explains the lifeless processes. When a magnet attracts iron shavings, no physicist will assume that there is a force at work in the magnet that aims toward the purpose of the attraction. When hydrogen and oxygen form water as a compound, the chemist does not interpret this process as if something in both substances had been actively striving toward the purpose of forming water. An explanation of living beings that is guided by a similar naturalistic mode of thinking must conclude that organisms become purpose-adjusted without anything in nature planning this purpose-conformity. This conformity comes to pass without being anywhere intended. Such an explanation was given by Charles Darwin. He took the point of view that there is nothing in nature that plans the design. Nature is never in a position to consider whether its products are adequate to a purpose or not. It produces without choosing between what is adequate to a purpose and what is not.

What is the meaning of this distinction anyhow? When is a

thing in conformity with a purpose? Is it not when it is so arranged that the external circumstances correspond to its needs, to its life conditions? A thing is inadequate to purpose when this is not the case. What will happen if, while a complete absence of plan in nature characterizes the situation, formations of all degrees of purpose-conformity, from the most to the least adequately adapted form, come into existence? Every being will attempt to adapt its existence to the given circumstances. A being well-adjusted to life will do so without much difficulty; one less adequately endowed will succeed only to a lesser degree. The fact must be added to this that nature is not a parsimonious housekeeper in regard to the production of living beings. The number of germs is prodigious. The abundant production of germs is backed up by inadequate means for the support of life. The effect of this will be that those beings that are better adapted to the acquisition of food will more easily succeed in their development. A well-adapted organic being will prevail in the strife for existence over a less adequately adjusted one. The latter must perish in this competition. The fit, that is to say, the one adapted to the purpose of life, survives; the unfit, that is, the one not so adapted, does not. This is the "struggle for life." Thus, the forms adequate to the purpose of life are preserved even if nature itself produces, without choice, the inadequate side by side with the adequate. Through a law, then, that is as objective and as devoid of any wise purpose as any mathematical or mechanical law of nature can be, the course of nature's evolution receives a tendency toward a purpose-conformity that is not originally inherent in it.

Darwin was led to this thought through the work of the social economist Malthus entitled *Essay on the Principle of Population* (1798). In this essay the view is advanced that there is a perpetual competition going on in human society because the population grows at a much faster pace than the supply of food. This law that Malthus had stated as valid for the history of mankind, was generalized by Darwin into a comprehensive law of the whole world of life.

Darwin now set out to show how this struggle for existence

becomes the creator of the various forms of living beings and that thereby the old principle of Linnaeus was overthrown, that "we have to count as many species in the animals and vegetable kingdoms as had been principally created." The doubt against this principle was clearly formed in Darwin's mind when, in the years 1831–36, he was on a journey to South America and Australia. He tells how this doubt took shape in him.

> When I visited the Galapagos Archipelago during my journey on *H.M.S. Beagle*, at a distance of about 500 miles from the shores of South America, I saw myself surrounded by strange species of birds, reptiles and snakes, which exist nowhere else in the world. Almost all of them bore the unmistakable stamp of the American continent. In the song of the mocking-thrush, in the sharp scream of the vultures, in the large candlestick-like opuntias I noticed distinctly the vicinity of America; and yet these islands were separated from the continent by many miles and were very different in their geological constitution and their climate. Even more surprising was the fact that most of the inhabitants of each of the individual islands of the small archipelago were specifically different although closely related. I often asked myself how these strange animals and men had come into being. The simplest way seemed to be that the inhabitants of the various islands were descended from one another and had undergone modifications in the course of their descent, and that all inhabitants of the archipelago were descendants of those of the nearest continent, namely, America, where the colonization naturally would have its origin. But it was for a long time an unexplainable problem to me how the necessary modification could have been obtained.

The answer to this question is contained in the naturalistic conception of the evolution of the living organism. As the physicist subjects a substance to different conditions in order to study its properties, so Darwin, after his return, observed the phenomena that resulted in living beings under different circumstances. He made experiments in breeding pigeons, chickens, dogs, rabbits and plants. Through these experiments it was shown that the living forms continuously change in the course of their propagation. Under certain circumstances some living organisms change so much after a few generations that in comparing the newly bred forms with their ancestors, one could speak of two completely different species, each of which follows its own design of organization. Such a variability of forms is used by the breeder in order to develop organisms through cultivation that answer certain demands. A breeder can produce a species of sheep with an especially fine wool if he allows only those specimens of his flock to be propagated that have the finest wool. The quality of the wool is then improved in the course of the generations. After some time, a species of sheep is obtained which, in the formation of its wool, has progressed far beyond its ancestors. The same is true with other qualities of living organisms. Two conclusions can be drawn from this fact. The first is that nature has the tendency to change living beings; the second, that a quality that has begun to change in a certain direction increases in that direction, if in the process of propagation of organic beings those specimens that do not have this quality are excluded. The organic forms then assume other qualities in the course of time, and continue in the direction of their change once this process has begun. They change and transmit the changed qualities to their descendants.

The natural conclusion from this observation is that change and hereditary transmission are two driving principles in the evolution of organic beings. If it is to be assumed that in the natural course of events in the world, formations that are adapted to life come into being side by side with those not adapted as well as others, it must also be supposed that the struggle for life takes place in the most diversified forms. This struggle effects, without a plan, what the breeder does with the aid of a preconceived plan. As the breeder excludes the specimen from the process of propagation that would introduce undesired qualities into the development, so the struggle for life eliminates the unfit. Only the fit survive in evolution. The tendency for perpetual perfection enters thus into the evolutionary process like a mechanical law. After Darwin had seen this and after he had thereby laid a firm foundation to a naturalistic world conception, he could write the enthusiastic words at the end of his work, *The Origin of Species*, which introduced a new epoch of thought:

> Thus, from the war of nature, from famine and death the most exalted object which we are capable of conceiving, namely, the production of the higher animals, directly follows. There is grandeur in this view of life, with its several powers having been originally breathed by the Creator into a few forms or into one; and that, whilst this planet has gone cycling on according to the fixed law of gravity, from so simple a beginning endless forms most beautiful and most wonderful have been and are being evolved.

At the same time one can see from this sentence that Darwin does not derive his conception from any anti-religious sentiment but merely from the conclusions that for him follow from distinctly significant facts. It was not hostility against the needs of religious experience that persuaded him to a rational view of nature, for he tells us distinctly in his book how this newly acquired world of ideas appeals to his heart.

> Authors of the highest eminence seem to be fully satisfied with the view that each species has been independently created. To my mind it accords better with what we know of the laws impressed in matter by the Creator that the production and extinction of the past and present inhabitants of the world should have been due to secondary causes, like those determining the birth and death of the individual. When I view all beings not as special creations, but as the linear descendants of some few beings which lived long before the first bed of the Cambrian system was deposited, they seem to me to become ennobled. . . . Hence, we may look with some confidence to a secure future of great length. And as natural selection works solely by and for the good of each being, all corporeal and mental endowments will tend to progress toward perfection.

Darwin showed in great detail how the organisms grow and spread, how, in the course of their development, they transmit their properties once they are acquired, how new organs are produced and change through use or through lack of use, how in this way the organic beings are adjusted to their conditions of existence and how finally through the struggle for life a natural selection takes place by means of which an ever increasing variety of more and more perfect forms come into being.

In this way an explanation of teleologically adjusted beings seems to be found that requires no other method for organic nature than that which is used in inorganic nature. As long as it was impossible to offer an explanation of this kind it had to be admitted, if one wanted to be consistent, that everywhere in nature where a purpose-adjusted being came into existence, the intervention of an extraneous power had to be assumed. In every such case one had to admit a miracle.

Those who for decades before the appearance of Darwin's work had endeavored to find a naturalistic world and life conception now felt most vividly that a new direction of thought had been given. This feeling is expressed by *David Friedrich Strauss* in his book, *The Old and the New Faith* (1872).

> One sees this is the way it must go; this is where the new banner is waving sprightly in the wind. It is a real joy in the sense of the loftiest joys of intellectual advance. We philosophers and critical theologians talked and talked to discredit the idea of a miracle. Our decree had no effect whatever, because we did not know how to demonstrate this idea as a superfluous one, because we did not know how to avoid it for we did not know of any energy of nature with which we could replace it where it seemed to be most necessary to be assumed. Darwin has demonstrated this energy of nature, this procedure of nature; he has opened the door through which a fortunate posterity will throw out the miracle once and for all times. Everyone who knows how much depends on miracles will praise him for that deed as one of the greatest benefactors of the human race.

Through Darwin's idea of fitness it is possible to think the concept of evolution really in the form of a natural law. The old doctrine of involution, which assumes that everything that comes into existence has been there in a hidden form before (compare pages 209–10 of the first volume of this book), had been deprived of its last hope with this step. In the process of evolution as conceived by Darwin, the more perfect form is in no way contained in the less perfect one, for the perfection of a higher being comes into existence through processes that have nothing whatsoever to do with the ancestors of this being. Let us assume that a certain evolutionary series has arrived at the marsupials. The form of the marsupials contains nothing at all of a higher, more perfect form. It contains only the ability to change at random in the course of its propagation. Certain circumstances then come to pass that are independent of any "inner" latent tendency of development of the form of the marsupials but that are such that of all possible variations (mutations) the prosimians survive. The forms of the marsupials contained that of the prosimians no more than the direction of a rolling billiard ball contains the path it will take after it has been deflected from its original course by a second billiard ball.

Those accustomed to an idealistic mode of thinking had no easy time in comprehending this reformed conception of evolution. *Friedrich Theodor Vischer,* a man of extraordinary acumen and subtlety of spirit who had come from Hegel's school, writes as late as 1874 in an essay:

> Evolution is an unfolding from a germ that proceeds from attempt to attempt until the picture that the germ contained latently as a possibility has become real. But once this is accomplished it stops and holds on to the form that is found, keeping it as a permanent one. Every concept as such would lose its firm outline if we were to consider the types that have existed on our planet for so many thousands of years as forever variable and above all if we were so to consider our own human type. We should then be unable any longer to trust our thoughts, the laws conceived by our thinking, our feelings, the pictures of our imagination, all of which are nothing but the clarifying imitations of forms of nature as it is known to us. Everything becomes questionable.

In another passage in the same essay he says:

> I still find it a little hard, for instance, to believe that we should owe our eye to the process of seeing, our ear to that of hearing. The

extraordinary weight that is given to the process of natural selection is something I am not quite satisfied with.

If Vischer had been asked whether or not he imagined that hydrogen and oxygen contained within themselves in a latent form a picture of water to make it possible for the latter to develop from the former, he would undoubtedly have answered, "No, neither in oxygen nor in hydrogen is there anything contained of the water that is formed; the conditions for the formation of this substance are given only when hydrogen and oxygen are combined under certain circumstances." Is the situation then necessarily different when, through the two factors of the marsupials and the external conditions, the prosimians came into being? Why should the prosimians be contained as a possibility, as a scheme, in the marsupials in order to be capable of being developed from them? What comes into being through evolution is generated as a new formation without having been in existence in any previous form.

Thoughtful naturalists felt the weight of the new teleological doctrine no less than Strauss. *Hermann Helmholtz* belongs, without doubt, among those who, in the eighteen-fifties and sixties, could be considered as representatives of such thoughtful naturalists. He stresses the fact that the wonderful purpose-conformity in the structure of living organisms, which becomes increasingly apparent as science progresses, challenges the comparison of all life processes to human actions. For human actions are the only series of phenomena that have a character that is similar to the organic ones. The fitness of the arrangements in the world of organisms does, according to our judgment, in most cases indeed far surpass what human intelligence is capable of creating. It therefore cannot surprise us that it has occurred to people to seek the origin of the structure and function of the world of living beings in an intelligence far superior to that of man. Helmholtz says:

> Before Darwin one could admit two kinds of explanations for the fact of organic purpose adjustment, both of which depended on an

interference of a free intelligence in the course of natural phenomena. One either considered, according to the vitalistic theory, the life-processes as perpetually guided by a life-soul; or one saw in each species an act of a super-natural intelligence through which it was supposed to have been generated. . . . Darwin's theory contains an essentially new creative thought. It shows that a purpose-adjustment of the form in the organisms can come to pass also without interference of an intelligence through the random effect of a natural law. This is the law of the transmission of individual peculiarities from the parents to the descendants, a law that was long known and recognized but was merely in need of a definite demarcation.

Helmholtz now is of the opinion that such a demarcation is given by the principle of natural selection in the struggle for existence. A scientist who, like Helmholtz, belongs to the most cautious naturalists of that time, *J. Henle,* said in a lecture, "If the experiences of artificial breeding were to be applied to the hypothesis of Oken and Lamarck, it would have to be shown how nature proceeds in order to supply the mechanism through which the experimental breeder obtains his result. This is the task Darwin set for himself and that he pursued with admirable industry and acumen."

The materialists were the ones who felt the greatest enthusiasm of all from Darwin's accomplishment. They had long been convinced that sooner or later a man like him would have to come along who would throw a philosophical light on the vast field of accumulated facts that was so much in need of a leading thought. In their opinion, the world conception for which they had fought could not fail after Darwin's discovery. Darwin approached his task as a naturalist. At first he moved within the limits reserved to the natural scientist. That his thoughts were capable of throwing a light on the fundamental problems of world conception, on the question of man's relation to nature, was merely touched upon in his book:

> In the future I see open fields for far more important researches. Psychology will be securely based on the foundation . . . of the necessary acquirement of each mental power and capacity by

gradation. Much light will be thrown on the origin of man and his history.

For the materialists, this question of the origin of man became, in the words of Buechner, a matter of most intimate concern. In lectures he gave in Offenbach during the winter of 1866–67, he says:

> Must the theory of transformation also be applied to our own race? Must it be extended to man, to us? Shall we have to submit to an application of the same principles or rules that have caused the life of all other organisms for the explanation of our own genesis and origin? Or are we—the lords of creation—an exception?

Natural science clearly taught that man could not be an exception. On the basis of exact anatomical investigations the English physiologist, T. H. Huxley, wrote in his book, *Man's Place in Nature* (1863):

> The critical comparison of all organs and their modification in the series of the monkeys leads us to one and the same result, that the anatomical differences that separate man from the gorilla and the chimpanzee are not as great as the differences that separate the anthropoid apes from the lower species of monkeys.

Could there still be a doubt in the face of such facts that natural evolution had also produced man—the same evolution that had caused the series of organic beings as far as the monkey through growth, propagation, inheritance, transmutation of forms and the struggle for life?

During the course of the century this fundamental view penetrated more and more into the mainstream of natural science. Goethe, to be sure, had in his own way been convinced of this, and because of this conviction he had most energetically set out to correct the opinion of his contemporaries, which held that man lacked an intermaxillary bone in his upper jaw. All animals were supposed to have this bone; only man, so one thought, did not have it. In its absence one saw the proof that man was anatomically different from the animals, that the plan of his structure was to be thought along different lines. The naturalistic mode of Goethe's thinking inspired him to undertake elaborate anatomical studies to abolish this error. When he had achieved this goal he wrote in a letter to Herder, convinced that he had made a most important contribution to the knowledge of nature; "I compared the skulls of men and animals and I found the trail, and behold, there it is. Now I ask you not to tell, for it must be treated as a secret. But I want you to enjoy it with me, for it is like the finishing stone in the structure of man; now it is complete and nothing is lacking. Just see how it is!"

Under the influence of such conceptions the great question of philosophy of man's relation to himself and to the external world led to the task of showing by the method of natural science what actual process had led to the formation of man in the course of evolution. Thereby the viewpoint from which one attempted to explain the phenomena of nature changed. As long as one saw in every organism including man the realization of a purposeful design of structure, one had to consider this purpose also in the explanation of organic beings. One had to consider that in the embryo the later organism is potentially indicated. When this view was extended to the whole universe, it meant that an explanation of nature fulfilled its task best if it showed how the later stages of evolution with man as the climax are prepared in the earlier stages.

The modern idea of evolution rejected all attempts of science to recognize the potential later phases in the earlier stages. Accordingly, the later phase was in no way contained in the earlier one. Instead, what was gradually developed was the tendency to search in the later phases for traces of the earlier ones. This principle represented one of the laws of inheritance. One can actually speak of a reversal of the tendency of explanation. This reversal became important for ontogenesis, that is, for the formation of the ideas concerning the evolution of the individual being from the egg to maturity. Instead of showing the predisposition of the later organs in the embryo, one set out to compare the various stages that an organism goes through in the course of its individual evolution from the egg to maturity with those of other forms of organisms. Lorenz Oken was already moving in this direction. In the fourth volume of his *General History of Nature for All Classes of Readers* he wrote:

> Years ago, through my physiological investigations, I arrived at the view that the developmental stages of the chicken in the egg have much similarity with different classes of animals. In the beginning it shows only the organs of infusoria, thereupon gradually assuming those of the polyps, jelly-fish, shellfish, snails and so forth. Conversely, then, I also had to consider the classes of animals as evolutionary stages that proceeded parallel to the developmental stages of the chicken. This view of nature challenged me to the most minute observation of those organs that are added as new forms to every higher class of animal, as well as of the ones that are developed one after the other during the developmental process. It is, of course, not easy to establish a complete parallelism with such a difficult object as a chick egg because its development is so incompletely known. But to prove that the parallelism actually exists is indeed not difficult. It is most distinctly shown in the transformation of the insects, which is nothing more than the development of the young going on before our eyes outside the egg, and actually in so slow a tempo that we can observe and investigate every embryonic stage at our leisure.

Oken compares the stages of transformation of the insects with the other animals and finds that the caterpillars have a great similarity with worms, and the cocoons with crustaceous animals. From such similarities this ingenious thinker draws the conclusion that "there is, therefore, no doubt that we are here confronted with a conspicuous similarity that justifies the idea that the evolutionary history in the egg is nothing but a repetition of the history of the creation of the animal classes." It came as a natural gift to this brilliant man to apprehend a great idea for which he did not even need the evidence of supporting facts. But it also lies in the nature of such subtle ideas that they have no great effect on those who work in the field of science.

Oken appears like a comet on the firmament of German philosophy. His thought supplies a flood of light. From a rich treasure of ideas he suggests leading concepts for the most divergent facts. His method of formulating factual connections, however, was somewhat forced. He was too much preoccupied with the point he wanted to make. This attitude also prevailed in his treatment of the law of the repetition of certain animal forms in the ontogeny of others mentioned above.

In contrast to Oken, *Karl Ernst von Baer* kept to the facts as firmly as possible when he spoke, in his *History of the Evolution of Animals* (1828), of the observations that had led Oken to his idea:

> The embryos of the mammals, birds, lizards and snakes, and probably also those of the turtles, in their earlier stages are extraordinarily similar to one another in their whole formation as well as in their individual parts. These embryos are so similar in fact that they can often only be distinguished by their sizes. I have in my possession two little embryos in alcohol that I forgot to label, and now I cannot possibly determine to what class they belong. They could be lizards, little birds or young mammals, so similar is the head and trunk formation of these animals. The extremities are still completely absent in these embryos and, even if they were there, at the first stages of their development they would not tell us anything because the feet of lizards and mammals, the wings and feet of birds, as well as the hands and feet of men, all develop from the same original form.

Such facts of embryological development excited the greatest interest of those thinkers who tended toward Darwinism. Darwin had proven the possibility of change in organic forms and, through transformation, the species now in existence might possibly be descended from a few original forms, or perhaps only one. Now it was shown that in their first phases of development the various living organisms are so similar to each other that they can scarcely be distinguished from one another, if at all. These two ideas, the facts of comparative embryology and the idea of descent, were organically combined in 1864 by

Fritz Müller (1821–97) in his thoughtful essay, *Facts and Arguments for Darwin*. Müller is one of those high-minded personalities who needs a naturalistic world conception because they cannot breathe spiritually without it. Also, in regard to his own action, he would feel satisfaction only when he could feel that his motivation was as necessary as a force of nature. In 1852 Müller settled in Brazil. For twelve years he was a teacher at the gymnasium in Desterro on the island of Santa Catharina, not far from the coast of Brazil. In 1867 he had to give up this position. The man of the new world conception had to give way to the reaction that, under the influence of the Jesuits, took hold of his school. Ernst Haeckel has described the life and activity of Fritz Müller in the *Jenaische Zeitschrift für Naturwissenschaft* (Vol. XXXI N.F. XXIV 1897).

Darwin called Müller the "prince of observers," and the small but significant booklet, *Facts and Arguments for Darwin*, is the result of a wealth of observations. It deals with a particular group of organic forms, the crustaceans, which are radically different from one another in their maturity but are perfectly similar at the time when they leave the egg. If one presupposes, in the sense of Darwin's theory of descent, that all crustacean forms have developed from one original type, and if one accepts the similarity in the early stages as an inherited element of the form of their common ancestor, one has thereby combined the ideas of Darwin with those of Oken pertaining to the repetition of the history of the creation of the animal species in the evolution of the individual animal form. This combination was accomplished by Fritz Müller. He thereby brought the earlier forms of an animal class into a certain law-determined connection with the later ones, which, through transformation, have formed out of them. The fact that at an earlier stage the ancestral form of a being now living has had a particular form caused its descendants at a later time to have another particular form. By studying the stages of the development of an organism one becomes acquainted with its ancestors whose nature has caused the characteristics of the embryonic forms. Phylogenesis and ontogenesis are, in Fritz Müller's book, connected as cause and effect. With this step a new element had entered the Darwinian trend of ideas. This fact retains its significance even though Müller's investigations of the crustaceans were modified by the later research of Arnold Lang.

Only four years had passed since the appearance of Darwin's *Origin of the Species* when Müller's book was published as its defense and confirmation. Müller had shown how, with one special class of animals, one should work in the spirit of the new ideas. Then, in 1866, seven years after the *Origin of the Species*, a book appeared that completely absorbed this new spirit. Using the ideas of Darwinism on a high level of scientific discussion, it threw a great deal of light on the problems of the interconnection of all life phenomena. This book was Ernst Haeckel's *General Morphology of Organisms*. Every page reflected his attempt to arrive at a comprehensive synopsis of the totality of the phenomena of nature with the help of new thoughts. Inspired by Darwinism, Haeckel was in search of a world conception.

Haeckel did his best in two ways to attempt a new world conception. First, he continually contributed to the accumulation of facts that throw light on the connection of the entities and energies of nature. Second, with unbending consistency he derived from these facts the ideas that were to satisfy the human need for explanation. He held the unshakable conviction that from these facts and ideas man can arrive at a fully satisfactory world explanation. Like Goethe, Haeckel was convinced in his own way that nature proceeds in its work "according to eternal, necessary and thereby divine laws, so that not even the deity could change it." Because this was clear to him, he worshipped his deity in these eternal and necessary laws of nature and in the substances in which they worked. As the harmony of the natural laws, which are with necessity interconnected, satisfies reason, according to his view, so it also offers to the feeling heart, or to the soul that is ethically or religiously attuned, whatever it may thirst for. In the stone that falls to the ground attracted by gravity there is a manifestation of the same divine order that is expressed in the blossom of a plant and in the human spirit that created the drama of *Wilhelm Tell*.

How erroneous is the belief that the feeling for the wonderful beauty of nature is destroyed by the penetration of reason into laws of nature is vividly demonstrated in the work of Ernst Haeckel. A rational explanation of nature had been declared to be incapable of satisfying the needs of the soul. Wherever man is disturbed in his inner life through knowledge of nature, it is not the fault of knowledge but of man himself. His sentiments are developed in a wrong direction. As we follow a naturalist like Haeckel without prejudice on his path as an observer of nature, we feel our hearts beat faster. The anatomical analysis, the microscopic investigation does not detract from natural beauty but reveals a great deal more of it. There is no doubt that there is an antagonism between reason and imagination, between reflection and intuition, in our time. The brilliant essayist, Ellen Key, is without doubt right in considering this antagonism as one of the most important phenomena of our time (compare Ellen Key, *Essays,* S. Fischer Verlag, Berlin, 1899). Whoever, like Ernst Haeckel, digs deep into the treasure mine of facts, boldly emerges with the thoughts resulting from these facts and climbs to the heights of human knowledge, can see in the explanation of nature only an act of reconciliation between the two contesting forces of reflection and intuition that "alternate in forcing each other into submission" (Ellen Key). Almost simultaneously with the publication of the book in which Haeckel presented with unflinching intellectual honesty his world conception derived from natural science, that is, with the appearance of his *Riddles of the Universe* in 1899, he began a serial publication called *Artforms of Nature*. In it he gives pictures of the inexhaustible wealth of wonderful formations that nature produces and that surpass "by far all artistic forms created by man" in beauty and in variety. The same man who introduces our mind to the law-determined order of nature leads our imagination to the beauty of nature.

The need to bring the great problems of world conception into direct contact with scientific, specialized research led Haeckel to one of the facts concerning which Goethe said that they represent the significant points at which nature yields the fundamental ideas for its explanation of its own accord, meeting us halfway in our search. This was realized by Haeckel as he investigated how Oken's thesis, which Fritz Müller had applied to the crustaceans, could be fruitfully applied to the whole animal kingdom. In all animals except the Protista, which are one-celled organisms, a cup- or jug-shaped body, the gastrula, develops from the zygote with which the organism begins its ontogenesis. This gastrula is an animal form that is to be found in the first stages of development of all animals from the sponges to man. It consists merely of skin, mouth and stomach. There is a low class of zoophytes that possess only these organs during their lives and therefore resemble gastrulae. This fact is interpreted by Haeckel from the point of view of the theory of descent. The gastrula form is an inherited form that the animal owes to the form of its common ancestor. There had been, probably millions of years before, a species of animals, the gastrae, that was built in a way similar to that of the lower zoophytes still living today—the sponges, polyps, etc. From this animal species all the various forms living today, from the polyps, sponges, etc., to man, repeat this original form in the course of their ontogenies.

In this way an idea of gigantic scope had been obtained. The path leading from the simple to the complicated, to the perfect form in the world of organisms, was thereby indicated in its tentative outline. A simple animal form develops under certain circumstances. One or several individuals of this form change to another form according to the conditions of life to which they are exposed. What has come into existence through this transmutation is again transmitted to descendants. There are then two different forms, the old one that has retained the form of the first stage, and a new one. Both of these forms can develop in different directions and into different degrees of perfection. After long periods of time an abundant wealth of species comes into existence through the transmission of the earlier form and through new formations by means of the process of adaptation to the conditions of life.

In this manner Haeckel connects today's processes in the world of organisms with the events of primeval times. If we want to explain some organ of an animal of the present age, we look back to the ancestors that had developed this organ under the circumstances in which they lived. What has come into existence through natural causes in earlier times has been handed down to our time through the process of heredity. Through the history of the species the evolution of the individual receives its explanation. The phylogenesis, therefore, contains the causes for the ontogenesis. Haeckel expresses this fact in his fundamental law of biogenetics: "The short ontogenesis or development of the individual is a rapid and brief repetition, an abbreviated recapitulation of the long process of phylogenesis, the development of the species."

Through this law every attempt at explanation through special purposes, all teleology in the old sense, has been eliminated. One no longer looks for the purpose of an organ; one looks for the causes through which it has developed. A given form does not point to a goal toward which it strives, but toward the origin from which it sprang. The method of explanation for the organic phenomena has become the same as that for the inorganic. Water is not considered the aim of oxygen, nor is man considered the purpose of creation. Scientific research is directed toward the origin of, and the actual cause for, living beings. The dualistic mode of conception, which declares that the organic and the inorganic has to be explained according to two different principles, gives way to a monistic mode of conception, to a monism that has only one uniform mode of explanation for the whole of nature.

Haeckel characteristically points out that through his discovery the method has been found through which every dualism in the above-mentioned sense must be overcome.

> Phylogenesis is the mechanical cause of ontogenesis. With this statement our basically monistic conception of organic evolution is

clearly characterized, and on the truth of this principle depends primarily the truth of the gastraea theory. . . . Every naturalist, who in the field of biogenesis is not satisfied with a mere admiration of strange phenomena but strives for an understanding of their significance, will, in the future, either have to side with or against this principle. It marks at the same time the complete break that separates the older teleological and dualistic morphology from the new mechanical and monistic one. If the physiological functions of inheritance and adaptation have been proven to be the only causes of the process of organic formation, then every kind of teleology, of dualistic and metaphysical mode of conception has thereby been eliminated from the field of biogenesis; the sharp contrast between the leading principles is clearly marked. Either a direct and causal connection between ontogeny and phylogeny exists or it does not. There is no third possibility! Either epigenesis and descent, or preformation and creation! (Compare also Vol. I, pp. 209ff. of this book.)

After Haeckel had absorbed Darwin's view of the origin of man he defended forcefully the conclusion that must be drawn from it. It was impossible for him just to hint hesitatingly, like Darwin, at this "problem of all problems." Anatomically and physiologically man is not distinguishable from the higher animals. Therefore, the same origin must be attributed to him as to them. Haeckel boldly defended this opinion and the consequences that followed from it for the conception of the world. There was no doubt for him that in the future the highest manifestations of man's life, the activities of his spirit, were to be considered under the same viewpoint as the function of the simplest living organism. The observation of the lowest animals, the protozoa, infusoria, rhizopods, taught him that these organisms had a soul. In their motions, in the indications of the sensations they show, he recognized manifestations of life that only had to be increased and perfected in order to develop into man's complicated actions of reason and will.

Beginning with the gastraea, which lived millions of years ago, what steps does nature take to arrive at man? This was the comprehensive question as stated by Haeckel. He supplied the answer in his *Anthropogenesis,* which appeared in 1874. In its first part, this book deals with the history of the individual (ontogenesis), in the second part, with that of the species (phylogenesis). He showed point by point how the latter contains the causes of the former. Man's position in nature had thereby been determined according to the principles of the theory of descent. To works like Haeckel's *Anthropogenesis,* the statement that the great anatomist, *Karl Gegenbauer,* made in his *Comparative Anatomy* (1870) can be justly applied. He wrote that in exchange for the method of investigation Darwin gave to science with his theory he received in return clarity and firmness of purpose. In Haeckel's view, the method of Darwinism had also supplied science with the theory of the origin of man.

What actually was accomplished by this step can be appreciated in its full measure only if one looks at the opposition with which Haeckel's comprehensive application of the principles of Darwinism was received by the followers of idealistic world conceptions. It is not even necessary to quote those who, blindly believing in the traditional opinion, turned against the "monkey theory," or those who believed that all finer, higher morality would be endangered if men were no longer convinced that they had a "purer, higher origin." Other thinkers, although quite open-minded with regard to new truths, found it difficult to accept *this* new truth. They asked themselves the question, "Do we not deny our own rational thinking if we no longer look for its origin in a general world reason over us, but in the animal kingdom below?" Mentalities of this sort eagerly attacked the points where Haeckel's view seemed to be without support of the facts. They had powerful allies in a number of natural scientists who, through a strange bias, used their factual knowledge to emphasize the points where actual experience was still insufficient to prove the conclusions drawn by Haeckel. The typical, and at the same time the most impressive, representative of this viewpoint of the naturalists was *Rudolf Virchow* (1821–1902). The opposition of Virchow and Haeckel can be characterized as follows. Haeckel puts his trust in the inner consistency of nature, concerning which Goethe is of the opinion that it is sufficient to make up for man's inconsistency. Haeckel, therefore, argues that if a principle of nature has been verified for certain cases, and if we still lack the experience to show its validity in other cases, we have no reason to hold the progress of our knowledge back. What experience denies us today, it may yield tomorrow. Virchow is of the opposite opinion. He wants to yield as little ground as possible to a comprehensive principle. He seems to believe that life for such a principle cannot be made hard enough. The antagonism between these two spirits was brought to a sharp point at the Fiftieth Congress of German naturalists and doctors in 1877. Haeckel read a paper there on the topic, *The Theory of Evolution of Today in Its Relation to Science in General.*

In 1894 Virchow felt that he had to state his view in the following way. "Through speculation one has arrived at the monkey theory; one could just as well have ended up with an elephant theory or a sheep theory." What Virchow demanded was incontestable proof of this theory. As soon as something turned up that fitted as a link in the chain of the argumentation, Virchow attempted to invalidate it with all means at his disposal.

Such a link in the chain of proof was presented with the bone remnants that Eugen Dubois had found in Java in 1894. They consisted of a skull and thigh bone and several teeth. Concerning this find, an interesting discussion arose at the Congress of Zoologists at Leyden. Of twelve zoologists, three were of the opinion that these bones came from a monkey and three thought they came from a human being; six, however, believed they presented a transitional form between man and monkey. Dubois shows in a convincing manner in what relation the being whose bone remnants were under discussion stood to the present monkey, on the one hand, and to man of today, on the other. The theory of evolution of natural science must claim such intermediary forms. They fill the holes that exist between numerous forms of organisms. Every new intermediary form constitutes a new proof for the kinship of all living organisms. Virchow objected to the view that these bone remnants came from such an intermediary form. At first, he declared that it was the skull of a monkey and the thigh bone of a man. Expert paleontologists, however, firmly pronounced, according to the careful report on the finding, that the remnants belonged together. Virchow attempted to support his view that the thigh bone could be only that of a human being with the statement that a certain growth in the bone proved that it must have had a disease that could only have been healed through careful human attention. The paleontologist, Marsch, however, maintained that similar bone extuberances occurred in wild animals as well. A further statement of Virchow's, that the deep incision between the upper rim of the eye socket and the lower skull cover of the alleged intermediary form proved it to be the skull of a monkey was then contradicted by the naturalist Nehring, who claimed that the same formation was found in a human skull from Santos, Brazil. Virchow's objections came from the same turn of mind that also caused him to consider the famous skulls of Neanderthal, Spy, etc., as pathological formations, while Haeckel's followers regarded them as intermediary forms between monkey and man.

Haeckel did not allow any objections to deprive him of his confidence in his mode of conception. He continued his scientific work without swerving from the viewpoints at which he had arrived, and through popular presentations of his conception of nature, he influenced the public consciousness. In his book, *Systematic Phylogenesis, Outline of a Natural System of Organisms on the Basis of the History of Species* (1894–96), he attempted to demonstrate the natural kinship of organisms in a strictly scientific method. In his *Natural History of Creation*, which, from 1868–1908, appeared in eleven editions, he gave a popular explanation of his views. In 1899, in his popular studies on monistic philosophy entitled, *The Riddles of the Universe*, he gave a survey of his ideas in natural philosophy by demonstrating without reserve the many applications of his basic thoughts. Between all these works he published studies on the most diverse specialized researches, always paying attention at the same time to the philosophical principles and the scientific knowledge of details.

The light that shines out from the monistic world conception is, according to Haeckel's conviction, to "disperse the heavy clouds of ignorance and superstition that have heretofore spread an impenetrable darkness over the most important one of all problems of human knowledge, that is, the problem concerning man's origin, his true nature and his position in nature." This is what he said in a speech given August 26, 1898 at the Fourth International Congress of Zoologists in Cambridge, *On Our Present Knowledge Concerning the Origin of Man*. In what respect his world conception forms a bond between religion and science, Haeckel has shown in an impressive way in his book, *Monism as a Bond between Religion and Science, Credo of a Naturalist*, which appeared in 1892.

If one compares Haeckel with Hegel, one can see distinctly the difference in the tendencies of world conception in the two halves of the nineteenth century. Hegel lives completely in the idea and accepts only as much as he needs from the world of facts for the illustration of his idealistic world picture. Haeckel is rooted with every fiber of his being in the world of facts, and he derives from this world only those ideas toward which these facts necessarily tend. Hegel always attempts to show that all beings tend to reach their climax of evolution in the human spirit; Haeckel continuously endeavors to prove that the most complicated human activities point back to the simplest origins of existence. Hegel explains nature from the spirit; Haeckel derives the spirit from nature. We can, therefore, speak of a reversal of the thought direction in the course of the century. Within German intellectual life, Strauss, Feuerbach and others began this process of reversal. In their materialism the new direction found a provisional extreme expression, and in Haeckel's thought world it found a strictly methodical-scientific one. For this is the significant thing in Haeckel, that all his activity as a research worker is permeated by a philosophical spirit. He does not at all work toward results that for some philosophical motivation or other are considered to be the aim of his world conception or of his philosophical thinking. What is philosophical about him is his method. For him, science itself has the character of a world conception. His very way of looking at things predestines him to be a monist. He looks upon spirit and nature with equal love. For this reason he could find spirit in the simplest organism. He goes even further than that. He looks for the traces of spirit in the inorganic particles of matter:

> Every atom possesses an inherent quantity of energy and in this sense is animate. Without assuming a soul for the atom, the simplest and most general phenomena of chemistry are unexplainable. Pleasure and displeasure, desire and aversion, attraction and repulsion must be a common property of all material atoms. For the motion of the atoms, which must take place in the formation and dissolution of every chemical compound can only be explained if we assume that they have sensation and will. On this assumption the generally accepted chemical doctrine of affinity is really based.

As he traces spirit down to the atom so he follows the purely material mechanism of events up to the most lofty accomplishments of the spirit:

> The spirit and soul of man are also nothing else but energies that are inseparably bound to the material substratum of our bodies. As the motion of our flesh is bound to the form elements of our muscles, so our mind's power of thinking is bound to the form elements of our brains. Our spiritual energies are simply functions of these physical organs just as every energy is a function of a material body.

One must not confuse this mode of conception with one that dreams souls in a hazy mystical fashion into the entities of nature and then assumes that they are more or less similar to that of man. Haeckel is a strict opponent of a world conception that projects qualities and activities of man into the external world. He has repeatedly expressed his condemnation of the humanization of nature, of anthropomorphism, with a clarity that cannot be misunderstood. If he attributes animation to inorganic matter, or to the simplest organisms, he means by that nothing more than the sum of energy manifestations that we observe in them. He holds strictly to the facts. Sensation and will are for him no mystical soul energies but *are* nothing more than what we observe as attraction and repulsion. He does not mean to say that attraction and repulsion are *really* sensation and will. What he means is that attraction and repulsion are on the lowest stage what sensation and will are on a higher one. For evolution is for him not merely an unwrapping of the higher stages of the spiritual out of the lower forms in which they are already contained in a hidden fashion, but a real ascent to new formations, an intensification of attraction and repulsion into sensation and will (compare page 300ff.).

This fundamental view of Haeckel agrees in a certain way with that of Goethe. He states in this connection that he had arrived at the fulfillment of his view of nature with his insight into the "two great springs of all nature," namely, polarity and intensification (*Polarität und Steigerung*), polarity "belonging to matter insofar as we think of it materially, intensification insofar as we think of it spiritually. The former is engaged in the everlasting process of attraction and repulsion, the latter in a continual intensification. As matter can never be and act without spirit, however, nor spirit without matter, so matter can also be intensified and the spirit will never be without attraction and repulsion."

A thinker who believes in such a world conception is satisfied to explain by other such things and processes, the things and processes that are actually in the world. The idealistic world conceptions need, for the derivation of a thing or process, entities that cannot be found within the realm of the factual. Haeckel derives the form of the gastrula that occurs in the course of animal evolution from an organism that he assumes really existed at some time. An idealist would look for ideal forces under the influence of which the developing germ becomes the gastrula. Haeckel's monism draws everything he needs for the explanation of the real world from the same real world. He looks around in the world of the real in order to recognize in which way the things and processes explain one another. His theories do not have the purpose for him, as do those of the idealist, to find a higher element in addition to the factual elements, but they merely serve to make the connection of the facts understandable. Fichte, the idealist, asked the question of man's destination. He meant by that something that cannot be completely presented in the form of the real, the factual; something that reason has to produce as an addition to the factually given existence, an element that is to make the real existence of man translucent by showing it in a higher light. Haeckel, the monistic contemplator of the world, asks for the origin of man, and he means by that the factual origin, the lower organism out of which man had developed through actual processes.

It is characteristic that Haeckel argues for the animation of the lower organisms. An idealist would have resorted to rational conclusions. He would present necessities of thought. Haeckel refers to what he has seen.

> Every naturalist, who, like me, has observed for many years the life activities of the one-celled protozoa, is positively convinced that they, too, possess a soul. This cellular soul consists also of a sum of sensations, perceptions and will activities; sensation, thinking and will of our human souls differ from those of the cellular soul only in degree.

The idealist attributes spirit to matter because he cannot accept the thought that spirit can develop from mere matter. He believes that one would have to deny the spirit if one does not assume it to exist before its appearance in forms of existence without organs, without brains. For the monist, such thoughts are not possible. He does not speak of an existence that is not manifested externally as such. He does not attribute two kinds of properties to things: those that are real and manifested in them and those that in a hidden way are latent in them only to be revealed at a higher stage of development. For him, there *is* what he observes, nothing else, and if the object of observation continues its evolution and reaches a higher stage in the course of its development, then these later forms are *there* only in the moment when they become visible.

How easily Haeckel's monism can be misunderstood in this direction is shown by the objections that were made by the brilliant thinker, *Bartholomaeus von Carneri* (1821–1909), who made lasting contributions for the construction of an ethics of this world conception. In his book, *Sensations and Consciousness, Doubts Concerning Monism* (1893), he remarks that the principle, "No spirit without matter, but also no matter without spirit," would justify our extending this question to the plant and even to the next rock we may stumble against, and to attribute spirit also to them. Without doubt such a conclusion would lead to a confusion of distinctions. It should not be overlooked that consciousness arises only through the cell activity in the cerebrum. "The conviction that there is no spirit without matter, that is to say, that all spiritual activity is bound to a material activity, the former terminating with the latter, is based on experience, while there is no experience for the statement that there is always spirit connected with matter." Somebody who would want to attribute animation to matter that does not show any trace of spirit would be like one who attributed the function to indicate time not to the mechanism of a watch but to the metal out of which it is made.

Properly understood, Haeckel's view is not touched by Carneri's criticism. It is safe from this criticism because Haeckel holds himself strictly within the bounds of observation. In his *Riddles of the Universe*, he says, "I, myself, have never defended the theory of atom-consciousness. I have, on the contrary, expressly emphasized that I think the elementary psychic activities of sensation and will, which are attributed to the atoms, as unconscious." What Haeckel wants is only that one should not allow a break in the explanation of natural phenomena. He insists that one should trace back the complicated mechanism by which spirit appears in the brain, to the simple process of attraction and repulsion of matter.

Haeckel considers the discovery of the organs of thought by *Paul Flechsig* to be one of the most important accomplishments of modern times. Flechsig had pointed out that in the gray matter of the brain there are to be found the four seats of the central sense organs, or four "inner spheres of sensation," the spheres of touch, smell, sight and hearing. "Between the sense centers lie thought centers, the 'real organs of mental life.' They are the highest organs of psychic activity that produce thought and consciousness. . . . These four thought centers, distinguished from the intermediate sense centers by a peculiar and highly elaborate nerve structure, are the true organs of thought, the only organs of our consciousness. Recently, Flechsig has proved that man has some especially complicated structures in some of these organs that cannot be found in the other mammals and that explain the superiority of human consciousness." (*Riddles of the Universe*, Chapt. X.)

Passages like these show clearly enough that Haeckel does not intend to assume, like the idealistic philosophers, the spirit as implicitly contained in the lower stages of material existence in order to be able to find it again on the higher stages. What he wanted to do was to follow the simplest phenomena to the most complicated ones in his observation, in order to show how the activity of matter, which in the most primitive form is manifested in attraction and repulsion, is intensified in the higher mental operations.

Haeckel does not look for a general spiritual principle for lack of adequate general laws explaining the phenomena of nature and mind. So far as his need is concerned, his general law is indeed perfectly sufficient. The law that is manifested in the mental activities seems to him to be of the same kind as the one that is apparent in the attraction and repulsion of material particles. If he calls atoms animated, this has not the same meaning that it would have if a believer in an idealistic world conception did so. The latter would proceed from the spirit. He would take the conceptions derived from the contemplation of the spirit down into the simplest functions of the atoms when he thinks of them as animated. He would explain thereby the natural phenomena from entities that he had first projected into them. Haeckel proceeds from the contemplation of the simplest phenomena of nature and follows them up to the highest spiritual activities. This means that he explains the spiritual phenomena from laws that he has observed in the simplest natural phenomena.

Haeckel's world picture can take shape in a mind whose observation extends exclusively to natural processes and natural entities. A mind of this kind will want to *understand* the connection within the realm of these events and beings. His ideal would be to see what the processes and beings themselves reveal with respect to their development and interaction, and to reject rigorously everything that might be added in order to obtain an explanation of these processes and activities. For such an ideal one is to approach all nature as one would, for instance, proceed in explaining the mechanism of a watch. It is quite unnecessary to know anything about the watchmaker, about his skill and about his thoughts, if one gains an insight into the mechanical actions of its parts. In obtaining this insight one has, within certain limits, done everything that is admissable for the explanation of the operation of the watch. One ought to be clear about the fact that the watch itself cannot be explained if another method of explanation is admitted, as, for instance, if somebody thought of some special spiritual forces that move the hour and minute hands according to the course of the sun. Every suggestion of a special life force, or of a power that works toward a "purpose" within the organisms, appears to Haeckel as an invented force that is added to the natural processes. He is unwilling to think about the natural processes in any other way than by what they themselves disclose to observation. His *thought* structure is to be derived directly from nature.

In observing the evolution of world conception, this thought structure strikes us, as it were, as the counter-gift from the side of natural science to the Hegelian world conception, which accepts in its thought picture *nothing* from nature but wants everything to originate from the soul. If Hegel's world conception said that the self-conscious ego finds itself in the experience of pure thought, Haeckel's view of nature could reply that the thought experience is a result of the nature processes, is, indeed, their highest product. If the Hegelian world conception would not be satisfied with such a reply, Haeckel's naturalistic view could demand to be shown some inner thought experience that does not appear as if it were a mirror reflection of events outside thought life. In answer to this demand, a philosophy would have to show how thought can come to life in the soul and can really produce a world that is not merely the intellectual shadow of the external world. A thought that is merely thought, merely the product of thinking, cannot be used as an effective objection to Haeckel's view. In the comparison mentioned above, he would maintain that the watch contains nothing in itself that allows a conclusion as to the personality, etc., of the watchmaker. Haeckel's naturalistic view tends to show that, as long as one is merely confronted with nature, one cannot make any statement concerning nature except what it records. In this respect this naturalistic conception is significant as it appears in the course of the development of world conception. It proves that philosophy must *create* a field for itself that lies in the realm of spontaneous creativity of thought life beyond the thoughts that are gained from nature.

Philosophy must take the step beyond Hegel that was pointed out in a previous chapter. It *cannot* consist of a method that moves in the same field with natural science. Haeckel himself probably felt not the slightest need to pay any attention to such a step of philosophy. His world conception does bring thoughts to life in the soul, but only insofar as their life has been stimulated by the observation of natural processes. The world picture that thought can create when it comes to life in the soul without this stimulus represents the kind of higher world conception that would adequately complement Haeckel's picture of nature. One has to go beyond the facts that are directly contained in the watch if one wants to know, for instance, something about the form of the watchmaker's face. But, for this reason, one has no right to demand that Haeckel's naturalistic view itself should not speak as Haeckel does when he states what positive facts he has observed concerning natural processes and natural beings.

CHAPTER III

The World as Illusion

Besides the current of world conception that, through the idea of evolution, wants to bring the conception of the phenomena of nature and that of the spirit into complete unity, there is another that expresses their opposition in the strongest possible form. This current also springs from natural science. Its followers ask, "What is our basis as we construct a world conception by means of thinking? We hear, see and touch the physical world through our senses. We then think about the facts that our senses supply concerning that world. We form our thoughts accordingly concerning the world at the testimony of the senses. But are the statements of our senses really to be trusted?"

Let us consult actual observations. The eye conveys to us the phenomena of light. We say an object sends us red light when the eye has the sensation of red. But the eye conveys sensations of light to us also in other cases. When it is pushed or pressed, or when an electric current flows through our head, the eye also has sensations of light. It is, therefore, possible that in cases in which we have the sensation of a light-sending body, something could go on in that object that has no semblance to our sensation of light. The eye, nevertheless, would transmit light to us.

The physiologist, Johannes Müller (1801–58), drew the conclusion from these facts that what man has as his actual sensation does not depend on the external processes but on his organization. Our nerves transmit sensations to us. As we do not have the sensation of the knife that cuts us but a state of our nerves that appears to us as pain, so we also do not have a sensation of the external world when something appears to us as light. What we then really have is a state of our optic nerve. Whatever may happen outside, the optic nerve translates this external event into the sensation of light. "The sensation is not a process that transmits a quality or a state of an external object to our consciousness but one that transmits a quality, a state of our nerves caused by an external event, to our consciousness. This Johannes Müller called "the law of specific sense energies." If that is correct, then our observations contain nothing of the external world but only the sum of our own inner conditions. What we perceive has nothing to do with the external world; it is a product of our own organization. We really perceive only what is in us.

Natural scientists of great renown regarded this thought as an irrefutable basis of their world conception. Hermann Helmholtz (1821–94) considered it as the Kantian thought—that all our knowledge had reference only to processes within ourselves, not to things in themselves—translated into the language of natural science (compare Vol. I of this book). Helmholtz was of the opinion that the world of our sensations supplies us merely with the signs of the physical processes in the world outside.

> I have been convinced that it is necessary to formulate the relation between the sensation and its object by declaring the sensation to be merely the sign of the effect of the object. The nature of the sign demands only that the same sign be always given to the same object. Beyond this requirement there is no more similarity necessary between the sensation and its object than between the spoken word and the object that we denote with it. We cannot even call our sense impression pictures, for a picture depicts the same by the same. In a statue we represent one bodily form through another bodily form; in a drawing we express the perspective view of an object by the same

perspective in the picture; in a painting we depict color through color.

Our sensations, therefore, must differ more from the events they represent than pictures differ from the objects they depict. In our sensual world picture we have nothing objective but a completely subjective element, which we ourselves produce under the stimulation of the effects of an external world that never penetrates into us. This mode of conception is supported from another side by the physicist's view of the phenomena of sensation. A sound that we hear draws our attention to a body in the external world, the parts of which are in a certain state of motion. A stretched string vibrates and we hear a tone. The string transmits the vibrations to the air. They spread and reach our ear; a tone sensation is transmitted to us. The physicist investigates the laws according to which the physical particles outside move while we hear these tones. He finds that the subjective tone sensation is based on the objective motion of the physical particles. Similar relations are observed by the physicist with respect to the sensations of light. Light is also based on motion, only this motion is not transmitted by the vibrating particles of the air, but by the vibrations of the ether, the thinnest matter that fills the whole space of the universe. By every light-emitting body, the ether is put into the state of undulatory vibrations that spread and meet the retina of our eye and excite the optic nerve, which then produces the sensation of light within us. What in our world picture appears as light and color is motion outside in space. Schleiden expresses this view in the following words:

> The light outside ourselves in nature is motion of the ether. A motion can be slow and fast; it can have this or that direction, but there is obviously no sense in speaking of light or dark, of green or red motion. In short, outside ourselves, outside the beings who have the sensation, there is no such thing as bright and dark, nor are there any colors.

The physicist expells colors and light from the external world because he finds only motion in it. The physiologist feels that he is forced to withdraw them into the soul because he is of the opinion that the nerve indicates only its own state of irritation no matter what might have excited it. The view that is given with these presuppositions is sharply delineated by *Hippolyte Taine* (1828–93) in his book, *Reason*. The external perception is, according to his opinion, nothing but hallucination. A person who, under the influence of hallucination, perceives a death skull three steps in front of him, has exactly the same perception as someone who receives the light rays sent out by a real skull. It is the same inner phantom that exists within us no matter whether we are confronted with a real skull or whether we have a hallucination. The only difference between the one perception and the other is that in one case the hand stretched out toward the object will grasp empty air, whereas in the other case it will meet some solid resistance. The sense of touch then supports the sense of sight. But does this support really represent an irrefutable testimony? What is correct for one sense is also valid for the other. The sensations of touch can also turn out to be hallucinations.

The anatomist Henle expresses the same view in his *Anthropological Lectures* (1876) in the following way:

> Everything through which we believe to be informed about an external world consists merely of forms of our consciousness for which the external world supplies merely the exciting cause, the stimulus, in the language of the physiologists. The external world has no colors, tones and tastes. What it really contains we learn only indirectly or not at all. How the external world affects a sense, we merely conclude from its behavior toward the other senses. We can, for instance, in the case of a tone, see the vibrations of the tuning fork with our eyes and feel it with our fingers. The nature of certain stimuli, which reveal themselves only to the one sense, as, for instance, the stimuli of the sense of smell, is still inaccessible to us. The number of the properties of matter depends on the number and on the keenness of the senses. Whoever lacks a sense loses a group of properties without a chance of regaining them. A person who would

have an extra sense would have an organ to grasp qualities of which we have no other inkling than the blind man has of color.

If one glances over the physiological literature from the second half of the nineteenth century, one sees that this view of the subjective nature of the world picture of our perceptions has gained increasing acceptance. Time and again one comes across variations of the thought that is expressed by J. Rosenthal in his *General Physiology of Muscles and Nerves* (1877). "The sensations that we receive through external impressions are not dependent on the nature of these impressions but on the nature of our nerve cells. We have no sensation of what exerts its effect on our body but only of the processes in our brain."

To what extent our subjective world picture can be said to give us an indication of the objective external world, is expressed by Helmholtz in his *Physiological Optics*:

> To ask the question if cinnabar is really red as we see it or if this is only a sense deception is meaningless. A red-blind person will see cinnabar as black or in a dark yellow-gray shade; this is also a correct reaction for the special nature of his eye. He must only know that his eye happens to be different from that of other people. In itself one sensation is neither more nor less correct or incorrect than the other, even if the people who see the red have the great majority on their side. The red color of cinnabar exists only insofar as the majority of men have eyes that are of a similar nature. One can say with exactly the same right that it is a quality of cinnabar to be black for red-blind people. It is a different question, however, if we maintain that the wave length of light that is reflected by cinnabar has a certain length. This statement, which we can make without reference to the special nature of our eye, is only concerned with the relations of the substance and the various systems of ether waves.

It is apparent that for such a conception all phenomena of the world are divided into two completely separated parts, into a world of motions that is independent of the special nature of our faculty of perception, and a world of subjective states that are there only within the perceiving subjects. This view has been expressed sharply and pointedly by the physiologist, Du Bois-Reymond (1818–96), in his lecture, *On the Limits of Natural Science*, which he gave at the forty-fifth assembly of German naturalists and physicians on August 14, 1872 in Leipzig. Natural science is the reduction of processes we perceive in the world to motions of the smallest physical particles of a "dissolution of natural processes into mechanics of atoms," for it is a "psychological fact of experience that, wherever such a dissolution is successful" our need for explanation is for the time being satisfied. Moreover, it is a known fact that our nervous system and our brain are of a material nature. The processes that take place within them can also be only processes of motion. When sound or light waves are transmitted to my sense organs and from there to my brain, they can here also be nothing but motions. I can only say that in my brain a certain process of motion goes on, and I have simultaneously the sensation "red." For if it is meaningless to say of cinnabar that it is red, it is not less meaningless to say of a motion of the brain particles that it is bright or dark, green or red. "Mute and dark in itself, that is to say, without qualities," such is the world according to the view that has been obtained through the natural scientific conception, which

> ... knows instead of sound and light only vibrations of a property-free fundamental matter that now can be weighed and then again is imponderable. ... The Mosaic word, "And there was light," is physiologically incorrect. Light came into being only when the first red eye spot of the infusoria differentiated for the first time between light and darkness. Without the substance of the optic and auditory sense this world, glowing in colors and resounding around us, would be dark and silent. (*Limits of Natural Science.*)

Through the processes in the substance of our optic and auditory senses a resounding and colorful world is, according to this view, magically called into existence. The dark and silent world is physical; the sounding and colorful one is psychic. Whereby does the latter arise out of the former; how does motion change into sensation? This is where we meet, according to Du Bois-Reymond, one of the "limits of natural science." In our brain and in the external world there are only motions; in our soul, sensations appear. We shall never be able to understand how the one can arise out of the other.

At first sight it appears as if, through the knowledge of material processes in the brain, certain processes and latent abilities can become understandable. I am thinking of our memory, the stream of the association of our thought pictures, the effect of exercise, specific talents and so forth. But a little concentration at this point tells us that this view is an error. We would only learn something concerning the inner conditions of our mental life that are approximately of the same nature as our sense impressions, but we should learn nothing that would explain how the mental life comes into existence through these conditions. What possible connections can there be between certain motions of certain atoms in my brain, on the one hand, and, on the other, such undeniable and undefinable facts expressed by the words: I feel pain; I am delighted; I taste something sweet, smell the scent of roses, hear the sound of an organ, see red, and also the certainty that immediately follows from all this, Therefore I am. It is altogether incomprehensible that it should not be a matter of perfect indifference to a number of atoms of carbon, hydrogen, nitrogen, oxygen, etc., what their position is and how they move, how this has been and how it will be.

There is no bridge for our knowledge that leads from motion to sensation. This is the credo of Du Bois-Reymond. From motion in the material world we cannot come into the psychical world of sensations. We know that sensation arises from matter in motion, but we do not know how this is possible. Also, in the world of motion we cannot go beyond motion. For our subjective perceptions we can point at certain forms of motions because we can infer the course of these motions from the process of our perceptions, but we have no conception of what it is that is moving outside in space. We say that matter moves. We follow its motions as we watch the reactions of our sensations, but as we do not observe the object in motion but only a subjective sign of it, we can never know what matter is. Du Bois-Reymond is of the opinion that we might be able to solve the riddle of sensation if the riddle of matter were disclosed. If we knew what matter is, we should probably also know how it produces sensations, but both riddles are inaccessible to our knowledge. Du Bois-Reymond meant to check those who wanted to go beyond this limit with the words, "Just let them try the only alternative that is left, namely, supra-naturalism, but be sure that science ends where supra-naturalism begins."

The results of modern natural science are two sharply marked opposites. One of them is the current of monism. It gives the impression of penetrating directly from natural science to the most significant problems of world conception. The other declares itself incapable of proceeding any further with the means of natural science than to the insight that to a certain subjective state there is a certain corresponding process of motion. The representatives of the two currents vehemently oppose each other. Du Bois-Reymond rejected Haeckel's *History of Creation* as fiction (compare Du Bois-Reymond's speech, *Darwin versus Galiani*). The ancestral trees that Haeckel constructs on the basis of comparative anatomy, ontogeny and paleontology appear to Du Bois-Reymond to be of "approximately the same value as are the ancestral trees of the Homeric heroes in the eyes of historical criticism." Haeckel, on the other hand, considers the view of Du Bois-Reymond to be an unscientific dilettantism that must naturally give support to the reactionary world conceptions. The jubilation of the spiritualists over Du Bois-Reymond's "Limitation Speech" was so much the more resonant and justified, as Du Bois-Reymond had, up to that time, been considered an important representative of the principle of scientific materialism.

What captivates many people in the idea of dividing the world dualistically into external processes of motion and inner, subjective processes of sensation and perception is the possibility of an application of mathematics to the external processes. If one assumes material particles (atoms) with energies to exist, one can calculate in which way such atoms have to move under the influence of these energies. What is so attractive in astronomy with its methods of strict calculations is carried into the smallest elements. The astronomer determines the motion of the celestial bodies by calculating the laws of the mechanics of the heavens. In the discovery of the planet Neptune we experienced a triumph of the mechanism of the heavens. One can also reduce the motions that take place in the external world when we hear a tone and see a color to laws that govern the motions of the celestial bodies. Possibly one will be able in the future to calculate the motion that goes on in our brain while we form the judgment, two times two is four. The moment when everything that can be expressed in mathematical formulas has been calculated will be the one in which the world has been explained mathematically. Laplace has given a captivating description of the ideal of such an explanation of the world in his *Essai Philosophique sur les Probabilités* (1814):

> A mind that would know for a given moment all forces that activate nature as well as the mutual position of the entities of which nature consists would, if its power of comprehension were otherwise sufficient, comprehend in the same formula the motions of the largest celestial body and of the lightest atom. Nothing would be uncertain for such a mind, and the future as well as the past would be within the scope of its perfect and immediate knowledge. Man's power of reasoning offers, with the perfection that it has given to astronomy, a feeble imitation of such a mind.

Du Bois-Reymond says in connection with these words:

> As the astronomer predicts the day on which a comet re-emerges from the depth of world space after years in the firmament of heaven, so would this mind read in its calculation the day when the Greek cross will shine from the mosque of the Hagia Sophia and when England will burn its last coal.

There can be no doubt that even the most perfect mathematical knowledge of a process of motion would not enlighten me with regard to the question of why this motion appears to me as a red color. When one ball hits another, we can explain the direction of the second ball but we cannot in this way determine how a certain motion produces the red color. All we can say is that when a certain motion is given, a certain color is also given. While we can *explain*, apparently, as opposed to merely describe, what can be determined through calculation, we cannot go beyond a mere description in anything that defies calculation.

A significant confession was made by *Gustav Robert Kirchhoff* (1824–87) when, in 1874, he defined the task of mechanics: "It is to describe the motions occurring in nature in the most complete and simple way." Mechanics applies mathematics. Kirchhoff confesses that with the help of mathematics no more can be obtained than a complete and simple description of the processes in nature.

To those personalities who demand of an explanation something essentially more than just a description according to certain points of view, the confession of Kirchhoff could serve as a confirmation of their belief that there are "limits to our knowledge of nature." Referring to Kirchhoff, Du Bois-Reymond praises the wise reserve of the master, who characterizes the task of mechanics as that of describing the motions of the bodies, and places this in contrast to Ernst Haeckel, who "speaks of atom souls."

* * *

An important attempt to base his world conception on the idea that all our perceptions are merely the result of our own organization has been made by *Friedrich Albert Lange* (1828–73) with his *History of Materialism* (1864). He had the boldness and consistency of thought that does not allow itself to be blocked by any obstacle but follows its fundamental conception to its last conclusion. Lange's strength lay in a forceful character that was expressed in many directions. His was a personality able to take up many things, and he had sufficient ability to carry them out.

One important enterprise was his renewal of Kant's conception that, with the support of modern natural science, we perceive things not as *they* require it, but as our *organization* demands it. Lange did not really produce any new conceptions, but he did throw light into given thought worlds that is rare in its brightness. Our organization, our brain, in connection with our senses, produces the world of sensation. I see "blue," or I feel "hardness," because I am organized in this particular way. I combine the sensations into objects. By combining the sensations of "white" and "soft," etc., I produce, for instance, the conception of wax. When I follow my sensation with my thoughts, I do not move in the external world. My intellect produces connections within the world of my sensations according to the laws of my reason. When I saw that the qualities I perceive in a body presuppose a matter with laws of motion, I also do not go outside of myself. I find that I am forced through my organization to add the thoughts of processes of motion to my sensations.

The same mechanism that produces our sensations also produces our conception of matter. Matter, equally, is only a product of my organization, just as color and tone. Even when we speak of things in themselves, we must be clearly aware of the fact that we cannot go beyond our own realm. We are so organized that we cannot possibly go beyond ourselves. Even what lies beyond our realm can be represented to ourselves only through *our* conception. We become aware of a limit to our world. We argue that there must be something beyond the limit that causes sensations in us. But we can only go as far as to that limit, even the limit we set ourselves because we can go no further. "A fish can swim in water in the pond, not in the earth, but it can hit its head against the bottom and the walls." In the same way we live within the realm of our conceptions and sensations, but not in the external things. We hit against a limit, however, where we cannot go any further, where we must say no more than that beyond this is the unknown. All conceptions we produce concerning this unknown are unjustified because we cannot do anything but relate the conceptions we have obtained within ourselves to the unknown. If we wanted to do this, we should be no wiser than a fish that would say, "Here I cannot go any further. Therefore, I want to go into some other kind of water in which I will try to swim in some other way." But the fact is that the fish can swim only in water and nowhere else.

This is supplemented by another thought that belongs with the first line of reasoning. Lange, as the spirit of an inexorable desire for consistency, linked them together. In what situation am I when I contemplate myself? Am I not as much bound to the laws of my own organization as I am when I consider something else? My eye observes an object. Without an eye there is no color. I believe that there is an object in front of me, but on closer inspection I find that it is my eye, that is to say, I, myself, that produces the object. Now I turn my observation to my eye itself. Can I do this in any other way except by means of my organs? Is not the conception that I obtain of myself also just my idea? The world of the senses is the product of our organization. Our visible organs are like all other parts of the phenomenal world, only pictures of an unknown object. Our real organization remains, therefore, as unknown to us as the objects of the external world. What we have before us is merely the product of both. Affected by an unknown world through an unknown ego, we produce a world of conceptions that is all we have at our disposal.

Lange asks himself the question: Where does a consistent materialism lead? Let all our mental conclusions and sense perceptions be produced by the activity of our brain, which is bound to material conditions, and our sense organs, which are also material. We are then confronted with the necessity of investigating our organism in order to see how it functions, but we can do this only by means of our organs. No color without an eye, but also no eye without an eye.

> The consistently materialistic view is immediately reversed into a consistently idealistic one. There is no break to be assumed in our nature. We must not attribute some functions of our being to a physical nature and others to a spiritual one, but we are justified to assume physical conditions for everything, including the mechanism

of our thinking, and we should not rest until we have found them. But we are as much justified if we consider as mere pictures of the really existing world, not only the external world as it appears to us, but also the organs with which we apprehend this world. The eye with which we believe we see is itself only a product of our imagination. When we find that our visual pictures are produced by the structure and function of the eye, we must never forget that the eye with all its contrivances—the optic nerve as well as the brain and the structures we may still discover in it as causes of our thinking—are only ideas that, to be sure, form a world that is consistent and interconnected in itself, but merely a world that points beyond itself. . . . The senses supply us, as Helmholtz says, with the effects of the things, not with faithful pictures, and certainly not with the things themselves. Among these effects are also the senses themselves as well as the brain and the molecular movements assumed in it. (*History of Materialism*, 1887.)

Lange, therefore, assumes a world beyond our world that may consist of the things in themselves or that may not even have anything to do with this "thing in itself," since even this concept, which we form at the limit of our own realm, belongs merely to the world of our ideas.

Lange's world conception, then, leads to the opinion that we have only a world of ideas. This world, however, forces us to acknowledge something beyond its own sphere. It also is completely incapable of disclosing anything about this something. This is the world conception of absolute ignorance, of agnosticism.

It is Lange's conviction that all scientific endeavor that does not limit itself to the evidence of the senses and the logical intellect that combines these elements of evidence must remain fruitless. That the senses and the intellect together, however, do not supply us with anything but a result of our own organization, he accepts as evidently following from his analysis of the origin of knowledge. The world is for him fundamentally a product of the fiction of our senses and of our intellects. Because of this opinion, he never asks the question of truth with regard to the ideas. A truth that could enlighten us about the essence of the world is not recognized by Lange. He believes he has obtained an open road for the ideas and ideals that are formed by the human mind and that he has accomplished this through the very fact that he no longer feels the need of attributing any truth to the knowledge of the senses and the intellect. Without hesitation he considered everything that went beyond sensual observation and rational combination to be mere fiction. No matter what the idealistic philosophers had thought concerning the nature of facts, for him it belonged to the realm of poetic fiction.

Through this turn that Lange gave to materialism there arose necessarily the question: Why should not the higher imaginative creations be valid if even the senses are creative? What is the difference between these two kinds of creation? A philosopher who thinks like this must have a reason for admitting certain conceptions that is quite different from the reason that influences a thinker who acknowledges a conception because he thinks it is true. For Lange, this reason is given by the fact that a conception has value for life. For him, the question is not whether or not a conception is true, but whether it is valuable for man. One thing, however, must be clearly recognized: That I see a rose as red, that I connect the effect with the cause, is something I have in common with all creatures endowed with the power of perception and thinking. My senses and my reason cannot produce any additional values, but if I go beyond the imaginative product of senses and reason, then I am no longer bound to the organization of the whole human species. Schiller, Hegel and every Tom, Dick and Harry sees a flower in the same way. What Schiller weaves in poetic imagination around the flower, what Hegel thinks about it, is not imagined by Tom, Dick and Harry in the same way. But just as Tom, Dick and Harry are mistaken when they think that the flower is an entity existing externally, so Schiller and Hegel would be in error if they took their ideas for anything more than poetic fiction that satisfied their spiritual needs. What is poetically created through the senses and the intellect belongs to the whole human race, and no one in this respect can be different from anybody else.

What goes beyond the creation of the senses and of reason is the concern of the individual. Nevertheless, this imaginative creation of the individual is also granted a value by Lange for the whole human race, provided that the individual creator "who produces it is normal, richly gifted and typical in his mode of thinking, and is, through his force of spirit, qualified to be a leader."

In this way, Lange believes that he can secure for the ideal world its value by declaring that also the so-called real world is a product of poetic creation. Wherever he may look, Lange sees only fiction, beginning with the lowest stage of sense perception where "the individual still appears subject to the general charactistics of the human species, and culminating with the creative power in poetry."

> The function of the senses and of the combining intellect, which produce what is reality for us, can be called a lower function if one compares them with the soaring flight of the spirit in the creative arts. But, in general and in their totality, these functions cannot be classified as a principally different activity of the mind. As little as our reality is a reality according to our heart's desire, it is nevertheless the firm foundation of our whole spiritual existence. The individual grows out of the soil of the species, and the general and necessary process of knowledge forms the only secure foundation for the individual's rise to an esthetic conception of the world. (*History of Materialism.*)

What Lange considers to be the error of the idealistic world conception is not that it goes beyond the world of the senses and the intellect with its ideas, but that it believes it possesses in these ideas more than the individual thinker's poetic fantasy. One should build up for oneself an ideal world, but one should be aware that this ideal world is no more than poetic imagination. If this idealism maintains it is more than that, materialism will rise time and again with the claim: I have the truth; idealism is poetry. Be that so, says Lange: Idealism is poetry, but materialism is also poetry. In idealism the individual is the creator, in materialism, the species. If they both are aware of their natures, everything is in its right place: the science of the senses and the intellect that provide proofs for the whole species, as well as the poetry of ideas with all its conceptions that are produced by the individual and still retain their value for the race.

> One thing is certain: Man is in need of an ideal world created by himself as a supplement of reality, and the highest and noblest functions of his spirit are actively combined in such creations. But is this free activity of the spirit to be allowed repeatedly to assume the deceptive form of a proof-establishing science? If so, materialism will emerge again and again to destroy the bolder speculations and try to satisfy reason's demand for unity with a minimum of elevation above the real and actually provable. (*History of Materialism.*)

In Lange's thinking, complete idealism is combined with a complete surrender of truth itself. The world for him is poetry, but a poetry that he does not value any less than he would if he could acknowledge it as reality.

Thus, two currents of a distinctly natural scientific character can be distinguished as abruptly opposing each other in the development of modern world conception: The monistic current in which Haeckel's mode of conception moved, and the dualistic one, the most forceful and consistent defender of which was Friedrich Albert Lange. Monism considers the world that man can observe to be a true reality and has no doubt that a thinking process that depends on observation can also obtain knowledge of essential significance concerning this reality. Monism does not imagine that it is possible to exhaust the fundamental nature of the world with a few boldly thought out formulas. It proceeds as it follows the facts, and forms new ideas in regard to the connections of these facts. It is convinced, however, that these ideas do supply a knowledge of a true reality. The dualistic conception of Lange divides the world into a known and an unknown part. It treats the first part in the same fashion as monism, following the lead of observation and reflective thought, but it believes that nothing at all can be known concerning the true essential core of the world through this observation and through this thought. Monism believes in the truth of the real and sees the human world of ideas best supported if it is based on the world of observations. In the ideas and ideals that the monist derives from natural existence, he sees something that is fully satisfactory to his feeling and to his moral need. He finds in nature the highest existence, which he does not only want to penetrate with his thinking for the purpose of knowledge, but to which he surrenders with all his knowledge and with all his love.

In Lange's dualism nature is considered to be unfit to satisfy the spirit's highest needs. Lange must assume a special world of higher poetry for this spirit that leads beyond the results of observation and its corresponding thought. For monism, true knowledge represents a supreme spiritual value, which, because of its truth, grants man also the purest moral and religious pathos. To dualism, knowledge cannot present such a satisfaction. Dualism must measure the value of life by other things, not by the truth it might yield. The ideas are not valuable because they participate in the truth. They are of value because they serve life in its highest forms. Life is not valued by means of the ideas, but the ideas are appreciated because of their fruitfulness for life. It is not for true knowledge that man strives but for valuable thoughts.

* * *

In recognizing the mode of thinking of natural science Friedrich Albert Lange agrees with monism insofar as he denies the uses of all other sources for the knowledge of reality, but he also denies this mode of thinking any possibility to penetrate into the essential of things. In order to make sure that he himself moves on solid ground he curtails the wings of human imagination. What Lange is doing in such an incisive fashion corresponds to an inclination of thought that is deeply ingrained in the development of modern world conception. This is shown with perfect clarity also in another sphere of thinking of the nineteenth century. This thinking developed, through various stages, viewpoints from which *Herbert Spencer* (1820–1903) started as he laid the foundations for a dualism in England. Spencer's dualism appeared at approximately the same time as Lange's in Germany, which strove for natural scientific knowledge of the world on the one hand and, on the other, confessed to agnosticism so far as the essence of things is concerned. When Darwin published his work, *The Origin of Species*, he could praise the natural scientific mode of thought of Spencer:

> Mr. Herbert Spencer, in an Essay (1852), has contrasted the theories of the Creation and the Development of organic beings with remarkable skill and force. He argues from the analogy of domestic production, from the changes which the embryos of many species undergo, from the difficulty of distinguishing species and varieties, and from the principle of general gradation that species have been modified; and he attributes the modification to the change of circumstances. The author (1855) has also treated Psychology on the principle of the necessary requirement of each mental power and capacity by gradation. (*The Origin of Species, Historical Sketch.*)

Also, other thinkers who followed the method of natural science felt attracted to Spencer because he tried to explain all reality from the inorganic to the psychological in the manner expressed in Darwin's words above. But Spencer also sides with the agnostics, so that Lange is justified when he says, "Herbert Spencer, whose philosophy is closely related to ours, believes in a materialism of the phenomenal world, the relative justification of which, within the realm of natural science, finds its limit in a thought of an unknowable absolute."

It is quite likely that Spencer arrived at his viewpoint from assumptions similar to those of Lange. He had been preceded in England by thinkers who were guided by a twofold interest. They wanted to determine what it is that man really possesses with his knowledge, but they also were resolved not to shatter by doubt or reason the essential substance of the world. They were all more or less dominated by the sentiment that Kant described when he said, "I had to suspend knowledge in order to make room for belief." (Compare the first volume of this book.)

The beginning of the development of the world conception of the nineteenth century in England is marked by the figure of *Thomas Reid* (1710–96). The fundamental conviction of this man can be expressed in Goethe's words as he describes his own activity as a scientist as non-speculative: "In the last analysis it seems to me that my method consists merely in the practical and self-rectifying operations of common sense that dares to practice its function in a higher sphere." (Compare Goethe's Werke, Vol. 38, p. 595 in Kürschner's *Deutsche National Literatur.*) This common sense does not doubt in any way that it is confronted with real essential things and processes as it contemplates the world. Reid believes that a world conception is viable only if it upholds this basic view of a healthy common sense. Even if one admitted the possibility that our observation could be deceptive and that the true nature of things could be different from the picture that is supplied to us by our senses and our intellect, it would not be necessary to pay any attention to such a possibility. We find our way through life only if we believe in our observation; nothing beyond that is our concern.

In taking this point of view Reid is convinced that he can arrive at really satisfactory truths. He makes no attempt to obtain a conception of things through complicated thought operations but wants to reach his aim by going back to the basic principles that the soul instinctively assumes. Instinctively, unconsciously, the soul possesses what is correct, before the attempt is made to illumine the mind's own nature with the torch of consciousness. It knows instinctively what to think in regard to the qualities and processes of the physical world, and it is endowed instinctively with the direction of moral behavior, of a judgment concerning good and evil. Through his reference to the truths innate in "common sense," Reid directs the attention of thought toward an observation of the soul. This tendency toward a psychological observation becomes a lasting and characteristic trait in the development of the English world conception.

Outstanding personalities within this development are *William Hamilton* (1788–1856), *Henry Mansel* (1820–71), *William*

Whewell (1794–1866), *John Herschel* (1792–1871), *James Mill* (1773–1836), *John Stuart Mill* (1806–73), *Alexander Bain* (1818–1903) and *Herbert Spencer* (1820–1903). They all place psychology in the center of their world conception.

William Hamilton also recognizes as truth what the soul from the beginning feels inclined to accept as true. With respect to fundamental truths proofs and comprehension ceases. All one can do is observe their emergence at the horizon of our consciousness. In this sense they are incomprehensible. But one of the fundamental manifestations of our consciousness is also that everything in this world depends on something that is unknown to us. We find in this world in which we live only dependent things, but not absolutely independent ones. Such independent things must exist, however. When a dependent thing is found, an independent thing is assumed. With our thinking we do not enter the independent entity. Human knowledge is meant for the dependent and it becomes involved in contradictions if its thoughts, which are well-suited to the dependent, are applied to the independent. Knowledge, therefore, must withdraw as we approach the entrance toward the independent. Religious belief is here in its place. It is only through his admission that he cannot know anything of the essential core of the world that man can be a moral being. He can accept a God who causes a moral order in the world. As soon as it has been understood that all logic has exclusively to do with the dependent, not the independent, no logic can destroy this belief in an infinite God.

Henry Mansel was a pupil and follower of Hamilton, but he expressed Hamilton's view in still more extreme forms. It is not going too far to say that Mansel was an advocate of belief who no longer judged impartially between religion and knowledge, but who defended religious dogma with partiality. He was of the opinion that the revealed truths of religion involve our knowledge necessarily in contradictions. This is not supposed to be the fault of the revealed truths but has its cause in the limitation of the human mind, which can never penetrate into regions from which the statements of revelation arise.

William Whewell believed that he could best obtain a conception concerning the significance, origin and value of human knowledge by investigating the method through which leading men of science arrived at their insights. In his *History of the Inductive Sciences* (1840), he set out to analyze the psychology of scientific investigation. Thus, by studying outstanding scientific discoveries, he hoped to find out how much of these accomplishments was due to the external world and how much to man himself. Whewell finds that the human mind always supplements its scientific observations. Kepler, for example, had the idea of an ellipse before he found that the planets move in ellipses. Thus, the sciences do not come about through a mere reception from without but through the active participation of the human mind that impresses its laws on the given elements. These sciences do not extend as far as the last entities of things. They are concerned with the particulars of the world. Just as everything, for instance, is assumed to have a cause, such a cause must also be presupposed for the whole world. Since knowledge fails us with respect to that cause, the dogma of religion must step in as a supplement. Herschel, like Whewell, also tried to gain an insight into the genesis of knowledge in the human mind through the observation of many examples. His *Preliminary Discourse on the Study of Natural Philosophy* appeared in 1831.

John Stuart Mill belongs with those thinkers who are deeply imbued with the conviction that one cannot be cautious enough in determining what is certain and uncertain in human knowledge. The fact that he was introduced to the most diversified branches of knowledge in his boyhood, most likely gave his mind its characteristic turn. As a child of three he received instructions in the Greek language, and soon afterwards was taught arithmetic. He was exposed to the other fields of instruction at a correspondingly early age. Of even greater importance was the method of instruction used by his father, James Mill, who was himself an important thinker. Through him vigorous logic became the second nature of John Stuart. From his autobiography we learn: "Anything which could be found out by thinking I was never told until I had exhausted my efforts to find it out for myself." The things that occupy the thinking of such a person must become his destiny in the proper sense of the word. "I have never been a child, I have never played cricket. It is, afterall, better to let nature take its own course," says John Stuart Mill as one whose destiny had so uniquely been to live almost exclusively in thinking. Because of his development, he had to experience to the fullest the problems concerning the significance of knowledge. How can knowledge, which for him was life, lead also to the source of the phenomena of the world? The direction in which Mill's thought developed in order to obtain clarity concerning these problems was probably determined early by his father. James Mill had proceeded by starting from psychological experience. He had observed the process by which idea is linked to idea in man's mind. Through connecting one concrete idea to another we obtain our knowledge of the world. We must then ask ourselves: What is the relation between the order in which the ideas are linked and the order of the things in the world? Through such a mode of conception our thinking begins to distrust its own power because man can associate ideas in a manner that is entirely different from the connection of the things in the external world. This mistrust is the basis of John Stuart Mill's logic, which appeared in 1843 as his chief work under the title, *System of Logic*.

In matters of world conception a more pronounced contrast is scarcely thinkable than that between Mill's *Logic* and Hegel's *Science of Logic*, which appeared twenty-seven years earlier. In Hegel we find the highest confidence in thinking, the full assurance that we cannot be deceived by what we experience within ourselves. Hegel experiences himself as a part, a member of the world, and what he experiences within himself must also belong to the world. Since he has the most direct knowledge of himself, he believes in the content of this knowledge and judges the rest of the world accordingly. He argues as follows: When I perceive an external thing, it is possible that the thing shows only its surface to me and that its essence remains concealed. This is not possible in my own case. I understand my own being.

I can then compare the things outside with my own being. If they reveal some element of my own essence on their surface, I am justified in attributing to them something of my own nature. It is for this reason that Hegel expects confidently to find outside in nature the very spirit and the thought connections that he finds within himself.

Mill, however, experiences himself not as a part of the world but as a spectator. The things outside are an unknown element to him and the thoughts that man forms concerning them are met by Mill with distrust. One observes men and learns from his observations that all men die. One forms the judgment that all men are mortal. The Duke of Wellington is a man; therefore, the Duke of Wellington is mortal. This is the conclusion the observer comes to. What gives him the right to do so? This is the question John Stuart Mill asks. If a single human being would prove to be immortal, the whole judgment would be upset. Are we justified in supposing that, because all men up to this time have died, they will continue to do so in the future? All knowledge is uncertain because we draw conclusions from observations we have made and transfer them to things we cannot know anything about, since we have not observed them directly. What would somebody who thinks like Hegel have to say about such a conception? It is not difficult to imagine the answer. We know from definite concepts that in every circle all diameters are equal. If we find a circle in the real world, we maintain that its diameters, too, are equal. If we observe it a quarter of an hour later and find that its diameters are unequal, we do not decide that under certain circumstances the diameter of a circle can also be unequal. But we say that what was formerly a circle has for some reason been elongated into an ellipse.

If we think like Hegel, this is the attitude we take toward the judgment, all men are mortal. It is not through observation but through an inner thought experience that we form the concept of man. For the concept of man, mortality is as essential as the equality of the diameters is for the concept of the circle. If we find a being in the real world that has all the other characteristics of man, we conclude that this being must also have that of mortality, in the same way that all other properties of the circle allow us to conclude that it has also that of the equality of diameters. If Hegel came across a being that did not die, he could only say, "That is not a man." He could not say, "A man can also be immortal." Hegel makes the assumption that the concepts in us are not arbitrarily formed but have their root in the essence of the world, as we ourselves belong to this essence. Once the concept of man has formed within us, it is clear that it has its origin in the essence of things, and we are fully justified in applying it to this essence. Why has this concept of mortal man formed within us? Surely only because it has its ground in the nature of things. A person who believes that man stands entirely outside of the order of things and forms his judgments as an outsider can argue that we have until now seen men die, and therefore we form the spectator concept: mortal men. The thinker who is aware that he himself belongs to the order of things and that it is they that are manifested within his thoughts, forms the judgment that up to this time all men have died; to die, then, is something that belongs to their nature, and if somebody does not die, he is not a man but something else. Hegel's logic has become a logic of things: For Hegel, the manifestation of logic is an effect of the essence of the world; it is not something that the human mind has added from an outside source to this essence. Mill's logic is the logic of a bystander, of a mere spectator who starts out by cutting the thread through which it is connected with the world.

Mill points out that the thoughts, which in a certain age appear as absolutely certain inner experiences, are nevertheless reversed in a later time. In the Middle Ages it was, for instance, believed that there could not possibly be antipodes and that the stars would have to drop from the sky if they did not cling to fixed spheres. Man will, therefore, only be capable of the right attitude toward his knowledge if he, in spite of his awareness that the logic of the world is expressed in this knowledge, forms in every individual case his judgment through a careful methodical examination of his conceptual connections guided by observation, a judgment that is always in need of correction.

It is the method of observation that John Stuart Mill attempts to determine with cool detachment and calculation. Let us take an example. Suppose a phenomenon had always occurred under certain conditions. In a given case a number of these conditions appear again, but a few of them are now missing. The phenomenon in question does not occur. We are forced to conclude that the conditions that were not provided and the phenomenon that failed to occur stood in a causal relationship. If two substances have always combined to form a chemical compound and this result fails to be obtained in a given case, it is necessary to inquire what condition is lacking that had always been present before. Through a method of this kind we arrive at conceptions concerning connections of facts that can be rightly considered as being grounded in the nature of things. Mill wants to follow the methods of observation in his analysis. Logic, which Kant maintained had not progressed a single step since Aristotle, is a means of orientation within our thinking itself. It shows how to proceed from one correct thought to the next. Mill's logic is a means of orientation within the world of facts. It intends to show how one obtains valid judgments about things from observation. He does not even admit mathematics as an exception. Mathematics must also derive its basic insights from observation. For example, in all observed cases we have seen that two intersecting straight lines diverge and do not intersect again. Therefore we conclude that they will never intersect again, but we do not have a perfect proof for this statement. For John Stuart Mill, the world is thus an alien element. Man observes its phenomena and arranges them according to what they announce to his conceptual life. He perceives regularities in the phenomena and through logical, methodical investigations of these regularities he arrives at the laws of nature. But there is nothing that leads him to the principle of the things themselves. One can well imagine that the world could also be entirely different. Mill is convinced that everybody who is used to abstraction and analysis and who seriously uses his abilities will, after a sufficient exercise of his imagination, have no difficulty with the idea that there could be another stellar system in which nothing could be found of the laws that have application to our own.

Mill is merely consistent in his bystander viewpoint of the world when he extends it to man's own ego. Mental pictures come and go, are combined and separated within his inner life; this is what man observes. He does not observe a being that remains identical with itself as "ego" in the midst of this constant flow of ideas. He has observed that mental pictures emerge within him and he assumes that this will continue to be the case. From this possibility, namely, that a world of perceptions can be grouped around a center, arises the conception of an "ego." Thus, man is a spectator also with respect to his own "ego." He has his conceptions tell him what he can know about himself. Mill reflects on the facts of memory and expectation. If everything that I know of myself is to consist of conceptual presentations, then I cannot say: *I remember a conception* that I have had at an earlier time, or I expect the occurrence of a certain experience, but I must say: *A present conception remembers itself* or expects its future occurrence. If we speak, so Mill argues, of the mind as of a sequence of perceptions, we must also speak of a sequence of perceptions that is aware of itself as becoming and passing. As a result, we find ourselves in the dilemma of having to say that either the "ego" or the mind is something to be distinguished from the perceptions, or else we must maintain the paradox that a mere sequence of perceptions is capable of an awareness of its past and future. Mill does not overcome this dilemma. It contains for him an insoluble enigma. The fact is that he has torn the bond between himself, the observer, and the world, and he is not capable of restoring the connection. The world for him remains an unknown beyond himself that produces impressions on man. All man knows of this transcendent unknown is that it can produce perceptions in him. Instead of having the possibility of knowing real things outside himself, he can only say in the end that there are opportunities for having perceptions. Whoever speaks of things in themselves uses empty words. We move on the firm ground of facts only as long as we speak of the continuous possibility of the occurrence of sensations, perceptions and conceptions.

John Stuart Mill has an intense aversion to all thoughts that are gained in any way except through the comparison of facts, the observation of the similar, the analogous, and the homogeneous elements in all phenomena. He is of the opinion that the human conduct of life can only be harmed if we surrender to the belief that we could arrive at any truth in any way except through observation. This disinclination of Mill demonstrates his hesitation to relate himself in his striving for knowledge to the things of reality in any other way than by an attitude of passivity. The things are to dictate to man what he has to think about them. If man goes beyond this state of receptivity in order to say something out of his own self *about* the things, then he lacks every assurance that this product of his own activity has anything to do *with* the things. What is finally decisive in this philosophy is the fact that the thinker who maintains it is unable to count his own spontaneous thinking as belonging to the world. The very fact that he himself is active in this thinking makes him suspicious and misleads him. He would best of all like to eliminate his own self completely, to be absolutely sure that no erroneous element is mixed into the objective statements of the phenomena. He does not sufficiently appreciate the fact that his thinking is a part of nature as much as the growth of a leaf of grass. It is evident that one must also examine one's own spontaneous thinking if one wants to find out something concerning it.

How is man, to use a statement of Goethe, to become acquainted with his relation to himself and to the external world if he wants to eliminate himself completely in the cognitive process? Great as Mill's merits are for finding methods through which man can learn those things that do not depend on him, a view concerning man's relation to himself and of his relation to the external world cannot be obtained by his methods. All these methods are valid only for the special sciences, not, however, for a comprehensive world conception. No observation can teach what spontaneous thinking is; only thinking can experience this in itself. As this thinking can only obtain information concerning its own nature through its own power, it is also the only source that can shed light on the relation between itself and the external world. Mill's method of investigation excludes the possibility of obtaining a world conception because a world conception can be gained only through *thinking* that is concentrated in itself and thereby succeeds in obtaining an insight into its own relation to the external world. The fact that John Stuart Mill had an aversion to this kind of self-supporting thinking can be well understood from his character. Gladstone said in a letter (compare Gompertz: John Stuart Mill, Vienna, 1889) that in conversation he used to call Mill the "Saint of Rationalism." A person who practices thinking in this way imposes rigorous demands on thinking and looks for the greatest possible precautionary measures so that it cannot deceive him. He becomes thereby mistrustful with respect to thinking itself. He believes that he will soon stand on insecure ground if he loses hold of external points of support. Uncertainty with regard to all problems that go beyond strictly observational knowledge is a basic trait in Mill's personality. In reading his books we see everywhere that Mill treats such problems as open questions concerning which he does not risk a sure judgment.

* * *

The belief that the true nature of things is unknowable is also maintained by *Herbert Spencer.* He proceeds by asking: How do I obtain what I call truths concerning the world? I make certain observations concerning things and form judgments about them. I observe that hydrogen and oxygen under certain conditions combine to form water. I form a judgment concerning this observation. This is a truth that extends only over a small circle of things. I then observe under what circumstances other substances combine. I compare the individual observations and thereby arrive at more comprehensive, more general truths concerning the process in which substances in general form chemical compounds. All knowledge consists in this; we proceed from particular truths to more comprehensive ones. We finally arrive at the highest truth, which cannot be subordinated to any other and which we therefore must accept without further explanation. In this process of knowledge we have, however, no means of penetrating to the absolute essence of the world, for thinking can, according to this opinion, do no more than compare the various things with one another and formulate general truths with respect to the homogeneous element in them. But the ultimate nature of the world cannot, because of its uniqueness, be compared to any other thing. This is why thinking fails with regard to the ultimate nature. It cannot reach it.

In such modes of conception we always sense, as an undertone, the thinking that developed from the basis of the physiology of the senses (compare above page 314ff.). In many philosophers this thought has inserted itself so deeply into their intellectual life that they consider it the most certain thought possible. They argue as follows: One can know things only by becoming aware of them. They then change this thought, more or less unconsciously, into: One can know only of those things that enter our consciousness, but it remains unknown how the things were before they entered our consciousness. It is for this reason that sense perceptions are considered as if they were in our consciousness, for one is of the opinion that they must first enter our consciousness and must become part of it in the form of conceptions if we are to be aware of them.

Also, Spencer clings to the view that the possibility of the process of knowledge depends on us as human beings. We therefore must assume an unknowable element beyond that which can be transmitted to us by our senses and our thinking. We have a clear consciousness of everything that is present in our mind. But an indefinite consciousness is associated with this clear awareness that claims that everything we can observe and think has as its basis something we can no longer observe and think. We know that we are dealing with mere appearances and not with full realities existing independently by themselves. But this is just because we know definitely that our world is only appearance, that we also know that an unimaginable real world is its basis. Through such turns of thought Spencer believes it possible to arrange a complete reconciliation between religion and knowledge. There is something that religion can grasp in belief, in a belief that cannot be shaken by an impotent knowledge.

The field, however, that Spencer considers to be accessible to knowledge must, for him, entirely take on the form of natural scientific conceptions. When Spencer himself ventures to explain, he does so in the sense of natural science.

Spencer uses the method of natural science in thinking of the process of knowledge. Every organ of a living being has come into existence through the fact that this being has adapted itself to the conditions under which it lives. It belongs to the human conditions of life that man finds his way through the world with the aid of thinking. His organ of knowledge develops through the adaptation of his conceptual life to the conditions of his external life. By making statements concerning things and processes, man adjusts himself to the surrounding world. All truths have come into being through this process of adaptation, and what is acquired in this way can be transmitted through inheritance to the descendants. Those who think that man, through his nature, possesses once and for all a certain disposition toward general truths are wrong. What appears to be such a disposition did not exist at an earlier stage in the ancestors of man, but has been acquired by adaptation and transmitted to the descendants. When some philosophers speak of truths that man does not have to derive from his own individual experience but that are given *a priori* in his organization, they are right in a certain respect. While it is obvious that such truths are acquired, it must be stressed that they are not acquired by man as an individual but as a species. The individual has inherited the finished product of an ability that has been acquired at an earlier age.

Goethe once said that he had taken part in many conversations on Kant's *Critique of Pure Reason* and that he had noticed how on those occasions the old basic problem had been renewed, "How much does our inner self contribute to our spiritual existence, how much the external world?" And Goethe goes on to say, "I had never separated the two; when I was philosophizing in my own way on things, I did so with an unconscious naivete and was really convinced that I saw with my eyes my opinion before me."

Spencer looks at this "old basic problem" from the point of view of natural science. He believed he could show that the developed human being also contributed to his spiritual existence through his own self. This self, is also made up of the inherited traits that had been acquired by our ancestors in their struggle with the external world. If we today believe we see with our eyes our opinions before us, we must remember that they were not always our opinions but that they were once observations that were really made by our eyes in the external world. Spencer's way of thinking, then, is, like that of John Stuart Mill, one that proceeds from psychology. But Mill does not go further than the psychology of the individual. Spencer goes from the individual back to his ancestors. The psychology of the individual is in the same position as the ontogenesis of zoology. Certain phenomena of the history of the individual are explainable only if they are referred back to phenomena of the history of the species. In the same way, the facts of the individual's consciousness cannot be understood if taken alone. We must go back to the species. We must, indeed, go back beyond the human species to acquisitions of knowledge that were accomplished by the animal ancestors of man. Spencer uses his great acumen to support this evolutionary history of the process of cognition. He shows in which way the mental activities have gradually developed from low stages at the beginning, through ever more accurate adaptations of the human mind to the external world and through inheritance of these adaptation. Every insight that the individual human being obtains through pure thought and without experience about things has been obtained by humanity or its ancestors through observation or experience. Leibniz thought he could explain the correspondence of man's inner life with the external world by assuming a harmony between them that was pre-established by the creator. Spencer explains this correspondence in the manner of natural science. The harmony is not pre-established, but gradually developed. We here find the continuation of natural scientific thinking to the highest aspects of human existence. Linnaeus had declared that every living organic form existed because the creator had made it as it is. Darwin maintained that it is as it is because it had gradually developed through adaptation and inheritance. Leibniz declared that thinking is an agreement with the external world because the creator had established this agreement. Spencer maintained that this agreement is there because it has gradually developed through adaptations and inheritance of the thought world.

Spencer was motivated in his thought by the need for a naturalistic explanation of spiritual phenomena. He found the general direction for such an explanation in Lyell's geology (compare page 267). In this geology, to be sure, the idea is still rejected that organic forms have gradually developed one from another. It nevertheless receives a powerful support through the fact that the inorganic (geological) formations of the earth's surface are explained through such a gradual development and through violent catastrophies. Spencer, who had a natural scientific education and who had for a time also been active as a civil engineer, recognized at once the full extent of the idea of evolution, and he applied it in spite of Lyell's opposition to it. He even applied this idea to spiritual processes. As early as 1850, in his book, *Social Statistics,* he described social evolution in analogy with organic evolution. He also acquainted himself with the studies of Harvey and Wolff in embryonic development (compare Vol. I of this book, pages 209ff.), and he plunged into the works of Karl Ernst von Baer (compare above pages 296ff.), which showed him that evolution proceeded from the development of a homogeneous uniform state to one of variety, diversity and abundance. In the early stages of embryological development the organisms are very similar; later they become different from one another (compare above pages 296ff.). Through Darwin this evolutionary thought was completely confirmed. From a few original organic forms the whole wealth of the highly diversified world of formations has developed.

From the idea of evolution, Spencer wanted to proceed to the most general truths, which, in his opinion, constituted the aim of all human striving for knowledge. He believed that one could discover manifestations of this evolutionary thought in the simplest phenomena. When, from dispersed particles of water, a cloud is formed in the sky, when a sand pile is formed from scattered grains of sand, Spencer saw the beginnings of an evolutionary process. Dispersed matter is contracted and concentrated to a whole. It is just this process that is presented to us in the Kant-Laplace hypothesis of world evolution. Dispersed parts of a chaotic world nebula have contracted. The organism originates in just this way. Dispersed elements are concentrated in tissues. The psychologist can observe that man contracts dispersed observations into general truths. Within this concentrated whole, articulation and differentiation take place. The original homogeneous mass is differentiated into the individual heavenly bodies of the solar system; the organism differentiates itself into the various organs.

Concentration alternates with dissolution. When a process of evolution has reached a certain climax, an equilibrium takes place. Man, for instance, develops until he has evolved a maximum of harmonization of his inner abilities with external nature. Such a state of equilibrium, however, cannot last; external forces will effect it destructively. The evolutionary process must be followed by a process of dissolution; what had been concentrated is dispersed again; the cosmic again becomes chaotic. The process of evolution can begin anew. Thus, Spencer sees the process of the world as a rhythmic play of motion. It is certainly not an uninteresting observation for the comparative history of the evolution of world conception that Spencer, from the observation of the genesis of world phenomena, reaches here a conclusion that is similar to one Goethe expressed in connection with his ideas concerning the genesis of life. Goethe describes the growth of a plant in the following way:

May the plant sprout, blossom or bear fruit, it is always by the same organs that the prescription of nature is fulfilled in various functions and under frequently changing forms. The same organ, which at the stem expands as a leaf and takes on a most differentiated shape, now contracts again in the calyx, spreads out in the petal, epitomizes in the organs of reproduction and finally once more swells as fruit.

If one thinks of this conception as being transferred to the whole process of the world, one arrives as Spencer's contraction and dispersion of matter.

* * *

Spencer and Mill exerted a great influence on the development of world conception in the second half of the nineteenth century. The rigorous emphasis on observation and the one-sided elaboration of the methods of observational knowledge of Mill, along with the application of the conceptions of natural science to the entire scope of human knowledge by Spencer could not fail to meet with the approval of an age that saw in the idealistic world conception of Fichte, Schelling and Hegel nothing but degeneration of human thinking. It was an age that showed appreciation only for the successes of the research work of natural science. The lack of unity among the idealistic thinkers and what seemed to many a perfect fruitfulness of a thinking that was completely concentrated and absorbed in itself, had to produce a deep-seated suspicion against idealism. One may say that a widespread view of the last four decades of the nineteenth century is clearly expressed in words spoken by Rudolf Virchow in his address, *The Foundation of the University of Berlin and the Transition from the Age of Philosophy into that of Natural Science* (1893): "Since the belief in magic formulas has been forced back into the most backward circles of the people, the formulas of the natural philosopher have met with little approval." And one of the most significant philosophers of the second half of the century, Eduard von Hartmann, sums up the character of his world conception in the motto he placed at the head of his book, *Philosophy of the Unconscious: Speculative Results Obtained by the Inductive Method of Natural Science.* He is of the opinion that it is necessary to recognize "the greatness of the progress brought about by Mill, through which all attempts of a deductive method of philosophy have been defeated and made obsolete for all times." (Compare Eduard von Hartmann, *Geschichte der Metaphysik,* 2 part, page 479.)

The recognition of certain limits of human knowledge that was shown by many naturalists was also received favorably by many religiously attuned souls. They argued as follows: The natural scientists observe the inorganic and organic facts of nature and they attempt to find general laws by combining the individual phenomena. Through these laws processes can be explained, and it is even possible to predetermine thereby the regular course of future phenomena. A comprehensive world conception should proceed in the same way; it should confine itself to the facts, establish general truths within moderate limits and not maintain any claim to penetrate into the realm of the "unknowable." Spencer, with his complete separation of the "knowable" and the "unknowable," met the demand of such religious needs to a high degree. The idealistic mode of thought was, on the other hand, considered by such religiously inclined spirits to be a fantastic aberration. As a matter of principle, the idealistic mode of conception cannot recognize an "unknowable," because it has to uphold the conviction that through the concentrated penetration into the inner life of man a knowledge can be attained that covers not merely the outer surface of the world but also its real core.

The thought life of some influential naturalists, such as Thomas Henry Huxley, moved entirely in the direction of such religiously inclined spirits. Huxley believed in a complete agnosticism with regard to the essence of the world. He declared that a monism, which is in general agreement with Darwin's results, is applicable only to external nature. Huxley was one of the first to defend the Darwinian conceptions, but he is at the same time one of the most outspoken representatives of those thinkers who believed in the limitation of that mode of conception. A similar view is also held by the physicist *Johaan Tyndall* (1820–93) who considered the world process to be an energy that is completely inaccessible to the human intellect. According to him, it is precisely the assumption that everything in the world comes into existence through a natural evolution that makes it impossible to accept the thought that matter, which is, afterall, the carrier of the whole evolution, should be no more than what our intellect can comprehend of it.

* * *

A characteristic phenomenon of his time is the personality of the English statesman, *James Balfour* (1840–1930). In 1879, in his book, *A Defense of Philosophical Doubt, Being an Essay on the Foundations of Belief,* he expressed a credo that is doubtless similar to that held by many other thinkers. With respect to everything that man is capable of explaining he stands completely on the ground of the thought of natural science. For him, there is no other knowledge but natural science, but he maintains at the same time that his knowledge of natural science is only rightly understood if it is clear that the needs of man's soul and reason can never be satisfied by it. It is only necessary to understand that, in the last analysis even in natural science, everything depends on faith in the ultimate truths for which no further proof is possible. But no harm is done in that this trend of thoughts leads us only to belief, because this belief is a secure guide for our action in daily life. We believe in the laws of nature and we master them through this belief. We thereby force nature to serve us for our purpose. Religious belief is to produce an agreement between the actions of man and his higher needs that go beyond his everday life.

The world conceptions that have been discussed under the title, "The World as Illusion," show that they have as their basis a longing for a satisfactory relationship of the self-conscious ego to the general world picture. It is especially significant that they do not consciously consider this search as their philosophical aim, and therefore do not expressly turn their inquiry toward that purpose. Instinctively as it were, they permit their thinking to be influenced by the direction that is determined by this unconscious search. The form that this search takes is determined by the conceptions of modern natural science. We approach the fundamental character of these conceptions if we fix our attention on the concept of "consciousness." This concept was introduced to the life of modern philosophy by Descartes. Before him, it was customary to depend more on the concept of the "soul" as such. Little attention was paid to the fact that only a part of the soul's life is spent in connection with conscious phenomena. During sleep the soul does not live consciously. Compared to the conscious life, the nature of the soul must therefore consist of deeper forces, which in the waking state are merely lifted into consciousness. The more one asked the question of the justification and the value of knowledge in the light of clear and distinct ideas, however, the more it was also felt that the soul finds the most certain elements of knowledge when it does not go beyond its own limits and when it does not delve deeper into itself than consciousness extends. The opinion prevailed that everything else may be uncertain, but what my consciousness is, at least, as such is certain. Even the house I pass may not exist without me; that the *image* of this house is now in my consciousness: *this* I may maintain. But as soon as we fix our attention on this consciousness, the concept of the ego inevitably grows together with that of the consciousness. Whatever kind of entity the "ego" may be outside the consciousness, the realm of the "ego" can be conceived as extending as far as the consciousness. There is no possibility of denying that the sensual world picture, which the soul experiences consciously, has come into existence through the impression that is made on man by the world. But as soon as one clings to this statement, it becomes difficult to rid oneself of it, for there is a tendency thereby to imply the judgment that the processes of the world are the causes, and that the content of our consciousness is the effect. Because one thinks that only the effect is contained in the consciousness, it is believed that the cause must be in a world *outside* man as an imperceptible "thing in itself." The presentation that is given above shows how the results of modern physiological research lead to an affirmation of such an opinion. It is just this opinion through which the "ego" finds itself enclosed with its subjective experiences within its own boundaries. This subtly produced intellectual illusion, once formed, cannot be destroyed as long as the ego does not find any clues within itself of which it knows that they refer to a being outside the subjective concsiousness, although they are actually depicted within that consciousness. The ego must, outside the sensual consciousness, feel a contact with entities that guarantee their being by and through themselves. It must find something *within* that *leads it outside itself.* What has been said here concerning thoughts that are brought to life can have this effect. As long as the ego has experienced thought only within itself, it feels itself confined with it within its own boundary. As thought is brought to life it emancipates the ego from a mere subjective existence. A process takes place that is, to be sure, experienced subjectively by the ego, but by its own nature is an objective process. This breaks the "ego" loose from everything that it can feel only as subjective.

So we see that also the conceptions for which the world is illusion move toward a point that is reached when Hegel's world picture is so transformed that its thought comes to life. These conceptions take on the form that is necessary for a world picture that is unconsciously driven by an impulse in that direction. But in them, thinking still lacks the power to work its way through to that aim. Even in their imperfection, however, these conceptions receive their general character from this aim, and the ideas that appear are the external symptoms of active forces that remain concealed.

Chapter IV

Echoes of the
Kantian Mode of Conception

Only a few personalities in the second half of the nineteenth century attempted to find a firm foundation for the relation of a conception of the self-conscious ego toward the general world picture by going deeply into Hegel's mode of thought. One of the best thinkers along these lines was *Paul Asmus* (1842–1876), who died as a young man. In 1873 he published a book entitled, *The Ego and the Thing in Itself.* In it he shows how it is possible, through Hegel's approach to thinking and the world of ideas, to obtain a relation of man toward the essence of things. He explains in an ingenious way that we have in man's thinking an element that is not alien to reality but full of life and fundamentally real, an element on which we only have to concentrate in order to arrive at the essence of existence. In a most illuminating way he describes the course of the evolution of world conception that began with Kant, who had seen in the "thing in itself" an element that was alien and inaccessible to man, and led to Hegel, who was of the opinion that thought comprised not only itself as an ideal entity but also the "thing in itself." Voices like this found scarcely a hearing. This became most poignantly clear in the slogan, "Back to Kant," which became popular in a certain current of philosophical life after

Eduard Zeller's speech at the University of Heidelberg, *On the Significance and Task of the Theory of Knowledge.*

The conceptions, partly conscious and partly unconscious, which led to this slogan, are approximately as follows. Natural science has shaken the confidence in spontaneous thinking that means to penetrate by itself to the highest questions of existence, but we cannot be satisfied with the mere results of natural science for they do not lead beyond the external view of things. There must be grounds of existence concealed behind this external aspect. Even natural science itself has shown that the world of colors, tones, etc., surrounding us is not a reality outside in the objective world but that it is produced through the function of our senses and our brain (compare above, pages 314ff.). For this reason, it is necessary to ask these questions: In what respect do the results of natural science point beyond their own limits toward the higher problems: What is the nature of our knowledge? Can this knowledge lead to a solution of that higher task? Kant has asked such questions with great emphasis. In order to find one's own position, one wanted to study how he had approached them. One wanted to think over with the greatest possible precision Kant's line of thought, attempting to avoid his errors and to find in the continuation of his ideas a way that led out of the general perplexity.

A number of thinkers endeavored to arrive at a tenable goal, starting from Kantian points of departure. The most important among them were *Hermann Cohen* (1842–1916), *Otto Liebmann* (1840–1912), *Wilhelm Windelband* (1848–1916), *Johannes Volkelt* (1842–1930) and *Benno Erdmann* (1851–1921). Much perspicacity can be found in the writings of these men. A great deal of work was done inquiring into the nature and extent of the human faculty of knowledge. Johannes Volkelt who, insofar as he was active as an epistomologist, lives entirely within this current, also contributed a thorough work on *Kant's Theory of Knowledge* (1879) in which all problems characterizing this trend of thought are discussed. In 1884 he gave the inaugural address for his professorship in Basel in which he made the statement that all thinking that goes beyond the results of the special empirical sciences of facts must have "the restless character of seeking and searching, of cautious trial, defensive reserve and deliberate admission." It should be an "advance in which one must partly withdraw again, a yielding in which one nevertheless holds on to a certain degree" (*On the Possibility of Metaphysics*, Hamburg & Leipzig, 1884).

This new attempt to start from Kant appears in a special light in Otto Liebmann. His writings, *Contributions Toward the Analysis of Reality* (1876), *Thoughts and Facts* (1882), *Climax of Theories* (1884), are veritable models of philosophical criticism. Here a caustic mind ingeniously discovers contradictions in the worlds of thought, reveals as half truths what appear as safe judgments, and shows what unsatisfactory elements the individual sciences contain when their results appear before the highest tribunals of thought. Liebmann enumerates the contradictions of Darwinism. He reveals its insufficiently founded assumptions and its defective thought connections, maintaining that something is needed to fill in the gaps to support the assumptions. On one occasion he ends an exposition he gives of the nature of living organisms with the words:

> Plant seeds do not lose their ability to germinate after lying dry for ages, and grains of wheat found in Egyptian mummy cases, after having been hermetically sealed and buried for thousands of years, when sowed in a moist soil, thrive excellently. Wheel animalcules (rotatoria) and other infusoria that have been gathered completely dried up from a gutter pipe are newly revived by rain water. Even frogs and fishes that have turned into ice cakes in freezing water revive when carefully thawed out. All these facts are capable of completely opposite interpretations. . . . In short, every form of categorical denial in this matter would be crude dogmatism. Therefore, we discontinue our argument.

This phrase, "We discontinue our argument," really expresses, even if it does not do so literally, every final thought of Liebmann's reflection. It is, indeed, the final conclusion of many recent followers and elaborators of Kantianism. They do not succeed in doing more than emphasize that they receive the things into their consciousness. Therefore, everything that they see, hear, etc., is not outside in the world but within themselves and they are incapable of deciding anything concerning the outside. A table stands before me, argues the Neo-Kantian, but, really, this only seems to be so. Only a person who is naively concerned with problems of philosophy can say, "Outside myself is a table." A person who has overcome that naivete says, "An unknown something produces an impression within my eye; this eye and my brain make out of the impression the sensation brown. As I have this sensation brown not merely at an isolated point but can let my eye run over a plane surface and four columnnar forms, so the brownness takes the shape of an object that is this table. When I touch this table, it offers resistance. It makes an impression on my sense of touch, which I express by attributing hardness to the picture that has been produced by the eye. At the suggestion of some "thing in itself" that I do not know, I have therefore created this table out of myself. The table is my mental content. It is only in my consciousness.

Volkelt presents this view at the beginning of his book on *Kant's Theory of Knowledge*:

> The first fundamental condition that the philosopher must clearly realize is the insight that, to begin with, our knowledge extends to nothing more than our conceptions. Our conceptions are the only things that we immediately and directly experience, and for just that reason that we experience them immediately, even the most radical doubt cannot deprive us of the knowledge of them. But the knowledge that goes beyond my faculty of conception is not protected from doubt. (I use this expression here always in its most comprehensive sense so that all physical events are included in the term.) Therefore, all knowledge that goes beyond the conceptions must be marked as doubtful at the outset of the philosophical reflection.

Otto Liebmann also uses this thought to defend the statement: Man can no more know that the things he conceives are *not*, than he can know positively that they *are*. "For the very reason that no conceiving subject can escape the sphere of its subjective imagination, because it can never grasp and observe what may exist or not exist outside its subjectivity, leaping thereby over its own consciousness and emancipating itself from itself. For this reason it would also be absurd to maintain that the object does *not* exist outside the subjective conception" (O. Liebmann, *Contributions toward the Analysis of Reality*).

Both Volkelt and Liebmann nevertheless endeavor to prove that man finds something in the world of his conceptions that is not merely observed or perceived, but that is added to the perception by thought—something that at least *points* toward the essence of things. Volkelt is of the opinion that there is a fact within the conceptual life that points to something that lies outside the life of conception. This fact consists in the logical necessity with which certain conceptions suggest themselves to man. In his book, *The Sources of Human Certainty* that appeared in 1906, we read Volkelt's view:

> If one seeks the basis of the certainty of our knowledge, one finds two points of origin, two sources of certainty. Even if an intimate cooperation of both sources of certainty is necessary if real knowledge is to result, it is nevertheless impossible to reduce one source to the other. The one source of certainty is the self-assurance of consciousness, the awareness of the facts of my consciousness. That I *am* consciousness is just as true as the fact that my consciousness testifies to the existence of certain processes and states, certain contents and forms. Without this source of certainty there would be no cognitive process; it supplies the material through the elaboration of which all knowledge is produced. The other source of certainty is the necessity of thought, the certainty of logical compulsion, the objective consciousness of necessity. With it something absolutely new is given that cannot possibly be derived from the certainty of our self-awareness in consciousness.

Concerning this second source of certainty, Volkelt expresses himself in his book mentioned above as follows:

> The immediate experience allows us to become aware of the fact that certain combinations of concepts show a peculiar form of

compulsion to be inherent in them that is essentially different from all other kinds of compulsion that are associated with conceptions. This compulsion forces us to think certain concepts as belonging together, not merely in the conscious process in which we are aware of them but also in a corresponding objective interconnection, independent of the conscious conceptions. Furthermore, this compulsion does not force us in a manner to suggest that we should forfeit our moral satisfaction or our inner happiness, our salvation and so forth, but it contains the suggestion that objective reality would have to annihilate itself in itself, would have to lose its possibility of existence if the opposite of what it prescribes as a necessity were to take place. What distinguishes this compulsion then is that the very thought of the opposite of that necessity forcing itself upon us, would be experienced as a call that reality should revolt against the conditions of its existence. This peculiar, immediately experienced compulsion is generally called logical compulsion or thought necessity. The logically necessary reveals itself directly as an announcement of the object itself. It is the peculiarly meaningful significance, the reason-guided illumination that is contained in everything logical, that bears witness with immediate evidence of the objective, real validity of the logical connections of concepts. (*Kant's Theory of Knowledge,* pp. 208 ff.)

Otto Liebmann confesses toward the end of his essay, *The Climax of Theories,* that in his opinion the whole thought structure of human knowledge, from the ground floor of the science of observation up to the most airy regions of the highest hypotheses of world conception, is permeated by thoughts that point beyond perception. "Fragments of percepts must first be supplemented by an extraordinary amount of non-observed elements linked together and connected in a definite order according to certain operations of the mind." But how can one deny that human thinking has the ability to know something through its own activity as long as it is necessary to resort to this acitivity even if one merely wants to obtain order among the facts of the observed precepts? Neo-Kantianism is in a curious position. It would like to confine itself within the boundaries of consciousness and within the life of conception, but it is forced to confess that it is impossible to take a step "within" these boundaries that does not lead in all directions beyond those limits. Otto Liebmann ends the second booklet of his *Thought and Facts* as follows:

> If, on the one hand, seen from the viewpoint of natural science, man were nothing but animated dust, then, on the other, all nature, as it appears in space and time, when seen from the only viewpoint that is immediately accessible and given to us, is an anthropocentric phenomenon.

There are many who hold the view that the world of observation is *merely* human conception in spite of the fact that it must extinguish itself if it is correctly understood. It is repeated again and again in the course of the last decades in many variations. *Ernst Laas* (1837–1885) forcefully defended the point of view that only positive facts of perception should be wrought into knowledge. *Alois Riehl* (1849–1924), proceeding from the same fundamental view, declares that there could be no general world conception at all, and that everything that goes beyond the various special sciences should only be a critique of knowledge. Knowledge is obtained only in the special sciences; philosophy has the task of showing how this knowledge comes about and of taking care that thought should not add any element that can not be justified by the facts. *Richard Wahle* in his book, *The Whole of Philosophy and Its End* (1894), eliminates with utmost scrutiny everything that the mind has added to the "occurrences" of the world until finally the mind stands in the ocean of occurrences that stream by, seeing itself in this ocean as one such occurrence, nowhere finding a point capable of providing a meaningful enlightenment concerning them. This mind would have to exert its own energy to produce order in the occurrences. But then it would be the mind itself that had introduced that order into nature. If the mind makes a statement about the essence of the occurrences, it derives this not from the things but from itself. This it could only do if it admitted that in its own activity something essential could go on. The assumption would have to be made that the mind's judgment could have significance also for things. But in its own judgment this confidence is something that, according to Wahle's world conception, the mind is not entitled to have. It must stand idly by and watch what flows past, around and inside itself, and it would only contribute to its own deception if it were to put any credence in a conception that it formed itself about the occurrences.

> What final answer could a mind find that looked into the world structure, tossing about within itself problems concerning the nature and purpose of events? As it seemed to occupy a firm stand in opposition to the surrounding world, it has had to experience that it dissolved into a flight of occurrences and flowed together with other occurrences. The mind did no longer "know" the world. It had to admit: I am not certain that there are "knowers," but there are simply occurrences. They do, to be sure, make their appearance in a manner that the concept of knowledge could emerge prematurely and without justification. . . . and "concepts" emerged and flitted by to bring light into the occurrences, but they were will-o'-the-wisps, specters of wishful thinking, miserable postulates whose evidence meant nothing, empty forms of knowledge. Unknown factors must rule the change. Darkness was spread over nature, occurrences are the veil of the true . . . (*The Whole of Philosophy and Its End*).

Wahle closes his book, which is to represent the "gifts" of philosophy to the individual sciences, theology, physiology, esthetics and civic education, with these words, "May the age begin when people will say: once was philosophy."

In the above mentioned book by Wahle, as well as in his other books, *Historical Survey of the Development of Philosophy* (1895) and *On the Mechanism of the Mental Life* (1906), we have one of the most significant symptoms of the evolution of world conception in the nineteenth century. The lack of confidence with respect to knowledge begins with Kant and leads, finally, as it appears in Wahle, to a complete disbelief in any philosophical world conception.

Chapter V

World Conceptions of Scientific Factuality

An attempt to derive a general view of world and life from the basis of strict science was undertaken in the course of the nineteenth century by *Auguste Comte* (1798–1857). This enterprise, which was presented as a comprehensive world picture in his *Cours de Philosophie Positive* (6 vols., 1830–42), was sharply antagonistic to the idealistic views of Fichte, Schelling and Hegel of the first half of the nineteenth century. It also opposed, although not to the same degree, all those thought structures that were derived from the ideas of evolution along the lines of Lamarck and Darwin. What occupied the central position of all world conception in Hegel, the contemplation and comprehension of man's own spirit, was completely rejected by Comte. He argues: If the human spirit wanted to contemplate itself, it would actually have to divide into two personalities; it would have to slip outside itself and place itself opposite its own being. Even a psychology that does not confine itself to the mere physiological view but intends to preserve the processes of the mind by themselves is not recognized by Comte. Anything that is to become an object of knowledge must belong to the objective inter-connections of facts, must be presented objectively as the laws of the mathematical sciences. From this position there follows Comte's objection to the attempts of Spencer and other thinkers whose world pictures followed the approach of scientific thinking adapted by Lamarck and Darwin. So far as Comte is concerned, the human species is given as a fixed and unchangeable fact; he refuses to pay any attention to Lamarck's theory. Simple, transparent natural laws as physics uses them for its phenomena are ideals of knowledge for him. As long as science does not work with such simple laws, it is unsatisfactory as knowledge for Comte. He has a mathematical bent of mind. If it cannot be treated clearly and simply like a mathematical problem, he considers it to be not ready for science. Comte has no feeling for the fact that one needs ideas that become increasingly more life-saturated as one rises from the purely mechanical and physical processes to the higher formations of nature and to man. His world conception owed a certain lifeless and rigid quality to this fact. The whole world appears to him like the mechanics of a machine. What escapes Comte everywhere is the element of life; he expells life and spirit from things and explains merely what is mechanical and machine-like. The concrete historical life of man appears in his presentation like the conceptual picture that the astronomer draws of the motions of the heavenly bodies. Comte constructed a scale of the sciences. Mathematics represents the lowest stage; it is followed by physics and chemistry and these again by the science of organisms; the last and concluding science in this sequence is sociology, the knowledge of human society. Comte strives to make all these sciences as simple as mathematics. The phenomena with which the individual sciences deal are supposed to be different in every case but the laws are considered to be fundamentally always the same.

* * *

The reverberations of the thought of Holbach, Condillac and others are still distinctly perceptible in the lectures on the relation between soul and body (*Les Rapports du Physique et du Moral de L'homme*) that *Pierre Jean Georges Cabanis* (1757–1808) gave in 1797 and 1798 in the medical school founded by the National Convention in Paris. Nevertheless, these lectures can be called the beginning of the development of the world conception of the nineteenth century in France. They express a distinct awareness of the fact that Condillac's mode of conception for the phenomena of the soul life had been too closely modelled after the conception of the mechanical processes of inorganic nature and their operation. Cabanis investigates the influence of age, sex, way of life and temperament on man's intellectual and emotional disposition. He develops the conception that the physical and the spiritual are not two separated entities that have nothing in common but that they constitute an inseparable whole. What distinguishes him from his predecessors is not his fundamental view but the way in which he elaborates it. His predecessors simply carry into the spiritual the views they have derived from the inorganic world. Cabanis is convinced that if we start by observing the world of the spiritual as open-mindedly as we observe the inorganic, it will reveal its relation to the rest of the natural phenomena.

Destutt de Tracy (1754–1836) proceeded in a similar way. He also wanted first to observe the processes of the spirit without bias as they appear when we approach them without philosophical or scientific prejudice. According to this thinker, one is in error if one conceives the soul as a mechanism as Condillac and his followers had done. This mechanistic character cannot be upheld any longer if one honestly observes oneself. We do not find in us an automaton, a being that is directed from without. We always find within us spontaneous activity and an inner self. We should actually not know anything of the effects of the external world if we did not experience a disturbance in our inner life caused by a collision with the external world. We experience our own being. We develop our activity out of ourselves, but as we do this we meet with opposition. We realize not only our own existence but also an external world that resists us.

Although they started from de Tracy, two thinkers—*Maine de Biran* (1766–1824) and *André-Marie Ampère* (1775–1826)were led by the self-observation of the soul in entirely different directions. Biran is a subtle observer of the human spirit. What in Rousseau seems to emerge as a chaotic mode of thought motivated by an arbitrary mood, we find in Biran in the form of clear and concrete thinking. Two factors of man's inner life are made the objects of observation by Biran who is a profoundly thoughtful psychologist: What man is through the nature of his being, his temperament, and what he makes out of himself through active work, his character. He follows the ramifications and changes of the inner life, and he finds the source of knowledge in man's inner life. The forces of which we learn through introspection are intimately known in our life, and we learn of an external world only insofar as it presents itself as more or less similar and akin to our inner world. What should we know of forces outside in nature if we did not experience within our self-active soul a similar force and consequently could compare this with what corresponds to it in the external world? For this reason, Biran is untiring in his search for the processes in man's soul. He pays special attention to the involuntary and the unconscious element in the inner life processes that exist long before the light of consciousness emerges in the soul. Biran's search for wisdom within the soul led him to a peculiar form of mysticism in later years. In the process of deriving the profoundest wisdom from the soul, we come closest to the foundation of existence when we dig down into our own being. The experience of the deepest soul processes then is an immersion in the well-spring of existence, into the God within us.

The attraction of Biran's wisdom lies in the intimate way in which he presents it. He could have found no more appropriate form of presentation than that of a *journal intime,* a form of diary. The writings of Biran that allow the deepest insight into his thought world were published after his death by E. Naville (compare Naville's book, *Maine de Biran. Sa vie et ses pensées,* 1857, and his edition, *Oeuvres inédités de Maine de Biran*). As old men, Cabanis and Destutt de Tracy belonged to a small circle of philosophers; Biran was a younger member among them. Ampère was among those who were acquainted with Biran's views. As a natural scientist, he became prominent through the extension of Oersted's observation concerning the relation of electricity to magnetism (compare above page 266). Biran's mode of conception is more intimate, that of Ampère more scientific-methodical. Ampère follows with interest the interrelationship of sensations and conceptions in the soul, and also the process through which the spirit arrives at a science of the world phenomena with the aid of thinking.

What is significant in this current of world conception, which chronologically represents the continuation of the teachings of Condillac, is the circumstance that the life of the soul itself is decidedly emphasized, that the self-activity of the inner personality of the human being is brought into the foreground of the investigation, and that all these thinkers are striving nevertheless for knowledge in the strict sense of natural science. Initially, they investigate the spirit with the methods of natural science, but they do not want to treat its phenomena as homogeneous with the other processes of nature. From these more materialistic beginnings there emerges finally a tendency toward a world conception that leans distinctly toward the spirit.

Victor Cousin (1792–1867) traveled through Germany several times and thus became personally acquainted with the leading spirits of the idealistic period. The deepest impression was made on him by Hegel and Goethe. He brought their idealism to France. As a professor at the École normale (1814), and later at the Sorbonne, he was able to do a great deal for this idealism through his powerful and fascinating eloquence that always produced a deep impression. Cousin received from the idealistic life of the spirit the conviction that it is not through the observation of the external world but through that of the human spirit that a satisfactory viewpoint for a world conception can be obtained. He based what he wanted to say on the self observation of the soul. He adopted the view of Hegel that spirit, idea and thought do not merely rule in man's inner life but also outside in nature and in the progress of the historical life, and that reason is contained in reality. Cousin taught that the character of a people of an age was not merely influenced by random happenings, arbitrary decisions of human individuals, but that a real idea is manifested in them and that a great man appears in the world merely as a messenger of a great idea, in order to realize it in the course of history. This produced a profound impression on Cousin's French audience, which in its most recent history had had to comprehend world historical upheavals without precedent, when they heard such a splendid speaker expound the role that reason played in the historical evolution in accordance with some great and fundamental ideas.

Comte, with energy and resolution, found his place in the development of French philosophy with his principle: only in the method of science, which proceeds from strict mathematical and directly observed truths as in physics and chemistry can the point of departure for a world conception be found. The only approach he considered mature was the one that fought its way through to this view. To arrive at this stage, humanity had to go through two phases of immaturity—one in which it believed in gods, and subsequently, one in which it surrendered to abstract ideas. Comte sees the evolution of mankind in the progression from theological thinking to idealistic thinking, and from there to the scientific world conception. In the first stage, man's thinking projected anthropomorphic gods into the processes of nature, which produce these processes in the same arbitrary manner in which man proceeds in his actions. Later, he replaces the gods with abstract ideas as, for instance, life force, general world reason, world purpose, and so forth. But this phase of development must give way to a higher one in which it must be understood that an explanation of the phenomena of the world can be found only in the method of observation and a strictly mathematical and logical treatment of the facts. For the purpose of a world conception, thinking must merely combine what physics, chemistry and the science of living organisms obtain through their investigation. Thinking must not add anything to the results of the individual sciences as theology had done with its divine beings and the idealistic philosophy with its abstract thoughts. Also, the conceptions concerning the course of the evolution of mankind, the social life of men in the state, in society, etc., will become clear only when the attempt is made to find in them laws like those found in the exact natural sciences. The causes that bring families, associations, legal views and state institutions into existence must be investigated in the same way as the causes that make bodies fall to the ground and that allow the digestive organs to operate. The science of human social life, of human development, sociology, is therefore what Comte is especially concerned with, and he tries to give it the exactness that the other sciences have gradually acquired.

In this respect he has a predecessor in *Claude-Henri de Saint-Simon* (1760–1825). Saint-Simon had presented the view that man would only learn to guide his own fate completely when he conceived of his own life in the state, in society and in the course of history in a strictly scientific sense, and when he arranged it like a process following a natural law. For awhile, Comte was on intimate terms with Saint-Simon. He parted ways with him when it seemed to him that Saint-Simon's views turned into all sorts of groundless dreams and utopias. Comte continued to work with a rare zeal in his original direction. His *Cours de Philosophie Positive* is an attempt to elaborate, in a style of spirit-alienation, the scientific accomplishments of his time into a world conception by presenting them merely in a systematized survey, and by developing sociology in the same way without the aid of theological and idealistic thoughts. Comte saw no other task for the philosopher than that of such a mere systematized survey. The philosopher would add nothing of his own to the picture that the sciences have presented as the connection of facts. Comte expressed thereby, in the most pointed manner, his view that the sciences alone, with their methods of observing reality, have a voice in the formulation of a world conception.

* * *

Within German spirit-life *Eugen Dühring* (1833–1921) appeared as a forceful champion of Comte's thought. This was expressed in 1865 in his *Natural Dialectic.* As a further exposition, he expounded his views in his book, *Course of Philosophy as a Strictly Scientific World Conception and Art of Life* (1875), and in numerous other writings in the fields of mathematics, natural science, philosophy, history of science and social economy. All of Dühring's work proceeds, in the strictest sense of the word, from a mathematical and mechanistic mode of thought. Dühring is outstanding in his endeavor to analyze his observations of nature in accordance with mathematical law, but where this kind of thinking is insufficient, he loses all possibility of finding his way through life. It is from this characteristic of his spirit that the arbitrariness and bias is to be explained with which Dühring judges so many things. Where it is necessary to judge the conflicts of life in accordance with higher ideas, he has, therefore, no other criterion than his sympathies and antipathies that have been aroused in him through accidental personal circumstances. This man, with his mathematically objective mind, becomes completely arbitrary when he undertakes to evaluate human accomplishments of the historical past or of the present. His rather unimaginative mathematical mode of conception led him to denounce a personality like Goethe as the most unscientific mind of modern times, whose entire significance consisted, in Dühring's opinion, in a few poetical achievements. It is impossible to surpass Dühring in his under-valuation of everything that lies beyond a drab reality as he does in his book, *The Highlights of Modern Literature.* In spite of this one-sidedness, Dühring is one of the most stimulating figures in the development of modern world conception. No one who has penetrated his thought-saturated books can help but confess that he has been profoundly affected by them.

Dühring uses rude language for all world conceptions that do not proceed from strictly scientific basic views. All such unscientific modes of thought "found themselves in the state of childish immaturity or feverish fits, or in the decadence of senility, no matter whether they infest entire epochs and parts of humanity under these circumstances or just occasionally individual elements or degenerated layers of society, but they always belong to the category of the immature, the pathological or that of over-ripeness that is already decomposed by putrefaction,"

(*Course of Philosophy*). What *Kant, Fichte, Schelling and Hegel* achieved, Dühring condemns as the outflow of a professorial wisdom of mountebanks; idealism as a world conception is for him a theory of insanity. He means to create a philosophy of reality that is alone adequate to nature because it "does away with all artificial and unnatural fictions, and for the first time makes the concept of reality the measure of all ideal conceptions"; reality is conceived in this philosophy "in a manner that excludes all tendencies toward a dream-like and subjectivistically limited world conception." (*Course of Philosophy*)

One should think like a real expert in mechanics, a real physicist who confines himself to the results of sense perception, of the logical combinations of the intellect and the operations of calculations. Anything that goes beyond this is idle playing with empty concepts. This is Dühring's verdict. Dühring means to raise this form of thinking, however, to its justified position. Whoever depends exclusively on that form of thinking can be sure that it supplies him with insight concerning reality. All brooding over the question of whether or not we actually can penetrate into the mysteries of the world process, all investigations, which, like Kant's, want to limit the faculty of knowledge, are caused by logical distortion. One should not yield to the temptation of a self-sacrificing self-denial of the mind that does not dare to make a positive statement about the world. What we can know is a real and untarnished presentation of the real.

> "The totality of things has a systematic order and an inner logically consistent structure. Nature and history have a constitution and a development that correspond to a large extent to the general logical relations of all concepts. The general qualities and relations of the concepts of thought with which logic deals must also be valid for the special case, that its object is the totality of being, together with its chief forms. Since the most general thinking decides to a large extent what can be and how it can be, the highest principles and the main forms of logic must set the standard for all reality and its forms. (*Course of Philosophy*)

Reality has produced for itself an organ in human thinking in which it can reproduce itself mentally in the form of thought in an ideal picture. Nature is everywhere ruled by an all-penetrating law that carries its own justification within itself and cannot be criticized. How could there be any meaning in an attempt to criticize the relevance of thinking, the organ of nature? It is mere foolishness to suppose that nature would create an organ through which it would reflect itself only imperfectly or incompletely. Therefore, order and law in this world must correspond to the logical order and law in human thinking. "The ideal system of our thought is the picture of the real system of objective reality; the completed knowledge has, in the form of thoughts, the same structure that the things possess in the form of real existence."

In spite of this general agreement between thinking and reality, there exists for the former the possibility to go beyond the latter. In the element of the idea, thinking continues the operations that reality has suggested to it. In reality all bodies are divisible, but only up to a certain limit. Thinking does not stop at this limit but continues to divide in the realm of the idea. Thought sweeps beyond reality; for thought, the body is divisible into infinity. Accordingly, to thought it consists of infinitely small parts. In reality, this body consists only of a definite, finite number of small, but not infinitely small parts. In this way all concepts of infinity that transcend reality come into existence. From every event we proceed to another event that is its cause; from this cause we go again to the cause of that cause and so forth. As soon as our thinking abandons the firm ground of reality, it sweeps on into a vague infinity. It imagines that for every cause a cause has to be sought in turn so that the world is without a beginning in time. In allotting matter to space, thinking proceeds in a similar way. In transversing the sky it always finds beyond the most distant stars still other stars; it goes beyond this real fact and imagines space as infinite and filled with an infinite number of heavenly bodies. According to Dühring, one ought to realize that all such conceptions of infinity have nothing to do with reality. They only occur through the fact that thinking, with the methods that are perfectly appropriate within the realm of reality, rises above this realm and thereby gets lost in the indefinite.

If in our thinking, however, we remain aware of this separation from reality, we need no longer refrain from applying our concepts borrowed from human action, to nature. Dühring, as he proceeds from such presuppositions, does not even hesitate to attribute to nature in its production an imagination any more than he does to man in his creation. "Imagination extends . . . into nature itself; it has its roots, as does all thinking in general, in the processes that precede the developed consciousness but do not produce any elements of subjective feelings" (*Course of Philosophy*). The thought upheld by Comte, that all world conception should be confined to a mere rearrangement of the purely factual, dominates Dühring so completely that he projects the faculty of imagination into the external world because he believes that he would simply have to reject it if it occurred merely in the human mind. Proceeding from these conceptions he arrives at other projections of such concepts as are derived from human activities. He thinks, for instance, that not only man could, in his actions, undertake fruitless attempts, which he then gives up because they do not lead to the intended aim, but that such attempts could also be observed in nature.

> The character of the tentative in the formations of nature is not at all alien to reality itself, and one cannot see why one should allow only one half of the parallelism between nature outside man and nature in man, just for the sake of pleasing a shallow philosophy. If subjective error of thinking and imagining springs from the relative separation and independence of this sphere, why should not a practical error or blunder of the objective and non-thinking nature be possibly the result of a relative separation and mutual alienation of its various parts and driving forces? A true philosophy that is not intimidated by common prejudices will finally recognize the perfect parallelism and the all-pervading unity of the constitution in both directions. (*Course of Philosophy*)

Dühring is not in the least shy when it is a question of applying the concepts to reality that thinking produces in itself. But since he has, because of his disposition, only a sense for mathematical conceptions, the picture he sketches of the world has a mathematical-schematic character. He rejects the mode of thought that was developed by Darwin and Haeckel and does not understand what motivates them to search for a reason to explain why one being develops from another. The mathematician places the forms of a triangle, square, circle and ellipse side by side; why should one not be satisfied with a similar schematic coordination in nature as well? Dühring does not aim at the genesis of nature but at the fixed formations that nature produces through the combinations of its energies, just as the mathematician studies the definite, strictly delineated forms of space. He finds nothing inappropriate in attributing to nature a purposeful striving toward such definite formations. Dühring does not interpret this purposeful tendency of nature as the conscious activity that develops in man, but he supposes it to be just as distinctly manifested in the operation of nature as every other natural manifestation. In this respect, Dühring's view is, therefore, the opposite pole of the one upheld by Friedrich Albert Lange. Lange declares the higher concepts, especially all those in which imagination has a share, to be justifiable poetic fiction; Dühring rejects all poetic imagination in concepts, but he attributes actual reality to certain higher ideas that are indispensable to him. Thus, it seems quite consistent for Lange to separate the foundation of the moral life entirely from all ideas that are rooted in reality (compare above, page 323). It is also consistent if Dühring wants to extend the ideas that he sees as valid in the realm of morality to nature as well. He is completely convinced that what happens in man and through man belongs to the natural events as much as do the inanimate processes. What in human life is right cannot be wrong in nature.

Such considerations contributed to making Dühring an energetic opponent to Darwin's doctrine of the struggle for existence.

If the fight of all against all were the condition of perfection in nature, it would have to be the same with man's life:

> Such a conception that claims to be scientific is the most immoral thing thinkable. The character of nature is in this way conceived in an anti-moral sense. It is not merely indifferent to the better morality of man but it is actually in agreement and in alliance with the bad moral principles that are followed by scoundrels. (*Course of Philosophy*)

According to Dühring's life-conception, what man feels as moral impulses must have its origin in nature. It is possible to observe in nature a tendency toward morality. As nature produces various forces that purposefully combine into stable formations, so it also plants into man instincts of sympathy. By them he allows himself to be determined in his social life with his fellow men. In man, the activity of nature is continued on an elevated level. Dühring attributes the faculty to produce sensations automatically out of themselves to the inanimate mechanical forces.

> The mechanical causality of the forces of nature becomes, so to speak, subjectified in the fundamental sensation. The fact of this elementary process of subjectification is evidently incapable of any further explanation, for somewhere and under some conditions the unconscious mechanism of the world must develop a feeling of itself. (*Course of Philosophy*)

But when the world arrives at this stage, it is not that a new law begins, a realm of the spirit, but merely a continuation occurs of what had already been there in the unconscious mechanism. This mechanism, to be sure, is unconscious, but it is nevertheless wise, for "the earth with all it produces, as well as all causes of life's maintenance that lie outside, especially in the sun and all influences that come from the whole surrounding world in general—this entire organization and arrangement must be thought of as essentially produced for man, which is to say, in agreement with his well-being." (*Course of Philosophy*)

* * *

Dühring ascribes thought and even aims and moral tendencies to nature without admitting that he thereby idealizes nature. But, for an explanation of nature, higher ideas are necessary that transcend the real. According to Dühring, however, there must be nothing like that; he therefore changes their meaning by interpreting them as facts. Something similar happened in the world conception of *Julius Hermann von Kirchmann* (1802–84), who published his *Philosophy of Knowledge* in 1864 at about the same time Dühring's *Natural Dialectic* appeared. Kirchmann proceeds from the supposition that only what is perceived is real. Man is connected with reality through his perception. Everything that he does not derive from perception he must eliminate from his knowledge of reality. He succeeds in doing this if he rejects everything that is contradictory. "Contradiction is not," is Kirchmann's second principle, which follows his first principle, "The perceived is."

Kirchmann admits only feelings and desires as the states of the soul of man that have an existence by themselves.

> Knowing forms a contrast to the other two states, to feeling and desire. . . . It is possible that there is in knowing something underlying, perhaps something similar to, pressure and tension, but if it is conceived in this way it cannot be grasped in its essence. As knowing, and it is only as such that it is to be investigated here, it merely makes itself into a mirror of another being. There is no better parable for this than the mirror. Just as the mirror is the more perfect the less it shows of itself and the more it reflects another being, so it is also with knowing. Its essence is the pure reflection of a being other than itself, without mixing in its own state of being. (*Philosophy of Knowledge, 1864*)

One cannot imagine a greater contrast to Hegel's mode of conception than this view of knowledge. While with Hegel the essence of a thing appears in thinking, in the element that the soul adds in spontaneous activity to the percept, Kirchmann's ideal of knowledge consists of a mirror picture of percepts from which all additions by the soul itself have been eliminated.

To judge Kirchmann's position in the intellectual life correctly, one must consider the great difficulty with which somebody who had the will to erect an independent structure of world conception was met in his time. The results of natural science, which were to produce a profound influence on the development of world conceptions, were still young. They were just sufficient to shake the belief in the classical idealistic world conception that had had to erect its proud structure without the aid of modern natural science. In the face of the wealth of detailed knowledge, it became difficult to reconstruct fundamental philosophical thoughts. The thread that led from the scientific knowledge of facts to a satisfactory total conception of the world was gradually lost in the general consciousness. A certain perplexity took hold of many. An understanding for the lofty flight of thought that had inspired the world conception of Hegel was scarcely to be found anywhere.

CHAPTER VI

Modern Idealistic World Conceptions

In the second half of the nineteenth century, the mode of conception of natural science was blended with the idealistic traditions from the first half, producing three world conceptions that show a distinctive individual physiognomy. The three thinkers responsible for this were *Rudolf Hermann Lotze* (1817–81), *Gustav Theodor Fechner* (1801–87), and *Eduard von Hartmann* (1842–1906).

In his work, *Life and Life-force,* which appeared in 1842 in Wagner's *Handwörterbuch der Physiologie,* Lotze opposed the belief that there is in living beings a special force, the life force, and defended the thought that the phenomena of life are to be explained exclusively through complicated processes of the same kind as take place in lifeless nature. In this respect, he sided entirely with the mode of conception of modern natural science, which tried to bridge the gap between the lifeless and the living. This attitude is reflected in his books that deal with subjects of natural science, *General Pathology and Therapy as Mechanical Sciences* (1842) and *General Physiology of the Physical Life* (1851). With his *Elements of Psychophysics* (1860) and *Propaedeutics of Esthetics* (1876), Fechner contributed works that show the spirit of a strictly natural scientific mode of conception. This was now done in fields that before him had been treated almost without exception in the sense of an idealistic mode of thinking. But Lotze and Fechner felt that need to construct for themselves an idealistic world of thought that went beyond the view of natural science. Lotze was forced to take this direction through the quality of his inner disposition. This demanded of him not merely an intellectual observation of the natural law in the world, but challenged him to seek life and inwardness of the kind that man feels within himself in all things and processes. He wanted to "struggle constantly against the conceptions that acknowledge only one half of the world, and the less important one at that, only the unfolding of facts into new facts, of forms into new forms, but not the constant reconversion of all those externalities into elements of inner relevance, into what alone has value and truth in the world, into bliss and despair, admiration and disgust, love and hatred, into joyful certainty and doubtful yearning, into all the nameless forms of suspense and fear in which life goes on, that alone deserves to be called life."

Lotze, like many others, has the feeling that the human picture of nature becomes cold and drab if we do not permeate it with the conceptions that are taken from the human soul (compare above pages . . .) What in Lotze is caused by his inner disposition of feeling, appears in Fechner as the result of a richly developed imagination that has the effect of always leading from a logical comprehension of things to a poetic interpretation of them. He cannot, as a natural scientific thinker, merely search for the conditions of man's becoming and for the laws that will cause his death again. For him, birth and death become events that draw his imagination to a life before birth and to a life after death. Fechner writes in his *Booklet on Life after Death*:

> Man lives on earth not once, but three times. His first stage of life is a continuous sleep; the second, an alternation between sleeping and waking; the third, an eternal waking. In the first stage, man lives in solitude and in the dark; in the second, he lives in fellowship and

as a separate being side by side and among others in a light that reflects the surface for him; in the third stage, his life interweaves with that of other spirits to a higher life in the highest spirit, and his sight penetrates the essence of the finite things. In the first phase, the body develops from its germ and produces the organs for the second; in the second phase, the spirit develops from its germ and produces its organ for the third; and in the third phase, the divine germ that lies in the spirit of every human being develops. It can be dimly felt and instinctively apprehended by a genius pointing toward a realm beyond, which is dark for us but bright as day for the spirit of the third phase. The transition from the first phase of life to the second is called birth; the transition from the second to the third is called death.

Lotze has given an interpretation of the phenomena of the world that is in keeping with the needs of his inner disposition in his works, *Microcosm* (1858–64), *Three Books of Logic* (1874) and *Three Books of Metaphysics* (1879). The notes taken from the lectures he gave on the various fields of philosophy also have appeared in print. He proceeds by following the strictly natural, law-determined course of the world and by interpreting this regularity in the sense of an ideal, harmonious, soul-filled order and activity of the world-ground. We see that one thing has an effect on another, but one could not produce the effect on the other if fundamental kinship and unity did not exist between them. The second thing would have to remain indifferent to the activity of the first if it did not possess the ability to behave in agreement with the action of the first and to arrange its own activity accordingly. A ball can be caused to move by another ball that hits it only if it meets the other ball with a certain understanding, so to speak, if it finds within itself the same understanding of motion as is contained in the first. The ability to move is something that is contained in the first ball as well as in the second, as common to both of them. All things and processes must have such common elements. That we perceive them as things and events is caused by the fact that we, in our observation, become acquainted only with their surface. If we were able to see their inner nature, we would observe not what separates them but what connects them to form a great world totality. There is only one being in our experience that we do not merely know from without but from within, that we cannot merely look *at,* but *into,* that our sight can penetrate. This is our own soul, the totality of our own spiritual personality. But since all things must possess a common element in their inner being, so they must also have in common with our soul the element that constitutes our soul's inner core. We may, therefore, conceive the inner nature of things as similar to the quality of our own soul. The world ground that rules as the common element of all things can be thought by us in no other way than as a comprehensible personality after the image of our own personality.

> Our heart's ardent desire to grasp the highest that it may divine can be satisfied by no other form of existence than that of the personality, no other form can be seriously considered. This aspiration of our heart is so much guided by the conviction that the living, self-possessed and self-enjoying form of the ego is the undeniable prerequisite and the only home of all good and all values. It is so much filled with a silent disdain of all existence that appears lifeless, that we always find the early phases of religion, when it is given to myth making, occupied with the attempt to transfigure the natural reality into a spiritual one. It has, however, never felt a need to reduce something that is spiritually alive to a blind reality as its firmer ground.

Lotze expresses his own feeling with regard to the things of nature as follows:

> I do not know them, these dead masses of which you speak; for me everything is life and inner alertness; rest and death are nothing but a dull transitory appearance of an ever active inner weaving.

If natural processes, as they appear in the observation, are only such dull transitory shadows, then one cannot expect to find their deepest essence in the regularity that presents itself to the observation, but in the "ever active weaving" of all inspiring, all comprehensive personality, its aims and purposes. Lotze, therefore, imagines that in all natural activity a personality's moral purpose is manifested toward which the world is striving. The laws of nature are the external manifestation of an all pervading ethical order of the world. This ethical interpretation of the world is in perfect harmony with what Lotze says concerning the continuous life of the soul after death:

> We have no other thought at our disposal than the general idealistic conviction that every created thing or being will remain in existence whose continuation is essential for the meaning of the world. Everything that serves only in a transitory phase of the course of the world will at some time cease to exist. That this principle does not justify certain rash applications need scarcely be mentioned. We certainly do not know the merits that would be adequate to earn the claim for eternal existence for one being, nor the defects that would deny it to others. (*Three Books of Metaphysics*)

At the point where Lotze's reflections touch the realm of the great enigmatic problems of philosophy, his thoughts show an uncertain and wavering character. One can notice that he does not succeed in securing from his two sources of knowledge, natural science and psychological self-observation, a reliable conception concerning man's relation to the course of the world. The inner force of self-observation does not penetrate to a thinking that could justify the ego feeling itself as a definite entity within the totality of the world. In his lectures, *Philosophy of Religion*, we read:

> The *belief in immortality* has no other sure foundation than the need for religion. For this reason it it also impossible to state anything beyond a simple metaphysical statement concerning the nature of continued existence. Such a statement would be: As we regard every entity to be merely a *creature of God*, there is no fundamentally valid *right* that the individual soul could claim, for instance, as a *substance,* to demand eternal individual existence. We can merely maintain that every entity is preserved by God only as long as its existence has a valuable significance for the totality of His world plan . . .

The indefinite character of such principles expresses the extent to which Lotze's ideas can penetrate into the realm of the great philosophical problems.

* * *

In his little book, *Life after Death*, Fechner says of the relation of man to the world:

> What does the anatomist see when he looks into man's brain? A tangle of white fibres, the meaning of which he cannot fathom. What does he see in himself? A world of lights, sounds, thoughts, reminiscences, fantasies, sentiments of love and hatred. In this way you must imagine the relationship of the side of the world that you see as you are externally confronted with it, to what this world sees in itself, and you must not demand that the inside and the outside of the world should show a greater similarity than in yourself, who is only a part of it. It is only the fact that you are a part of this world that allows you to see within yourself a part of what the world experiences inwardly.

Fechner imagines that the world spirit stands in the same relation to the world of matter as the human spirit does to the human body. He then argues: Man speaks of himself when he speaks of his body, but he also speaks of himself when he deals with his spirit. The anatomist who investigates the tangle of dead brain fibres is confronted with the organ that once was the source of thoughts and imaginations. When the man, whose brain the anatomist observes, was still alive, he did not have before him in his mind the fibres of his brain and their physical function, but a world of mental contents. What has changed then when, instead of a man who experiences his inner soul content, the anatomist looks at the brain, the physical organ of that soul? Is it not in both cases the same being, the same man that is inspected? Fechner is of the opinion that the object is the same, merely the point of view of the observer has changed. The anatomist observes from outside what was previously viewed by man from inside. It is as if one looks at a circle first from without and then from within. In the first case, it appears convex, in the second, concave. In both cases, it is the same circle. So it is also with man. If he looks at himself from within, he is spirit; if the natural scientist looks at him from without, he is body, matter.

According to Fechner's mode of conception, it is of no use to ponder on how body and spirit effect each other, for they are not two entities at all; they are both one and the same thing. They appear to us only as different when we observe them from different viewpoints. Fechner considers man to be a body that is spirit at the same time. From this point of view it becomes possible for Fechner to imagine all nature as spiritual, as animated. With regard to his own being, man is in the position to inspect the physical from within and thus to recognize the inside directly as spiritual. Does not the thought then suggest itself that everything physical, if it could be inspected from within, would appear as spiritual? We can see the plant only from without, but is it not possible that it, too, if seen from within, would prove to be a soul? This notion grew in Fechner's imagination into the conviction that everything physical is spiritual at the same time. The smallest material particle is animated, and the combination of particles to form more perfect material bodies is merely a process viewed from the outside. There is a corresponding inner process that would, if one could observe it, present itself as the combination of individual souls into more comprehensive souls. If somebody had the ability to observe from within the physical processes of our earth with the plants, animals and men living on it, the totality would appear to him as the soul of the earth. So it would also be with the solar system, and even with the whole world. The universe seen from without is the physical cosmos; seen from within, it is the all-embracing spirit, the most perfect personality, God.

A thinker who wants to arrive at a world conception must go beyond the facts that present themselves to him without his own activity. But what is achieved by this going beyond the results of direct observation is a question about which there are the most divergent views. Kirchhoff expressed his view (compare above, page 323) by saying that even through the strictest science one cannot obtain anything but a complete and simple description of the actual events. Fechner proceeds from an opposite viewpoint. It is his opinion that this is "the great art, to draw conclusions from *this world to the next,* not from reasons that we do not know nor from presuppositions that we accept, but from facts with which we are acquainted, to the greater and higher facts of the world beyond, and thereby to fortify and support from below the belief that depends on higher viewpoints and to establish for it a living relationship toward life. (*The Booklet on Life after Death*) According to this opinion, Fechner does not merely look for the connection of the outwardly observed physical phenomena with the inwardly experienced spiritual processes, but he adds to the observed soul phenomena others, the earth spirit, the planetary spirit, the world spirit.

Fechner does not allow his knowledge of natural science, which is based on a firm foundation, to keep him from raising his thoughts from the world of the senses into regions where they envisage world entities and world processes, which, if they exist, must be beyond the reach of sense perception. He feels stimulated to such an elevation through his intimate contemplation of the world of the senses, which reveals to his thinking more than the mere sense perception would be capable of disclosing. This "additional content" he feels inclined to use in imagining extrasensory entities. In *his* way, he strives thus to depict a world into which he promises to introduce thoughts that have come to life. But such a transcendence of sensory limits did not prevent Fechner from proceeding according to the strictest method of natural science, even in the realm that borders that of the soul. It was he who created the scientific methods for this field.

Fechner's *Elements of Psychophysics* (1860) is the fundamental work in this field. The fundamental law on which he based psychophysics states that the increase of sensation caused in man through an increase of external impressions, proceeds proportionately slower than the intensification of the stimulating impressions. The greater the strength of the stimulus at the outset, the less the sensation grows. Proceeding from this thought, it is possible to obtain a measured proportion between the external stimulus (for instance, the strength of physical light) and the sensation (for instance, the intensity of light sensation). The continuation of this method established by Fechner has resulted in the elaboration of the discipline of psychophysics as an entirely new science, concerned with the relation of stimuli toward sensations, that is to say, of the physical to the psychical.

Wilhelm Wundt, who continued to work in Fechner's spirit in this field, characterizes the founder of the science of psychophysics in an excellent description:

> Probably none of his other scientific achievements show in such a splendid way the rare combination of gifts that were at Fechner's disposal as do his psychophysical works. To produce a work like his *Elements of Psychophysics*, it was necessary to be intimately acquainted with the principles of the exact method of mathematical physics and at the same time to possess an inclination to probe the most profound problems of being, a combination that was realized only in him. For this purpose he needed the originality of thinking that enabled him to adapt freely the inherited research methods to fit his own needs, and the courage never to show any hesitation to proceed along new and untrodden paths. The observations of *E. H. Weber*, which were admirable for their ingenious simplicity but limited in their scope, the isolated and often more arbitrary than deliberately devised experimental methods and results of other physiologists—these formed the modest material out of which he built a new science.

Important insights into the inter-relation between body and soul have resulted from the experimental method suggested by Fechner. Wundt characterizes this new science in his *Lectures on the Human and Animal Soul* (1863) as follows:

> I shall show in the following exposition that the experiment is the chief instrument in psychology. It leads us from the facts of consciousness to those processes that prepare the conscious life in the dark background of the soul. Self-observation provides, as does observation in general, merely the composite phenomena. It is only through the experiment that we free the phenomenon of all accidental circumstances to which it is bound in nature. Through the

experiment we produce the phenomenon synthetically out of the conditions we ourselves control. Change these conditions and we thereby also change, in a measurable way, the phenomenon itself. In this way, it is always the experiment that leads us to the laws of nature because only in the experiment can we observe simultaneously the causes and the results.

It is doubtless only in a borderline territory of the field of psychology that the experiment is really fruitful, that is, in the territory where the conscious processes lead to the backgrounds of the soul life where they are no longer conscious but material processes. The psychical phenomena in the proper sense of the word can, after all, only be obtained by a purely spiritual observation. Nevertheless, E. Kräpelin, a psychophysicist, is fully justified when he says "that the young science will always be capable of maintaining its independent position side by side with the other branches of the natural sciences and particularly the science of physiology" (*Psychological Works*, published by E. Kräpelin, Vol. I, part 1, page 4).

* * *

When *Eduard von Hartmann* published his *Philosophy of the Unconscious* in 1869 he did not so much have in mind a world conception based on the results of modern natural science but rather one that would raise to a higher level the ideas of the idealistic systems of the first half of the nineteenth century, since these appeared to him insufficient in many points. It was his intention to free these ideas of their contradictions and to develop them completely. It seemed to him that Hegel's, Schelling's and Schopenhauer's thoughts contained potential truths that would only have to be fully developed. Man cannot be satisfied by merely observing facts if he intends to know things and processes of the world. He must proceed from facts to ideas. These ideas cannot be considered to be an element that our thinking arbitrarily adds to the facts. There must be something in them that corresponds to the things and events. This corresponding element cannot be the element of conscious ideas, for these are brought about only through the material processes of the human brain. Without a brain there is no consciousness. We must, therefore, assume that an unconscious ideal element in reality corresponds to the conscious ideas of the human mind.

Hartmann, like Hegel, considers the idea as the real element in things that is contained in them beyond the perceptible, that is to say, beyond the accessible to sense observation. But the mere content of the ideas would never be capable of producing a real process within them. The idea of a ball cannot collide with the idea of another ball. The idea of a table cannot produce an impression on the human eye. A real process requires a real force. In order to gain a conception of such a force, Hartmann borrows from Schopenhauer. Man finds in his soul a force through which he imparts reality to his thought and to his decisions. This force is the will. In the form in which it is manifest in the human soul the will presupposes the existence of the human organism. Through the organism it is a conscious will. If we want to think of a force as existing in things, we can conceive of it only as similar to the will, the only energy with which we are immediately acquainted. We must, however, think of this will as something without consciousness. Thus, outside man an unconscious will rules in things that endows them with the possibility of becoming real. The world's content of idea and will in their combination constitutes its unconscious basis.

Although the world, without doubt, presents a logical structure because of its content of ideas, it nevertheless owes its real existence to a will that is entirely without logic and reason. Its content is endowed with reason; that this content is a *reality* is caused by unreason. The rule of unreason is manifested in the existence of the pain by which all beings are tortured. Pain out-balances pleasure in the world. This fact, which is to be philosophically explained from the non-logical will element, Eduard von Hartmann tries to establish by careful investigations of the relation of pleasure and displeasure in the world. Whoever does not indulge in illusions but observes the evils of the world objectively cannot arrive at any other result than that there is much more displeasure in the world than pleasure. From this, we must conclude that non-being is preferable to being. Non-being, however, can be attained only when the logical-reasonable idea annihilates being. Hartmann, therefore, regards the world process as a gradual destruction of the unreasonable will by the reasonable world of ideas. It must be the highest moral task of man to contribute to this conquest of the will. All cultural progress must aim at this final conquest. Man is morally good if he participates in the progress of culture, if he demands nothing for himself but selflessly devotes himself to the great work of liberation from existence. He will without doubt do that if he gains the insight that pain must always be greater than pleasure and that happiness is for this reason impossible. Only he who believes happiness to be possible can maintain an egotistic desire for it. The pessimistic view of the preponderance of pain over pleasure is the best remedy against egotism. Only in surrendering to the world process can the individual find his salvation. The true pessimist is led to act unegotistically.

What man does consciously, however, is merely the unconscious, raised into consciousness. To the *conscious* contribution of human work to the cultural progress, there corresponds an *unconscious* general process consisting of a progressive emancipation of the primordial substance of the world from will. The beginning of the world must already have served this aim. The primordial substance had to create the world in order to free itself gradually with the aid of the idea from the power of the will.

> Real existence is the incarnation of the godhead. The world process is the history of the passion of the incarnate God and at the same time the path for the redemption of the God crucified in the flesh. Morality is the co-operating work for the shortening of this path of passion and redemption. (Hartmann, *Phenomenology of the Moral Consciousness*, 1879, Page 871.)

Hartmann elaborated his world conception in a series of comprehensive works and in a great number of monographs and articles. These writings contain intellectual treasures of extraordinary significance. This is especially the case because Hartmann knew how to avoid being tyrannized by his basic thoughts in the treatment of special problems of science and life, and to maintain an unbiased attitude in the contemplation of things. This is true to a particularly high degree in his *Phenomenology of the Moral Consciousness* in which he presents the different kinds of human doctrines of morality in logical order. He gives in it a kind of "natural history" of the various moral viewpoints, from the egotistical hunt for happiness through many intermediate stages to the selfless surrender to the general world process through which the divine primordial substance frees itself from the bondage of existence.

Since Hartmann accepts the idea of purpose for his world conception, it is understandable that the mode of thinking of natural science that rests on Darwinism appears to him as a one-sided current of ideas. To Hartmann the idea tends in the whole of the world process toward the aim of non-being, and the ideal content is for him purposeful also in every specific phase. In the evolution of the organism Hartmann sees a purpose in self-realization. The struggle for existence with its process of natural selection is for him merely auxiliary functions of the purposeful rule of ideas (*Philosophy of the Unconscious*, 10. Ed., Vol. III, Page 403).

* * *

The thought life of the nineteenth century leads, from various sides, to a world conception that is characterized by an uncertainty of thought and by an inner hopelessness. Richard Wahle declares definitely that thinking is incapable of contributing anything to the solution of "transcendent" questions, or of the highest problems, and Eduard von Hartmann sees in all cultural work nothing but a detour toward the final attainment of the ultimate purpose—complete deliverance from existence. Against the currents of such ideas, a beautiful statement was written in 1843 by the German linguist, Wilhelm Wackernagel in his book, *On the Instruction in the Mother Tongue*. Wackernagel says that doubt cannot supply the basis for a world conception; he considers it rather as an "injury" that offends not only the person who wants to know something, but also the things that are to be known. "Knowledge," he says, "begins with confidence."

Such confidence for the ideas that depend on the research methods of natural science has been produced in modern times, but not for a knowledge that derives its power of truth from the self-conscious ego. The impulses that lie in the depths of the development of the spiritual life require such a powerful will for the truth. Man's searching soul feels instinctively that it can find satisfaction only through such a power. The philosophical endeavor strives for such a force, but it cannot find it in the thoughts that it is capable of developing for a world conception. The achievements of the thought life fail to satisfy the demands of the soul. The conceptions of natural science derive their certainty from the observation of the external world. Within one's soul one does not find the strength that would guarantee the same certainty. One would like to have truths concerning the spiritual world concerning the destiny of the soul and its connection with the world that are gained in the same way as the conceptions of natural science.

A thinker who derived his thoughts as much from the philosophical thinking of the past as from his penetration of the mode of thinking of natural science was *Franz Brentano* (1828–1912). He demanded of philosophy that it should arrive at its results in the same manner as natural science. Because of this imitation of the methods of natural science, he hoped that psychology, for instance, would not have to renounce its attempts to gain an insight into the most important problem of soul life.

> But for the hopes of a Plato and Aristotle to attain sure knowledge concerning the continued life of our better part after the dissolution of our body, the laws of the association of ideas, the development of convictions and opinions and of the origin and development of pleasure and love would be anything but a true compensation. If this

new natural scientific method of thinking would really bring about the elimination of the problem of immortality, this would have to be considered as significant for psychology.

This is Brentano's statement in his *Psychology from the Empirical Standpoint*, (1870, page 20).

Symptomatic of the weakness of a psychology that intends to follow the method of natural science entirely is the fact that such a serious seeker after truth as Franz Brentano did not write a second volume of his psychology that would really have taken up the highest problems after the first volume that dealt only with questions that had to be considered as "anything but a compensation for these highest questions of the soul life." The thinkers of that time lacked the inner strength and elasticity of mind that could do real justice to the demand of modern times. Greek thought mastered the conception of nature and the conception of the soul life in a way that allowed both to be combined into one total picture. Subsequently, human thought life developed independently of and separated from nature, within the depths of the soul life, and modern natural science supplied a picture of nature. From this fact the necessity arose to find a conception of the soul life within the self-conscious ego that would prove strong enough to hold its own in conjunction with the image of nature in a general world picture. For this purpose, it is necessary to find a point of support within the soul itself that carried as surely as the results of natural scientific research. Spinoza believed he had found it by modelling his world conception after the mathematical method; Kant relinquished the knowledge of the world of things in themselves and attempted to gain ideas that were to supply, through their moral weight, to be sure, not knowledge, but a certain belief.

Thus we observe in these searching philosophers a striving to anchor the soul life in a total structure of the world. But what is still lacking is the strength and elasticity of thought that would form the conceptions concerning the soul life in a way to promise a solution for the problems of the soul. Uncertainty concerning the true significance of man's soul experiences arises everywhere. Natural science in Haeckel's sense follows the natural processes that are perceptible to the senses and it sees the life of the soul only as a higher stage of such natural processes. Other thinkers find that we have in everything the soul perceives only the effects of extra-human processes that are both unknown and unknowable. For these thinkers, the world becomes an "illusion," although an illusion that is caused by natural necessity through the human organization.

> As long as the art of looking around corners has not been invented, that is, to conceive without conceptions, the proud self-restrictions of Kant, that we can know of reality only *that* it is, not *what* it is, will have to be acknowledged as the final decision.

This is the judgment of Robert Zimmermann, a philosopher of the second half of the nineteenth century. For such a world conception the human soul, which cannot have any knowledge of its own nature of *"what* it is," sails into an ocean of conceptions without becoming aware of its ability to find something in this vast ocean that could open vistas into the nature of existence. Hegel had been of the opinion that he perceived in thinking itself the inner force of life that leads man's ego to reality. For the time that followed, "mere thinking" became a lightly woven texture of imaginations containing nothing of the nature of true being. When, in the search for truth, an opinion ventures to put the emphasis on thinking, the suggested thoughts have a ring of inner uncertainty, as can be seen in this statement of Gideon Spicker: "That thinking in itself is correct, we can never know for sure, neither empirically nor logically . . ." (Lessing's *Weltanschauung*, 1883, page 5).

In a most persuasive form, Philipp Mainländer (1841–1876) gave expression to this lack of confidence in existence in his *Philosophy of Redemption.* Mainländer sees himself confronted by the world picture toward which modern natural science tends so strongly. But it is in vain that he seeks for a possibility to anchor the self-conscious ego in a spiritual world. He cannot achieve through this self-conscious ego what had first been realized by Goethe, namely, to feel in the soul the resurrection of an inner living reality that experiences itself as spiritually alive in a living spiritual element behind a mere external nature. It is for this reason that the world appears to Mainländer without spirit. Since he can think of the world only as having originated from the spirit, he must consider it as a remainder of a past spiritual life. Statements like the following are striking:

> Now we have the right to give to this being the well-known name that always designates what no power of imagination, no flight of the boldest fantasy, no abstract thinking however profound, no intently devout heart, no enraptured and transported spirit ever attained: *God.* But this simple oneness *is of the past;* it is no longer. In a transformation of its nature, it has dispersed itself into a world of diversity. (Compare Max Seiling's essay, *Mainländer.*)

If, in the existing world, we find only reality without value or merely the ruins of value, then the aim of the world can only be its destruction. Man can see his task only in a contribution to this annihilation. (Mainländer ended his life by suicide.) According to Mainländer, God created the world only in order to free himself from the torture of his own existence. "The world is the means for the purpose of non-being, and it is the only possible means for this purpose. God knew that he could change from a state of super-reality into non-being only through the development of a real world of multiformity. *(Philosophie der Erlösung)*

This view, which springs from mistrust in the world, was vigorously opposed by the poet, Robert Hamerling (1830–89) in his posthumously published philosophical work, *Atomism of Will.* He rejects logical inquiries concerning the value or worthlessness of the world and starts from an original inner experience:

> Almost all men with very few exceptions want to live at any price, no matter whether they are happy or unhappy. The main thing is not whether they are *right* in wanting this, but *that* they want this; this is simply undeniable. Yet the doctrinarian pessimists do not consider

this decisive fact. They only balance, in learned reflections, pleasure and pain as life brings them in its particular instances. Since pleasure and pain are matters of feeling, it is feeling and not intellect that is decisive in striking the balance of pleasure and pain. This balance is actually to be found in all humanity, one can even say in everything that has life, and is in favor of the pleasure of existence. That everything alive wants to live and wants this under all circumstances, wants to live at any price, is the great fact against which all doctrinarian talk is powerless.

Hamerling then contemplates the thought: There is something in the depth of the soul that clings to existence, expressing the nature of the soul with more truth than the judgments that are encumbered by the mode of conception of modern natural science as they speak of the value of life. One could say that Hamerling feels a spiritual point of gravity in the depth of the soul that anchors the self-conscious ego in the living and moving world. He is, therefore, inclined to see in this ego something that guarantees its existence more than the thought structures of the philosophers. He finds a main defect in modern world conception in the opinion "that there is too much sophistry in the most recent philosophy directed against the ego," and he would like to explain this "from the *fear* of the soul, of a special soul-entity or even a thing-like conception of a soul." Hamerling points significantly to the really important question, "The ideas of the ego are interwoven with the elements of feeling. . . . What the spirit has not experienced, it is also incapable of thinking. . . ." For Hamerling, all higher world conception hinges on the necessity of feeling the act of thinking itself, of experiencing it inwardly. The possibility of penetrating into those soul-depths in which the living conceptions can be attained that lead to a knowledge of the soul entity through the inner strength of the self-conscious ego is, according to Hamerling, barred by a layer of concepts that originated in the course of the development of modern world conception, and change the world picture into a mere ocean of ideas. He introduces his philosophy, therefore, with the following words:

> Certain stimuli produce odors within our organ of smell. Thus, the rose has no fragrance if nobody smells it. Certain air vibrations produce sounds in the ear. Sound then does not exist without an ear. A gunshot would not ring out if nobody heard it.

Such conceptions have in the course of modern thought development become so definite a part of thinking that Hamerling added to the quoted exposition the words:

> If this, dear reader, does not seem plausible to you, if your mind stirs like a shy horse when it is confronted with this fact, do not bother to read another line; leave this book and all others that deal with philosophical things unread, for you lack the ability that is necessary for this purpose, that is, to apprehend a fact without bias and to adhere to it in your thoughts. *(Atomism of Will)*

Hamerling's last poetic effort was his *Homunculus*. In this work he intended to present a criticism of modern civilization. He portrayed in a radical way in a series of pictures what a humanity is drifting to that has become soul-less and believes only in the power of external natural laws. As the poet of *Homunculus*, he knows no limit to his criticism of everything in this civilization that is caused by this false belief. As a thinker, however, Hamerling nevertheless capitulates in the full sense of the word to the mode of conception described in this book in the chapter, "The World as Illusion." He does not hesitate to use words like the following.

> The extended spatial corporeal world as such exists only insofar as we perceive it. Anyone who adheres to this principle will understand what a naive error it is to believe that there is, in addition to the impression *(Vorstellung)* that we call *"horse"* still another horse, which is actually the real horse and of which our inner impression is only a kind of copy. Outside of myself, let it be said again, there is only the sum total of those conditions that produce within my senses an idea *(Anschauung)* that I call horse.

With respect to the soul life, Hamerling feels as if nothing of the world's own nature could ever penetrate into the ocean of its thought pictures. But he has a feeling for the process that goes on in the depths of modern soul development. He feels that the knowledge of modern man must vigorously light up with its own power of truth within the self-conscious ego, as it had manifested itself in the perceived thought of the Greeks. Again and again he probes his way toward the point where the self-conscious ego feels itself endowed with the strength of its true being that is at the same time aware of standing within the spiritual life of the world. But he only senses this and thus fails to arrive at any further revelation. So he clings to the feeling of existence that pulsates within his soul and that seems to him more substantial, more saturated with reality than the mere conceptions of the ego, the mere thought of the ego. "From the awareness or feeling of *our own being* we gain a concept of being that goes far beyond the status of being merely an object of thought. We gain the concept of a being that not merely *is* thought, but *thinks*."

Starting from this ego that apprehends itself in its feeling of existence, Hamerling attempts to gain a world picture. What the ego experiences in its feeling of existence is, according to him, "the atom-feeling within us" *(Atomgefühl)*. The ego knows of itself, and it knows itself as an "atom" in comparison with the world. It must imagine other beings as it finds itself in itself: as atoms that experience and feel themselves. For Hamerling, this seems to be synonymous with atoms of will, with will-endowed *monads*. For Hamerling's *Atomism of Will*, the world becomes a multitude of will-endowed monads, and the human soul is one of the will-monads. The thinker of such a world picture looks around himself and sees the world as spiritual, to be sure, but all he can discover of the spirit is a manifestation of the will. He can say nothing more about it. This world picture reveals nothing that would answer the questions concerning the human soul's position in the evolutionary process of the world, for whether one considers the soul as what it appears before all philosophical thinking, or whether one characterizes it according to this thinking as a monad of will, it is necessary to raise the same enigmatic questions with regard to both soul-conceptions. If one thought like *Brentano,* one could say, "For the hopes of a Plato and Aristotle to attain sure knowledge concerning the continued life of our better part after the dissolution of our body, the knowledge that the soul is a monad of will among other monads of will is anything but a true compensation."

In many currents of modern philosophical life one notices the instinctive tendency (living in the subconsciousness of the thinkers) to find in the self-conscious ego a force that is unlike that of *Spinoza, Kant, Leibniz* and others. One seeks a force through which this ego, the core of the human soul can be so conceived that man's position in the course and the evolution of the world can become revealed. At the same time, these philosophical currents show that the means used in order to find such a force have not enough intensity in order to fulfill "the hopes of a Plato and Aristotle" (in Brentano's sense) to do justice to the modern demands of the soul. One succeeds in developing opinions, for instance, concerning the possible relation of our perceptions to the things outside, or concerning the development and association of ideas, of the genesis of memory, and of the relation of feeling and will to imagination and perception. But through one's own mode of conception one locks the doors to questions that are concerned with the "hopes of Plato and Aristotle." It is believed that through everything that could be thought with regard to these "hopes," the demands of a strictly scientific procedure would be offended that have been set as standards by the mode of thinking of natural science.

The ideas of the philosophical thought picture of Wilhelm Wundt (1832–1920) aim no higher than their natural scientific basis permits. For Wundt, philosophy is "the general knowledge that has been produced by the special sciences" (Wundt, *System of Philosophy*). By the methods of such a philosophy it is only possible to continue the lines of thought created by the special sciences, to combine them, and to put them into a clearly arranged order. This Wundt does, and thus he allows the general form of his ideas to become entirely dependent on the habits of conception that develop in a thinker who, like Wundt, is acquainted with the special sciences, that is, a person who has been active in some particular field of knowledge such as the psychophysical aspect of psychology. Wundt looks at the world picture that the human soul produces through sense experience and at the conceptions that are experienced in the soul under the influence of this world picture. The scientific method considers sense perceptions as effects of processes outside man. For Wundt, this mode of conception is, in a certain sense, an unquestioned matter of course. He considers as external reality, therefore, what is inferred conceptually on the basis of sense perceptions. This external reality as such is not inwardly experienced; it is assumed by the soul in the same way that a process is assumed to exist outside man that effects the eye, causing, through its activity, the sensation of light. Contrary to this process, the processes in the soul are *immediately* experienced. Here our knowledge is in no need of conclusions but needs only *observations* concerning the formation and connection of our ideas and their relation to our feelings and will impulses. In these observations we deal only with soul activities that are apparent in the stream of consciousness, and we have no right to speak of a special soul that is manifested in this stream of consciousness. To assume matter to be the basis of the natural phenomena is justifiable for, from sense perceptions, one must conclude, by means of concepts, that there are material processes. It is not possible in the same sense to infer a soul from the psychic processes.

> The auxiliary concept of matter is . . . bound to the indirect or conceptual nature of all natural science. It is impossible to conceive how the direct and intuitive inner experience should demand such an auxiliary concept as well. . . . (Wundt, *System of Philosophy*).

In this way, the question of the nature of the soul is, for Wundt, a problem to which in the last analysis neither the observation of the inner experience nor any conclusions from these experiences can lead. Wundt does not observe a soul; he perceives only psychical activity. This psychical activity is so manifested that whenever it appears, a parallel physical process takes place at the same time. Both phenomena, the psychical activity and the physical process, are parts of one reality: they are in the last analysis the same thing; only man separates them in his observation. Wundt is of the opinion that a scientific experience can recognize only such spiritual processes as are bound to physical processes. For him, the self-conscious ego dissolves into the psychical organism of the spiritual processes that are to him identical with the physical processes, except that these appear as spiritual-psychical when they are seen from within.

But if the ego tries to find what it can consider as characteristic for its own nature, it discovers its will-activity. Only by its *will* does it distinguish itself as a self-dependent entity from the rest of the world. The ego thus sees itself induced to acknowledge in *will* the fundamental character of being. Considering its own nature, the ego admits that it may assume will-activity as the source of the world. The *inner nature* of the things that man observes in the external world remains concealed behind the observation. In his own being he recognizes the will as the essence and may conclude that what meets his will from the external world is of a nature homogeneous with his will. As the will activities of the world meet and affect one another, they produce in one another the ideas, the inner life of the units of will. This all goes to show how Wundt is driven by the fundamental impulse of the self-conscious ego. He goes down into man's own entity until he meets the ego that manifests itself as will and, taking his stand within the will-entity of the ego, he feels justified to attribute to the entire world the same entity that the soul experiences within itself. In this world of will, also, nothing answers the "hopes of Plato and Aristotle."

Hamerling approaches the riddles of the world and of the soul as a man of the nineteenth century whose disposition of mind is enlivened by the spiritual impulses that are at work in his time. He feels these spiritual impulses in his free and deeply human being to which it is only natural to ask questions concerning the riddle of human existence, just as it is natural for ordinary man to feel hunger and thirst. Concerning his relation to philosophy, he says:

> I felt myself above all as a human being, as a whole and full human being, and it was thus that the great problems of existence and life were my most intimate spiritual interest. I did not turn suddenly toward philosophy. It was not that I accidentally developed an inclination in that direction, nor because I wanted to try myself out in a new field. I have been occupied with the great problems of human knowledge from my early youth through the natural and irresistible bent that drives man in general to the inquiry of the truth and to the solution of the riddles of existence. Nor could I ever regard philosophy as a special science, which one could take up or neglect as one would statistics or forestry. But I always considered it to be the investigation of questions of the most intimate, the most important and the most interesting human concern. (*Atomism of Will*)

In the course that his philosophical investigations take, Hamerling becomes affected by forces of thought that had, in Kant, deprived knowledge of the power to penetrate to the root of existence and that led during the nineteenth century to the opinion that the world was an illusion of our mind. Hamerling did not surrender unconditionally to this influence but it does encumber his view. He searched within the self-conscious ego for a point of gravity in which reality was to be experienced and he believed he had found this point in the will. Thinking was not felt by Hamerling as it had been experienced in Hegel. Hamerling saw it only as "mere thinking" that is powerless to seize upon reality. In this way, Hamerling appraised the will in which he believed he experienced the force of being. Strengthened by the will apprehended in the ego as a real force, he meant to plunge into a world of will-monads.

Hamerling starts from an experience of the world riddles, which he feels as *vividly and as directly* as a hunger of the soul. Wundt is driven to these questions by the results to be found in the broad field of the special sciences of modern times. In the manner in which he raises his questions on the basis of these sciences, we feel the specific power and the intellectual disposition of these sciences. His answers to these problems are, as in Hamerling, much influenced by the directing forces of modern thought that deprive this form of thinking of the possibility to feel itself within the well-spring of reality. It is for this reason that Wundt's world picture becomes a "mere ideal survey" of the nature picture of the modern mode of conception. For Wundt also, it is only the *will* in the human soul that proves to be the element that cannot be entirely deprived of all being through the impotence of thinking. The will so obtrudes itself into the world conception that it seems to reveal its omnipotence in the whole circumference of existence.

In Hamerling and Wundt two personalities emerge in the course of the development of philosophy who are motivated by forces that attempt to master by thought the world riddles with which the human soul finds itself confronted through its own experience as well as through the results of science. But in both personalities these forces have the effect of finding within themselves nothing that would allow the self-conscious ego to feel itself within the source of reality. These forces rather reach a point where they can no longer uphold the contact with the great riddles of the universe. What they cling to is the will, but from this world of will nothing can be learned that would assure us of the "continued life of our better part after the dissolution of the body," or that would even touch on the riddles of the soul and the world. Such world conceptions originate from the natural irrepressible bent "that drives man in general to the investigation of the truth and to the solution of the riddles of existence." Since they use the means that, according to the opinion of certain temporary tendencies, appear as the only justifiable ones, they arrive at a mode of conception that contains no elements of experience to bring about the solution.

It is apparent that man sees himself at a given time confronted with the problems of the world in a definite form; he feels instinctively what he has to do. It is his responsibility to find the means for the answer. In using these means he may not be equal to the challenge presenting itself from the depths of the spiritual evolution. Philosophies that work under such conditions represent a *struggle* for an aim of which they are not quite consciously aware. The aim of the evolution of the modern world conception is to experience something within the self-conscious ego that gives being and reality to the ideas of the world picture. The characterized philosophical trends prove powerless to attain such life and such reality. Thought no longer gives to the ego or the self-conscious soul, the inner support that insures existence. This ego has moved too far away from the ground of nature to believe in such a guarantee as was once possible in ancient Greece. It has not as yet brought to life within itself what this ground of nature once supplied without demanding a spontaneous creativity of the soul.

Chapter VII

*Modern Man
and His World Conception*

The Austrian thinker, Bartholomaeus Carneri (1871–1909) attempted to open wide perspectives of world conception and ethics on the ground of Darwinism. Eleven years after the appearance of Darwin's *Origin of Species,* he published his work, *Morality and Darwinism* (1871), in which he used the new world of ideas as the basis of an ethical world conception in a comprehensive way. (Compare his books, *Foundation of Ethics,* 1881, *Man as His Own Purpose,* 1878, and *Modern Man, Essays on Life Conduct,* 1891.) Carneri tries to find in the picture of nature the elements through which self-conscious ego is conceivable within this picture. He would like to think this world picture so wide and so comprehensive as to contain the human soul within its scope. He aims at the reunion of the ego with the mother ground of nature, from which it has become separated. He represents in his world conception the opposite tendency to the philosophy for which the world becomes an illusion of the imagination and which, for that reason, renounces all connection with the reality of the world so far as knowledge is concerned.

Carneri rejects all moral philosophy that intends to proclaim for man other moral commandments than those that result from his own nature. We must remember that man is not to be understood as a special being beside all other things of nature but that he is a being that has gradually developed from lower entities according to purely natural laws. Carneri is convinced that all life is like a chemical process. "The digestion in man is such a process as well as the nutrition of the plant." At the same time, he emphasizes that the chemical process must be raised to a higher form of evolution if it is to become plant or animal.

> Life is a chemical process of a special kind; it is the individualized chemical process, for the chemical process can reach a point where it can maintain itself without certain conditions . . . that it formerly needed.

It is apparent that Carneri observes that lower processes are transformed into higher ones, that matter takes on higher forms of existence through the perfection of its functions.

> As matter, we conceive the substance insofar as the properties that result from its divisibility and its motion effect our senses physically, that is to say, as mass. If this division or differentiation goes so far as to produce phenomena that are no longer sensually perceptible but only perceptible to our thinking, we say the effect of the substance is spiritual.

Also, morality does not exist as a special form of reality; it is a process of nature on a higher level. Therefore, the question cannot be raised: What is man to do to comply with some special moral commandment that is valid for him? We can only ask: What appears as morality when the lower processes develop into the higher spiritual ones?

> While moral philosophy proclaims certain moral laws and commands that they are to be kept so that man may be what he ought to be, our ethics develops man as he is. It wants to do no more than to show him what he may at some time become. While the former moralizing philosophy knows of duties to be enforced by punishments, our ethics uphold an ideal from which any compulsion would

merely distract because it can be approached only on the path of knowledge and of freedom.

As the chemical process individualizes itself into a living being on a higher level, so on a still higher level life is transformed into self-consciousness. The entity that has become self-conscious no longer merely looks out into nature; it looks back into itself.

> The awakened self-consciousness constituted, if conceived dualistically, a break with nature, and man felt himself separated from nature. This breach existed only for him, but for him it was complete. It had not developed as suddenly as it is taught in Genesis, just as the days of creation must not be taken literally as days. But with the completion of self-consciousness, the breach was a fact and with the feeling of boundless lonesomeness that overcame man in this state, his ethical development began.

Up to a certain point nature leads life. At this point, self-consciousness arises, man comes into existence. "His further development is his own work and what keeps him on the course of progress is the power and the gradual clarification of his wishes." Nature takes care of all other beings, but it endows man with desires and expects him to take care of their fulfillment. Man has within himself the impulse to arrange his existence in agreement with his wishes. This impulse is his desire for happiness:

> This impulse is unknown to the animal. It knows only the instinct for self-preservation; to develop that instinct into the desire for happiness, the human self-consciousness is necessary as a fundamental condition.

The striving for happiness is the basis of all action:

> The martyr who sacrifices his life, be it for his scientific conviction or for his belief in God, aims for nothing but his happiness. He finds it in the first case in his loyalty of conviction, and in the second case he expects it in a better world. To everyone happiness is the last aim and no matter how different the picture may be that the individual

has of this happiness, it is to every sentient living being the beginning and the end of all his thinking and feeling.

As nature gives man only the need for happiness, this image of happiness must have its origin within man himself. Man creates for himself the pictures of his happiness. They spring from his ethical fantasy. Carneri finds in this fantasy the new concept that prescribes the ideals of our action to our thinking. The "good" is, for Carneri, "identical with progressive evolution, and since evolution is pleasure . . . happiness not merely constituted the aim but also the moving element that drives toward that aim."

Carneri attempted to find the way that leads from the natural order to the sources of morality. He believed he had found the ideal power that propels the ethical world order as spontaneously from one moral event to the next as the material forces on the physical level develop formation after formation and fact after fact.

Carneri's mode of conception is entirely in agreement with the idea of evolution that does not permit the notion that a later phase of development is already preformed in an earlier one, but considers it as a really new formation. The chemical process does not contain implicitly animal life, and happiness develops as an entirely new element on the ground of the animal's instinct for self-preservation. The difficulty that lies in this thought caused a penetrating thinker, W. H. Rolph, to develop the line of reasoning that he set down in his book, *Biological Problems, an Attempt at the Development of a Rational Ethics* (1884). Rolph asks himself, "What is the reason that a form of life does not remain at a given stage but develops progressively and becomes more perfect?" This problem presents no difficulty for a thinker who maintains that the later form is already implicitly contained in the earlier one. For him, it is quite clear that what is at first implicit will become explicit at a certain time. But Rolph was not willing to accept this answer. On the other hand, however, he was also not satisfied with the "struggle for existence" as a solution of the problem. If a living being fights only for the satisfaction of its necessary needs, it will, to be sure, over-power its weaker competitors, but it will itself remain what it is. If one does not want to attribute a mysterious, mystical tendency toward perfection to this being, one must seek the cause of this perfection in external, natural circumstances. Rolph tries to give an explanation by stating that, whenever possible, every being satisfies its needs to a greater extent than is necessary.

> Only by introducing the idea of insatiability does the Darwinian principle of perfection in the struggle for life become acceptable, for it is only thus that we have an explanation for the fact that the creature acquires, whenever it can do so, more than it needs for maintaining its status quo, and that it grows excessively whenever the occasion is given for it. (*Biological Problems*)

What takes place in this realm of living beings is, in Rolph's opinion, not a struggle for acquisition of the necessary means of life but a "struggle for *surplus* acquisition." "While the Darwinist knows of no life struggle as long as the existence of the creature is not threatened, I consider this struggle as ever present. It is simply primarily a struggle for life, a struggle for the increase of life, not a struggle for existence." Rolph draws from these natural scientific presuppositions the conclusions for his ethics:

> Expansion of life, not its mere preservation, struggle for advantage, not for existence, is the rallying cry. The mere acquisition of life's necessities and sustenance is not sufficient; what must also be gained is comfort, if not wealth, power and influence. The search and striving for continuous improvement of the condition of life is the characteristic impulse of animal and man. (*Biological Problems*)

Rolph's thoughts stimulated *Friedrich Nietzsche* (1844–1900) to produce his own ideas of evolution after having gone through other phases of his soul life. At the beginning of his career as an author, the idea of evolution and natural science in general had been far from his thoughts. He was at first deeply impressed by the philosophy of Arthur Schopenhauer, and from him he adopted the conception of pain as lying at the bottom of all existence. Unlike Schopenhauer and Eduard von Hartmann, Nietzsche did not seek the redemption from this pain in the fulfillment of moral tasks. It was his belief rather that the transformation of life into a work of art that leads beyond the pain of existence. Thus, the Greeks created a world of beauty and appearance in order to make this painful existence bearable. In Richard Wagner's musical drama he believed he found a world in which beauty lifts man beyond pain. It was in a certain sense a world of illusion that was quite consciously sought by Nietzsche in order to overcome the misery of the world. He was of the opinion that, at the root of the oldest Greek culture, there had been the will of man to forget the real world through a state of intoxication.

> Singing and dancing man manifests himself as a member of a higher community. He has forgotten to walk and to speak and, in his dance, he is about to fly up into the air. (*The Birth of Tragedy*, 1872)

With these words Nietzsche describes and explains the cult of the ancient worshippers of Dionysos, in which he saw the root of all art. Nietzsche maintained of Socrates that he had over-powered this Dionysian impulse by placing reason as judge over them. The statement, "Virtue is teachable," meant, according to Nietzsche, the end of a comprehensive, impulsive culture and the beginning of a much feebler phase dominated by thinking. Such an idea arose in Nietzsche under the influence of Schopenhauer, who placed the untamed, restless will higher than the systematizing thought life, and under the influence of Richard Wagner who, both as a man and as an artist, followed Schopenhauer. But Nietzsche was, by his own inclination, also a contemplative nature. After having surrendered for awhile to the idea of the redemption of the world through beauty as mere appearance, he felt this conception as a foreign element to his own nature, something that had been implanted in him through the influence of Richard Wagner, with whom he had been connected by friendship. Nietzsche tried to free himself from this trend of ideas and to come to terms with a conception of reality that was more in agreement with his own nature. The fundamental trait of his character compelled him to experience the ideas and impulses of the development of a modern world conception as a direct personal fate. Other thinkers formed pictures of a world conception and the process of this formative description constituted their philosophic activity. Nietzsche is confronted with the world conceptions of the second half of the nineteenth century, and it becomes his destiny to experience personally all the delight but also all the sorrows that these world conceptions can cause if they affect the very substance of the human soul. Not only theoretically but with his entire individuality at stake, Nietzsche's philosophical life developed in such a way that representative world conceptions of modern times would completely take hold of him, forcing him to work himself through to his own solutions in the most personal experiences of life.

How can one live if one must think that the world is as Schopenhauer and Richard Wagner imagine it to be? This became the disturbing riddle for him. It was not, however, a riddle for which he sought a solution by means of thinking and knowledge. He had to experience the solution of this problem with every fibre of his nature. Others *think* philosophy; Nietzsche had to *live* philosophy. The modern life of world conception becomes completely personal in Nietzsche. When an observer meets the philosophies of other thinkers, he feels inclined to judge; this is one-sided, that is incorrect, etc. With Nietzsche such an observer finds himself confronted with a world conception within the life of a human being, and he sees that one idea makes this human being healthy while another makes him ill. For this reason, Nietzsche becomes more and more a poet as he presents his picture of world and life. It is also for this reason that a reader who cannot agree with Nietzsche's presentation insofar as his philosophy is concerned, can still admire it because of its poetic power.

What an entirely different tone comes into the modern history of philosophy through Nietzsche as compared to Hamerling, Wundt and even Schopenhauer! These thinkers search contemplatively for the ground of existence and they arrive at the will, which they find in the depths of the human soul. In Nietzsche this will is alive. He absorbs the philosophical ideas, sets them aglow with his ardent will-nature and then makes something entirely new out of them: A life through which will-inspired ideas and idea-illumined will pulsate. This happens in Nietzsche's first creative period, which began with his *Birth of Tragedy* (1870), and had its full expression in his four *Untimely Meditations: David Strauss Confessor and Author; On the Use and Disadvantage of History for Life; Schopenhauer as Educator; Richard Wagner in Bayreuth.* In the second phase of his life, it was Nietzsche's destiny to experience deeply what a life and world conception based exclusively on the thought habits of natural science can be to the human soul. This period is expressed in his works, *Human, All Too Human* (1878), *The Dawn of Day* (1881), and *Gay Science* (1882).

Now the ideals that inspired Nietzsche in his first period have cooled; they appear to him as bubbles of thought. His soul now wants to gain strength, to be invigorated in its feeling by the "reality" of the content that can be derived from the mode of conception of natural science. But Nietzsche's soul is full of life; the vigor of this inner life strives beyond anything that it could owe to the contemplative observation of nature. The contemplation of nature shows that the animal becomes man. As the soul feels its inner power of life, the conception arises: The animal bore man in itself; must not man bear within himself a higher being, the *superman?* Nietzsche's soul experiences in itself the superman wresting himself free from man. His soul revels in lifting the modern idea of evolution that was based on the world of the senses to the realm that the senses do not perceive, a realm that is felt when the soul experiences the meaning of evolution within itself. "The mere acquisition of life's necessities and sustenance is not sufficient; what must also be gained is comfort, if not wealth, power and influence. The search and striving for a continuous improvement of the condition of life is the characteristic impulse of animal and man." This conviction, which in Rolph was the result of contemplative observation, becomes in Nietzsche an inner experience, expressed in a grandiose hymn of philosophic vision. The knowledge that represents the external world is insufficient to him; it must become inwardly increasingly fruitful. Self-observation is poverty. A creation of a new inner life that outshines everything so far in existence, everything man is already, arises in Nietzsche's soul. In man, the superman is born for the first time as the meaning of existence. Knowledge itself grows beyond what it formerly had been; it becomes a creative power. As man *creates,* he takes his stand in the midst of the meaning of life. With lyrical ardor Nietzsche expresses in his *Zarathustra* (1884) the bliss that his soul experiences in creating "superman" out of man. A knowledge that feels itself as creative perceives more in the ego of man than can be lived through in a single course of life; it contains more than can be exhausted in such a single life. It will again and again return to a new life. In this way the idea of "eternal recurrence" of the human soul thrusts itself on Nietzsche to join his idea of "superman."

Rolph's idea of the "enhancement of life" grows in Nietzsche into the conception of the "Will to Power," which he attributes to all being and life in the world of animal and of man. This "Will to Power" sees in life "an appropriation, violation, over-powering of the alien and weaker being, its annexation or at least, in the mildest case, its exploitation." In his book, *Thus Spake Zarathustra*, Nietzsche sang his hymn of praise to his faith in the reality and the development of man into "superman." In his unfinished work, *Will to Power, Attempt at a Revaluation of all Values*, he wanted to re-shape all conceptions from the viewpoint that no other will in man held higher sway than the will for power.

The striving for knowledge becomes in Nietzsche a real force that comes to life in the soul of man. As Nietzsche feels this animation within himself, life assumes in him such an importance that he places it above all knowledge and truth that has not been stirred into life. This again led him to renounce all truth and to seek in the will for power a substitute for the will for truth. He no longer asks, "Is what we know true?" but rather, "Is it sustaining and furthering life?"

"What matters in all philosophizing is never 'the truth' but something entirely different, let us call it health, the future, power, life . . ." What man really strives for is always power; he only indulged himself in the illusion that he wanted "truth." He confused the means with the end. Truth is merely a means for the purpose. "The fact that a judgment is wrong is no objection to it." What is important is not whether a judgment is true or not, but "the question to what degree it advances and preserves life, preserves a race, perhaps even breeds a race." "Most thinking of a philosopher is done secretly by his instincts and thus forced into certain channels." Nietzsche's world conception is the expression of a personal feeling as an individual experience and destiny.

In Goethe the deep impulse of modern philosophical life became apparent; he felt the idea come to life within the self-conscious ego so that with this enlivened idea this ego can know itself in the core of the world. In Nietzsche the desire exists to let man develop his life beyond himself; he feels that then the meaning of life must be revealed in what is inwardly self-created being, but he does not penetrate essentially to *what* man creates beyond himself as the meaning of life. He sings a grandiose hymn of praise to the superman, but he does not form his picture; he *feels* his growing reality but he does not *see* him. Nietzsche speaks of an "eternal recurrence," but he does not describe what it is that recurs. He speaks of raising the form of life through the will to power, but where is the description of the heightened form of life? Nietzsche speaks of something that must be there in the realm of the unknown, but he does not succeed in going further than pointing at the unknown. The forces that are unfolded in the self-conscious ego are also not sufficiently strong in Nietzsche to outline distinctly a reality that he knows as weaving and breathing in human nature.

We have a contrast to Nietzsche's world conception in the materialistic conception of history and life that was given its most pregnant expression by *Karl Marx (1818–83)*. Marx denied that the idea had any share in historical evolution. For him, the real factors of life constituted the actual basis of this evolution, and from them are derived opinions concerning the world that men have been able to form according to the various situations of life in which they find themselves. The man who is working physically and under the power of somebody else has a world conception that differs from that of the intellectual worker. An age that replaces an older economic form with a new one brings also different conceptions of life to the surface of history. If one wants to understand a historical age, one must, for its explanation, go back to its social conditions and its economic processes. All political and cultural currents are only surface-reflectings of these deeper processes. They are essentially ideal effects of real facts, but they have no share in those facts. A world conception, therefore, that is caused by ideal factors can have no share in the progressive evolution of our present conduct of life. It is rather our task to take up the real conflicts of life at the point at which they have arrived, and to continue their development in the same direction.

This conception evolved from a materialistic reversal of Hegelianism. In Hegel, the ideas are in a continuous progress of evolution and the results of this evolution are the actual events of life. What Auguste Comte derived from natural scientific conceptions as a conception of society based on the actual events of life, Karl Marx wants to attain from the direct observation of the economic evolution. Marxism is the boldest form of an intellectual current that starts from the historical phenomena as they appear to external observation, in order to understand the spiritual life and the entire cultural development of man. This is modern "sociology." It in no way accepts man as an individual but rather as a member of social evolution. Man's conceptions, knowledge, action and feeling are all considered to be the result of social powers under the influence of which the individual stands.

Hippolyte Taine (1828–93) calls the sum total of the forces determining every cultural event the "milieu." Every work of art, every institution, every action is to be explained from preceding and simultaneous circumstances. If we know the race, the milieu and the moment through and in which a human achievement comes into being, we have explained this work. *Ferdinand Lasalle* (1825–65), in his *System of Acquired Rights* (1861), showed how conditions of rights and laws, such as property, contract, family, inheritance, etc., arise and develop. The mode of conception of the Romans created a kind of law that differed from that of the Germans. In none of these thoughts is the question raised as to what arises in the human individual, what does he produce through his own inner nature? The question that is always asked is: What are the causes in the general social conditions for the life of the individual? One can observe in this thought tendency an opposite inclination to the one prevailing at the beginning of the nineteenth century with regard to the question of man's relation to the world. It was then customary to ask: What rights can man claim through his own nature (natural rights), or in what way does man obtain knowledge in accordance with his own power of reason as an individual? The sociological trend of thought, however, asks: What are the legal and intellectual concepts that the various social groupings cause to arise in the individual?

The fact that I form certain conceptions concerning things does not depend on my power of reasoning but is the result of the historical development that produced me. In Marxism the self-conscious ego is entirely deprived of its own nature; it finds itself drifting in the ocean of facts. These facts develop according to the laws of natural science and of social conditions. In this world conception the *impotence* of modern philosophy with regard to the human soul approaches a maximum. The "ego," the self-conscious human soul, wants to find in itself the entity through which it can assert its own significance within the existence of the world, but it is unwilling to dive *into its own depths*. It is afraid it will not find in its own depths the support of its own existence and essence. It wants to derive its own being from an entity that lies *outside* its own domain. To do this, the ego follows the thought habits developed in modern times under the influence of natural science, and turns either to the world of material events or to that of social evolution. It believes it understands its own nature in the totality of life if it can say to itself, "I am, in a certain way, conditioned by these events, by this evolution."

Such philosophical tendencies show that there are forces at work in the souls of which they are dimly aware, but which cannot at first be satisfied by the modern habits of thought and research. Concealed from consciousness, spiritual life works in human souls. It drives these souls to go so deep into the self-conscious ego that this ego can find in its depths what leads to the source of world existence. In this source the human soul feels its kinship with a world entity that is *not* manifested in the mere phenomena and entities of nature. With respect to these phenomena and entities modern times have arrived at an ideal of research with which the scientist feels secure in his endeavor. One would now also like to feel this security in the investigation of the nature of the human soul. It has been shown above that, in leading thinkers, the striving for such security resulted in world pictures that no longer contain any elements from which satisfactory conceptions of the human soul could be derived. The attempt is made to treat philosophy according to the method of natural science, but in the process of this treatment the meaning of the philosophical question itself is lost. The task with which the human soul is charged from the very depth of its nature goes far beyond anything that the thinkers are willing to recognize as safe methods of investigation according to the modern habits of thought.

In appraising the situation of the development of modern world conception thus characterized, one finds as the most outstanding feature the *pressure* that the mode of thought of natural science has exerted on the minds of people ever since it attained its full stature. One recognizes as the reason for this pressure the fruitfulness, the efficiency of this mode of thinking. An affirmation of this is to be found in the work of a natural scientist like *T. H. Huxley* (1825–95). He does not believe that one could find anything in the knowledge of natural science that would answer the last questions concerning the human soul. But he is convinced that our search for knowledge must confine itself to the limits of the mode of conception of natural science and we must admit that man simply has no means by which to acquire a knowledge of what lies behind nature. The result of this opinion is that natural science contains no insight concerning man's highest hopes for knowledge, but it allows him to feel that in this mode of conception the investigation is placed on secure ground. One should, therefore, abandon all concern for everything that does not lie within the realm of natural science, or one should consider it as a matter of belief.

The effect of this pressure caused by the method of natural science is clearly expressed in a thought current called pragmatism that appeared at the turn of the century and intended to place all striving for truth on a secure basis. The name "pragmatism" goes back to an essay that Charles Peirce published in the American journal, *Popular Science*, in 1878. The most influential representatives of this mode of conception are *William James* (1842–1910) in America and *F. C. Schiller* (1864–1937) in England, who uses the word "humanism." Pragmatism can be called disbelief in the power of thought. It denies that thinking that would remain within its own domain is capable of producing anything that can be proved as truth and knowledge justifiable by itself. Man is confronted with processes of the world and must act. To accomplish this, thinking serves him in an auxiliary function. It sums up the facts of the external world into ideas and combines them. The best ideas are those that help him to achieve the right kind of action so that he can attain his purpose in accordance with the facts of the world. These ideas man recognizes as his truth. Will is the ruler of man's relation to the world, not thinking. James deals with this matter in his book, *The Will to Believe*. The will determines life; this is its undeniable right. Therefore, will is also justified in influencing thought. It is, to be sure, not to exert its influence in determining what the facts are in a particular case; here the intellect is to follow the facts themselves. But it will influence the understanding and interpretation of reality as a whole. "If our scientific knowledge extended as far as to the end of things, we might be able to live by science alone. But since it only dimly lights up the edges of the dark continent that we call the universe, and since we must form, at our own risk, some sort of thought of this universe to which we belong with our lives, we shall be justified if we form such thoughts as agree with our nature—thoughts that enable us to act, hope and live."

According to this conception, our thought has no life that could possibly concentrate and deepen in itself and, in Hegel's sense, for example, penetrate to the source of existence. It merely emerges in the human soul to serve the ego when it takes an active part in the world with its will and life. Pragmatism deprives thought of the power it possessed from the rise of the Greek world conception. Knowledge is thus made into a product of the human will. In the last analysis, it can no longer be the element into which man plunges in order to find himself in his true nature. The self-conscious ego no longer penetrates into its own entity with the power of thinking. It loses itself in the dark recesses of the will in which thought sheds no light on anything except the aims of life. But these, as such, do not spring from thought. The power exerted by external facts on man has become excessively strong. The conscious ability to find a light in the inner life of thought that could illumine the last questions of existence has reached the zero point. In pragmatism, the development of modern philosophy falls shortest of what the spirit of this development really demands: that man may find himself as a thinking and self-conscious ego in the depths of the world in which this ego feels itself as deeply connected with the well-spring of existence, as the Greek truth-seeker did through his perceived thought. That the spirit of modern times demands this becomes especially clear through pragmatism. It places man in the focal point of his world picture. In *man,* it was to be seen how reality rules in existence. Thus, the chief question was directed toward the element in which the self-conscious ego rests. But the power of thought was not sufficient to carry light into this element. Thought remained behind in the upper layers of the soul when the ego wanted to take the path into its own depth.

In Germany *Hans Vaihinger* (1852–1933) developed his *Philosophy of As-If* (1911) along the same lines as pragmatism. This philosopher regards the leading ideas that man forms about the phenomena of the world not as thought images through which, in the cognitive process, the soul places itself into a spiritual reality, but as fictions that lead him to find his way in the world. The "atom," for instance, is imperceptible. Man forms the thought of the "atom." He cannot form it in order to know something of a reality, but merely *"as if"* the external phenomena of nature had come to pass through compound actions of atoms. If one imagines that there are atoms, there will be order in the chaos of perceived natural phenomena. It is the same with all leading ideas. They are assumed, not in order to depict facts that are given solely by perception. They are invented, and reality is then interpreted "as if" the content of these imagined concepts really were the basis of reality. The impotence of thought is thus consciously made the center of this philosophy. The power of the external facts impresses the mind of the thinker so overwhelmingly that he does not dare to penetrate with his "mere thought" into those regions from which the external reality springs. But as we can only hope to gain an insight into the nature of man if we have spiritual means to penetrate into the characterized regions, there can be no possibility of approaching the highest riddles of the universe through the "As-If Philosophy."

We must now realize that both "pragmatism" and the "As-If Philosophy" have grown out of the thought practice of the age that is dominated by the method of natural science. Natural science can only be concerned with the investigation of the connection of external facts, of facts that can be observed in the field of sense perception. In natural science it cannot be a question of making the connections themselves, at which its investigation aims, sensually perceptible, but merely of *establishing* these connections in the indicated field. By following this basic principle, modern natural science became the *model* for all scientific cognition and, in approaching the present time, it has gradually been drawn into a thought practice that operates in the sense of "pragmatism" and the "As-If Philosophy." Darwinism, for instance, was at first driven to proclaim a line of evolution of living beings from the most imperfect to the most perfect and thus to conceive man as a higher form in the evolution of the anthropoid apes. But the anatomist, Carl Gegenbauer, pointed out as early as 1870 that it is the *method of investigation* applied to such an idea of evolution that constitutes the fruitful part of it. The use of this method of investigation has continued to more recent times, and one is quite justified in saying that, while it remained faithful to its original principle, it has led beyond the views with which it was originally connected. The investigation proceeded "as if" man had to be sought within the line of descent of the anthropoid apes. At the present time, one is not far from recognizing that this cannot be so, but that there must have been a being in earlier times whose true descendants are to be found in man, while the anthropoid apes developed away from this being into a less perfect species. In this way the original modern idea of evolution has proved to be only an auxiliary step in the process of investigation.

While such a thought practice holds sway in natural science, it seems quite justified for natural science to deny that, in order to solve world riddles, there is any scientific cognitive value in an investigation of pure thought carried out by means of a thought contemplation in the self-conscious ego. The natural scientist feels that he stands on secure ground when he considers thinking only as a means to secure his orientation in the world of external facts. The great accomplishments to which natural science can point at the turn of the twentieth century agree well with such a thought practice. In the method of investigation of natural science, "pragmatism" and the "As-If Philosophy" are actually at work. If these modes of conception now appear to be special philosophical thought tendencies also, we see in this fact that modern philosophy has basically taken on the form of natural science.

For this reason, thinkers who instinctively feel how the demand of the spirit of modern world conception is secretly at work will quite understandably be confronted with the question: How can we uphold a conception of the self-conscious ego in the face of the *perfection* of the natural scientific method? It may be said that natural science is about to produce a world picture in which the self-conscious ego does not find a place, for what natural science can give as a picture of the external man contains the self-conscious soul only in the manner in which the magnet contains its energy. There are now two possibilities. We either delude ourselves into believing that we produce a serious statement when we say, "Our brain thinks," and then accept the verdict that "the spiritual man" is merely the surface expression of material reality, or we recognize in this "spiritual man" a self-dependent essential reality and are thus driven out of the field of natural science with our knowledge of man. The French philosophers, *Émile Boutroux* (1845–1921) and *Henri Bergson* (1859–1941), are thinkers who accept the latter possibility.

Boutroux proceeds from a criticism of the modern mode of conception that intends to reduce all world processes to the laws of natural science. We understand the course of his thought if we consider that a plant, for example, contains processes that, to be sure, are regulated by laws effective also in the mineral world, but that it is quite impossible to imagine that these mineral laws themselves cause this plant life through their own content. If we want to recognize that plant life develops on the basis of mineral activity, we must presuppose that it is a matter of perfect indifference to the mineral forces if plant life develops from this basis. There must be a spontaneously creative element added to the mineral agencies if plant life is to be produced. There is, therefore, a creative element everywhere in nature. The mineral realm is there but a creative element stands behind it. The latter produces the plant life based on the ground of the mineral world. So it is in all the spheres of natural order up to the conscious human soul, indeed, including all sociological processes. The human soul does not spring from mere biological laws, but directly from the fundamental creative element and it assimilates the biological processes and laws to its own entity. The fundamental creative element is also at work in the sociological realm. This brings human souls into the appropriate connections and interdependence. Thus, in Boutroux's book, *On the Concept of Natural Laws in the Science and Philosophy of Today* (1895), we find:

> Science shows us a hierarchy of laws, which we can, to be sure, bring closer and closer together but which we cannot blend into a single law. It shows us, furthermore, besides this relative dissimilarity of the laws, a mutual influence of these laws on each other. The physical laws affect the living being, but the biological laws are at work at the same time.

Boutroux turns his attention from the natural laws represented in the thinking of natural science to the creative process behind these laws. Emerging directly from this process are the entities that fill the world. The behavior of these entities to one another, their mutual effect on each other, can be expressed in laws that are conceivable in thought. What is thus conceived becomes, as it were, a basis of the natural laws for this mode of conception. The entities are real and manifest their natures according to laws. The sum total of these laws, which in the final analysis constitute the unreal and are attached to an intellectually conceived existence, constitutes matter. Thus, Boutroux can say:

> Motion (what he means is the totality of everything that happens between entities according to natural laws) is, in itself, obviously as much an abstraction as thinking in itself. Actually, there are only living entities, their nature being halfway between the pure concepts of thinking and motion. These living entities form a hierarchy and activity circulates in them from above to below and from below to above. The spirit moves matter neither directly nor indirectly, for there is no raw matter and what constitutes the nature of matter is closely connected with what constitutes the nature of the spirit.

But if natural laws are only the sum total of the interrelation of the entities, then the human soul also does not stand in the world as a whole in such a way that it could be explained from natural laws; from its own nature it adds its manifestations to the other laws. With this step, freedom, the spontaneous self-revelation, is secured for the soul. One can see in this philosophical mode of thinking the attempt to gain clarity concerning the true essence of nature in order to acquire an insight into the relation of the human soul to it. Boutroux arrives at a conception of the human soul that can only spring from its self-manifestation. In former times, according to Boutroux, one saw in the mutual influences of the entities, the manifestation of the "capriciousness and arbitrariness" of spiritual beings. Modern thinking has been freed from this belief by the knowledge of natural laws. As these laws exist only in the cooperative processes of the entities, they cannot contain anything that might determine the entities.

> The mechanical natural laws that have been discovered by modern science are, in fact, the bond that connects the external world with the inner realm. Far from constituting a necessity, they are our liberators; they allow us to add to the contemplation in which the ancients were locked up, a *science of action*.

These words point to the demand of the spirit of modern world conception that has repeatedly been mentioned in this book. The ancients were limited to contemplation. To them, the soul was in the element of its true nature when it was in thought contemplation. The modern development demands a "science of action." This science, however, could only come into being if the soul could, in thinking, lay hold of its own nature in the self-conscious ego, and if it could arrive, through a spiritual experience, at inner activities of the self with which it could see itself as being grounded in its own entity.

Henri Bergson tries to penetrate to the nature of the self-conscious ego in a different way so that the mode of conception of natural science does not become an obstacle in this process. The *nature of thinking* itself has become a world riddle through the development of the world conceptions from the time of the Greeks to the present age. Thought has lifted the human soul out of the world as a whole. Thus, the soul lives with the thought element and must direct the question to thought: How will you lead me again to an element in which I can feel myself really sheltered in the world as whole? Bergson considers the scientific mode of thinking. He does not find in it the power through which it could swing itself into a true reality. The thinking soul is confronted with reality and gains thought images from it. It combines these images, but what the soul acquires in this manner is not rooted within reality; it stands outside reality. Bergson speaks of thinking as follows:

> It is understood that fixed concepts can be extracted by our thoughts from the mobile reality, but there is no means whatever of reconstituting the mobility of the real with the fixity of concepts. (*Introduction to Metaphysics*)

Proceeding from thoughts of this kind, Bergson finds that all attempts to penetrate reality by means of thinking had to fail because they undertook something of which thinking, as it occurs in life and science, is quite incapable to enter into true reality. If, in this way, Bergson believes he recognizes the impotence of thinking, he does not mean to say that there is no way by means of which the right kind of experience in the self-conscious ego may reach true reality. For the ego, there is a way outside of thinking—the way of immediate experience, of intuition.

> To philosophize means to reverse the normal direction of the workings of thought . . . Symbolic knowledge is relative through pre-existing concepts, which goes from the fixed to the moving, but not so intuitive knowledge, which establishes itself in the moving reality and adopts the life itself of things. (*Introduction to Metaphysics*)

Bergson believes that a transformation of our usual mode of thinking is possible so that the soul, through this transformation, will experience itself in an activity, in an intuitive perception, in which it *unites* with a reality that is deeper than the one that is perceived in ordinary knowledge. In such an intuitive perception the soul experiences itself as an entity that is not conditioned by the physical processes, which produce sensation and movement. When man perceives through his senses, and when he moves his limbs, a corporeal entity is at work in him, but as soon as he *remembers* something a purely psychic-spiritual process takes place that is *not* conditioned by corresponding physical processes. Thus, the whole inner life of the soul is a specific life of a psychic-spiritual nature that takes place in the body and in connection with it, but not through the body. Bergson investigated in detail those results of natural science that seemed to oppose his view. The thought indeed seems justified that our physical functions are rooted in bodily processes when one remembers how, for instance, the disease of a part of the brain causes an impediment of speech. A great many facts of this kind can be enumerated. Bergson discusses them in his book, *Matter and Memory*, and he decides that all these facts do not constitute any proof against the view of an independent spiritual-psychical life.

In this way, modern philosophy seems through Bergson to take up its task that is demanded by the time, the task of a concentration of the experience of the self-conscious ego, but it accomplishes this step by declaring thought as impotent. Where the ego is to experience itself in its own nature, it cannot make use of the power of thinking. The same holds for Bergson insofar as the investigation of life is concerned. What must be considered as the driving element in the evolution of the living being, what places these beings in the world in a series from the imperfect to the perfect, we cannot know through a thoughtful contemplation of the various forms of the living beings. But if man experiences himself in himself as psychical life, he stands in the element of life that lives in those beings and knows itself in him. This element of life first had to pour itself out in innumerable forms to prepare itself for what it later becomes in man. The effusion of life (*élan vital*), which arouses itself into a thinking being in man, is there already manifested in the simple living entity. In the creation of all living beings it has so spent itself that it retains only a part of its entire nature, the part, to be sure, that reveals itself as the fruit of all previous creations of life. In this way, the entity of man exists *before* all other living beings, but it can live its life as man only after having ejected all other forms of life, which man then can observe from without as *one* form among all others. Through his intuitive knowledge Bergson wants to vitalize the results of natural science so that he can say:

> It is as if a vague and formless being, whom we may call, as we will, *man* or *superman,* had sought to realize himself, and had succeeded only by abandoning a part of himself on the way. The losses are represented by the rest of the animal world, and even by the vegetable world, at least in what these have that is positive and above the accidents of evolution. (*Creative Evolution*)

From lightly woven and easily attainable thoughts like this, Bergson produces an idea of evolution that had been expressed previously in a profound mode of thought by *W. H. Preuss* in his book, *Spirit and Matter* (1882). Preuss also held that man has not developed from the other natural beings but is, from the beginning the fundamental entity, which had first to eject his preliminary stages into the other living beings before he could give himself the form appropriate for him on earth. We read in the above-mentioned book:

> The time should have come . . . to establish a theory of origin of organic species that is not based solely on one-sidedly proclaimed theorems from descriptive natural science, but is also in agreement with the other natural laws that are at the same time the laws of human thinking. What is necessary is a theory that is *free from all hypothesizing* and that rests solely on strict conclusions from natural scientific *observations* in the widest sense of the word; a theory that saves the concept of the species according to the actual possibility, but at the same time adapts Darwin's concept of evolution to its own field and tries to make it fruitful. The center of this new theory is

man, the species *unique on our planet: Homo sapiens*. It is strange that the older observers began with the objects of nature and then went astray to such an extent that they did not find the way that leads to the human being. This aim had been attained by Darwin only in an insufficient and unsatisfactory way as he sought the ancestor of the lord of creation among the animals, while the naturalist should begin with himself as a human being *in order to proceed through the entire realm of existence and of thinking and to return finally to humanity*. . . . It was not by accident that the human nature resulted from the entire terrestrial evolution, but by necessity. Man is the aim of all telluric processes and every other form that occurs beside him has borrowed its traits from him. Man is the first-born being of the entire cosmos. . . . When his germinating state (man in his potentiality) had come into being, the remaining organic substance no longer had the power to produce further human possibilities. What developed thereafter became animal or plant. . . .

Such a view attempts to recognize man as placed on his ground by the development of modern world conception, that is to say, outside nature, in órder to find something in such a knowledge of man that throws light on the world surrounding him. In the little known thinker from Elsfleth, W. H. Preuss, the ardent wish arises to gain a *knowledge of the world* at once through an *insight into man*. His forceful and significant ideas are immediately directed to the human being. He sees how this being struggles its way into existence. What it must leave behind on its way, what it must slough off, remains as nature with its entities on a lower stage of evolution surrounding man as his environment. The way toward the riddles of the world in modern philosophy must go through an investigation of the human entity manifested in the self-conscious ego. This becomes apparent through the development of this philosophy. The more one tries to enter into its striving and its search, the more one becomes aware of the fact that this search aims at such experiences in the human soul that do not only produce an insight into the human soul itself, but also kindles a light by means of which a certain knowledge concerning the world outside man can be secured. In looking at the views of Hegel and related thinkers, more recent philosophers came to doubt that there could be the power in the *life of thought* to spread its light beyond the realm of the soul itself. The element of thought seemed not strong enough to engender an activity that could explain the being and the meaning of the world. By contrast, the natural scientific mode of conception demanded a penetration into the core of the soul that rested on a firmer ground than thought can supply.

Within this search and striving the attempts of Wilhelm Dilthey (1833–1911) take a significant position. In writings like his *Introduction to the Cultural Sciences*, and his Berlin Academy treatise, *Contributions to the Solution of the Problem of Our Belief in the Reality of the External World and Its Right* (1890), he offered expositions that are filled with all the philosophical riddles that weigh on the modern development of world conception. To be sure, the form of his presentation, which is given in the modern terminology used by scholars, prevents a more general impression being created by what he has to say. It is Dilthey's view that through the thoughts and imaginations that appear in his soul man cannot even arrive at the certainty that the perceptions of the senses correspond to a reality independent of man. Everything that is of the nature of thought, ideation and sense perception is picture. The world that surrounds man could be a dream without a reality independent of him if he were exclusively dependent on such pictures in his awareness of the real world. But not only these pictures present themselves in the soul. In the process of life the soul is filled with will, activity and feeling, all of which stream forth from it and are recognized as an immediate experience rather than intellectually. In willing and feeling the soul experiences itself as reality, but if it experienced itself *only* in this manner, it would have to believe that its own reality were the only one in the world. This assumption could be justified only if the will could radiate in all directions without finding any *resistance.* But that is not the case. The intentions of the will cannot unfold their life in that way. There is something obtruding itself in their path that they have not produced but that must nevertheless be accepted by them.

To "common sense" such a thought development of a philosopher can appear as hair-splitting. The historical account must not be deflected by such judgment. It is important to gain an insight into the difficulty that modern philosophy had to create for itself in regard to a question that seems so simple and in fact superfluous to "common sense," that is, if the world man sees, hears, etc., may rightly be called *real*. The "ego" that had, as shown above in our historical account of the development of philosophical world riddles, separated itself from the world, strives to find its way back into the world from what appears in its own consciousness as a state of loneliness. It is Dilthey's opinion that this way cannot be found back into the world by saying that the soul experiences pictures (thoughts, ideas, sensations), and since these pictures appear in our consciousness they must have their causes in a real external world. A conclusion of this kind would not, according to Dilthey, give us the right to speak of a real external world, for such a conclusion is drawn *within the soul* according to the needs of this soul, and there is no guarantee that there really *is* in the external world what the soul *believes* in following its own needs. Therefore, the soul cannot *infer* an external world; it would expose itself to the danger that its conclusion might have a life only within the soul but without any significance for an external world. Certainty concerning an outer world can be gained by the soul only if this external world penetrates into the inner life of the "ego," so that *within* this "ego" not only the "ego" but also the external world itself unfolds its life. This happens, according to Dilthey, when the soul experiences in its *will* and its *feeling* something that does not spring from within. Dilthey attempts to decide from the most self-evident facts a question that is for him a fundamental problem of all world conception. A passage like the following may illustrate this:

> As a child presses his hand against a chair in order to move it, he measures his power against the resistance; his own life and the object are experienced together. But now let the child be locked up. It is in vain that he rattles against the door; now his entire excited

will becomes aware of the compulsion of an overwhelming powerful external world that hinders and restricts, and compresses, as it were, his own self-willed life. The desire to escape from the displeasure and to gratify his impulses is followed by the consciousness of obstruction, displeasure and dissatisfaction. What the child thus experiences follows him through his entire adult life. The resistance becomes pressure. We seem to be everywhere surrounded by walls of actual facts through which we cannot break. The impressions remain, no matter how much we would like to change them; they vanish although we strive to cling to them; impulses of motion directed by the idea of avoiding something that causes pain are, under certain circumstances always followed by emotions that hold us within the realm of pain. Thus, the reality of the external world grows, so to speak, progressively more dense around us.

Why is such a reflection, which seems unimportant for many people, developed in connection with the highest problems of philosophy? It seems hopeless to gain an insight into man's position in the world as a whole from such points of departure. What is essential, however, is the fact that philosophy arrived at reflections of this kind on its way, to use Brentano's words once more, to "gain certainty for the hopes of Plato and Aristotle concerning the continued life of our better part after the dissolution of our body." To attain sure knowledge of this kind seems to become more difficult the more the intellectual development advances. The "self-conscious ego" feels itself more and more ejected from the world; it seems to find in itself less and less the elements that connect it with the world in a way different from that of our "body," which is subject to "dissolution." While this "self-conscious ego" searched for a certain knowledge concerning its connection with an eternal world of the spirit, it lost the certainty of an insight in its connection with the world as revealed through the perception of the senses. In our discussion of Goethe's world conception, it was shown how Goethe searched for such experiences of the soul that carry it into a reality lying behind sense perception as a spiritual world. In this world conception the attempt is made to experience something *within* the soul through which it no longer lives exclusively within its own confines in spite of the fact that it feels the experienced content as its own. The soul searches for world experiences *in itself* through which it participates with its experience in an element that it cannot reach through the mediation of the mere physical organs. Although Dilthey's mode of reflection may appear to be quite unnecessary, his efforts must be considered as belonging to the same current of the philosophical development. He is intent on finding an element *within* the soul that does not *spring from the soul* but belongs to an independent realm. He would like to prove that the world enters the experience of the soul. Dilthey does not believe that such an entrance can be accomplished by the thought element. For him, the soul can assimilate in its entire life content, in will, striving and feeling, something that is not only soul but part of the real external world. We recognize a human being in our soul as real not by forming a representative thought picture of the person we see before us, but by allowing his will and his feeling to enter into our own will and sentiment. Thus, a human soul, in Dilthey's opinion, acknowledges a real external world not because this outer world conveys its reality through the thought element, but because the soul as a self-conscious ego, *experiences inwardly in itself* the external world. In this manner he is led to acknowledge the spiritual life as something of a higher significance than the mere natural existence. He produces a counterbalance to the natural scientific mode of conception with his view, and he even thinks that nature as a real external world can be acknowledged only because it can be experienced by the spiritual part of our soul. The experience of the natural is a subdivision of our general soul experience, which is of a spiritual nature, and spiritually our soul is part of a general spiritual development on earth. A great spiritual organism develops and unfolds in cultural systems in the spiritual experience and creative achievement of the various peoples and ages. What develops its forces in this spiritual organism permeates the individual human souls. They are embedded in the spiritual organism. What they experience, accomplish and produce receives its impulses not from the stimulations of nature, but from the comprehensive spiritual life. Dilthey's mode of conception is full of understanding for that of natural science. He often speaks in his discussions of the results of the natural scientists, but, as a counter-balance to his recognition of natural development, he insists on the independent existence of a spiritual world. Dilthey finds the content of a science of the spiritual in the contemplation of the cultures of different peoples and ages.

Rudolf Eucken (1864–1926) arrives at a similar recognition of an independent spiritual world. He finds that the natural scientific mode of thought becomes self-contradictory if it intends to be more than a *one-sided* approach to reality, if it wants to proclaim what it finds within the possible grasp of its own knowledge as the only reality. If one only observed nature as it offers itself to the senses, one could never obtain a comprehensive conception of it. In order to explain nature, one must draw on what the spirit can experience only through itself, what it can never derive from external observation. Eucken proceeds from the vivid feeling that the soul has of its own spontaneous work and creation when it is occupied in the contemplation of external nature. He does not fail to recognize in which way the soul is dependent on what it perceives through its sense organs and how it is determined through everything that has its natural basis in the body. But he directs his attention to the autonomous regulating and life-inspiring activity of the soul that is independent of the body. The soul gives direction and conclusive connection to the world of sensations and perceptions. It is not only determined by stimuli that are derived from the physical world but it experiences purely spiritual impulses in itself. Through these impulses the soul is aware that it has its being in a real spiritual world. Into its experiences and creations flow the forces from a spiritual world to which it belongs. This spiritual world is directly experienced as real in the soul that knows itself as one with that world. In this way, the soul sees itself, according to Eucken, supported by a living and creative spiritual world. It is his opinion that the thought element, the intellectual forces, are not powerful enough to fathom the depths of this spiritual world. What streams from the spiritual world into man pours itself into his entire comprehensive soul life, not only into his intellect. This world of the spirit is endowed with the character of personality of a substantial nature. It also impregnates the thought element but it is not confined to it. The entire soul may feel itself in a substantial spiritual connection.

Eucken, in his numerous writings, knows how to describe in a lofty and emphatic way this spiritual world as it weaves and has its being: *The Struggle for a Spiritual Content of Life* (1896), *Truth Content of Religion* (1901), *Basic Outlines of a New Life Conception, Spiritual Currents of the Present Time, Life Conceptions of the Great Thinkers,* and *Knowledge and Life.* In these books he tries to show from different points of view how the human soul, as it experiences itself and as it understands itself in this experience, is aware of being permeated and animated by a creative, living spiritual substance of which it is a part and a member. Like Dilthey, Eucken describes, as the content of the independent spiritual life, what unfolds in the civilizations of humanity in the moral, technical, social and artistic creations of the various peoples and ages.

In a historical presentation as is herein attempted, there is no place for criticism of the described world conceptions. But it is not criticism to point out how a world conception develops new questions through its own character, for it is thus that it becomes a part of the historical development. Dilthey and Eucken speak of an independent spiritual world in which the individual human soul is embedded. Their theory of this spiritual world, however, leaves the following questions open: What is this spiritual world and in what way does the human soul belong to it? Does the individual soul vanish with the dissolution of the body after it participated within that body in the development of the spiritual life manifested in the cultural creations of the different peoples and ages? One can, to be sure, answer these questions from Dilthey's and Eucken's point of view by saying that what the human soul can know in its own life does not lead to results with respect to these questions. But this is precisely what can be said to characterize such world conceptions that they lead, through their mode of conception, to *no* means of cognition that could guide the soul or the self-conscious ego beyond what can be experienced in connection with the body. In spite of the intensity with which Eucken stresses the independence and reality of the spiritual world, what the soul experiences according to his world conception of this spiritual world, and in connection with it, is experienced through the body. The hopes of Plato and Aristotle, so often referred to in this book, with regard to the nature of the soul and its independent relation to the spiritual world are not touched by such a world conception. No more is shown than that the soul, as long as it appears within the body, participates in a spiritual world that is quite rightly called real. What it is in the spiritual world as an independent spiritual entity cannot be discussed within this philosophy. It is characteristic of these modes of conception that they do, to be sure, arrive at a recognition of a spiritual world and also of the spiritual nature of the human soul. But no knowledge results from this recognition concerning the position of the soul, the self-conscious ego, in the reality of the world, apart from the fact that it acquires a consciousness of the spiritual world through the life of the body.

The historical position of these modes of conception in the development of philosophy appears in its right light if one recognizes that they produce questions that they cannot answer with their own means. They maintain emphatically that the soul becomes in itself conscious of a spiritual world that is independent of itself. But how is this consciousness acquired? Only through the means of cognition that the soul has in and through its existence in the body. *Within this form of existence* a certainty of a real spiritual world arises. But the soul finds no way to experience its own self-contained entity in the spirit *outside the body*. What the spirit manifests, stimulates and creates *within the soul* is perceived by it as far as the physical existence enables it to do so. What it is *as a spirit* in the spiritual world and, in fact, whether or not it is a separate entity within that world, is a question that cannot be answered by the mere recognition of the fact that the soul *within the body* can be conscious of its connection with a living and creative spiritual world. To obtain an answer of this kind it would be necessary for the self-conscious human soul, while it advances to a knowledge of the spiritual world, to become aware of its own mode of life in the world of the spirit, independent of the conditions of its bodily existence. The spiritual world would not only have to enable the soul entity to recognize its reality but it would have to convey something of its own nature to the soul. It would have to reveal to the soul in what way it is different from the world of the senses and in what manner it allows the soul entity to participate in this different mode of existence.

A feeling for this question lives in those philosophers who want to contemplate the spiritual world by directing their attention toward something that *cannot*, according to their opinion, be found within the mere observation of nature. If it could be shown that there is something with regard to which the natural scientific mode of conception would prove to be powerless, then this could be considered to guarantee the justification of assuming a spiritual world. A mode of thought of this kind had already been indicated by Lotze (compare page 375ff. of this volume). It found forceful representatives later in *Wilhelm Windelband* (1848–1915), *Heinrich Rickert* (1863–1936) and others. These thinkers are of the opinion that there is an element entering into the world conception that is inaccessible to the natural scientific mode of thought. They consider this element to be the "values" that are of decisive importance in human life. The world is no dream but a reality if it can be shown that certain experiences of the soul contain something that is independent of this soul. The actions, endeavors and will impulses of the soul are no longer sparks that light up and vanish in the ocean of existence, if one must recognize that there is something that endows them with *values* independent of the soul. Such *values*, however, the soul must acknowledge for its will impulses and its actions just as much as it must recognize that its perceptions are not merely produced by its own effort. Action and will impulses of man do not simply occur like facts of nature; they must be considered from the point of view of a legal, moral, social, esthetic or scientific *value*. It is quite right to insist that during the evolution of civilizations in different ages and of different peoples, man's views concerning the values of right, morality, beauty and truth have undergone changes. If Nietzsche could speak of a "revaluation of all values," it must be acknowledged that the value of actions, thoughts and will intentions is determined from without in a similar way to the way perceptual ideation receives the character of reality from without. In the sense of the "philosophy of values" one can say: As the *pressure* or *resistance* of the natural external world make the difference between an idea that is a mere picture of fantasy or one that represents reality, so the light and approbation that fall on the soul life from an external spiritual world decide whether or not an impulse of the will, an action and a thought endeavor have a *value* in the world as a whole or are only arbitrary products of the soul. As a stream of values, the spiritual world flows through the lives of men in the course of history. While the human soul feels itself as living in a world determined by values, it experiences itself in a spiritual element. If this mode of conception were seriously carried out, all statements that man could make concerning the spiritual would have to take on the form of value judgments. The only thing one could then say about anything not revealed in nature and therefore not to be known through the natural scientific mode of conception, would be in which way and in what respect it possessed an independent value in the whole of the world. The question would then arise: If one disregards everything in the human soul that natural science has to say about it, is it then valuable as a member of the spiritual world, and does it have a significant independent value? Can the riddles of philosophy concerning the soul be solved if one cannot speak of its *existence but only of its value*? Will not the philosophy of values always be forced to adopt a language similar to that of Lotze when he speaks of the continuation of the soul?

> Since we consider every being only as a *creature of God*, there is no fundamentally valid *right* on which the individual soul, for instance

as a "substance," could base its claim in order to demand an eternal, individual, continued existence. Perhaps we can only maintain that every being will be *preserved by God as long* as its existence is of a valuable significance for the whole of His world plan. . . . (Compare page 379 of this volume.)

Here the *"value"* of the soul is spoken of as its decisive character. Some attention, however, is also paid to the question of how this value may be connected with the *preservation of existence*. One can understand the position of the philosophy of value in the course of the development of philosophy if one considers that the natural scientific mode of conception is inclined to claim all *knowledge of existence for itself.* If that is granted, philosophy can do nothing but resign itself to the investigation of something else, and such a "something else" is seen in these "values." The following question, as an unsolved problem, can be found in Lotze's statement: Is it at all possible to go no further than to define and characterize values and to renounce all knowledge concerning the *form of existence* of the values?

* * *

Many of the most recent schools of thought prove to be attempts to search within the self-conscious ego, which in the course of the philosophical development feels itself more and more separated from the world, for an element that leads back to a reunion with the world. The conceptions of Dilthey, Eucken, Windelband, Rickert and others are such attempts. They want to do justice both to the demands of natural science and to the contemplation of the experience of the soul so that a science of the spirit appears as a possibility beside the science of nature. The same aims are followed by the thought tendencies of *Herman Cohen* (1842–1918) (compare page 352 of this volume), *Paul Natorp* (1854–1924), *August Stadler* (1850–1910), *Ernst Cassirer* (1874–1945), *Walter Kinkel* (born 1871) and others who share their philosophical convictions. In directing their attention to the processes of thinking itself, they believe that in this highest activity of the self-conscious ego the soul gains hold on an inner possession that allows it to penetrate into reality. They turn their attention to what appears to them as the highest fruit of thinking. A simple example of this would be the thinking of a circle in which specific representative thought pictures of any circle are disregarded entirely. As much can be embraced in this way by *pure* thinking as can be encompassed by the power of our soul through which we can penetrate into reality. For what we can think in this way manifests its own nature through thinking in the consciousness of man. The sciences strive to arrive, by means of their observations, experiments and methods, at such results concerning the world as can be seized in pure thinking. They will have to leave the fulfillment of this aim to a far distant future, but one can nevertheless say that insofar as they endeavor to have pure thought, they also strive to convey the true essence of things to the possession of the self-conscious ego. When man makes an observation in the sensual external world, or in the course of historical life, he has, according to this conception, no true reality before him. What the observation of the senses offers is merely the challenge to search for a reality, not a reality in itself. Only when, through the activity of the soul, a thought appears, so to speak, to reveal itself at the very place where the observation has been made, is the living reality of the observed object integrated into real knowledge. The progressively developing knowledge replaces with thought what has been observed in the world. What the observation showed in the beginning was there only because man with his senses, with his everyday imagination, realizes at first for himself the nature of things in his own limited way. What he has at his disposal in this way has significance only for himself. What he substitutes as thought for the observation is no longer troubled by his own limitation. It is as it is thought, for thought determines its own nature and reveals itself according to its own character in the self-conscious ego. Thought does not allow the ego to determine its character in any way.

There lives in this world conception a subtle feeling for the development of thought life since its first philosophical flowering within Greek intellectual life. It was the thought experience that gave to the self-conscious ego the power to be vigorously conscious of its own self-dependent entity. In the present age this power of thought can be experienced in the soul as the impulse that, seized within the self-conscious ego, endows this ego with the awareness that it is not a mere external observer of things but that it lives essentially in an intimate connection with their reality. It is in thought itself that the soul can feel it contains a true and self-dependent reality. As the soul thus feels itself interwoven with thought as a content of life that breathes reality, it can again experience the supporting power of the thought element as this was experienced in Greek philosophy. It can be experienced again as strongly as it was felt in the philosophy that took thought as a perception. It is true that in the world conception of Cohen and kindred spirits, thought cannot be considered as a perception in the sense of Greek philosophy. But in this conception the inner permeation of the ego with the thought world, which the ego acquired through its own work, is such that this experience includes, at the same time, the awareness of its reality.

The connection with Greek philosophy is emphasized by these thinkers. Cohen expresses himself on this point as follows. "The relation that Parmenides forged as the identity of thinking and being must persist." Another thinker who also accepts this conception, Walter Kinkel, is convinced that "only thinking can know being, for both thinking and being are, fundamentally understood, one and the same." It is through this doctrine that Parmenides became the real creator of scientific idealism (*Idealism and Realism*).

It is also apparent from the presentations of these thinkers *how* the formulation of their thoughts presupposes the century-long effect of the thought evolution since the Greek civilization. In spite of the fact that these thinkers start from Kant, which could have fostered in them the opinion that thought lives only within the soul, outside true reality, the supporting power of thought exerts itself in them. This thought has gone beyond the Kantian limitation and it forces these thinkers who contemplate its nature to become convinced that thought itself is reality, and that it also leads the soul into reality if it acquires this element rightly in inner work and, equipped with it, seeks the way into the external world. In this philosophical mode of thinking thought proves intimately connected with the world contemplation of the self-conscious ego. The fundamental impulse of this thought tendency appears like a discovery of the possible service that the thought element can accomplish for the ego. We find in the followers of this philosophy views like these: "Only thinking itself can produce what may be accepted as being." "Being is the being of thinking" (Cohen).

Now the question arises: Can these philosophers expect of their thought experience, which is produced through the conscious work in the self-conscious ego, what the Greek philosopher expected of it when he accepted thought as a perception? If one believes to perceive thought, one can be of the opinion that it is the real world that reveals it. As the soul feels itself connected with thought as a perception, it can consider itself as belonging to the element of the world that is thought, indestructible thought, while the sense perception reveals only destructible entities. The part of the human being that is perceptible to the senses can then be supposed to be perishable, but what emerges in the human soul as thought makes it appear as a member of the spiritual, the true reality. Through such a view the soul can conceive that it belongs to a truly real world. This could be achieved by a modern world conception only if it could show that the thought experience not only leads *knowledge* into a true reality, but also develops the power to free the soul from the world of the senses and to place it into true reality. The doubts that arise in regard to this question cannot be counter-acted by the insight into the reality of the thought element if the latter is considered as acquired by perception actively produced through the work of the soul. For, from what could the certainty be derived that what the soul produces actively in the world of the senses, can also give it a real significance in a world that is not perceived by senses? It could be that the soul, to be sure, could procure a knowledge of reality through its actively produced thoughts, but that nevertheless the soul itself was not rooted in this reality. Also, this world conception merely points to a spiritual life, but it cannot prevent the unbiased observer from finding philosophical riddles at its end that demand answers and call for soul experiences for which this philosophy does not supply the foundations. It can arrive at the conviction that thought is real, but it cannot find through thought a guarantee for the reality of the soul.

* * *

The philosophical thinking at which *A. v. Leclaire* (born 1848), *Wilhelm Schuppe* (1836–1913), *Johannes Rehmke* (1848–1930), *von Schubert-Soldern* (born 1852), and others arrived, shows how philosophical inquiry can remain confined to the narrow circle of the self-conscious ego without finding a possibility to make the transition from this region into the world where this ego could link its own existence to a world reality. There are certain differences among these philosophies, but what is characteristic of all of them is that they all stress that everything man can count as belonging to his world must manifest itself within the realm of *his consciousness.* On the ground of their philosophy the thought cannot be conceived that would even presuppose anything about a territory of the world if the soul wanted to transcend with its conceptions beyond the realm of consciousness. Because the "ego" must comprise everything to which its knowledge extends within the folds of its consciousness, because it holds it within the consciousness, it therefore appears necessary to this view that the entire world *is within the limits* of this awareness. That the soul should ask itself: How do I stand with the possession of my consciousness in a world that is independent of this consciousness, is an impossibility for this philosophy. From its point of view, one would have to decide to give up all questions of this kind. One would have to become blind to the fact that there *are* inducements within the realm of the conscious soul life to look beyond that realm, just as in reading one does not look for the meaning *in* the forms that are visible on the paper, but to the significance that is expressed *by* them. As in reading, it is a question not of studying the *forms* of the letters as it is of no importance for the conveyed meaning to consider the nature of these forms themselves, so it could be irrelevant for an insight into true reality that within the sphere of the "ego" everything capable of being known has the character of consciousness.

The philosophy of *Carl du Prel* (1839–99) stands as an opposite pole to this philosophical opinion. He is one of the spirits who have deeply felt the insufficiency of the opinion that considers the natural scientific mode of conception to which so many people have grown accustomed to be the only possible form of world explanation. He points out that this mode of conception unconsciously sins against its own statements, for natural science must admit on the basis of its own results

> that we never perceive the objective processes of nature but rather their effect on us, not vibrations of the ether but light, not air vibrations but sounds. We have then, so to speak, a subjectively falsified world picture, but this does not interfere with our practical orientation because this falsification shows no individual differences and proceeds in a constant manner and according to law. . . . Materialism itself has proved through natural science that the world transcends beyond our senses. It has undermined its own foundation and it has sawed off the branch on which it had been sitting. As a philosophy, however, it still continues to sit on that branch. Materialism, therefore, has no right at all to call itself a philosophy. . . . It has only the justification of a branch of knowledge; furthermore, the world, the object of its study, is a world of mere appearance. To try to build a world conception on this foundation is an obvious self-contradiction. The real world is entirely different, qualitatively as well as quantitatively, from the one that is known to materialism, and only the real world can be the object of a philosophy. (Carl du Prel, *The Riddle of Man.*)

Such objections are necessarily caused by the materialistically colored mode of thought of natural science. Its weakness is noticed by many people who share the point of view of du Prel. The latter can be considered as a representative of a pronounced trend of modern philosophy. What is characteristic of this trend is the way in which it tries to penetrate into the realm of the *real* world. This way still shows the after-effect of the natural scientific mode of conception, although the latter is at the same time most violently criticized. Natural science starts from the facts that are accessible to the sensory consciousness. It finds itself forced to refer to a supersensible element, for only the light is sensually perceptible, not the vibrations of the ether. The vibrations then belong to a realm that is, at least, extra-sensory in its nature. But has natural science the right to speak of an extra-sensory element? It means to *limit* its investigations to the realm of sense perceptions. Is anyone justified to speak of supersensible elements who restricts his scientific endeavors to the results of the consciousness that is bound to the senses and therefore to the body?

Du Prel wants to grant this right of investigating the supersensible only to a thinker who seeks the nature of the human soul outside the realm of the senses. What he considers as the chief demand in this direction is the necessity to demonstrate manifestations of the soul that prove the soul is also active when it is not bound to the body. Through the body the soul develops its *sensual consciousness.* In the phenomena of hypnotism, hypnotic suggestion and somnambulism, it becomes apparent that the soul is active when the sensual consciousness is eliminated. The soul life, therefore, extends further than the realm of consciousness. It is here that du Prel arrives at the diametrically opposite position to those of the characterized philosophers of the all-embracing consciousness who believe that the limits of consciousness define at the same time the entire realm of philosophy. For du Prel, the nature of the soul is to be sought *outside* the circle of this consciousness. If, according to him, we observe the soul when it is active without the usual means of the senses, we have the proof that it is of a supersensible nature.

Among the means through which this can be done, du Prel and many others count, besides the observation of the above-mentioned "abnormal" psychic phenomena, also the phenomena of spiritualism. It is not necessary to dwell here on du Prel's opinion concerning this field, for what constitutes the mainspring of his view becomes apparent also if one considers only his attitude toward hypnotism, hypnotic suggestion and somnambulism. Whoever wants to prove the spiritual nature of the human soul cannot limit himself to showing that the soul has to refer to a supersensible world in its cognitive process. For natural science could answer that it does not follow that the soul is itself *rooted* in the supersensible realm because it has a *knowledge* of a supersensible world. It could very well be that knowledge of the supersensible could also be dependent on the activity of the body and thus *be of significance* only for a soul that is bound to a body. It is for this reason that du Prel feels it necessary to show that the soul not only *knows* the supersensible while it is itself bound to the body, but that it *experiences* the supersensible while it is outside the body. With this view, he also arms himself against objections that can be raised from the viewpoint of the natural scientific mode of thinking against the conceptions of Eucken, Dilthey, Cohen, Kinkel and other defenders of a knowledge of a spiritual world. He is, however, not protected against the doubts that must be raised against his own procedure.

Although it is true that the soul can find an access to the supersensible only if it can show how it is itself active *outside* the sensual realm, the emancipation of the soul from the sensual world is not assured by the phenomena of hypnotism, somnambulism and hypnotic suggestion, nor by all other processes to which du Prel refers for this purpose. In regard to all these phenomena it can be said that the philosopher who wants to explain them still proceeds only with the means of his ordinary consciousness. If this consciousness is to be useless for a real explanation of the world, how can its explanations, which are applied to the phenomena *according to the conditions of this consciousness*, be of any decisive significance for these phenomena? What is peculiar in du Prel is the fact that he directs his attention to certain facts that point to a supersensible element, but that he, nevertheless, wants to remain entirely on the ground of the natural scientific mode of thought when he explains those facts. But should it not be necessary for the soul to enter the supersensible in its *mode of thinking* when the supersensible becomes the *object* of its interest? Du Prel looks at the supersensible, but *as an observer* he remains within the realm of the sensual world. If he did not want to do this, he would have to demand that only a hypnotized person can say the right things concerning his experiences under hypnosis, that only in the state of somnambulism could knowledge concerning the supersensible be acquired and that what the not-hypnotized, the non-somnambulist must think concerning these phenomena is of no validity. If we follow this thought consistently, we arrive at an impossibility. If one speaks of a transposition of the soul outside the realm of the senses into another form of existence, one must intend to acquire the knowledge of this existence *within* that other region. Du Prel points at a path that must be taken in order to gain access to the supersensible. But he leaves the question open regarding the means that are to be used on this path.

* * *

A new thought current has been stimulated through the transformation of fundamental physical concepts that has been attempted by *Albert Einstein* (1879–1955). The attempt is of significance also for the development of philosophy. Physics previously followed its given phenomena by thinking of them as being spread out in empty three dimensional space and in one dimensional time. Space and time were supposed to exist outside things and events. They were, so to speak, self-dependent, rigid quantities. For things, distances were measured in space. For events, duration was determined in time. Distance and duration belong, according to this conception, to space and time, not to things and events. This conception is opposed by the theory of relativity introduced by Einstein. For this theory, the distance between two things is something that belongs to those things themselves. As a thing has other properties it has also the property of being at a certain distance from a second thing.

Besides these relations that are given by the nature of things there is no such thing as space. The assumption of space makes a geometry that is thought for this space, but this same geometry can be applied to the world of things. It arises in a mere thought world. Things have to obey the laws of this geometry. One can say that the events and situations of the world must follow the laws that are established *before* the observation of things. This geometry now is dethroned by the theory of relativity. What exists are only things and they stand in relations to one another that present themselves geometrically. Geometry thus becomes a part of physics, but then one can no longer maintain that their laws can be established *before* the observation of the things. No thing has any *place* in space but only distances relative to other things.

The same is assumed for time. No process takes place at a definite time; it happens in a time-distance relative to another event. In this way, temporal distances in the relation of things and spatial intervals become homogenous and flow together. Time becomes a fourth dimension that is of the same nature as the three dimensions of space. A process in a thing can be determined only as something that takes place in a temporal and spatial distance relative to other events. The motion of a thing becomes something that can be thought only in relation to other things.

It is now expected that only this conception will produce unobjectionable explanations of certain physical processes while such processes lead to contradictory thoughts if one assumes the existence of an independent space and independent time.

If one considers that for many thinkers a science of nature was previously considered to be something that can be mathematically demonstrated, one finds in the theory of relativity nothing less than an attempt to declare any real science of nature null and void. For just this was regarded as the scientific nature of mathematics that it could determine the laws of space and time without reference to the observation of nature. Contrary to this view, it is now maintained that the things and processes of nature *themselves* determine the relations of space and time. They are to supply the mathematical element. The only certain element is surrendered to the uncertainty of space and time observations.

According to this view, every thought of an essential reality that manifests its nature in existence is precluded. Everything is only in relation to something else.

Insofar as man considers himself within the world of natural things and events, he will find it impossible to escape the conclusions of this theory of relativity. But if he does not want to lose himself in mere relativities, in what may be called an impotence of his inner life, if he wants to experience his own entity, he must not seek what is "substantial in itself" in the realm of *nature* but in *transcending nature*, in the realm of the spirit.

It will not be possible to evade the theory of relativity for the physical world, but precisely this fact will drive us to a knowledge of the spirit. What is significant about the theory of relativity is the fact that it proves the necessity of a science of the spirit that is to be sought in spiritual ways, independent of the observation of *nature*. That the theory of relativity forces us to think in this way constitutes its value within the development of world conception.

* * *

It was the intention of this book to describe the development of what may be called philosophical activity in the proper sense of the word. The endeavor of such spirits as Richard Wagner, Leo Tolstoi and others had for this reason to be left unconsidered, significant as discussion of their contribution must appear when it is a question of following the currents that lead from philosophy into our general spiritual culture.

CHAPTER VIII

*A Brief Outline
of an Approach to Anthroposophy*

If one observes how, up to the present time, the philosophical world conceptions take form, one can see under-currents in the search and endeavor of the various thinkers, of which they themselves are not aware but by which they are instinctively moved. In these currents there are forces at work that give direction and often specific form to the ideas expressed by these thinkers. Although they do not want to focus their attention on the forces directly, what they have to say often appears as if driven by hidden forces, which they are unwilling to acknowledge and from which they recoil. Forces of this kind live in the thought worlds of Dilthey, Eucken and Cohen. They are led by cognitive powers by which they are unconsciously dominated but that do not find a conscious development within their thought structures.

Security and certainty of knowledge is being sought in many philosophical systems, and Kant's ideas are more or less taken as its point of departure. The outlook of natural science determines, consciously or unconsciously, the process of thought formation. But it is dimly felt by many that the source of knowledge of the external world must be sought in the self-conscious soul. Almost all of these thinkers are dominated by the question: How can the self-conscious soul be led to regard its inner experiences as a true manifestation of reality? The ordinary world of sense perception has become "illusion" because the self-conscious ego has, in the course of philosophical development, found itself more and more isolated with its subjective experiences. It has arrived at the point where it regards even sense perception merely as inner experience that is powerless to assure being and permanence for them in the world of reality. It is felt how much depends on finding a point of support within the self-conscious ego. But the search stimulated by this feeling only leads to conceptions that do not provide the means of submerging with the ego into a world that provides satisfactory support for existence.

To explain this fact, one must look at the attitude toward the reality of the external world taken by a soul that has detached itself from that reality in the course of its philosophical development. This soul feels itself surrounded by a world of which it first becomes aware through the senses. But then it also becomes conscious of its own activity, of its own inner creative experience. The soul feels, as an irrefutable truth, that no light, no color can be revealed without the eye's sensitivity for light and color. Thus, it becomes aware of something creative in this activity of the eye. But if the eye produces the color by its spontaneous creation, as it must be assumed in such a philosophy, the question arises: Where do I find something that exists in itself, that does not owe its existence to my own creative power? If even the manifestations of the senses are nothing but results of the activity of the soul, must this not be true to even a higher degree with our thinking, through which we strive for conceptions of a true reality? Is this thinking not condemned to produce pictures that spring from the character of the soul life but can never provide a sure approach to the sources of existence? Questions of this kind emerge everywhere in the development of modern philosophy.

It will be impossible to find the way out of the confusion resulting from these questions as long as the belief is maintained that the world revealed by the senses constitutes a complete, finished and self-dependent reality that must be investigated in order to know its inner nature. The human soul can arrive at its insights only through a spontaneous inner creativity. This conviction has been described in a previous chapter of this book, "The World as Illusion," and in connection with the presentation of Hamerling's thoughts. Having reached this conviction, it is difficult to overcome a certain impasse of knowledge as long as one thinks that the world of the senses contains the real basis of its existence *within itself* and that one therefore has to copy with the inner activity of the soul what lies outside.

This impasse will be overcome only by accepting the fact that, by its very nature, sense perception does not present a finished self-contained reality, but an unfinished, incomplete reality, or a half-reality, as it were.

As soon as one presupposes that a full reality is gained through perceptions of the sensory world, one is forever prevented from finding the answer to the question: What has the creative mind to add to this reality in the act of cognition? By necessity one shall have to sustain the Kantian option: Man must consider his knowledge to be the inner product of his own mind; he cannot regard it as a process that is capable of revealing a true reality. If reality lies *outside* the soul, then the soul cannot produce anything that corresponds to this reality, and the result is merely a product of the soul's own organization.

The situation is entirely changed as soon as it is realized that the human soul does not deviate from reality in its creative effort for knowledge, but that prior to any cognitive activity the soul conjures up a world that is *not* real. Man is so placed in the world that by the nature of his being he changes things from what they really are. Hamerling is partly right when he says:

> Certain stimuli produce the odor within our organ of smell. The rose, therefore, has no fragrance if nobody smells it. . . . If this, dear reader, does not seem plausible to you, if your mind stirs like a shy horse when it is confronted with this fact, do not bother to read another line; leave this book and all others that deal with philosophical things unread, for you lack the ability that is necessary for this

purpose, that is, to apprehend a fact without bias and to adhere to it in your thoughts. (Compare pages 393ff. of this volume.)

How the sensory world *appears* when man is confronted with it, depends without a doubt on the nature of the soul. Does it not follow then that this appearance of the world is a *product of man's soul*? An unbiased observation shows, however, that the unreal character of the external sense world is caused by the fact that when man is directly confronted by things of the world, he suppresses something that really belongs to them. If he unfolds a creative inner life that lifts from the depths of his soul the forces that lie dormant in them, he adds something to the part perceived by the senses and thereby turns a half-reality to its entirety. It is due to the nature of the soul that, at its first contact with things, it *extinguishes* something that belongs to them. For this reason, things appear to the senses not as they are in reality but as they are modified by the soul. Their delusive character (or their mere appearance) is caused by the fact that the soul has deprived them of something that really belongs to them.

Inasmuch as man does not merely observe things, he adds something to them in the process of knowledge that reveals their full reality. The mind does not add anything to things in the process of cognition that would have to be considered as an unreal element, but prior to the process of knowledge it has deprived these things of something that belongs to their true reality. It will be the task of philosophy to realize that the world accessible to man is an "illusion" *before it is approached in the process of cognition.* This process, however, leads the way toward a full understanding of reality. The knowledge that man creates during the process of cognition seems to be an inner manifestation of the soul only because he must, before the act of cognition, reject what comes from the nature of things. He cannot see at first the real nature of things when he encounters them in mere observation. In the process of knowledge he unveils what was first concealed. If he regards as a reality what he had at first perceived, he will now realize that he has added the results of his cognitive activity to reality. As soon as he recognizes that what was apparently produced by himself has to be sought in the things themselves, that he merely failed to see it previously, he will then find that the process of knowing is a real process by which the soul progressively unites with world reality. Through it, it expands its inner isolated experience to the experience of the world.

In a short work, *Truth and Science*, published in 1892, the author of the present book made a first attempt to prove philosophically what has been briefly described. Perspectives are indicated in this book that are necessary to the philosophy of the present age if it is to overcome the obstacles it has encountered in its modern development. A philosophical point of view is outlined in this essay in the following words:

> The initial form in which reality confronts the ego is not its true manifestation but the final form, which the ego fashions out of it, is. The first form is altogether without significance for the objective world; it is of importance only as a basis for the processes of cognition. Therefore, it is not the form of the world that is presented by theory that must be considered subjective but the one the ego encounters initially as in mere perception.

A further exposition of this point of view is given in the author's later philosophical work, *The Philosophy of Freedom* (1894) (translated also with the title, *The Philosophy of Spiritual Activity*). There an attempt is made to give the philosophical foundations for a conception that was outlined in *Truth and Science*.

> It is not due to the objects that they are given to us at first without their corresponding concept, but to our mental organization. Our whole being functions in such a way that from every real thing the relevant elements come to us from two sources, from perceiving and from thinking. The way I am organized for apprehending the things has nothing to do with the nature of the things themselves. The gap between perceiving and thinking exists only from the moment that I, as a spectator, confront the things.

And later on it is stated:

The percept is that part of reality that is given objectively; the concept the part that is given subjectively, through intuition. Our mental organization tears the reality apart into these two factors. The one factor presents itself to perception, the other to intuition. Only the union of the two, that is, the percept fitting systematically into the universe, constitutes the full reality. If we take mere percepts by themselves we have no reality but rather disconnected chaos. If we take by itself the law and order connecting the percepts then we have nothing but abstract concepts. Reality is not contained in the abstract concept. It is, however, contained in thoughtful observation, which does not one-sidedly consider either concept or percept alone, but rather the union of the two.

In accepting this point of view we shall be able to think of mental life and of reality as united in the self-conscious ego. This is the conception toward which philosophical development has tended since the Greek era and that has shown its first distinctly recognizable traces in the world conception of Goethe. The awareness arises that this self-conscious ego does not experience itself as isolated and divorced from the objective world, but its detachment from this world is experienced merely as an illusion of its consciousness. This isolation can be overcome if man gains the insight that at a certain stage of his development he must give a provisional form to his ego in order to suppress from his consciousness the forces that unite him with the world. If these forces exerted their influences in his consciousness without interruption, he would never have developed a strong, independent self-consciousness. He would be incapable of experiencing himself as a self-conscious ego. The development of self-consciousness, therefore, actually depends on the fact that the mind is given the opportunity to perceive the world without that part of reality that is *extinguished* by the self-conscious ego prior to an act of cognition.

The world forces belonging to this part of reality withdraw into obscurity in order to allow the self-conscious ego to shine forth in full power. The ego must realize that it owes its self-knowledge to a fact that spreads a veil over the knowledge of the world. It follows that everything that stimulates the soul to a vigorous, energetic experience of the ego, conceals at the same time the deeper foundations in which this ego has its roots. All knowledge acquired by the ordinary consciousness tends to strengthen the self-conscious ego. Man feels himself as a self-conscious ego through the fact that he perceives an external world with his senses, that he experiences himself as being outside this external world and that, at a certain stage of scientific investigation, he feels himself in relation to this external world in such a way that it appears to him as "illusion." Were it not so, the self-conscious ego would not emerge. If, therefore, in the act of knowledge one attempts merely to copy what is observed before knowledge begins, one does not arrive at a true experience of *full reality,* but only at an image of a *"half reality."*

Once this is admitted to be the situation, one can no longer look for the answer of the riddles of philosophy within the experiences of the soul that appear on the level of ordinary consciousness. It is the function of this consciousness to strengthen the self-conscious ego. To achieve this it must cast a veil over the connection of the ego with the objective world, and it therefore cannot show how the soul is connected with the true world. This explains why a method of knowledge that applies the means of the natural scientific or similar modes of conception must always arrive at a point where its efforts break down. This failing of many modern thinkers has previously been pointed out in this book, for, in the final analysis, all scientific endeavor employs the same mode of thinking that serves to detach the self-conscious ego from the true reality. The strength and greatness of modern science, especially of natural science, is based on the unrestrained application of this method.

Several philosophers such as Dilthey, Eucken and others, direct philosophical investigation toward the self-observation of the soul. But what they observe are those experiences of the soul that form the basis for the self-conscious ego. Thus, they do not penetrate to the sources in which the experiences of the soul originate. These sources cannot be found where the soul first observes itself on the level of ordinary consciousness. If the soul is to reach these sources, it must go beyond this ordinary consciousness. It must experience something in itself that ordinary consciousness cannot give to it. To ordinary thinking, such an experience appears at first like sheer nonsense. The soul is to experience itself *knowingly* in an element without carrying its consciousness into that element. One is to transcend consciousness and yet be conscious! But in spite of all this, we shall either continue to get nowhere, or we shall have to open new aspects that will reveal the above mentioned "absurdity" to be only apparently so since it really indicates the direction in which we must look for help to solve the riddles of philosophy.

One will have to recognize that the path into the "inner region of the soul" must be entirely different from the one that is taken by many philosophies of modern times. As long as soul experiences are taken the way they present themselves to ordinary consciousness, one will not reach down into the depths of the soul. One will be left merely with what these depths release. Such is the case with Eucken's world conception. It is necessary to penetrate below the surface of the soul. This is, however, not possible by means of the ordinary experiences. The strength of these rests precisely in the fact that they remain in the realm of the ordinary consciousness. The means to penetrate deeper into the soul can be found if one directs one's attention to something that is, to be sure, also at work in the ordinary consciousness, but does not enter it while it is active.

While man thinks, his consciousness is focused on his thoughts. He wants to conceive something by means of these thoughts; he wants to think correctly in the ordinary sense. He can, however, also direct his attention to something else. He can concentrate his attention on the activity of thinking as such. He can, for instance, place into the center of his consciousness a thought that refers to nothing external, a thought that is conceived like a symbol that has no connection to something external. It is now possible to hold onto such a thought for a certain length of time. One can be entirely absorbed by the concentration on this thought. The important thing with this exercise is not that one lives in thoughts but that one experiences the activity of thinking. In this way, the soul breaks away from an activity in which it is engaged in ordinary thinking.

If such an inner exercise is continued long enough, it will become gradually apparent to the soul that it has now become involved in experiences that will separate it from all those processes of thinking and ideation that are bound to the physical organs. A similar result can be obtained from the activities of feeling and willing and even for sensation, the perception of external things. One can only be successful with this approach if one is not afraid to admit to oneself that self-knowledge cannot be gained by mere introspection, but by concentrating on the inner life that can be revealed only through these exercises. Through continued practice of the soul, that is, by holding the attention on the inner activity of thinking, feeling and willing, it is possible for these "experiences" to become "condensed." In this state of "condensation" they reveal their inner nature, which cannot be perceived in the ordinary consciousness. It is through such exercises that one discovers how our soul forces must be so "attenuated" or weakened in producing our ordinary form of consciousness, that they become imperceptible in this state of "attenuation." The soul exercises referred to consist in the *unlimited increase* of faculties that are also known to the ordinary consciousness but never reach such a state of concentration. The faculties are those of *attention* and of *loving surrender to the content of the soul's experience.* To attain the indicated aim, these abilities must be increased to such a degree that they function as entirely new soul forces.

If one proceeds in this manner, one arrives at a real inner experience that by its very nature is independent of bodily conditions. This is a life of the spirit that must not be confused with what Dilthey and Eucken call the spiritual world. For what *they* call the spiritual world is, after all, experienced by man when he depends on his physical organs. The spiritual life that is here referred to does not exist for a soul that is bound to the body.

One of the first experiences that follows the attainment of this new spiritual life is a true insight into the nature of the ordinary mental life. This is actually not produced by the body but proceeds outside the body. When I see a color, when I hear a sound, I experience the color and the sound not as a result of my body, but I am connected with the color, with the sound, as a self-conscious ego, outside my body. My body has the task to function in a way that can be compared with the action of a mirror. If, in my ordinary consciousness, I only have a mental connection with a color, I cannot perceive it because of the nature of this consciousness, just as I cannot see my own face when I look out into space. But if I look into a mirror, I perceive this face as part of a body. Unless I stand in front of the mirror, I *am* the body and experience myself as such. Standing in front of the mirror, I perceive my body as a reflection. It is like this also with our sense perceptions, although we must, of course, be aware of the insufficiency of the analogy. I live with a color *outside* my body; through the activity of my body, that is, my eye and my nervous system, this color is transformed for me into a conscious perception. The human body is not the producer of perceptions and of mental life in general, but a mirroring device of psychic and spiritual processes that take place outside the body.

Such a view places the theory of knowledge on a promising basis. In a lecture called, *The Psychological Foundations and Epistemological Position of Spiritual Science*, delivered before the Philosophical Congress in Bologna on April 18, 1911, the author of this book gave the following account of a view that was then forming in his mind.

> On the basis of epistemology one can reach a conception of the ego only if one does not think of it as being inside the bodily organization and as receiving impression "from outside." One should conceive this "ego" as having its being *within* the general order (*Gesetzmässigkeit*) of the things themselves, and regard the organization of the body merely as a sort of mirror through which the organic processes of the body reflect back to the ego what this ego perceives outside the physical body as it lives and weaves within the true essence of the world.

During sleep the mirror-like relation between body and soul is interrupted; the "ego" *lives* only in the sphere of the spirit. For the ordinary consciousness, however, mental life does not exist as long as the body does not reflect the experiences. Sleep, therefore, is an unconscious process. The exercises mentioned above and other similar ones establish a consciousness that differs from the ordinary consciousness. In this way, the faculty is developed not merely to *have* purely spiritual experiences, but to *strengthen* these experiences to such a degree that they become spiritually perceptible without the aid of the body, and that they become reflected within themselves. It is only in an experience of this kind that the soul can obtain true self-knowledge and become consciously aware of its own being. Real experiences that do not belong to the sense world, but to one in which the soul weaves and has its being, now rise in the manner in which memory brings back experiences of the past. It is quite natural that the followers of many modern philosophies will believe that the world that thus rises up belongs in the realms of error, illusion, hallucination, auto-suggestion, etc. To this objection one can only answer that a serious spiritual endeavor, working in the indicated way, will discipline the mind to a point where it will clearly differentiate illusion from spiritual reality, just as a *healthy* mind can distinguish a product of fantasy from a concrete perception. It will be futile to seek theoretical proofs for this spiritual world, but such proofs also do not exist for the reality of the world of perceptions. In both cases, actual *experience* is the only true judge.

What keeps many men from undertaking the step that, according to this view, can alone solve the riddles of philosophy, is the fear that they might be led thereby into a realm of unclear mysticism. Unless one has from the beginning an inclination toward unclear mysticism, one will, in following the described path, gain access to a world of spiritual experience that is as crystal clear as the structures of mathematical ideas. If one is, however, inclined to seek the spiritual in the "dark unknown," in the "inexplicable," one will get nowhere, either as an adherent or as an opponent of the views described here.

One can easily understand why these views will be rejected by personalities who consider the methods used by natural science for obtaining knowledge of the sense world as the only true ones. But whoever overcomes such one-sidedness will be able to realize that the genuinely scientific way of thinking constitutes the real basis for the method that is here described. The ideas that have been shown in this book to be those of the modern scientific method, present the best subject matter for mental exercises in which the soul can immerse itself, and on which it can concentrate in order to free itself from its bondage to the body. Whoever uses these natural scientific ideas in the manner that has been outlined above, will find that the thoughts that first seem to be meant to depict only natural processes will really set the soul free from the body. Therefore, the spiritual science that is here referred to must be seen as a continuation of the scientific way of thinking provided it is inwardly experienced in the right way.

* * *

The true nature of the human soul can be *experienced directly* if one seeks it in the characterized way. In the Greek era the development of the philosophical outlook led to the birth of thought. Later development led through the experience of thought to the experience of the self-conscious ego. Goethe strove for experiences of the self-conscious ego, which, although actively produced by the human soul, at the same time place this soul in the realm of a reality that is inaccessible to the senses. Goethe stands on this ground when he strives for an idea of the plant that cannot be perceived by the senses but that contains the supersensible nature of all plants, making it possible, with the aid of this idea, to invent new plants that would have their own life.

Hegel regarded the experience of thought as a "standing in the true essence of the world"; for him the world of thoughts became the inner essence of the world. An unbiased observation of philosophical development shows that thought experience was, to be sure, the element through which the self-conscious ego was to be placed on its own foundation. But it shows also that it is necessary to go beyond a life in mere thoughts in order to arrive at a form of inner experience that leads beyond the ordinary consciousness. For Hegel's thought experience still takes place within the field of this ordinary consciousness.

In this way, a view of a reality is opened up for the soul that is inaccessible to the senses. What is experienced in the soul through the penetration into *this* reality, appears as the true entity of the soul. How is it related to the external world that is experienced by means of the body? The soul that has been thus freed from its body feels itself to be weaving in an element of soul and spirit. It knows that also in its ordinary life it is outside that body, which merely acts like a mirror in making its experiences perceptible. Through this experience the soul's spiritual experience is heightened to a point where the reality of a new element is revealed to the soul.

To Dilthey and Eucken the spiritual world is the sum total of the cultural experiences of humanity. If this world is seen as the only accessible spiritual world, one does not stand on a ground firm enough to be comparable to the method of natural science. For the conception of natural science, the world is so ordered that the physical human being in his individual existence appears as a unit toward which all other natural processes and beings point. The cultural world is what is created by this human being. That world, however, is not an individual entity of a higher nature than the individuality of the human being.

The spiritual science that the author of this book has in mind points to a form of experience that the soul can have independent from the body, and in this experience an individual entity is revealed. It emerges like a higher human nature for whom the physical man is like a tool. The being that feels itself as set free, through spiritual experience, from the physical body, is a spiritual human entity that is as much at home in a spiritual world as the physical body in the physical world. As the soul thus experiences its spiritual nature, it is also aware of the fact that it stands in a certain relation to the body. The body appears, on the one hand, as a cast of the spiritual entity; it can be compared to the shell of a snail that is like a counter-picture of the shape of the snail. On the other hand, the spirit-soul entity appears in the body like the sum total of the forces in the plant, which, after it has grown into leaf and blossom, contract into the seed in order to prepare a new plant. One cannot experience the inner spiritual man without knowing that he contains something that will develop into a new physical man. This new human being, while living within the physical organism, has collected forces through experience that could not unfold as long as they were encased in that organism. This body has, to be sure, enabled the soul to have experiences in connection with the external world that make the inner spiritual man different from what he was before he began life in the physical body. But this body is, as it were, too rigidly organized for being transformed by the inner spiritual man according to the pattern of the new experiences. Thus there remains hidden in the human shell a spiritual being that contains the disposition of a new man.

Thoughts such as these can only be briefly indicated here. They point to a spiritual science that is essentially constructed after the model of natural science. In elaborating this spiritual science one will have to proceed more or less like the botanist when he observes a plant, the formation of its root, the growth of its stem and its leaves, and its development into blossom and fruit. In the fruit he discovers the seed of the new plant-life. As he follows the development of a plant he looks for its origin in the seed formed by the previous plant. The investigator of spiritual science will trace the process in which a human life, apart from its external manifestation, develops also an inner being. He will find that external experiences die off like the leaves and the flowers of a plant. Within the inner being, however, he will discover a spiritual kernel, which conceals within itself the potentiality of a new life. In the infant entering life through birth he will see the return of a soul that left the world previously through the gate of death. He will learn to observe that what is handed down by heredity to the individual man from his ancestors is merely the material that is worked upon by the spiritual man in order to bring into physical existence what has been prepared seedlike in a preceding life.

Seen from the viewpoint of this world conception, many facts of psychology will appear in a new light. A great number of examples could be mentioned here; it will suffice to point out only one. One can observe how the human soul is transformed by experiences that represent, in a certain sense, repetitions of earlier experiences. If somebody has read an important book in his twentieth year and reads it again in his fortieth, he experiences it as if he were a different person. If he asks without bias for the reason for this fact, he will find that what he learned from his reading twenty years previous has continued to live in him and has become a part of his nature. He has within him the forces that live in the book, and he finds them again when he re-reads the book at the age of forty. The same holds true with our life experiences. They become part of man himself. They live in his "ego." But it is also apparent that within the limits of one life this inner strengthening of the higher man must remain in the realm of his spirit and soul nature. Yet one can also find that this higher human being strives to become strong enough to find expression in his physical nature. The rigidity of the body prevents this from happening within a single life span. But in the central core of man there lives the potential predisposition that, together with the fruits of one life, will form a new human life in the same way that the seed of a new plant lives in the plant.

Moreover, it must be realized that following the entry of the soul into an independent spirit world the results of this world are raised into consciousness in the same way that the past rises into memory. But these realities are seen as extending beyond the span of an individual life. The content of my present consciousness represents the results of my earlier physical experiences; so, too, a soul that has gone through the indicated exercises faces the whole of its physical experience and the particular configuration of its body as originating from the spirit-soul nature, whose existence preceded that of the body. This existence appears as a life in a purely spiritual world in which the soul lived before it could develop the germinal capacities of a preceding life into a new one. Only by closing one's mind to the obvious possibility that the faculties of the human soul are capable of development can one refuse to recognize the truthfulness of a person's testimony that shows that as a result of inner work one can really know of a spiritual world beyond the realm of ordinary consciousness. This knowledge leads to a spiritual apprehension of a world through which it becomes evident that the true being of the soul lies behind ordinary experiences. It also becomes clear that this soul being survives death just as the plant seed survives the decay of the plant. The insight is gained that the human soul goes through repeated lives on earth and that in between these earthly lives it leads a purely spiritual existence.

This point of view brings reality to the assumption of a spiritual world. The human souls themselves carry into a later cultural epoch what they acquired in a former. One can readily observe how the inner dispositions of the soul develop if one refrains from arbitrarily ascribing this development merely to the laws of physical heredity. In the spiritual world of which Eucken and Dilthey speak the later phases of development always follow from the immediately preceding ones. Into this sequence of events are placed human souls who bring with them the results of their preceding lives in the form of their inner soul disposition. They must, however, acquire in a process of learning what developed in the earthly world of culture and civilization while they were in a purely spiritual state of existence.

A historical account cannot do full justice to the thoughts exposed here. I would refer anyone who seeks more information to my writings on spiritual science. These writings attempted to give, in a general manner, the world conception that is *outlined* in the present book. Even so, I believe that it is possible to recognize from it that this world conception rests on a serious philosophical foundation. On this basis it strives to gain access to a world that opens up to sense-free observation acquired by inner work.

One of the teachers of this world conception is the history of philosophy itself. It shows that the course of philosophical thought tends toward a conception that cannot be acquired in a state of ordinary consciousness. The accounts of many representative thinkers show how they attempt in various ways to comprehend the self-conscious ego with the help of the ordinary consciousness. A theoretical exposition of why the means of this ordinary consciousness must lead to unsatisfactory results does not belong to a historical account. But the historical facts show distinctly that the ordinary consciousness, however we may look at it, cannot solve the questions it nevertheless must raise. This final chapter was written to show why the ordinary consciousness and the usual scientific mind lack the means to solve such questions. This chapter was meant to describe what the characterized world conceptions were unconsciously striving for. From one certain point of view this last chapter no longer belongs to the history of philosophy, but from another point of view, its justification is quite clear. The message of this book is that a world conception based on spiritual science is virtually demanded by the development of modern philosophy as an answer to the questions it raises.

To become aware of this one must consider specific instances of this philosophical development. Franz Brentano in his *Psychology* points out how philosophy was deflected from the treatment of the deeper riddles of the soul (compare page 390 of this volume). He writes, "Apparent as the necessity for a restriction of the field of investigation is in this direction, it is perhaps no more than only apparent." David Hume was most emphatically opposed to the metaphysicists who maintained that they had found within themselves a carrier for all psychic conditions. He says:

> For my part, when I enter most intimately into what I call myself, I always stumble on some particular perception or other, of heat or cold, light or shade, love or hatred, pain or pleasure. I can never catch *myself* at any time without a perception and never can observe anything but perceptions. When my perceptions are removed for any time, as by sound sleep, so long am I insensible of *myself* and may truly be said not to exist. (*Treatise of Human Nature*, Part IV, Sect. 6.)

Hume only knows the kind of psychological observation that would approach the soul without any inner effort. An observation of this kind simply cannot penetrate to the nature of the soul. Brentano takes up Hume's statement and says, "This same man, Hume, nevertheless, observes that all proofs for the immortality of the soul possess the same power of persuasion as the opposing traditional views." But here we must add that only faith, and not knowledge, can support Hume's view that the soul contains nothing more than what he finds there. For how could any continuity be guaranteed for what Hume finds as the content of the soul? Brentano continues by saying:

> Although it is obvious that a denial of a soul substance eliminates the possibility to speak of an immortality in the proper sense of the word, it is still not true that the question of immortality loses all meaning if a supporting substance for psychic activity is denied.

This becomes immediately evident if one considers that, with or without supporting substance, one cannot deny that our psychic life here on earth has a certain continuity. If one rejects the idea of a soul substance, one has the right to assume that this continuity does not depend on a supporting substance. The question as to whether our psychic life would continue after the destruction of our body will be no less meaningful for such a thinker than it is for others. It is really quite inconsistent if thinkers of this school reject the essential question of immortality as meaningless also in this important sense on the basis of the above-mentioned reason. It should then, however, be referred to as the immortality of life rather than that of the soul. (Brentano, *Psychology from the Empirical Standpoint*, Bk. I, Chap. 1.)

This opinion of Brentano's, however, is without support if the world conception outlined above is rejected. For where can we find grounds for the survival of psychic phenomena after the dissolution of the body if we want to restrict ourselves to the ordinary consciousness? *This* consciousness can only last as long as its reflector, the physical body, exists. What may survive the loss of the body cannot be designated as substance; it must be *another* form of consciousness. But this other consciousness can be discovered only through the inner activity that frees the soul from the body. This shows us that the soul can experience consciousness even without the mediation of the body. Through such activity and with the help of *supersensible perception,* the soul will experience the condition of the complete loss of the body. It finds that it had been the body, itself, that obscured that higher consciousness. While the soul is incarnated, the body has such a strong effect on the soul that this other consciousness cannot become active. This becomes a matter of direct experience when the soul exercises indicated in this chapter are successfully carried out. The soul must then consciously suppress the forces that originate in the body and extinguish the body-free consciousness. This extinction can no longer take place after the dissolution of the body. It is the other consciousness, therefore, that passes through successive lives and through the purely spiritual existence between death and birth. From this point of view, there is reference to a nebulous soul substance. In terms that are comparable to ideas of natural science, the soul is shown how it continues its existence because in one life the seed of the next is prepared, as the seed is prepared in the plant. The present life is shown as the reason for a future life, and the true essence of what continues when death dissolves the body is brought to light.

Spiritual science as described here nowhere contradicts the methods of modern natural science. But science has to admit that with its methods one cannot gain insight into the realm of the spiritual. As soon as the existence of a consciousness other than the ordinary one is recognized, one will find that by it one is led to conceptions concerning the spiritual world that will give to it a cohesion similar to that that natural science gives to the physical world.

It will be of importance to eliminate the impression that this spiritual science has borrowed its insights from any older form of religion. One is easily misled to this view because the conception of reincarnation, for instance, is a tenet of certain creeds. For the modern investigator of spiritual science, there can be no borrowing from such creeds. He finds that the devotion to the exercises described above will lead to a consciousness that enters the spiritual world. As a result of this consciousness he learns that the soul has its standing in the spiritual world in the way previously described.

A study of the history of philosophy, beginning with the awakening of thought in Greek civilization, indicates the way that leads to the conviction that the true being of the soul can be found below the surface of ordinary experience. Thinking has proved to be the educator of the soul by leading it to the point at which it is alone with itself. This experience of solitude strengthens the soul whereby it is able to delve not only into its own being but also to reach into the deeper realities of the world. The spiritual science described in this chapter does not attempt to lead behind the world of the senses by using the means of ordinary consciousness, such as reflection and theorizing. It recognizes that the spiritual world must remain concealed from that consciousness and that the soul must, through its own inner transformation, rise into the supersensible world before it can become conscious of it.

In this way, the insight is also gained that the origin of moral impulses lies in the world that the soul perceives when it is free of the body. From there also the driving forces originate that do not stem from the physical nature of man but are meant to determine his actions independent from this nature.

When one becomes acquainted with the fact that the "ego" with its spiritual world lives outside the body and that it, therefore, carries the experiences of the external world to the physical body, one will find one's way to a truly spiritual understanding of the riddle of human destiny. A man's inner life is deeply connected with his experiences of destiny. Just consider the state of a man at the age of thirty. The real content of his inner being would be entirely different if he had lived a different kind of life in his preceding years. His "ego" is inconceivable without the experiences of these years. Even if they have struck him serious blows of fate, he has become what he is through them. They belong to the forces that are active in his "ego." They do not merely strike him from outside. As man lives in his soul and spirit with color that is perceptible only by means of its mirror-effect of the body, so he lives in union with his destiny. With color he is united in his soul life, but he can only perceive it when the body reflects it. Similarly, he becomes one with the effect of a stroke of destiny that results from a previous earth life, but he experiences this blow only inasmuch as the soul plunges *unconsciously* into events that spring from these causes. In his ordinary consciousness man does not know that his *will* is bound up with his destiny. In his newly acquired body-free consciousness he finds that he would be deprived of all initiative if that part of his soul that lives in the spiritual world had not willed its entire fate, down to the smallest details. We see that the riddles of human destiny cannot be solved merely by theorizing about them, but only by learning to understand how the soul grows together with its fate in an experience that proceeds beyond the *ordinary consciousness.* Thus, one will gradually realize that the causes for this or that stroke of destiny in the present life must be sought in a previous one. To the ordinary consciousness our fate does not appear in its true form. It takes its course as a result of previous earthly lives, which are hidden from ordinary consciousness. To realize one's deep connection with the events of former lives means at the same time that one becomes *reconciled* with one's destiny.

For a fuller coverage of the philosophical riddles like these, the author must refer to his other works on spiritual science. We can only mention the more important *results* of this science but not the specific ways and means by which it can become convincing.

Philosophy leads by its own paths to the insight that it must pass from a study of the world to an *experience* of it, because mere reflection cannot bring a satisfactory solution to all the riddles of life. This method of cognition is comparable to the seed of a plant. The seed can work in a twofold way when it becomes ripe. It can be used as human food or as seed for a new plant. If it is examined with respect to its usefulness, it must be looked at in a way different from the observation that follows the cycle of reproducing a new plant.

Similarly, man's spiritual experiences can choose either of two roads. On the one hand, it serves the contemplation of the external world. Examined from this point of view, one will be inclined to develop a world conception that asks above all things: How does our knowledge penetrate to the nature of things? What knowledge can we derive from a study of the nature of things? To ask these questions is like investigating the nutritional value of the seed. But it is also possible to focus attention on the experiences of the soul that are not diverted by outside impressions, but lead the soul from one level of being on to another. These experiences are seen as an implanted driving force in which one recognizes a higher man who uses this life to prepare for the next. One arrives at the insight that this is the fundamental impulse of all human soul experience and that *knowledge* is related to it as the use of the seed of the plant for food is comparable to the development of the grain into a new plant. If we fail to understand this fact, we shall live under the illusion that we could discover the nature of knowledge by merely observing the soul's experiences. This procedure is as erroneous as it is to make only a chemical analysis of the seed with respect to its food value and to pretend that this represents its real essence. Spiritual science, as it is meant here, tries to avoid this error by revealing the inner nature of the soul's experience and by showing that it can also serve the process of knowledge, although its true nature does not consist in this contemplative knowledge.

The "body-free soul consciousness" here described must not be confused with those enhanced mental conditions that are not acquired by means of the characterized exercises but result from states of lower consciousness such as unclear clairvoyance, hypnotism, etc. In these conditions no body-free consciousness can be attained but only an abnormal connection between body and soul that differs from that of the ordinary life. Real spiritual science can be gained only when the soul finds, in the course of its own disciplined meditative work, the transition from the ordinary consciousness to one with which it awakens in and becomes directly aware of the spiritual world. This inner work consists in a heightening, not a lowering of the ordinary consciousness.

Through such inner work the human soul can actually *attain* what philosophy aims for. The latter should not be under-estimated because it has not attained its objective on the paths that are usually followed by it. Far more important than the philosophical results are the forces of the soul that can be developed in the course of philosophical work. These forces must eventually lead to the point where it becomes possible to recognize a "body-free soul experience." Philosophers will then recognize that the "world riddles" must not merely be considered scientifically but need to be *experienced* by the human soul. But the soul must first attain to the condition in which such an experience is possible.

This brings up an obvious question. Should ordinary knowledge and scientific knowledge deny its own nature and recognize as a world conception only what is offered from a realm lying outside its own domain? As it is, the experiences of the characterized consciousness are convincing at once also to this ordinary consciousness as long as the latter does not *insist* upon locking itself up within its own walls. The supersensible truths can be *found* only by a soul that enters into the supersensible. Once they are found, however, they can be fully understood by the ordinary consciousness. For they are in complete and necessary agreement with the knowledge that can be gained for the world of the senses.

It cannot be denied that, in the course of the history of philosophy, viewpoints have repeatedly been advanced that are similar to those described in this final chapter. But in former ages these tendencies appeared only like *by-ways* of the philosophical inquiry. Its first task was to work its way through everything that could be regarded as a continuation of the awakening thought experience of the Greeks. It then could point the way toward supersensible consciousness on the strength of its own initiative and in awareness of what it can and what it cannot attain. In former times this consciousness was accepted, as it were, without philosophical justification. It was not demanded by philosophy itself. But modern philosophy demands it in response to what it has achieved already *without* the assistance of this consciousness. Without this help it has succeeded in leading the spiritual investigation into directions that will, if rightly developed, lead to the recognition of supersensible consciousness. That is why this final chapter did not start by describing the way in which the soul speaks of the supersensible when it stands within its realm. Quite to the contrary, an attempt was made to outline philosophically the tendencies resulting from the modern world conceptions, and it was shown how a pursuit of *these innate tendencies* leads the soul to the recognition of its own supersensible nature.

INDEX

Index

A

Agnosticism, 326, 331, 348
Ammonius Sakkas (c. 175–242), 48
Ampère, André-Marie (1775–1836), 362, 363, 364
Anaxagoras (c. 500 B.C.), 30, 32, 63
Anaximander (611–550 B.C.), 24, 28
Anaximenes (c. 600 B.C.), 24, 26
Angelus Silesius (Johann Scheffler, 1624–1677), 60
Anselm of Canterbury (1033–1109), 56, 57
Anthropomorphism, 163, 307
Apollonius of Tyana (c. 50 A.D.), 48, 49
Archytas (c. 400–365 B.C.), 23
Aristophanes (c. 450–385 B.C.), 33
Aristotle (384–322 B.C.), 7, 41ff., 44, 46, 47, 53, 56, 59, 61, 64, 66, 82, 84, 105, 110, 131, 338, 388, 395, 397, 427, 431
Asmus, Paul (1842–1876), 352
Atomists, 32, 33
Augustine, St. Aurelius (354–430), 55, 56
Averroës (1126–1198), 53

B

Baader, Franz Xaver Benedikt von (1765–1841), 158, 203, 253
Bacon, Francis (1561–1626), 64ff., 70, 74
Baer, Carl Ernst von (1792–1876), 267, 279, 296
Bain, Alexander, (1818–1903), 333
Balfour, Arthur James (1848–1930), 349
Basilides (c. 130 A.D.), 51

471

Bauer, Bruno (1809–1882), 224ff.
Beck, Jakob Sigismund (1761–1840), 122
Bergson, Henri (1859–1941), 418, 420ff.
Berkeley, George (1684–1753), 77ff.
Bernadinus Telesius, see Telesius
Boehme, Jakob (1575–1624), 61ff., 63, 203
Boutroux, Emile (1845–1921), 418
Brentano, Franz (1838–1917), 254, 388ff., 395, 427, 461
Bruno, Giordano (1548–1600), 9, 63ff.
Buechner, Ludwig (1824–1899), 262ff., 265ff., 268, 270, 293
Burdach, Karl Friedrich (1776–1847), 267

C

Cabanis, Pierre Jean Georges (1757–1808), 79, 362
Cardanus, Hieronymus (1501–1576), 71
Carneri, Bartholomäus von (1821–1909), 310ff., 401ff.
Cassirer, Ernst (1874–1945), 434
Chalybäs, Heinrich Moritz (1796–1862), 204
Chrysippus (280–208 B.C.), 44
Clemens of Alexandria (died 211 A.D.), 52
Cohen, Hermann (1842–1918), 353, 434, 436ff., 441, 445
Comte, Auguste (1798–1857), 360ff., 365ff., 370, 411

Condillac, Etienne Bonnot de Mably de (1715–1780), 78, 362
Copernicus, Nicholas (1473–1543), 63, 70, 71, 93, 100, 224, 282
Cousin, Victor (1792–1867), 364ff.
Cratylus (Plato's teacher), 27
Critias (Pupil of Socrates), 33
Cusanus, Nicolaus, 60
Cuvier, Georges Baron de (1769–1832), 234
Czolbe, Heinrich (1819–1873), 270ff.

D

Dante Alighieri (1265–1321), 57
Darwin, Charles (1809–1882), 234, 281, 284ff., 302, 331, 345, 348, 354, 360, 371ff., 387, 401, 417
Democritus (c. 460–371 B.C.), 32
Descartes, René (1596–1650), 9, 67ff., 72, 94, 95ff., 252, 350
Destutt de Tracy, Antoine Louis Claude (1754–1836), 362ff., 363
Deutinger, Martin von (1815–1864), 203, 206, 207
Diderot, Denis (1713–1784), 79
Dilthey, Wilhelm (1833–1911), 425ff., 430, 434, 445, 451, 453
Dionysius the Areopagite, 52, 53
Dubois, Eugen (1858–1940), 304
Du Bois-Reymond, Emil (1815–1896), 319ff., 322

Dühring, Eugen (1833–1921), 366ff., 373

E

Echtermeyer, Ernst Theodor 1805–1844), 208
Eckhard, Meister, see Meister Eckhard
Einstein, Albert (1879–1955), 442ff.
Eleatics, 29
Empedocles (483–424 B.C.), 31ff.
Encyclopedists, 263
Epicureans, 44
Epicurus (342–270 B.C.), 44
Erdmann, Benno (1851–1921), 353
Erdmann, Johann Eduard (1805–1892), 177
Eucken, Rudolf (1846–1926), 429ff., 434, 441, 445, 451, 453, 457

F

Faraday, Michael (1791–1867), 266
Fechner, Gustav Theodor (1801–1887), 279, 375ff., 376, 380, 383
Feuerbach, Ludwig (1804–1872), 209ff., 214, 221, 224, 226, 262, 273, 306
Fichte, Immanuel Hermann (1797–1879), 203, 204, 207
Fichte, Johann Gottlieb (1762–1814), 4, 91, 120ff., 122ff., 131, 141, 147, 149, 151ff., 163, 188, 192, 194, 195, 199, 215, 220, 233, 253, 272, 282, 309, 347, 360, 368

Fischer, Karl Philip (1824–1908), 204
Flechsig, Paul (born 1847), 310, 311
Forberg, Friedrich (1770–1848), 122
Frantz, Constantin (1817–1891), 254
Fries, Jakob Friedrich (1773–1843), 177, 253

G

Galilei, Galileo (1564–1642), 63, 65, 66, 70, 71, 143, 282
Gegenbaur, Karl (1826–1903), 303, 417
Geoffroy de St. Hilaire, Etienne (1772–1844), 234, 276
Gladstone, William Ewart (1809–1898), 341
Gnosis, 51ff.
Goethe, Johann Wolfgang von (1749–1832), 14, 18, 65, 66, 88, 90, 91ff., 97ff., 110ff., 129, 131, 136, 138, 139, 140, 141, 142ff., 149, 151, 155, 163, 167, 174, 179, 183ff., 188, 195ff., 211, 220, 233, 234, 258, 263, 268, 276, 282, 283, 293, 300, 308, 332, 340, 343, 346, 364, 367, 391, 410, 427, 450, 456
Gomperz, Theodor (1832–1912), 341
Gorgias (died after 399 B.C.), 33
Grillparzer, Franz (1791–1872), 180
Gunther, Anton (1783–1863), 203, 205

H

Haeckel, Ernst (1834–1919), xiv, xv, xvi, 163, 298, 299ff., 321, 329, 371, 390

Haller, Albrecht von (1708–1777), 114, 209, 210

Hamann, Johann Georg (1730–1788), 85, 86

Hamerling, Robert (1830–1889), 391ff., 398ff., 407, 447

Hamilton, William (1788–1856), 333

Hartmann, Eduard von (1842–1906), 347, 375, 384ff., 387, 406

Harvey, William (1578–1657), 345

Hegel, Georg Wilhelm Frederich (1770–1831), xv, xvi, 122, 168ff., 185, 188, 191, 192, 195, 198, 201–208, 211, 212, 215, 218, 220, 221, 225, 227, 229, 233, 242ff., 254, 256–260, 266, 272, 273, 281, 282, 283, 290, 306, 312, 313, 327, 335, 336, 337, 347, 351, 352, 360, 364, 368, 373, 374, 384, 390, 398, 411, 415, 424, 456

Heinroth, Johann Christian (1773–1843), 142

Helmholtz, Hermann von (1821–1894), 197, 291, 292, 315ff., 318, 326

Helvetius, Claude Adrien (1715–1771), 78

Hemsterhuis, Franz (1721–1790), 89

Henle, Jakob (1809–1885), 292, 317

Heraclitus (c. 540–480 B.C.), 24ff., 26ff.

Herbart, Johann Friedrich (1776–1841), 122, 185ff., 205, 253

Herder, Johann Gottfried (1744–1803), 83ff., 86, 87, 88, 116, 294

Herschel, John (1792–1871), 333, 334

Hippias (c. 400 B.C.), 33

Hobbes, Thomas (1588–1679), xxiv

Hoff, Karl von (1771–1837), 268

Hoffman, Franz (1804–1881), 204

Holbach, Paul Heinrich Dietrich von (1723–1789), 78, 263, 361

Humbold, Alexander von (1769–1859), 261

Humboldt, Wilhelm von (1767–1835), 93, 253

Hume, David (1711–1776), 80ff., 99ff., 461, 462

Huxley, Thomas Henry (1825–1895), 293, 348, 413

I

Iamblichus (c. 330 A.D.), 48

J

Jacobi, Friedrich Heinrich (1743–1819), 83ff., 84, 86, 97, 98, 99, 114, 145, 146, 253

James, William (1842–1910), 414ff.

Jean Paul, see Richter

K

Kant, Immanuel (1724–1804), xxiii, 81, 90, 91ff., 103–122, 131, 132, 136, 137, 144–147, 162, 163, 186, 192–195, 216, 217, 220, 244, 245, 253, 315, 331, 346, 352, 353, 357, 359, 368, 389, 390, 395, 398, 436, 445, 447

Kepler, Johannes (1571–1630), 63, 70, 100

Key, Ellen (1849–1926), 299

Kinkel, Walter (born 1871), 434, 436, 441

Kirchhoff, Gustav Robert (1824–1887), 323ff., 381

Kirchmann, Julius Heinrich (1807–1884), 373ff.

Kleanthes, 44

Kraepelin, Emil (1856–1926), 384

Krause, Karl Christian Friedrich (1781–1832), 203, 204, 207, 253

L

Laas, Ernst (1837–1885), 358

Lamarck, Jean (1749–1829), 233, 275, 278, 292, 360, 361

La Mettrie, Julien de (1709–1751), 78, 79

Lang, Arnold, 298

Lange, Friedrich Albers (1828–1875), 259, 323ff., 326, 330, 331, 371

Laplace, Pierre Simone (1749–1827), 322, 346

Lassalle, Ferdinand (1825–1864), 412

Lavoisier, Antoine Laurent (1743–1794), 282

Leclair, Anton von (born 1845), 438

Leibniz, Gottfried Wilhelm von (1646–1716), 9, 74ff., 76, 77, 95ff., 141, 165, 189, 210, 252, 272, 344, 395

Leonardo da Vinci (1452–1519), 71

Lessing, Gotthold Ephraim (1729–1781), 22, 81ff., 84, 85, 86, 96, 247

Leucippus (c. 450 B.C.), 32

Lichtenberg, Georg Christoph (1742–1799), 121ff., 214ff., 223

Liebmann, Otto (1840–1912), 353ff.

Linnaeus, Karl von (1707–1778), 115, 286, 345

Locke, John (1632–1704), 76, 77, 78, 86, 252

Lotze, Hermann (1817–1881), 271, 280, 375ff., 432

Lucretius, Carus (96–55 B.C.), 45

Lyell, Charles (1797–1875), 267ff., 345

M

Mackay, John Henry (1864–1933), 230, 232

Maimon, Salomon (1753–1800), 122

Maimonides (1135–1204), 53

Mainländer, Philipp (1841–1876), 390

Maine de Biran, François Pierre

Gauthier (1766–1824), 362, 363
Malthus, Thomas Robert (1766–1834), 285
Mansel, Henry (1820–1871), 333
Marcion (died c. 170 A.D.), 51
Marsch, 305
Marx, Karl (1818–1883), 411ff.
Mayer, Julius Robert (1814–1878), 266
Meister Eckhard (1260–1327), 60, 203
Melissos (c. 450 B.C.), 28
Mendelssohn, Moses (1729–1786), 86, 87
Mettrie, see La Mettrie
Michelet, Carl Ludwig (1801–1893), 258ff., 277
Mill, James (1773–1836), 333, 334
Mill, John Stuart (1806–1873), 333, 334ff., 344, 347
Moderatus (1st Century A.D.), 49
Moleschott, Jacob (1822–1893), 262ff., 265ff., 268, 270, 281
Mueller, Fritz, 297, 298
Mueller, Johannes (1801–1858), 276, 278, 314, 315

N

Natorp, Paul (1854–1924), 434
Naville, Jules Ernest (1816–1909), 363
Nehring, Alfred (1845–1904), 305
Neo-Platonism, 46
Newton, Isaac (1642–1727), 108, 195, 196, 197, 198ff., 203

Nietzsche, Friedrich (1844–1900), 405ff.
Nigidius Figulus (c. 95–45 B.C.), 49
Nominalism, 8, 57ff., 70
Novalis (Friedrich Georg von Hardenberg) (1772–1801), 149

O

Oken, Lorenz (1779–1851), 233, 278, 292, 295, 296, 297, 300
Oersted, Hans Christian (1777–1851), 266, 364
Origines (c. 183–252), 52
Orphies, 18

P

Paracelsus (1493–1541), 61, 203
Parmenides (born c. 540 B.C.), 28, 29, 33, 436
Peirce, Charles (1839–1914), 414
Pherekydes of Syros (6th Century B.C.), 6, 7, 12ff., 16ff., 22, 24, 25, 28, 34
Philo of Alexandria (20–50 A.D.), 47
Philolaus (c. 450 B.C.), 23
Planck, Karl Christian (1819–1880), 260ff., 272ff.
Plato (427–347 B.C.), 7, 29, 36, 39ff., 42, 43, 46, 47, 49, 59, 66, 84, 85, 89, 105, 110, 131, 173, 193, 194, 198, 253, 272, 388, 395, 397, 427, 431
Plotinus (205–270), 46ff., 50, 60, 61
Porphyrius (232–304), 48
Post-Kantians, 163
Pragmatism, 414ff.

Prel, Carl du (1839–1899), 439
Pruess, Wilhelm Heinrich (born 1909), 423ff.
Prodicus (contemporary of Socrates), 33
Proclus (410–485), 48
Protagoras (c. 480–410 B.C.), 33
Pyrrho (360–270 B.C.), 45
Pythagoras (582–493 B.C.), 21ff., 24, 49, 60

R

Realism, 9, 57ff., 70
Rehmke, Johannes (1848–1930), 438
Reid, Thomas (1710–1756), 332ff.
Reinhold, Karl Leonhard (1758–1823), 125, 253
Relativity, Theory of, 442
Reuschle, Karl Gustav, 266
Rickert, Heinrich (1863–1936), 432ff.
Richter, Jean Paul Friedrich 1763–1825), 93, 146, 147
Riehl, Aloys (1844–1924), 358
Rolph, W. H., 404ff., 409
Romanticism, 147
Roscellin, Johannes (c. 1050–1123), 58
Rosenkrantz, Karl (1805–1879), 202, 243, 253
Rosenthal, Isidor (1836–1915), 318
Rousseau, Jean Jacques (1712–1778), 80, 363
Ruge, Arnold (1802–1880), 208

S

Saint-Simon, Claude-Henri de (1760–1825), 366
Schelling, Friedrich Wilhelm Josef (1775–1854), 122, 151ff., 164, 165, 166, 178, 188, 192, 195, 203, 215, 220, 233, 259, 272, 282, 347, 360, 368, 384
Schiller, Ferdinand Canning Scult (1864–1937), 414
Schiller, Friedrich (1759–1805), 92ff., 112ff., 131ff., 144, 148, 149, 151, 188, 220, 233, 327
Schlegel, Friedrich (1772–1829), 148
Schleiden, Matthias Jacob (1804–1881), 267, 316
Schleiermacher, Friedrich Ernst (1768–1834), 122ff., 167, 253
Schopenhauer, Arthur (1788–1860), 122, 192ff., 384, 385, 406
Schubert-Soldern, Richard von (born 1852), 438
Schulze, Gottlob Ernst (1761–1833), 121, 193, 194
Schuppe, Wilhelm (1836–1913), 438
Schwann, Theodore (1810–1882), 267
Scotus Erigena (c. 810–877), 7, 8, 50ff., 68, 69, 72
Seiling, Max, 391
Sengler, Jacob (1799–1878), 204
Shaftesbury, Anthony Ashley Cooper (1671–1713), 89
Shakespeare (1564–1616), 70
Scepticism, 45, 58, 121ff.
Socrates (469–399 B.C.), 29, 33, 35ff., 46, 406
Solger, Karl Wilhelm Ferdinand (1780–1819), 148ff., 253
Sophists, 32ff., 58

477

Soret, Friedrich Jacob (1795–1865), 276
Spencer, Herbert (1820–1903), 331ff., 341ff., 347, 348, 361
Spicker, Gideon (1840–1912), 390
Spinoza, Baruch (1632–1677), 9, 67, 72ff., 83, 85, 87ff., 94, 96, 97, 100ff., 114, 161ff., 165, 252, 389, 395
Stadler, August (1850–1910), 434
Steffens, Henrik (1773–1845), 233
Stirner, Max (1806–1856), 225, 229ff., 231, 232, 233, 274
Stoics, 44
Strauss, David Friedrich (1808–1874), 221ff., 266, 289, 291, 306, 408
Suso, Heinrich (c. 1300–1366), 60

T

Taine, Hippolyte (1828–1893), 317, 411
Tauler, Johannes (c. 1300–1361), 60, 203
Telesius, Bernardinus (1508–1588), 71
Tetens, Johann Nikolaus (1736–1807), 89
Thales (c. 625–545 B.C.), 6, 7, 24ff., 34
Theology, German, 60
Thomas Aquinas (1227–1274), 56ff., 70
Thrahndorff, Karl Friedrich Eusebius (1782–1863), 203, 206
Thrasymachus (contemporary of Socrates), 33
Tolstoi, Leo (1828–1910), 444
Treitschke, Heinrich von (1834–1896), 232
Trendelenburg, Friedrich Adolf (1802–1872), 259
Troxler, Ignaz Paul Vitalis (1780–1866), 254ff.
Tyndall, John (1820–1893), 349

U

Ulrici, Hermann (1806–1884), 203, 204

V

Vaihinger, Hans (1852–1933), 416ff.
Valentinus (died c. 160 A.D.), 51
Virchow, Rudolf (1821–1903), 303, 304, 305, 347
Vischer, Friedrich Theodor (1807–1887), 251, 264, 290, 291
Vogt, Carl (1817–1895), 262ff., 268, 269, 280
Volkalt, Johannes (1848–1930), 353
Volta, Alessandro (1743–1827), 282
Voltaire, Jean Marie Aroriet (1694–1778), 79, 80

W

Wackernagel, Wilhelm (1806–1869), 387
Wagner, Richard (1813–1883), 406, 407ff., 444
Wagner, Rudolf (1805–1864), 253, 268ff., 375

Wahle, Richard (died 1857), 358, 359, 387
Weber, Ernst Heinrich (1795–1878), 383
Weisse, Christian Hermann (1801–1866), 203, 205, 207, 257
Whewell, William (1794–1866), 333, 334
Wieland, Christoph Martin (1733–1813), 192
Winckler, Johann Heinrich (1703–1770), 97
Windelband, Wilhelm (1848–1915), 353ff., 432ff., 434
Windischmann, Karl Joseph Hieronymus (1775–1839), 253
Wirth, 204
Wohler, Friedrich (1800–1882), 264
Wolff, Casper Friedrich (1733–1794), 209ff., 220, 345
Wolff, Christian (1679–1754), 80, 86, 97, 99
Wundt, Wilhelm (1832–1920), 383, 396ff., 399ff., 407

X

Xenophon (c. 500 B.C.), 35, 37
Xenophanes (born c. 580 B.C.), 28

Z

Zeller, Eduard (1814–1908), 353
Zeno of Elea (c. 500 B.C.), 28, 29
Zeno of Kition (342–270 B.C.), 44
Zimmerman, Robert (1824–1898), 190ff., 390

www.ingramcontent.com/pod-product-compliance
Lightning Source LLC
Chambersburg PA
CBHW031700230426
43668CB00006B/61